The Tocq

About the Editors

Olivier Zunz is Commonwealth Professor of History at the University of Virginia and president of the Tocqueville Society. He is the author of *The Changing Face of Inequality* (1982), *Making America Corporate* (1990), and *Why the American Century?* (1998). He is also the editor of *Reliving the Past* (1985), and coeditor of *The Landscape of Modernity* (1992) and *Social Contracts under Stress* (2002). Professor Zunz has held visiting appointments at the École des Hautes Études en Sciences Sociales and the Collège de France and is currently at work on a history of American philanthropy.

Alan S. Kahan is Associate Professor of History at Florida International University. He is the author of *Aristocratic Liberalism, The Social and Political Thought of Jacob Burckhardt, John Stuart Mill, and Alexis de Tocqueville* (1992, 2001), and the translator of Tocqueville's *The Old Regime and the Revolution* (vol. 1: 1998, vol. 2: 2001). He is currently at work on a history of intellectuals' antagonism to capitalism.

Charles Feigenoff, who revised the excerpts of the public-domain translation of *Democracy in America* published in this volume, holds a Ph.D. in nineteenth-century American literature from the University of Virginia. He is a freelance writer and editor who lives in Charlottesville, Virginia.

The Tocqueville Reader

A Life in Letters and Politics

Edited by

Olivier Zunz and Alan S. Kahan

Blackwell
Publishing

Editorial Offices:
108 Cowley Road, Oxford OX4 1JF, UK
Tel: +44 (0)1865 791100
350 Main Street, Malden, MA 02148–5018, USA
Tel: +1 781 388 8250

Library of Congress Cataloging-in-Publication Data
Tocqueville, Alexis de, 1805–1859.
The Tocqueville reader / edited by Olivier Zunz and Alan S. Kahan.
    p. cm.
Includes bibliographical references and index.
ISBN 0-631-21545-X (hb : alk. paper) — ISBN 0-631-21546-8 (pb : alk. paper)
    1. Political science. 2. Sociology. I. Zunz, Olivier. II. Kahan, Alan S. III. Title.
JC229 .T775 2002
320′.092—dc21   2002020851

A catalogue record for this title is available from the British Library

Typeset in 10.5 on 12.5 Bembo
by SetSystems Ltd, Saffron Walden, Essex
Printed and bound in Great Britain
by MPG Books Limited, Bodmin, Cornwall

For further information on
Blackwell Publishers, visit our website:
www.blackwellpublishers.co.uk

To the memory of François Furet

Contents

PART III   The Years in Politics

Note on Sources and Translations

Part I   The Discovery of *Democracy in America*

Chapter 1

1a–1b: Alexis de Tocqueville [hereafter AdT], *Selected Letters on Politics and Society*, ed. R. Boesche, trans. J. Toupin and R. Boesche, University of California Press, Berkeley, 1985, copyright © The Regents of the University of California, [hereafter BO], 37–41, 45–59
1c: AdT, *Œuvres complètes*, Éditions Gallimard, Paris, 1991 [hereafter O.C.], XIV, 143–44

Chapter 2

2a–2g: AdT, *Journey to America*, trans. G. Lawrence, ed. J. P. Mayer, Double-day and Co., Anchor books, New York, 1971, reprinted by permission of Éditions Gallimard, Paris, 217–18, 46–48, 154–55, 62–69, 267–68, 251–57, 320–21.

Chapter 3

3a–3b; 6a–6d: AdT, *Democracy in America*, vol. 1, 1835, vol. 2, 1840, trans. Henry Reeve, revised by Francis Bowen and further revised by Phillips Bradley, with an introduction by Daniel J. Boorstin, Vintage Books, New York, 1990.
3c: O.C. XV.1, 52–54.

Part II Great Britain, France and the United States

Chapter 4

4a: AdT, *Memoir on Pauperism* trans. Seymour Drescher, with an introduction by Gertrude Himmelfarb, Ivan R. Dee, Chicago, 1997, 51–63, 69–72 (courtesy of Seymour Drescher).
4b: *Alexis de Tocqueville's Journey in Ireland*, trans. and ed. Emmet Larkin, Catholic University of America Press, Washington, DC, 1990, 24–26, 51, 79. Reprinted by permission.
4c: O.C. XVI, 146–47.

Chapter 5

5a: O.C., XIV, 387–388
5b: *Œuvres complètes*, ed. Gustave de Beaumont, Michel Lévy Frères, Paris, 1864–66, [hereafter Beaumont], 5: 428–33
5c: O.C. XIII, 1, 387–90.
5d: BO, 112–15.
5e: O.C., VI, 1, 52–53.
5f: BO, 153–57.

Chapter 6

6a–d: see above, notes on chapter 3.
6e: O.C., VI, 1, 329–31.

Part III The Years in Politics

Chapter 7

7a: partly published by Pierre Roland-Marcel, in *Essai politique sur Alexis de Tocqueville*, Alcan, Paris, 1910, 336–39. Complete text in Tocqueville archives (courtesy of Françoise Mélonio).
7b: O.C., III, 2, 87.
7c: O.C., X, 698–99.

7d: *O.C.*, III, 2, 738–41.
7e: *O.C.*, III, 2, 742–44.

Chapter 8

8a: partly published in AdT, *Writings on Empire and Slavery* trans. Jennifer Pitts, The Johns Hopkins University Press, Baltimore, 2001, 16, 59, 60–61; in André Jardin, *Tocqueville: A Biography*, trans. Lydia Davis with Robert Hemenway, The Johns Hopkins University Press, Baltimore, 1988, 322; complete text in *O.C.*, III, 1, 173–74 and in *O.C.*, IX, 68–69.
8b: *O.C.*, III, 1, 443–44, 447–48.

Chapter 9

9a and b: Alexis de Tocqueville, *Recollections* trans. G. Lawrence, ed. J. P. Mayer, Doubleday and Co., Anchor Books, New York, 1971, 1–8, 12–17, 61–68, 133–35, 136–37, 155–57.
9c: *O.C.*, XIV, 528–31.
9d: *O.C.*, III, 3, 192.
9e: *O.C.*, III, 3, 196.
9f: BO, 230–33.
9g: *O.C.*, XV, 1, 255–58.

Chapter 10

10a: BO, 252–58.
10b: *O.C.*, XV, 2, 41–43.
10c: *O.C.*, XIV, 271–72.
10d: *O.C.*, III, 3, 469–70.
10e: *O.C.*, XV, 2, 53–56.
10f: BO, 297–301.
10g: *O.C.*, XV, 2, 105–109.
10h: *O.C.*, XV, 2, 267–69.
10i: Beaumont, 6: 332–33.

Part IV   The Return to *The Old Regime and the Revolution*

Chapters 11 and 12

AdT, *The Old Regime and the Revolution* trans. Alan S. Kahan, ed. François Furet and Françoise Mélonio 2 vols. The University of Chicago Press, 1998, 2001.

Chapter 13

13a: *O.C.*, XV, 2, 313–16.
13b: Beaumont, 6, 406–407.
13c: *O.C.*, XIV, 341–43.
13d: *O.C.*, VIII, 3, 542–46.

For this volume, Alan S. Kahan has translated from the French sections 4c, 5b, 5c, 7a, 7b, 7e, 9g, 10b, 10d, 10g, 10i, 13a, 13b, 13d, Olivier Zunz sections 1c, 3c, 5a, 6e, 7c, 7d, 8a (in part), 8b, 9c, 9d, 9e, 10c, 10e, 10h, 13c, and Charles Feigenoff has revised sections 3a–3b and 6a–6d from the public domain English-language edition.

Introduction

Democracy in America (1835, 1840) and *The Old Regime and the Revolution* (1856) are the beginning and ending points of Alexis de Tocqueville's comparative reflections on the difficulty of combining freedom and equality in the modern world. This preoccupation arose directly from Tocqueville's deeply personal reactions to the collapse of the French Old Regime and the spread of democratic ideals. Tocqueville was an aristocrat at heart but one who investigated vastly different settings to evaluate the meaning of liberty for his generation.

Tocqueville lived a short but very full life. He went to America in 1831 when he was only 25 and spent nine months exploring its cities and its frontier villages and speaking to some of the most influential Americans of the period. The subsequent publication of *Democracy in America* in 1835 and 1840 made him famous. Tocqueville, however, was not satisfied with being a man of letters. He served as representative in the French national assembly for twelve years where he fought hard for freedom and against the specter of absolute rule. When absolute rule returned in the form of the Second Empire in 1851, Tocqueville retired from politics and devoted his last years to his second masterpiece.

The constant throughout Tocqueville's life was liberty, for which he had an abiding passion. For him, liberty involves far more than the protection of individuals' life and property inscribed in bills of rights. It appears where the habits of citizens lead them to act spontaneously, without awaiting orders from a higher authority, to do the things they need for themselves. Above all in a society resting on liberty, citizens act in cooperation with others. Bonds of association are always alive and active in a free society. [See selection 11d3 for Tocqueville's definition of freedom]

Tocqueville reflected at length on the problem of liberty and its vicissitudes in the France of his days. Did it exist anywhere? Here was the great surprise for him and many of his contemporaries. In America, Tocqueville discovered a system of decentralized government and religious institutions, almost all based on ideals of self-governance, individual participation, free association, and equality. For him, the role of equality in America came as a shock, because in Tocqueville's aristocratic world, equality signified leveling and was the work of royal despotism. All subjects are equal in their subservience to a monarch. In America, by contrast, equality seemed consistent with liberty, although Tocqueville remained cautious about the effects in democratic practice of a tyranny of the majority.

By the time Tocqueville wrote *The Old Regime*, he feared that France would never attain a lasting freedom. To Tocqueville, the origins of France's loss of freedom were quite clear. The French society of his day was marked by individualism – some say he coined the term – by which Tocqueville meant that persons were egoistic, self-regarding, ambitious for themselves alone, and fully independent of the ties to others that liberty requires. [See selection 6c2] Why? Others in his milieu blamed the Revolution, the terror, Napoleon. Tocqueville disagreed. For him, as he pursued his research in writing, the villain that emerged was the old monarchical state. That state had been suspicious of local groups. It destroyed local administrative structures and replaced them by a system of purchased privileges that only generated conflict and frustration. Tocqueville described the paradox of a society in which subjects, isolated by their often frivolous privileges, felt equality only in their powerlessness.

He pursued the same themes in all his writings. In addition to his two great books, Tocqueville left behind him a huge paper trail of political memoranda, recollections, especially those of the 1848 revolution, and extensive travel notes. Among the latter, most noteworthy are his records of travel to Great Britain and to Algeria, where Tocqueville monitored the progress of French colonization. As a thinker who had committed his life to comparisons among countries, Tocqueville envisioned going to India to measure the British colonial experience against that of his own country. The project did not materialize but his substantial preparatory readings added depth to his reflection on social hierarchies.

Tocqueville was also an indefatigable correspondent. Although not easily approachable, he had a gift for forming deep and enduring friendships both early and late in life, nurtured by extensive correspondence. His letters to a close-knit network of friends, including leading French, British, and American intellectuals, as well as family members and constituents, contain some of his best thoughts. Some letters were drafts of longer texts. Others include traces of unfinished projects.

Tocqueville has been regarded by posterity as an analyst so perceptive that he seems to have prophetic powers. For instance, Tocqueville talked about the unavoidable progress of "equality of conditions." By this, Tocqueville rarely meant economic leveling. He usually meant equal legal status at birth, for all, *and* everyone's ability to undertake, alone or in a group, the tasks of society. In this book, however, we have tried to free Tocqueville from the status of oracle and allow him to return as an intellectual struggling to come to grips with a few essential and complex ideas on freedom, equality, aristocracy, and democracy. We have organized this selection of his writings chronologically rather than thematically because Tocqueville was as loyal to his intellectual pursuits as he was loyal to his friends. Each work is like a preliminary formulation of the next one. Only in this case, Tocqueville started out with a masterpiece and kept improving on it as he achieved ever greater mastery of concepts and evidence.

The Young Tocqueville

Tocqueville was born in Paris on July 29, 1805. The most important trait he inherited from his parents was his status as an aristocrat. This was something he never forgot, and which readers often ignore. Despite the Revolution, social barriers remained strong in France, and Tocqueville always knew himself to be of a class born apart. Tocqueville's observations about democracy, and his reasoned attachment to it, were those of an outsider, one to whom equality was instinctively foreign. [7b] Nevertheless Tocqueville recognized that the society of orders, the aristocratic conception of society in which everyone was ranked from birth according to an accepted hierarchy, was Europe's past, and that democracy, a society based on equality of status at birth, was its future. The tension between Tocqueville's emotional and social identity as an aristocrat and his intellectual and moral engagement with democracy animates Tocqueville's critique of modern society.

There were many tensions and contradictions in Tocqueville's life, and they were reflected in his works. Even his aristocratic heritage was complicated. The family of Hervé de Tocqueville (1772–1856), Alexis's father, was old and distinguished, but not very rich, although their long pedigree was a source of prestige. For several centuries the family had been established at the château of Tocqueville, in Normandy, not far from Cherbourg. They were of the *noblesse d'épée*, aristocrats whose nobility derived originally from their military services. One of Tocqueville's paternal ancestors fought at the Battle of Hastings in 1066. Marshal Vauban, Louis XIV's master of military fortification, was another ancestor. Hervé himself served the restored Bourbon monarchy as an administrator. Tocqueville's mother, Louise-Madeleine Le Peletier de Rosanbo (1772–1836), was descended from a recently ennobled family of the *noblesse de robe*, those aristocrats who derived nobility from their positions in the judiciary and royal bureaucracy. They were much more politically prominent. Tocqueville's maternal great-grandfather was Malesherbes (1721–1794), who had been both a reformist government minister and a leader in resistance to royal authority before the French Revolution. Before the Revolution, *noblesse de robe* and *noblesse d'épée* were often hostile to one another. But since the *noblesse de robe* frequently had the cash and the connections, while the *noblesse d'épée* had the prestige and the lineage, they sometimes married.

Tocqueville's family, while not very wealthy by aristocratic standards, was thus both old and prominent. This prominence was costly during the Revolution. Malesherbes came out of retirement to act as Louis XVI's defense attorney when the king was tried in 1792, and not only paid for it with his life in 1794 but had to watch his daughter be executed before he was guillotined. Tocqueville's parents themselves were arrested and saved from the guillotine only by Robespierre's fall. This imprisonment under threat of death marked the family deeply. Tocqueville's enduring hatred of the arbitrary exercise of power may well have derived from it. The fact that he accepted the Revolution's outcome despite the family history was yet another of the emotional strains behind his magisterial intellectual front.

After the Revolution, many of Tocqueville's relatives continued to be prominent. A maternal aunt married the elder brother of Chateaubriand, the Romantic writer and sometime politician. Later Chateaubriand introduced Tocqueville to the salons of the literary elite and helped launch *Democracy in America*. Tocqueville was related to a number of other political figures of widely varying stripe, including many partisans of the Bourbon monarchy (known as Legitimists), as well as Napoleonic officials. One of the latter was his cousin Count Molé, who went on to serve King Louis-Philippe as prime minister and attempted to persuade Tocqueville to support his conservative government. But Molé was unable to recruit Tocqueville, despite offering to find him a seat in the Chamber. Tocqueville was always intellectually independent, and always put his political principles ahead of family connections. Tocqueville was the only member of his immediate family to break with the hereditary loyalty to the Bourbon dynasty although he paid an emotional price for doing so. Unlike his father, Tocqueville saw the Bourbon attempt to revive an aristocratic regime in France as an anachronism.

Tocqueville recognized that aristocracy could be anachronistic as early as his late teens. His childhood education had been confided to Abbé Lesueur, a conservative priest of Jansenist leanings.[1] The abbé won Tocqueville's enduring affection. Although he did not leave any strong intellectual imprint on his pupil, he taught him French composition and most likely introduced him to the writings of Pascal. In 1821, at the age of 16, Tocqueville entered the lycée at Metz, where his father was serving as "prefect."[2] Tocqueville spent the next three years there, and they were intellectually and emotionally important. He fought a duel, had a love affair with an unsuitable girl (neither noble nor wealthy), and, most importantly, discovered his father's library. Hervé de Tocqueville was a widely-read man. His library contained many of the writings of the *philosophes*, the eighteenth-century French Enlightenment intellectuals who had often questioned the idea of hereditary inequality. It was in this library, we may conjecture, that Tocqueville decided aristocratic society was dead. Here he may first have acquired his intimate knowledge of Rousseau and Montesquieu, and in this library, we know from his much later confessions to the Russian mystic and Parisian society figure Madame Swetchine, Tocqueville lost his religion. [13a] After reading the rationalist assaults on dogma of the eighteenth century, Tocqueville emerged as something of a Deist, and certainly no longer a Christian. He retained a belief in God and in an afterlife in which good and evil were rewarded and punished, but he held no further religious convictions. He deeply regretted this, for he had a profound desire for religious certainty (perhaps related to his early reading of Pascal), but he was never able to recapture his boyhood faith as a Catholic. He struggled with religious questions throughout his life but kept this struggle hidden from almost everyone.

Upon graduating from the lycée, Tocqueville went to law school in Paris from 1824 to 1826, and in 1827 was appointed a *juge auditeur* (apprentice judge) at Versailles. Tocqueville was not a very successful lawyer, and he was passed over for promotion at least once. But his career was altered by events. In 1830 Charles X, the last Bourbon king, was overthrown. The Revolution of 1830 put an end to Charles' flirtation with absolutism and installed the constitutional monarchy of his cousin King Louis-Philippe, with a parliamentary government. Tocqueville took the oath of obedience required of public

---

1　The Jansenists originated in seventeenth-century France as a reform movement within the Catholic Church. Pascal was affiliated with them. They were condemned by the Pope and many of their writings banned because of similarities with Protestantism. Later Jansenism persisted as a current within French Catholicism emphasizing strict morality and inward faith.

2　A representative of central authority in each French department.

officials and remained in government service. This chilled relations with his pro-Bourbon family for some time and helped him decide to travel to America with his friend and legal colleague, Gustave de Beaumont.

"He Began to Think Before He Knew Anything"

This well-known remark about Tocqueville by the nineteenth-century literary critic Sainte-Beuve refers to the fact that Tocqueville must have had a great many ideas in mind *before* he set off for America in 1831, or he could not have written *Democracy in America*.[3] As Tocqueville wrote in 1835, the year *Volume one* was published: "Nearly ten years ago I was already thinking about parts of the things I have just now set forth."[4]

The twin problems that preoccupied Tocqueville were those of equality and freedom. It is important to understand that he often used the words *equality* and *democracy* interchangeably. By equality or democracy, Tocqueville did not mean simply a political system in which everyone votes. He meant something broader and deeper. For Tocqueville, *democracy* was a social state based not only on the premise that all people are equal at birth but also that they can share in the task of organizing society. For this, they needed freedom. Tocqueville's work was largely devoted to working out the vast implications of this seemingly simple postulate.

Tocqueville strove all his life, both as a writer and a politician, to make a secure place for freedom within a democratic world. For he realized that freedom and equality do not coexist easily. He thought it easier if the habit of freedom preceded the growth of equality, as in America. But if equality came first, as in France, it was often at the expense of freedom. Equality is not inimical to freedom, in Tocqueville's view, but it can exist without freedom. For Tocqueville, the combination of equality and freedom is the best possible human condition, while equality without freedom is among the worst. The world faced a choice between two extremes, and Tocqueville was always trying to understand both the threats to and opportunities for freedom in a democratic world.

---

3   Sainte-Beuve, *Moniteur Universel*, December 31, 1860, republished in *Causeries du Lundi* (Paris: Garnier Frères, 1862), XV: 105n1.
4   Letter probably to Eugène Stoffels, although identified as to Louis de Kergorlay, January 1835, in Roger Boesche, ed., *Alexis de Tocqueville, Selected Letters on Politics and Society* (Berkeley: University of California Press, 1985), p. 95. For the identification of the recipient, see André Jardin, *Tocqueville, a Biography* (Baltimore: Johns Hopkins University Press, 1988), trans. Lydia Davis with Robert Hemenway, p. 93.

Tocqueville's formal education and brief legal career were important in developing these ideas. He retained throughout his work an interest in law codes and judicial forms. Most importantly, he was exposed during his time in the law to many of the broader intellectual influences that stamped his thought. It was while an apprentice judge in 1829–30 that Tocqueville attended lectures on the history of France and European civilization given by François Guizot, then a leader of the liberal opposition to the Bourbons as well as one of the great historians of the nineteenth century. Tocqueville found Guizot's lectures "truly *extraordinary*."[5] Guizot taught Tocqueville about democracy as a rising social state. Equally important, Guizot set the pattern for Tocqueville's writing. Like Tocqueville, Guizot preferred analysis over narrative. Guizot wrote about "civilization," not events, and for Guizot, civilization meant an ensemble of laws, mores, and opinion. Guizot helped Tocqueville see political developments as intimately related to a swathe of underlying and overlapping conditions. The impact of factors such as democracy and centralization on civilization, which Guizot emphasized, were of continuing concern for Tocqueville. Later Guizot would be a dominant political figure during the July Monarchy, prime minister when it fell in 1848, and the subject of Tocqueville's bitter contempt. [5f] But in the 1820s, Guizot's conception of history and the political theories he presented along with a group of post-Revolutionary exponents of constitutional monarchy, known as the Doctrinaires, were of crucial importance to Tocqueville.[6] The Doctrinaires, who were trying to find a way to avoid the excesses of either the Revolution or of absolute monarchy, helped teach Tocqueville to think about the social and intellectual foundations of a free political system that would avoid these pitfalls. Another Doctrinaire, Pierre-Paul Royer-Collard, a member of the French parliament under both the Restoration and the July Monarchy, and a friend and mentor to Tocqueville, added something to Tocqueville's intellectual formation not found in Guizot: hostility to the obsession with material well-being typical of democratic society. The aristocrat Tocqueville was doubtless predisposed to think this, but Royer-Collard confirmed it for him while, like Tocqueville, accepting the advent of democracy as inevitable and just.

The Doctrinaires were not the only important intellectual influences on Tocqueville. Older authors, who had encouraged Tocqueville's love for

---

5 Letter to Beaumont, August 30, 1829, *Œuvres complètes* (Paris: Gallimard, 1959–) [hereafter *O.C.*], vol. 8, pt. 1, p. 80.
6 On Tocqueville and the Doctrinaires, see Aurelian Craiutu, "Tocqueville and the Political Thought of the French Doctrinaires" *History of Political Thought*, 20 (1999), pp. 456–93.

freedom as well as his understanding of equality when he was still an adolescent in his father's library, continued to influence him as an adult. As he wrote to his relative and lifelong friend Louis de Kergorlay: "there are three men with whom I live a little daily, they are Pascal, Montesquieu and Rousseau."[7] Rousseau, and in particular Rousseau's "Discourse on the Origins and Foundations of Inequality" (also known as the "Second Discourse"), had particular impact on Tocqueville's ideas about the fundamental meanings and implications of equality. Tocqueville's works are scattered with unacknowledged references to Rousseau. Since Rousseau was strongly associated with the era's radical left, with whom Tocqueville did not want to be identified, it would have been counterproductive for him to make explicit reference to Rousseau, but the traces are there. Tocqueville strongly disagreed with Rousseau's prescriptions for a direct democracy representing the "general will," but Tocqueville's recognition of universal human impulses towards freedom and equality, and his depiction of human nature, owed much to Rousseau.[8] Even the *Social Contract* finds occasional echoes in the *Democracy*, as when Tocqueville reproduces Rousseau's claim that citizens in democracies are sometimes free only at the moment when they vote. [6d6]

Although quoted in *Democracy*, Pascal's influence on Tocqueville is more difficult to pin down.[9] He clearly helped Tocqueville think about religion. His ideas about the combination of greatness and triviality in the human soul also appear in Tocqueville's writings. [5c] If Tocqueville's psychological acuity has a source outside his own soul, Pascal as well as Rousseau are part of it. Nevertheless, Tocqueville would never have suggested, as Pascal did, that all human troubles come from our inability to sit still in our room – what use would freedom be then? Tocqueville valued action too much to accept any form of quietism.

Montesquieu was perhaps the most important influence on Tocqueville. The parallels in their sociological analysis of law and principles of national character were noted at the time. After the publication of the first volume of *Democracy in America*, Tocqueville was hailed as the modern Montesquieu.[10] The most obvious similarity in subject and method between Tocqueville and

---

7   Letter to Kergorlay, November 12, 1836, in Alexis de Tocqueville, *O.C.*, vol. 13, pt. 1, p. 418.

8   Tocqueville's description of the native Americans in *Democracy*, *Volume one* owes much to Rousseau's *Discourse on Inequality*, and his description of democratic mores in part 3 of *Volume two* owes much to *Emile*.

9   *Democracy*, II, section 3, chapter 19.

10   See Françoise Mélonio, *Tocqueville and the French* (Charlottesville: University Press of Virginia, 1998), trans. Beth G. Raps, p. 74.

Montesquieu lies in the latter's *Spirit of the Laws*. However, Tocqueville also read closely Montesquieu's *Considerations on the Greatness and Decline of the Romans*. [10a] Although Tocqueville rejected Montesquieu's equation of democracy with virtue, he imitated Montesquieu's methods, in particular his habit of following the consequences of a basic principle, such as democracy or centralization, through a multitude of different contexts and unexpected ramifications.[11]

But Tocqueville's writing was not that of an eighteenth-century author, not even one transformed by the French Revolution and the political theory of the Doctrinaires. He was very much a child of his own time, and his writing often betrays the influence of Romanticism. *Democracy in America* in particular contains descriptive passages, often centered around natural scenes associated with emotions of loss and the passing of time, that are very Romantic in tone. His descriptions of native Americans, the lost French nation of Quebec, and the former homestead of some French refugees from the Terror, are notable examples of the Romantic Tocqueville.[12]

1831–1832: The American Voyage

How, then, did *Democracy in America* come to be? Career prospects were not very good in France in 1831 for a 25 year-old lawyer who had sworn a loyalty oath to an uncertain constitutional monarchy. Friends and family disapproved of the new regime and of his willingness to accommodate himself to it. Given his position in the judicial system and a mounting interest in prison reform in official circles, an investigation of the American penitentiary system seemed like a good way to gain time. Tocqueville and his friend Gustave de Beaumont, whom he had met at the court in Versailles, managed to convince

11   On Montesquieu's influence see Melvin Richter, "Comparative Political Analysis in Montesquieu and Tocqueville" *Comparative Politics*, 1 (1969), pp. 129–60 and "The Uses of Theory: Tocqueville's Adaptation of Montesquieu" in Richter, ed., *Essays in Theory and History* (Cambridge: Harvard University Press, 1970). On Rousseau, see Harvey Mitchell, *Individual Choice and the Structures of History: Alexis de Tocqueville as Historian Reappraised* (New York: Cambridge University Press, 1996). On Pascal see Luis Diez del Corral, *La mentalidad politica de Tocqueville con especial referencia a Pascal* (Madrid: Real Academia de Ciencias Morales y Politicas, 1965).

12   See also "Fortnight in the Wilderness," written on the steamboat *The Superior*, begun August 1, 1831, beautifully translated in George W. Pierson, *Tocqueville in America* [first published in 1938 as *Tocqueville and Beaumont in America*] (Baltimore: Johns Hopkins University Press, 1996), 231–82.

the Ministry of the Interior to let them undertake an official mission to study American prisons.

America was a special place for Tocqueville beyond its presumably remarkable penitentiary system. Tocqueville saw America as a laboratory where he could observe the simultaneous benefits and abuses of equality – the strengths and pitfalls of democracy. He conceived of this important voyage as a way to work through his personal dilemma. If he were to live in a society ever becoming more egalitarian, he had to see one. Rather than adopting the reactionary mood of his fellow aristocrats, who were defeated by the French revolution, displaced by the Empire, and discouraged by a failed Restoration, Tocqueville wanted to engage the modern world. By going to America, he combined adventure with the search for his future – and the world's.

On April 2, 1831, Tocqueville and Beaumont sailed from Le Havre; they landed at Newport, Rhode Island, on May 9. Although the two friends had practiced their English with the other passengers on the boat and taken some preliminary notes, these conversations did not prepare them for the surprises that awaited them. Echoing some of Rousseau's images of man in the state of nature, Tocqueville writes his friend Chabrol on arrival and asks him to imagine a society without "roots," without "memories," without "prejudices," without "routines," without even "common ideas," not to mention "national character," "yet a hundred times happier than our own." [1a]

The initial idea was for Tocqueville and Beaumont to write a joint book on America in addition to the official prison report. But, as it turned out, Tocqueville kept most of the notes and also did most of the translations during the journey. Beaumont, who had a fine talent for drawing, kept a sketchbook and eventually chose to write a fanciful novel, *Marie; or, Slavery in the United States* (1835), about the improbable love story of a French immigrant and an American woman of mulatto ancestry, followed by documentary appendices on race relations.

Tocqueville was extraordinarily observant throughout the journey. Encounters, conversations, and observations were often more important to him than reading in forming his judgments. He listened carefully to what his American informers were telling him while also paying attention to how they expressed themselves. He reconstructed their thoughts and imagined their history. Tocqueville was remarkably systematic in asking questions on topics close to his heart and in following leads from one informant to the next. [1c] He meticulously recorded conversations in his notebooks, while already formulating some of the connections on which he would later elaborate. Often he pursued his ideas in long letters to friends, asking them to keep the letters so he could refer to them on his return. He confided additional thoughts to his diaries. Large sections of *Volume one* are direct transcriptions of these conversations with over two hundred Americans, but it is only by reading Tocqueville's detailed travel notes and correspondence that one can track their origins. [2a–2g] In so doing, historians have been able not only to retrace Tocqueville's travel steps but also his process of intellectual creation. [1a–1c] They have generally divided the voyage into six distinct geographic areas, each corresponding to a new stage in Tocqueville's conceptualization and understanding of democracy in America.[13]

New York State was the site of the initial encounter. It was a short steamboat ride from Rhode Island, where the two friends landed, to New York City, where they established their base before heading for Albany and Buffalo. Tocqueville and Beaumont were moved by the effusiveness of American hospitality. Although they had secured letters of introduction, they had little opportunity to use them as local dignitaries spontaneously threw parties in their honor. There were some awkward moments as when their American hosts toasted Lafayette without realizing that, in Tocqueville's family circle of Legitimists, the Marquis was considered a traitor. But Tocqueville suffered through these moments with good grace. More importantly, he met some of the most accomplished Americans of the day, like Albert Gallatin, the Swiss-born statesman who had been Jefferson's Treasury Secretary.

Tocqueville and Beaumont took the steamer to Albany, the state capital, where they attended their first independence day parade, went by stage to Utica, and, then, on horseback to Syracuse. They were impressed by America's excellent transportation facilities: steamboat and stagecoach carried mail and newspapers as well as people, a fact not lost on Tocqueville, who was interested in how democratic ideas circulated and public opinion formed.

To understand equality as a social condition, Tocqueville encouraged his informants to talk about the ways American institutions affected social practices. The first focused discussion of institutions and mores took place at the home of state legislator John Spencer in Canandaigua, in upstate New York. Beaumont thought Spencer was their first real informant.[14] Spencer shared his detailed knowledge of the workings of the judiciary. He impressed Tocqueville with several ideas which were included in the final volume. Spencer explained that the freedom of the press in America was balanced by the heavy fines to which newspapers were subjected if convicted of false statements. Tocqueville, who had just witnessed the collapse of the last Bourbon king after he had thoroughly restricted the freedom of the press, listened intently. Spencer insisted that religion was on the side of political

---

13 The most important book remains Pierson's *Tocqueville in America*.
14 Gustave de Beaumont, *Lettres d'Amérique. 1831–1832* ed. André Jardin and George W. Pierson (Paris: Presses Universitaires de France, 1973), p. 98.

freedom in America. Again, Tocqueville who knew first hand the disastrous consequences of the French clergy's support of the King's divine rights, felt he was grasping an important aspect of American life. [3a2] Spencer promoted bicameralism or the "resolution to two tests." Tocqueville made it an axiom of political science.

The two travelers also adhered to their official purpose of studying prisons. In Syracuse, they interviewed Elam Lynds, the retired warden of both Sing Sing and Auburn prisons, which they had visited. In both places, they had observed inmates required to perform collective physical labor in total silence, under the threat of the whip, and return to solitary confinement at night. Nothing like that existed in France, where prisoners could freely interact with one another, a condition that, Tocqueville believed, discouraged them from reforming. American silence came at a price – the whip, which Tocqueville and Beaumont loathed. Yet they were in awe of the inmates' orchestrated peaceful movements back and forth from private cells to collective workspace.

Their New York trip also gave them their first exposure to Indians, near Buffalo. Tocqueville, "full of memories of M. de Chateaubriand and of Cooper," had imagined noble savages bearing the "marks" of "proud virtues" and "liberty."[15] These Romantic and Rousseauian expectations were greatly disappointed when encountering a broken people given to alcoholism and hand outs.

The journey to the Great Lakes and Canada – the second part of the trip – provided a different set of observations that were to be woven into the fabric of *Democracy in America*. On the American frontier, Tocqueville had an important realization. He found himself observing the most advanced form of political life – self-government by free associations – in the most backward of environments. In pioneer Michigan, he discovered that although frontier society was rough, the inhabitants of these areas were free, well informed, and governed themselves. The contrast with France, with its refined mores but oppressive political system, could not have been greater. The refinements of the old world were, he decided, irrelevant to the emergence of modern politics.

As it turned out, Tocqueville did not have to wait until his return to France to pursue his comparison of new and old regimes. Next door was French Canada, where the two friends stopped on their way back east, after taking a look at Niagara Falls. In Quebec, although they appreciated the friendly hospitality dispensed to them, they did not like the bastardized language they heard and felt people lacked spark. They blamed the Catholic

---

15 Alexis de Tocqueville, *Journey to America* trans. George Lawrence, ed. Jean-Pierre Mayer (Garden City, NY: Doubleday and Co., Anchor Books, 1971), p. 204.

church for discouraging individualism and education, hence effectively reducing the political effects of a broad electoral base. They also uncovered anachronistic if limited remnants of French feudal taxation and landholding practices.

It was during the third part of Tocqueville's voyage, in New England, that the concept of equality came into sharp focus. Tocqueville cultivated his ideas on equality and what he would call the "tyranny of the majority." As a result, the New England experience was arguably the most important of the voyage. He owed much of this conceptual breakthrough to the many conversations he had with ex-federalists and proto-Whig politicians who had not reconciled themselves to Andrew Jackson's presidential victory of 1828. They were well-bred members of the elite who believed that it was their job to lead and were struggling with an American version of Tocqueville's personal dilemma. How could power, they asked, shift from educated, cultured people like themselves to a group of Jacksonian adventurers? As the New Englanders faced the unforeseen social consequences of their parents' political revolution, Tocqueville felt a deep sense of kinship with them.

The New Englanders strengthened Tocqueville's conviction that democracy was both inevitable and dangerous. Jared Sparks, Unitarian minister and Harvard history professor, [2b] whom Tocqueville had met before in Paris, instilled in his visitor's mind the idea of the tyranny of the majority, only to complain later that Tocqueville was making altogether too much of it.[16] Perhaps Tocqueville had gone too far when he wrote: "I know of no other country in which there is so little independence of mind and real freedom of discussion as in America." [3b7]

The high point of the New England visit was dinner at the home of Bostonian diplomat Alexander Everett, where Tocqueville was seated next to John Quincy Adams, the sixth president, who had lost his reelection bid to General Jackson. The two spoke in French, and the issue which dominated their wide-ranging conversation was slavery. Adams characterized white Southerners as a "class" with "all the ideas, all the passions, all the prejudices of an aristocracy," finding work "dishonorable" even though there was nothing in the Southern climate that should prevent them from working.[17] So Americans too had an aristocracy to contend with. Tocqueville soaked up the conversation and put all of it in *Democracy*. [3a2, 3b10]

In the fourth part of his trip, centered mostly around Philadelphia and

16 Sparks wrote: "I think he is entirely mistaken. His ideas are not verified by experience." See Herbert B. Adams, "Jared Sparks and Alexis de Tocqueville," *Johns Hopkins University Studies in Historical and Political Science* XVI, 12 (1898): p. 43.
17 Tocqueville, *Journey to America*, pp. 48–51.

Baltimore, Tocqueville reinforced many of the impressions he had acquired previously but also learned much more about American prisons. During their two-week stay in Philadelphia, Tocqueville made eight visits to the Eastern State penitentiary in Cherry Hill, where he interviewed each of the prisoners individually. He became deeply impressed by the Quaker-inspired emphasis on the prisoners' repentance by means of uninterrupted solitary confinement in cells large enough to provide an individual work space.

This fourth moment in the voyage brought only minor conceptual advances for *Democracy* but it had a major influence on Tocqueville's agenda as a political reformer during the 1840s. Philadelphia, like Boston, was a center of the abolitionist movement. Slavery was on everybody's mind as Nat Turner, who had led a violent slave rebellion in Virginia in the summer of 1831, had just been sentenced to death. In town, Tocqueville paid special attention to race relations. He went over many points already covered in the conversations of the previous months as he reviewed American institutions, population movements, and mores. He met also with Nicholas Biddle, who ran the Second Bank of the United States, and Joel Poinsett, a close associate of Jackson. A little further south, in Baltimore, the center of American Catholicism, Tocqueville visited the old Charles Carroll, who had been among the signers of the Declaration of Independence. Part of their conversation, on the frontier, appears in *Volume one*.[18] So do John H. B. Latrobe's opinions on political parties and lawyers. [2d] By now, Tocqueville was ready for the Southern or fifth part of the tour.

The two friends decided to enter the slave states from the West. They went to Pittsburgh to take a steamboat to Cincinnati, Ohio, where Tocqueville discussed universal suffrage at length with young abolitionist Salmon Portland Chase, who later became Chief Justice of the US Supreme Court. Then came the much anticipated entrance into slave territory. The shocking disparity between the two states of Ohio and Kentucky inspired Tocqueville to contrast them. [3b10] On the Northern bank of the Ohio river was work, on the Southern, idleness; on one merit, on the other birth; on one freedom, on the other slavery; on one democracy, on the other still aristocracy.

The Southern part of the trip was difficult and ultimately had to be aborted. November and December 1831 were exceptionally cold, and traveling proved hard. A steamboat accident forced the two friends to an adventurous inland detour including a twenty-five mile walk in the snow and further direct exposure to the elements on a one-horse open coach from Nashville to

18 See James T. Schleifer, *The Making of Tocqueville's "Democracy in America"* (Chapel Hill: University of North Carolina Press, 1980), p. 50.

Memphis. Tocqueville had to stop in a local inn for three days to recover from illness before he could move on.

In the South, the optimistic mood of the Northwest frontier gave way to pessimistic speculations on the future of the Indian tribes and on American governance. Tocqueville was deeply moved at the sight of Choctaw Indians displaced by the Federal government. The latter, he charged, was prosecuting under the legal guise of treaties the cruel extinction of an entire population. [3b10] On December 20, Tocqueville confided in his diary that he could not understand why the people of Tennessee had put an adventurer like Davy Crockett in office. [2e] On December 31, on the steamboat bound for New Orleans, he met heavy-drinking, uneducated Sam Houston who had been "the choice of the people" for governor of Tennessee. Houston, dubbed the White Cherokee for his years among Indians, actually instructed Tocqueville on native Americans more astutely than anybody else. [2f]

Tocqueville and Beaumont hurried though the Southern part of their journey. After a brief look at New Orleans, they decided to leave the South without having set foot on a plantation to observe the workings of slavery. For reasons which have remained obscure, the French government wanted the two commissioners back. Tocqueville, in turn, was getting worried about a young English woman named Marie Mottley whom he had met before leaving France, as early news reached him of the spreading cholera epidemic in Europe.

In the sixth and last segment of the trip, Tocqueville and Beaumont spent twelve days traveling by way of various stagecoaches across Alabama, Georgia, South Carolina, and North Carolina to reach Norfolk, Virginia, on their way to Washington, DC. There Tocqueville had a brief interview with President Jackson. It was also time to collect as much additional information as possible, a task made easier by Edward Livingston, an expert on the penal system in Louisiana who had become Jackson's secretary of state and who invited Beaumont and Tocqueville to every session of Congress he attended. Livingston saw to it that the two travelers had the books and publications they requested. Tocqueville, who, like most nineteenth-century French authors, rarely named specific informants in his writings, made an exception for Livingston, who became the only informant acknowledged as such by Tocqueville in the preface to *Volume one* of *Democracy*.[19]

Tocqueville and Beaumont embarked in New York for Le Havre on February 20, 1832.

---

19   In the second note, not reproduced here.

1832–1839: Becoming an Author, a Reformer,
and a Politician

Upon his return, the demands of friendship and personal loyalty quickly overwhelmed Tocqueville's intention to begin writing. Tocqueville took friendship seriously. Thus, despite his lack of sympathy for another Bourbon restoration, Tocqueville pleaded the case of his childhood companion Kergorlay, who was imprisoned in April 1832 for his participation in the Duchess of Berry's Legitimist plot to overthrow the July monarchy.

After he had helped to rescue Kergorlay from imprisonment, other tasks continued to keep Tocqueville away from *Democracy*. It was becoming urgent to complete the penitentiary assignment by turning in the report to the Ministry of the Interior. But it proved no easier for Tocqueville to come to grips with the prison system than with the larger American experience. Although the two friends had collaborated on every aspect of the penal investigation in America, Tocqueville now felt unfocused, perhaps even despondent about his future, and Beaumont, as a result, took on the responsibility of writing the report while Tocqueville submitted to the less demanding task of answering in writing his friend's questions. The report and subsequent book, which the friends cosigned, was a documentary history of American prisons. It was also a plea for the implementation in France of some measure of solitary confinement so as to avoid perpetuating "the society of villains" that had taken root in prisons. The report, which recommended balancing just punishment with individual repentance, launched Tocqueville's career as a social reformer.

Tocqueville finally overcame his writer's block after going to England, with Beaumont, in August and September 1833. Tocqueville had been thinking of visiting England ever since he had attended Guizot's lectures. His experience in Great Britain proved to be a powerful catalyst, highlighting the contrasts between France and America and giving him a better understanding of the American system. England was especially important in thinking comparatively. Two big ideas energized Tocqueville during this short visit. Tocqueville realized how influential the British aristocracy was in all aspects of life, making the country so different from the democratic America he had left behind. Conversely, the British practice of administrative decentralization, which contrasted so markedly with that of centralized France, helped Tocqueville place American institutions in their proper context. [6c5]

Returning to Paris from England, Tocqueville recognized that the time had come to draft the American book. What he needed to do was finally digest all his detailed travel notes and fill the gaps in his knowledge of

American history and government. [1c] He hired two young Americans living in Paris to provide him with summaries of over two hundred authorities, from Justice Story's *Commentary on the Constitution* to Jefferson's *Notes on Virginia* to *The Federalist Papers*, as well as the many documents Livingston had helped assemble and the long memorandum Jared Sparks had written for him. For the first time, Tocqueville came fully to grips with the Harvard professor's long disquisition on the political history of New England townships as the source of American democracy. [3a2] He also reflected on such thorny problems as ways of reconciling Montesquieu's emphasis on small republics with Madison's bold assurance that size did not impede democracy.

His friends and family were important influences as he completed the manuscript, albeit less on the substance of his ideas than on their form. Tocqueville read aloud drafts of his work and submitted manuscripts to them for corrections which he frequently accepted. After a year of writing in a Parisian attic, Tocqueville brought out *Volume one* in 1835. He was still only 29.

The book is often seen as one of the first works of modern political science. Indeed Tocqueville himself seems to have viewed it in this way, announcing in his introduction that "We need a new science of politics for a world completely new." [3a1] Tocqueville combined political reporting on the United States of 1831–32 with a full-scale analysis of the social consequences of politics and the political consequences of social practices. He reflected at length on the inevitable rise of equality, on the political and social benefits of administrative decentralization, on the freedom of political associations and the press, but also on the tyranny of the majority.

Tocqueville was not able to overcome the misgivings he had about the conclusions that he came to in the book. He painted America as the prototype of a society formed by the dual principles of equality and freedom, a society built on the voluntary associations of free and equal individuals in a weak state. But he feared that too much equality endangered freedom. An aristocrat at heart, his commitment to democracy was the determined surrender to an unavoidable future which, if properly managed, would be better than the aristocratic past. In a rare display of self-doubt, he wrote to Kergorlay, the friend he had just saved from prison, "the best thing for me would be if no one read my book."[20]

But that was not for him to decide. The success of *Volume one* brought him much praise, immediate fame, and instant recognition, including induction into the illustrious Académie des Sciences Morales et Politiques. The same year, 1835, Tocqueville married Marie Mottley, whom he had met

20 *O.C.*, January 1835, vol. 13, pt. 1, p. 374.

when he was a young lawyer at the courthouse in Versailles. As a commoner and a foreigner, she was never fully accepted by his family, and their married life was tumultuous. Although the two remained deeply in love, [5a] they had no children and frequent arguments. Alexis could not stop his "blood boiling at the sight of a woman" while Marie never accepted "the least deviation on my part."[21] "Deviate," however, he constantly did. Tocqueville resolved contradictions supremely well intellectually but it was more difficult for him to address them on a personal and emotional level.

A career change was also in order. Although now a well-known author, Tocqueville wrote to Kergorlay in 1837: "Do not believe that I have a blind enthusiasm, or indeed any kind of enthusiasm, for the intellectual life."[22] For Tocqueville, thought always came second to action. He rejected Royer-Collard's advice that he would be more useful as a writer and intellectual than as a politician. Marie, however, was supportive of his efforts to jump into politics, something he had wanted to do ever since his student years. After his mother's death in 1836, Tocqueville received the family estate of Tocqueville in Normandy, which had been unoccupied since the French Revolution, and turned the nearby town of Valognes into the electoral base for his political career. He then ran for election to the Chamber of Deputies.

What political party Tocqueville would join was not clear at first. He wished to be independent. But whom would he support after he won? Tocqueville was a self-described "liberal of a new kind" with a program that did not easily fit the pattern of either right or left. [5b and 5d] When he was elected in 1839 (after an initial failure in 1837), he insisted on sitting on the left of the Chamber to avoid being labeled a Legitimist.

A second trip to England, extended by a visit to Ireland shortly after the publication of *Volume one*, was instrumental in keeping Tocqueville on the path of social reform. This time, he devoted his attention exclusively to industrialization and poverty, two problems he had neglected in America but had begun to study in England with the help of Nassau William Senior, the prominent British economist who was revising the Poor Laws.[23] Tocqueville did not like the idea of public charity initially and thought that British laws tended to generate poverty. In the prison report, he and Beaumont had written that "any help given to an abandoned child" resulted "only in the

21 Letter to Kergorlay, September 27, 1843, *O.C.*, vol. 13, pt. 2, p. 121.
22 Letter to Kergorlay, October 4, 1837, *O.C.*, vol. 13, pt. 1, p. 479. See also the letter to Royer-Collard of November 20, 1838, *O.C.*, vol. 11, p. 74.
23 The British new poor law of 1834 limited relief payments to sick and aged paupers and established workhouses where able-bodied paupers were put to work. The law also ended the system of giving charitable relief to laborers as supplement to wages.

abandonment of another one."[24] Tocqueville came back from England, however, with a greater appreciation for the field of "pauperism," that is, the formulation of policies to fight poverty. He lectured on pauperism at the local Royal Academic Society of Cherbourg and argued the case for charity on behalf of only those poor who could not fend for themselves. On another occasion, he reflected on ways in which French workers could insure themselves a modicum of economic security through association. [4a–4c] Tocqueville, then, became a social reformer on his way to becoming a full-fledged politician.

In the span of a few years, then, Tocqueville had become a literary celebrity, a cautious reformer, a politician, and a local notable. With all this activity, Tocqueville found it difficult to find the time to write. As he lamented in 1839 while looking at the unfinished manuscript of *Volume two*: "I must at all costs finish this book. It and I have a duel to the death—I must kill it or it must kill me."[25] Tocqueville won, but he was by then several steps removed from his experience in America. Democracy as a social model had become his dominant subject. While *Volume one* was concerned mostly with American politics, *Volume two* focused on how the principle of equality affected society and culture. It contains some of Tocqueville's best generalizations on the nature of individualism, self-interest properly understood as social good, and the benefits of voluntary associations. Tocqueville forcefully argued that democracy was better served when the experience of political freedom preceded that of social equality, so as to control it and prevent its abuses. He presented a sustained comparison of aristocratic and democratic societies by outlining the consequences of different political regimes for language, science, and the arts, among many other topics. As Tocqueville himself put it to his British friend and reviewer John Stuart Mill, "I have meant to depict the general features of democratic societies, for which there is not yet a complete model." [6e] But as he also recognized, it was harder for the reader to follow him in these speculations. Historians have often wondered whether *Volume two* was the continuation of *Volume one*, as its title says, or a whole new and different book despite Tocqueville's view that the two were one. [6a] Sociologists have found in the Tocqueville of *Volume two* one of the first practitioners of their methods.[26] In its own time, however, this second volume suffered from being more abstract and difficult for readers to under-

---

24 Gustave de Beaumont and Alexis de Tocqueville, *Système pénitentiaire aux États-Unis et son application en France* (1833, 1836, 1845), *O.C.*, vol. 4, pt. 1, p. 152.
25 Letter to Beaumont, October 8, 1839, *O.C.*, vol. 8, pt. 1, p. 380.
26 Raymond Aron, *Main currents in sociological thought*, trans. Richard Howard and Helen Weaver (New York: Basic Books, 1965).

stand than the first. Although Mill praised it, many of the other reviews were unfavorable. As Tocqueville wrote to Royer-Collard: "I cannot hide from myself the fact that the book is not much read and not well understood by the great public."[27]

1840–1848: French Politics, Colonization, and Slavery

Even though Tocqueville was only modestly successful as a politician, his years in politics were the second great adventure of his life and played a major role in his thinking and later in his writing. Especially, he demonstrated that he loved freedom much more than equality. [7a and 7b] As a member of the Chamber of Deputies from 1839 to 1848, Tocqueville confronted three great issues: political reform, colonization, and slavery. He cannot be said to have been very effective at dealing with any of them, but then neither was the regime.

As an elected representative, Tocqueville was very much a member of the French political elite. Less than three per cent of the French adult male population was wealthy enough to have the right to vote and only one tenth of these voters were eligible for office by virtue of their still greater wealth. During much of Tocqueville's political career efforts to broaden suffrage played a leading role in politics, but Tocqueville did not support them, although he complained that voting was too restricted. He heralded the American example of universal male suffrage in his book, but proved shy about bringing it to France. He deemed France not ready, and he remained apprehensive of the tyranny of the majority.

Like almost all liberals of his time, Tocqueville maintained a distinction between civil rights, theoretically accessible to all, and political rights, limited to the few. Moreover, he thought that it was easier for Americans, who had the experience of political freedom, to implement equality than for the French, who were still struggling with the concept of liberty. Tocqueville himself remained haunted by the excesses of radicals during the Terror and was convinced they would surely abuse political power if they had it again.

Nevertheless, Tocqueville considered himself generally in favor of political reform. In the 1840s he supported Odilon Barrot's pro-monarchial center-left party, opposed to the immobilism of the conservative ministries led by Guizot. Tocqueville consistently opposed the regime by pushing in the Chamber for those basic freedoms which the July Monarchy had written into its own constitutional Charter, but had already severely limited by the time he was

27   Letter of August 25, 1840 *O.C.*, vol. 11, pp. 92–93.

elected. After 1835, no criticism of the king or of the form of government was tolerated in the newspapers. Public meetings were strictly controlled. Fighting against such restrictions on the freedom of the press and associations had already been a strong undercurrent of *Volume two* of *Democracy*. In the Chamber, Tocqueville challenged his old teacher minister Guizot, the strong-man of the regime, whom he admired as a historian, but who as politician gave only lip service to freedom and democracy. Tocqueville detested this later Guizot for what he saw as his lack of principle, his willingness to govern by corrupting deputies, and for his rejection of all political reforms, especially those designed to limit political corruption. But although aligned with the left, Tocqueville was one of its more moderate members. [7a]

Tocqueville was not a major parliamentary figure. He failed at attempts to create a "young left" party of his own. Tocqueville lacked two essential parliamentary qualities: ready comradeship with his colleagues, and great talent as a public speaker, the latter partly because tuberculosis had weakened his voice.

Tocqueville did, however, play a prominent role in the Chamber on certain issues, in particular on the colonization of Algeria. With the French experience in Quebec in mind, Tocqueville had at first questioned the desire of French people to leave their birthplace for distant colonies. But as a politician, he changed his mind and supported colonization as one of the great challenges of his generation. For Tocqueville, colonization was both a way of bringing political freedom to declining civilizations and of pushing complacent Frenchmen out of their bourgeois mediocrity.

When Tocqueville began writing on Algeria in 1837, he imagined that French and Arabs could eventually peacefully cohabit. When he visited the country in 1841, he felt that he had to support a brutal conquest in the face of Arab resistance. But when he returned in 1847 as member of a parliamen-tary commission, he denounced French military rule. His report to the Chamber contributed to precipitate Marshal Bugeaud's resignation as governor-general of the colony. By then, Tocqueville stood firmly for an emerging community of interests among colonizers and local peoples in lieu of the existing army dictatorship. Passionate as ever for decentralization, he advocated accommodating local customs, despite his deep dislike for the Koran. [8a] But he stood virtually alone in this position as French politicians and colonists alike could conceive of nothing better than replacing French military rule by French centralized administrative practice.

The French experience in Algeria led Tocqueville to look for comparisons with other colonial histories. Contrasting French agrarian colonization with the more flexible rule of British merchants in India, Tocqueville marveled at the British ability not only to play one local Indian prince against the other, control the economy by indirect rule, and implement a new administrative and legal structure, but to do all of this while accommodating local life. He credited the British advance to the absence of a French-style grand administrative design which would have proven too rigid and therefore crippling. As part of his notes on the British colony, his brief reflections on the Indian caste system were an important addition to his lifelong investigation of social hierarchies, which has shaped much of modern social science. [8b]

The abolition of slavery is the third great issue Tocqueville confronted as a politician. It was in debating the future of slavery that Tocqueville solidified his views of race relations. An abolitionist, he campaigned for ending slavery in the French colonies, as the British had done in theirs already in 1833. In 1839, a parliamentary committee for which Tocqueville was spokesman demanded the immediate emancipation of all slaves, but the matter never came to a vote. In 1843 the matter came up again, without any action being taken. Only with the Revolution of 1848 was slavery finally abolished.

When we examine his entire record, Tocqueville appears as a firm Eurocentric reformer, a supporter of exporting superior European cultures, but at the same time an advocate of local autonomy and political freedom. Moreover he strongly rejected any concept of biological hierarchy. He had a chance to make his position on this last point abundantly clear a few years later when demolishing the premises of Arthur de Gobineau's famous *Essay on the Inequality of the Human Races* (1853). For Tocqueville, arguments about the superiority of one blood over another were yet another form of predestination and denial of human freewill, which he rejected in the name of freedom. [10f]

1848–1851: In the Second Republic

Meanwhile, restrictions on freedom were increasingly felt at home. By the late 1840s, Tocqueville had become keenly aware of growing popular opposition to the regime and other similar movements in Europe. He talked about "the air of revolution" overtaking France in one of his few memorable speeches in the Chamber of Deputies in January 1848. But always on the side of order, he refused to join the "banquet campaign" – disguised political meetings held by the opposition in public halls and parks to push for enlarging the electorate, among other reforms. The revolution that broke out after the prohibition of the demonstration and banquet of February 22 resulted in Louis-Philippe's abdication and improvised departure for England two days later.

What was unfolding under Tocqueville's own eyes was an extraordinary rerun of a cycle of freedom and repression Tocqueville knew all too well from his reflections on the Revolution and First Empire of Napoleon I. Only this time, he was caught in the midst of it.

At first, Tocqueville's hope was that the nine year-old Comte de Paris would be declared the new king with the liberal Duchess of Orleans acting as regent. But there was little support for this solution. Instead, the Second Republic was solemnly declared on February 27. Tocqueville decided to support it. As he put it in his *Recollections*, he plunged "headlong into the fray, risking wealth, peace of mind and life to defend, not any particular government, but the laws that hold society together."[28]

Tocqueville ran again for election, and the peasants in his district, voting for the first time under universal male suffrage, returned him to office in April. A month later, he supported General Cavaignac's quelling of the vast June 1848 insurrection which the new regime had provoked by ending its program of public works, depriving tens of thousands of their livelihood.

Despite his personal prominence, Tocqueville's influence in the Second Republic remained limited. While serving on the committee writing the new Republican constitution, where his friend Beaumont had also been appointed, Tocqueville resisted his colleagues' design for centralized rule to no avail. To increase the leverage of local elites, he proposed a bicameral system after the American model, but the other members rejected this idea. Beaumont, however, successfully proposed that the president serve only one term. This measure would soon have the unintended effect of enticing Louis Napoleon, elected president of the Republic in December 1849, to stage a military coup on December 2, 1851.

Tocqueville served for five months in 1849 as minister of foreign affairs, where he appointed the young and impecunious poet Gobineau, with whom he later argued about race, as his private secretary. In the ministry, he inherited a difficult situation in Rome, where a French contingent had just reinstated Pope Pius IX, forced to flee as a result of revolution. He chose a devout Catholic, his friend Francisque de Corcelle who had so perceptively endorsed *Volume one* back in 1835, as his ambassador to the Vatican, with instructions to suggest democratic reforms. But it was wishful thinking to believe the pontiff capable of them. [9g] The year of revolution, 1848, was already over in Paris, in Rome, and elsewhere. [9f]

In his unfinished but beautifully written *Recollections* of these years, Tocqueville underscored the "class struggle" [9b9] in the French Second Republic. Tocqueville never read Marx, and unlike him, Tocqueville did not interpret

---

28 Alexis de Tocqueville, *Recollections*. trans. G. Lawrence, ed. J. P. Mayer (Garden City, NY: Doubleday and Co., 1971), p. 85.

the events of June 1848 as the rebellion of the proletariat against the bourgeoisie. Yet like Marx and also Proudhon, he saw in the revolution the unmistakable sign of a lasting class challenge to property rights. [7d, 9a]

Louis-Napoleon's coup sent a resisting Tocqueville to jail for a few days. More importantly, it ended his political career for good. Tocqueville could accept a republic, but not another empire legalized by plebiscite. With the French willingly relinquishing their freedom to an adventurer, who happened to be the nephew of the first Napoleon, an oppressive centralized regime was back, and with it the all too familiar cycle in French history of oscillating between the anarchy of revolution and the oppression of a despot. [9a and 9b]

Tocqueville and the Second Empire

Tocqueville's opposition to the Second Empire did not waver. To his dying day he lived in a kind of internal exile, refusing to swear the oath of loyalty to Napoleon III. This made him ineligible to hold public office. He refused to change his mind even when Napoleon III sounded him out in 1853 about returning as foreign minister. Not surprisingly, Tocqueville had great contempt for former liberals who went over to the new regime, as well as for place-hunting ex-Legitimist aristocrats and submissive clergymen. In *The Old Regime* he would compare the docile clergy of 1852, the first to bow before the new monarch, with the stiff-necked clergy of the eighteenth century, who often took the lead in resisting royal despotism. Tocqueville himself took part in skirmishes in the two prestigious societies of which he was a member – the Académie française and that of sciences morales et politiques – to make sure Bonapartist candidates for membership were defeated. It is a measure of Tocqueville's hatred of Napoleon III's coup d'état that he broke relations with people who supported it, including his own brother Edouard, who ran for election in 1852 on a platform defending the coup.

These events made Tocqueville increasingly pessimistic about the chances of lasting political freedom ever being established in France. He feared that France would merely alternate between periods of authoritarian despotism and anarchy. [13d] His own political philosophy did not change, but his belief in the ability of France to embody it had been shaken. [compare 5b to 10d] So Tocqueville turned to his pen. As he had already written in 1837: "I cannot understand how when the route of *action* is closed, one does not throw oneself with all one's strength towards *thought*."[29] The object of that thought

29   Letter to Kergorlay, October 4, 1837, *O.C.*, vol. 13, pt. 1, p. 479.

was the causes and consequences of the French Revolution, and the result was *The Old Regime and the Revolution*.

The Old Regime and the Revolution

In 1850, when the Second Republic was still in existence, Tocqueville had already foreseen a time when he would return to writing. His experience and his self-critical honesty led him to think less of his own political abilities than he had in the 1830s. [10a] After Napoleon III's coup, Tocqueville once again felt compelled to express his views on modern democratic society and its probable future. But he did not want to write an abstract treatise of political theory. He decided to use the French Revolution as the vehicle for his ideas. In Tocqueville's eyes, the Revolution begun in 1789 was still unresolved. [12c2] Writing about the France of the Revolution enabled him, like many nineteenth-century intellectuals, to write freely about the world of his own day.

The year 1850 was not the first time Tocqueville had thought seriously about the Revolution of 1789. In 1836 he had written an essay, "The Social and Political State of France Before and After 1789," for John Stuart Mill's *London and Westminster Review*. But the work of the 1850s differs from the earlier work in many respects, not least in its point of departure. Although *The Old Regime* would become a book about the period preceding the Revolution, it started out as a study of Napoleon I. Watching a Second Empire succeeding a Second Republic, Tocqueville could use the unfolding events in the late eighteenth century as parallels for himself and his contemporaries in the middle of the nineteenth. In the summer of 1852 he wrote two chapters about 1799, "How the Republic was Ready to Receive a Master," [12c1] and "How the Nation, While No Longer Republican, Had Remained Revolutionary." The dominant tone of these chapters is somber. Tocqueville knew that history repeating itself is both farce and tragedy. He described the farce in his *Recollections*. The tragedy of French history was reserved for *The Old Regime*, once Tocqueville had decided that neither Napoleon nor the Revolution could be understood without an understanding of the France from which they emerged.

Seeing the continuity with the American work, Beaumont suggested "Democracy and Freedom in France" as the title for the work we know as *The Old Regime*.[30] *The Old Regime* was Tocqueville's final attempt to work out the precarious relationship between democracy and freedom in the

---

30   Beaumont to Tocqueville, see *O.C.*, vol. 8, pt. 3, pp. 372–73.

modern world, and in this regard it is certainly a continuation of *Democracy in America*. But the political context described in *The Old Regime*, a despotism rather than a democracy, was much more pessimistic. Had France given up its freedom? More importantly, how could France regain it? *The Old Regime* describes how the French monarchy created the preconditions for despotism, while Tocqueville desperately looks around for a means of escape.

The fundamental influences on *The Old Regime* are the same as those on *Democracy in America*: Rousseau and Montesquieu, Guizot and the Doctrinaires. But Tocqueville rejected the Doctrinaires' account of the Revolution as the triumph of the middle classes (which much influenced the Marxist interpretation of the Revolution). The middle class is not the major player in *The Old Regime*; it takes a back seat to both the monarchy and the intellectuals.[31] One important new influence on Tocqueville, however, is the Revolution's great English opponent, Edmund Burke. Burke published his classic *Reflections on the Revolution in France* in 1790. It was a combination of probing analysis and brilliant counter-revolutionary rhetoric. Comparison of *The Old Regime* and the *Reflections* shows how much of Tocqueville's book was constructed as a running dialogue with Burke. At a number of points in *The Old Regime*, Tocqueville explicitly refutes Burke, taking pleasure in pointing out his rival's blind spots: "Burke does not realize that what stands before his eyes is . . ." [11b5] What Tocqueville studiously does not mention is how much he borrows from Burke, how often their analyses agree. The famous chapter on the Revolution as religion especially owes Burke a great deal. [11b3]

Tocqueville's methods as a writer are also similar in the *Democracy* and *The Old Regime*, but they have been perfected in the later work. Tocqueville in *The Old Regime* is constantly weaving back and forth between the particular and the general. There is no fact that is not chosen to illustrate a particular argument, and rarely an argument that is not embodied in a fact or telling anecdote. Often the facts are used to reveal previously unsuspected consequences of earlier generalizations, while the new consequence is then used to link to apparently separate arguments or causal chains. *The Old Regime* is a masterpiece of literary construction.

The three Books of *The Old Regime* follow a clear plan.[32] In the first book,

---

31 Although there are indications that the middle class would have played a greater role in the projected second Book of the projected second volume. See Alan S. Kahan, "Tocqueville's Two Revolutions," *Journal of the History of Ideas*, 46 (1985): pp. 585–96.

32 As we have it today, *The Old Regime* is divided into three Books. Tocqueville made this division in the second edition – originally Books two and three were not separated. Before publication, Tocqueville subdivided several chapters. But Tocqueville never changed the order in which he presented his ideas.

Tocqueville enunciates what has become known as the "continuity thesis," the idea that the French Revolution, despite the rhetoric of the moment, occurred more in continuity with past trends than in opposition to them. [11a and 11b] This idea so arrests readers that they often stop and accuse Tocqueville of ignoring the vastly innovative character of the Revolution, something he never did, as can be seen, for example, in *Book one*, chapter 3, where he discusses how the Revolution in practice became something utterly new, a political religion. [11a] Tocqueville wants us to hold both of these seemingly contradictory viewpoints – the Revolution is old, the Revolution is new – at the same time, for only then can we begin to understand it.

Centralization is the great theme of *Book two* on long-term causes. *Book two* develops the idea that bureaucratic centralization under royal authority, and the destruction of local governments and freedoms that went with it, was a long-term cause of the Revolution. [11c] Paradoxically, the history of centralized France is sometimes explicitly described as that of decentralized America gone wrong, as when Tocqueville compares the New England township with the eighteenth-century French village: "They resembled each other, in a word, as much as the living could resemble the dead."[33] Much of *Book two* derives from the year Tocqueville spent at Tours, from June 1853 until May 1854, reading about life in eighteenth-century France as captured in the files of the royal administration of the province of Touraine. He was among the first to use such archives. Critics of Tocqueville often note that he exaggerated the extent of the monarchy's success in making France uniform. But the critics usually omit Tocqueville's awareness of regional differences, as can be seen in the appendix to *The Old Regime* devoted to Languedoc (not included here). For Tocqueville, the course of the Revolution in 1789–99 demonstrated that differences were of less importance than similarities.

Book three on more recent causes opens with the famous chapter on the role of intellectuals in bringing about the revolution. [11d1] It describes their unique position in French society and argues that intellectuals too demanded equality more often than freedom. In Tocqueville's view the monarchy, by depriving the nobility, the Third Estate, and even the royal administration of any real experience with politics, had opened the way for intellectuals to exercise political influence and shape public opinion, unbridled by any practical experience, either on their own part or on that of their audience. Afterwards *Book three* discusses additional sources of political discontent: the growing irreligion of the upper classes, the growing dissatisfaction of the poor as their oppression became a matter of public debate, even how growing

---

33 *The Old Regime*, trans. Alan S. Kahan, ed. François Furet and Françoise Mélonio (Chicago: University of Chicago Press, 1998) 1: p. 129.

economic prosperity made people less tolerant of old practices. By the end of
the book, revolution seems a natural consequence of an accumulation of long-
and medium-term factors. Centralization, while destroying freedom and self-
government, encourages equality. This equality leads not to greater harmony
but to greater social antagonism, as vestigial privileges and distinctions seem
more objectionable than ever. While revolution seems inevitable, lasting
freedom seems anything but likely, although Tocqueville, by force of will,
refuses to despair. [11d8]

Tocqueville is on the side of freedom, and he refuses to let the Revolution,
especially in its initial inspiration, be on the other side. *Book one* of the
projected second volume praises the Revolution's shining moments. The key
to overcoming the legacy of absolutism lies in the spirit of freedom embodied
in the first meetings of the Estates-General in 1789, and in the Declaration of
the Rights of Man and the Citizen. [12a7] How Tocqueville would have
concluded the second volume will never be known. It is hard to imagine a
happy ending, with Napoleon on the way. Tocqueville is highly critical of
the path followed by supporters of the Revolution, who agreed ultimately to
compromise liberty in the name of equality. Tocqueville, however, always
rejected fatalism. Perhaps it was the difficulty of finding hope in the Revolution that prevented Tocqueville from finishing his work. Certainly in 1857–58
he was often discouraged about his progress. But Tocqueville had sounded
discouraged before. Maybe the more prosaic explanation of his discouragement is the better one – by the time he grew seriously worried about the
progress of *Volume two*, in the spring of 1858, Tocqueville was a dying man.

When *The Old Regime and the Revolution* was published in 1856, it was
accorded an enthusiastic reception. *The Old Regime* was acknowledged as a
towering achievement even by political opponents. It was also recognized as
a work of the liberal opposition to Napoleon III, and gave Tocqueville
renewed political prominence. In the years immediately after his death in
1859, Tocqueville served, on the strength of *The Old Regime*, as the liberals'
figurehead.

Tocqueville's *Old Regime* completed his contribution to a European
political tradition of aristocratic liberalism.[34] Other notable figures in this
tradition were Gustave Flaubert and Ernest Renan in France, John Stuart Mill
and Matthew Arnold in England, and the Swiss–German historian Jacob
Burckhardt. Aristocratic liberals prized political freedom and individuality
while harboring a good deal of contempt for middle-class materialism. Unlike

---

34   See Alan S. Kahan, *Aristocratic Liberalism: the Social and Political Thought of Jacob
Burckhardt, John Stuart Mill and Alexis de Tocqueville* (New Brunswick: Transaction Publishers, 2001).

the Doctrinaires and most other nineteenth-century European liberals, Tocqueville, Mill, and like-minded thinkers did not identify political liberty with the middle class. This aristocratic liberalism existed throughout Europe in the mid nineteenth century, although it was never the dominant current. Even celebrated authors like Tocqueville and Mill considered themselves intellectually isolated. Tocqueville and Mill had much in common. Although the relationship between the two of them had cooled due to disagreements about French foreign policy and Harriet Mill's dislike of Tocqueville, Mill sent Tocqueville a copy of his newly-published *On Liberty* just a few months before Tocqueville's death in 1859. Unfortunately, Tocqueville died before he was able to comment on it as he had promised.

Tocqueville's Last Days

Tocqueville, who never enjoyed robust health, died on April 16, 1859, at the age of 53. Contemporaries often noted his sickly complexion when they first met him, and from his youth he suffered from migraines, digestive problems, and general poor health. It was not bad enough to keep him from traveling all over America on horseback and by carriage, in very strenuous conditions, nor from going on long cross-country walks in Normandy. Nevertheless, it is likely that Tocqueville was a victim of tuberculosis long before his first episode of spitting blood in March 1850. Despite the remissions characteristic of the disease, Tocqueville was never afterwards in good health for long. Tocqueville's letters in this volume often make reference to his health, and with reason. Even his time in the Tours archives was prompted by his doctor's insistence that he avoid the colder, damper winter climate of Normandy.

In April 1858 Tocqueville went to Paris, planning to spend considerable time consulting the libraries there for his work on *Volume two* of *The Old Regime*. By May he felt so ill he had to give up work and return to his manor at Tocqueville. In late October he and his wife moved south to Cannes, on the warm French Riviera, in the hope that the mild winter climate would do him good. It did not. As he wished, his body was taken back to Normandy for burial in the village cemetery of Tocqueville.

Tocqueville's death has prompted a certain amount of controversy over whether he returned to Catholicism in his last days. His wife, a devout convert to Catholicism, certainly did her best to persuade him to confess before his death, and afterwards encouraged the impression that he had died a Catholic. Tocqueville, however, had always outwardly observed Catholic forms, despite holding Deist beliefs, setting an example of the alliance of religion and liberal political beliefs his works always held up as ideal.[35] It seems most probable that Tocqueville never recovered his Catholic faith. The one god he had always worshiped was Freedom.

This Reader

Democracy in America and *The Old Regime and the Revolution* are part of Tocqueville's enduring quest to understand the relationship between equality and freedom in the modern world. As Tocqueville demonstrated in both works, equality could enhance freedom in some contexts and under the right circumstances, but seriously imperil it in others. When written, these two books were linked to specific political events and experiences that inspired their author. Yet the two works have been separated in posterity as these events have lost their immediacy for subsequent generations.

Each book has had an important afterlife of its own. Suffice it to say that, as the United States changed from a society committed to local forms of voluntary associations to one dominated by national organizations, *Democracy* lost much of its appeal. It was largely neglected by the reading public until American social scientists of the 1950s rediscovered the old idea of national character. They found inspiration in Tocqueville but appropriated his book for their own purposes, whether celebrating America as the only country born modern or exposing its mass society.[36] In France, the ruling political battles of the Third and Fourth Republics, and the increasingly prevalent Marxist interpretation of the Revolution in academic circles overshadowed the *Old Regime* even longer, until the 1970s. As political passions over the French Revolution finally faded into the new technocratic and modernizing program of the Fifth Republic, intellectuals rediscovered Tocqueville for his comparative methods and brilliant interpretation of the Revolution. They found his explanations powerful antidotes to what François Furet once called "the Revolutionary catechism" associated with Marxism.[37]

The subsequent collapse of the Soviet Union has contributed to a dramatic

35   Doris S. Goldstein, *Trial of Faith: Religion and Politics in Tocqueville's Thought* (New York: Elsevier, 1975), gives a good account of the debate. See also Jardin, *Tocqueville*, pp. 528–33.

36   Seymour Martin Lipset, *The First New Nation: the United States in Historical and Comparative Perspective* (New York: Basic Books, 1963); David Riesman, in coll. with Reuel Denney and Nathan Glazer, *The Lonely Crowd: a Study of the Changing American Character* (New Haven: Yale University Press, 1950).

37   François Furet, *Interpreting the French Revolution*, trans. Elborg Forster (New York: Cambridge University Press, 1981).

revitalization in Europe, including Eastern Europe, of Tocqueville's ideas on civil society as a necessary foundation of self government. In the United States the same event has prompted a new and still ongoing examination of the broad debates on the merits of American civil society, many of which were initiated by *Democracy*. In this reader, our only ambition is to show how Tocqueville himself understood these connections.

Editors' Acknowledgments

The editors owe thanks to David A. Bell, David D. Bien, Charles Feigenoff, Maurice Kriegel, Pap Ndiaye, and Sophia Rosenfeld for their precious counsel in writing this introduction, and to Françoise Mélonio for her help throughout, not least in bringing the editors together. Alan Kahan is grateful to Florida International University for granting him leave in which to work on this volume; Olivier Zunz to the University of Virginia electronic text center for scanning the initial French or English version of the selected texts, and to his students of HIST 403, *Reading Tocqueville*, as well as his colleagues of the University of Virginia Center on Religion and Democracy, for many stimulating conversations.

OZ and ASK

Chronology of Alexis de Tocqueville's Life and Some of the Principal Events which Affected it

1750   Conventional date for the beginning of French Enlightenment.

July 4, 1776   American Independence.

May, 1789   Meeting of the Estates-General at Versailles.

July 14, 1789   Fall of the Bastille.

August, 1789   Abolition of Feudalism, Declaration of the Rights of Man and the Citizen.

1792   Deposition of the king, creation of the French Republic.

1793–94   Terror, rule of Robespierre and the Committee of Public Safety. Imprisonment of Tocqueville's parents, execution of his great grandfather, Malesherbes.

1795–99   France governed by the Directory.

Brumaire 18 (November 9), 1799   Napoleon leads coup and comes to power as First Consul.

1803   Napoleon proclaimed Emperor.

July 29, 1805   Birth of Alexis de Tocqueville.

December, 1805   Battle of Austerlitz.

1815   Battle of Waterloo, end of First Empire.

1815–30   Bourbon Restoration. King Louis XVIII (1815–24). Hervé de Tocqueville (Alexis' father) prefect and peer.

1824–30   Reign of Charles X, attempt to revive absolute monarchy.

1824–26   Alexis at law school at Paris.

1827–32   Alexis apprentice judge at Versailles.

July, 1830   Revolution overthrows Charles X, creates July Monarchy, King Louis-Philippe.

1831–32   Tocqueville's trip to America, with Gustave de Beaumont, ostensibly to investigate the prison system.

1833   Tocqueville and Beaumont publish their report on American penitentiaries.

1833   Tocqueville's first trip to England.

1835   Tocqueville marries Marie Mottley.

1835   *Democracy in America*, Volume one, published.

1835   Trip to England and Ireland.

1837   Tocqueville narrowly misses being elected to the Chamber of Deputies.

1838   Tocqueville elected to the Académie des Sciences Morales et Politiques.

1839   Tocqueville elected to the Chamber as the representative of Valognes, a small town near Cherbourg and Tocqueville. He will continue to represent this district until he leaves public life in 1852.

1840   *Democracy in America*, Volume two, published.

1841   Tocqueville elected to the Académie Française.

1841   First trip to Algeria.

1846   Second trip to Algeria.

February 24–25, 1848   Revolution proclaims Second Republic.

June 23–26, 1848   Insurrection of Paris lower classes suppressed.

1849   First trip to Germany.

June–October, 1849   Tocqueville Minister for Foreign Affairs.

1850   Tocqueville writes his *Recollections* about the events of 1848–50 while in Italy recuperating from severe attack of tuberculosis.

December 2, 1851   Coup by President Louis-Napoleon Bonaparte. Tocqueville briefly imprisoned.

December 2, 1852   Louis-Napoleon proclaims himself Emperor Napoleon III. Second Empire established.

1854   Second trip to Germany.

1856   *The Old Regime and the Revolution* published.

1859   Tocqueville dies of tuberculosis at Cannes.

Part I

The Discovery of
Democracy in America

Preliminary Note

This section presents the first five years of Tocqueville's work, from the American voyage in 1831–32 to the publication and reception of volume one of *Democracy in America* in 1835. In letters to friends Ernest de Chabrol and Louis de Kergorlay, and to his mother, Tocqueville sketches out his first impressions of America (1a–c). Throughout the trip he confides in his diaries his thoughts on politics, law, society, and mores. He also carefully transcribes conversations with his informants. We have selected transcriptions of conversations with Unitarian minister and Harvard history professor Jared Sparks, Baltimore lawyer John H. B. Latrobe, and former Tennessee Governor Sam Houston, later President of The Republic of Texas (2a–g). The reader can catch a glimpse of the creation of *Democracy* by comparing the 1835 book with some of Tocqueville's initial views.

Sampling *Democracy* entailed difficult choices. Because Tocqueville was correct about so many things, big and small, he is often viewed as a particularly shrewd pundit and prophet. But Tocqueville had no supernatural powers and his conclusions were of necessity closely tied to the events of 1831–32 as he understood them. To take only one example, Jared Sparks, Joel R. Poinsett, Nicholas Biddle, Charles Carroll, John H. B. Latrobe, and other informants all agreed that great political parties had disappeared in the United States. Tocqueville reported this news faithfully, just before the rise of mass political parties in the 1840s. Even his most famous prediction, that of the growing parallel power of the United States and Russia in the modern world (3b10), was actually commonplace in the French press of the 1830s.

Rather than deciding when Tocqueville was visionary or mistaken, we concentrated on those passages most representative of Tocqueville's own intellectual quest: the exploration of the tense relationship between equality and freedom. Thus we have included his reflections on the inevitable rise of equality, on the benefits of administrative decentralization, and on the tyranny of the majority (3a–b). As Tocqueville was a committed abolitionist, we have included also a large part of his powerful chapter on American race relations (3b10).

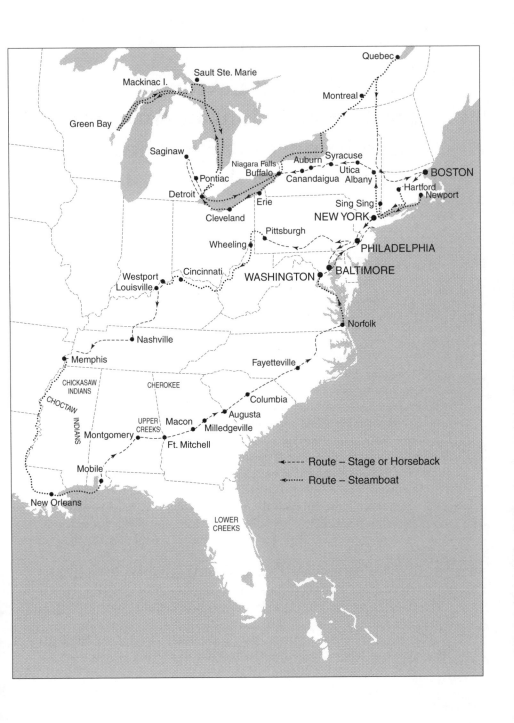

Quebec

Sault Ste. Marie

Mackinac I.

Montreal

Green Bay

Saginaw

Auburn Syracuse

BOSTON

Niagara Falls

Utica

Pontiac Buffalo

Canandaigua Albany

Hartford

Detroit

Erie

Newport

Cleveland

Sing Sing

NEW YORK

Pittsburgh

Wheeling

PHILADELPHIA

Westport Cincinnati

WASHINGTON BALTIMORE

Louisville

Norfolk

Nashville

Fayetteville

Memphis

CHICKASAW
INDIANS

CHEROKEE

Columbia

CHOCTAW
INDIANS

UPPER
CREEKS Macon Augusta

Montgomery Milledgeville

Ft. Mitchell

Mobile

LOWER
CREEKS

New Orleans

←----- Route – Stage or Horseback

←······ Route – Steamboat

I

Travel Letters:
First Impressions of America
and Important Sketches of
Democracy in America, 1831

1a   To Ernest de Chabrol[1]

New York, June 9, 1831

Imagine, my dear friend, if you can, a society formed of all the nations of the world: English, French, Germans . . . people having different languages, beliefs, opinions: in a word, a society without roots, without memories, without prejudices, without routines, without common ideas, without a national character, yet a hundred times happier than our own; more virtuous? I doubt it. That is the starting point: What serves as the link among such diverse elements? What makes all of this into one people? Interest. That is the secret. The private interest that breaks through at each moment, the interest that, moreover, appears openly and even proclaims itself as a social theory.

In this, we are quite far from the ancient republics, it must be admitted, and nonetheless this people is republican, and I do not doubt that it will be so for a long time yet. And for this people a republic is the best of governments.

I can explain this phenomenon only by thinking that America finds itself, for the present, in a physical situation so fortunate, that private interest is never contrary to the general interest, which is certainly not the case in Europe.

What generally inclines men to disturb the state? On the one hand, the desire to gain power; on the other, the difficulty of creating a happy existence

---

1   A young lawyer who shared an apartment with Tocqueville and Beaumont in Versailles in 1828.

for themselves by ordinary means. Here, there is no public power, and, to tell the truth, there is no need for it. The territorial divisions are so limited; the states have no enemies, consequently no armies, no taxation, no central government; the executive power is nothing; it confers neither money nor power. As long as things remain this way, who will want to torment his life in order to attain power?

Now, looking at the other part of my assertion, one arrives at the same conclusion; because, if political careers are more or less closed, a thousand, ten thousand others are open to human activity. The whole world here seems a malleable material that man turns and fashions to his liking. An immense field, of which the smallest part has yet been traversed, is here open to industry. There is no man who cannot reasonably expect to attain the comforts of life: there is none who does not know that with love of work, his future is certain.

Thus, in this fortunate country, nothing attracts the restlessness of the human spirit toward political passions; everything, on the contrary, draws it toward activity that poses no danger to the state. I would wish that all of those who, in the name of America, dream of a republic for France, could come see for themselves what it is like here.

This last reason that I just gave you, to my mind the prime reason, explains equally well the only two outstanding characteristics that distinguish this people: its industrial spirit and the instability of its character.

Nothing is easier than becoming rich in America; naturally, the human spirit, which needs a dominant passion, in the end turns all its thoughts toward gain. As a result, at first sight this people seems to be a company of merchants joined together for trade, and as one digs deeper into the national character of the Americans, one sees that they have sought the value of everything in this world only in the answer to this single question: how much money will it bring in?

As for the instability of character, it breaks through in a thousand places; an American takes up, quits and takes up again ten trades in his lifetime; he changes his residence ceaselessly and continually forms new enterprises. Less than any other man in the world he fears jeopardizing a fortune once he has acquired it, because he knows with what ease he can acquire a new one.

Besides, change seems to him the natural state of man, and how could it be otherwise? Everything is ceaselessly astir around him – laws, opinions, public officials, fortunes – the earth itself here changes its face every day. In the midst of the universal movement that surrounds him, the American could not stay still.

One must not look here either for that family spirit, or for those ancient traditions of honor and virtue, that distinguish so eminently several of our old societies of Europe. A people that seems to live only to enrich itself could not be a virtuous people in the strict meaning of the word; but it is *well ordered*. All of the trifles that cling to idle riches it does not have: its habits are regular, there is little or no time to devote to women, and they seem to be valued only as mothers of families and managers of households. Mores are pure; this is incontestable. The *roué* of Europe is absolutely unknown in America; the passion for making a fortune carries away and dominates all others.

1b   To Louis de Kergorlay[2]

Yonkers, June 29, 1831
20 miles from New York

I am beginning my letter here, my dear friend, but I do not know when or where I will finish it. I have not written you earlier because I have not had anything in particular to tell you; I dislike talking of France from so far away. You would have nearly forgotten the events to which my letter referred by the time it reached you; the things I would be discussing would have changed ten times in the interim. On the other hand, before talking to you about this country, I wanted to know it a little better than I did when I had first arrived. I see that I have not gained much by waiting. The people of every foreign country have a certain external appearance that one perceives at first glance and retains very readily. When one wants to penetrate a little further, one finds real difficulties that were not expected, one proceeds with a discouraging slowness, and doubts seem to grow the more one progresses. I feel at this moment that my head is a chaos into which a throng of contradicting notions are pell-mell making their way. I am wearing myself out looking for some perfectly clear and conclusive points, and not finding any. In this state of mind, it is both agreeable and useful for me to be writing you. Maybe my ideas will untangle themselves a little under the obligation of explaining them; moreover, were I to find only hollow musings and doubts, I would still send them to you without any qualms. One of the advantages of our friendship is that we know each other so perfectly and we are so sure of our truthfulness toward each other that we can express to each other the *beginnings* of opinions without fearing interpretations; we are quite sure that the mind of the one who is writing is exactly in the position in which it reveals itself to be, neither more nor less.

You ask me in your last letter if there are *beliefs* here. I do not know what

2   A distant cousin, best friend since childhood.

precise sense you attach to that word; what strikes me is that the immense majority of people are united in regard to certain *common opinions*. So far, that is what I have envied most about America. To begin with, I have not yet been able to overhear in a conversation with anyone, no matter to what rank in society they belong, the idea that a republic is not the best possible government, and that a people does not have the right to give itself whatever government it pleases. The great majority understands republican principles in the most democratic sense, although among some one can see a certain aristocratic tendency piercing through that I will try to explain to you below. But that a republic is a good government, that it is natural for human societies, no one seems to doubt – priests, magistrates, businessmen, artisans. That is an opinion that is so general and so little discussed, even in a country where freedom of speech is unlimited, that one could almost call it a belief. There is a second idea that seems to me to be of the same character; the immense majority has *faith* in human wisdom and good sense, faith in the doctrine of human perfectibility. That is another point that finds little or no contradiction. That the majority can be fooled once, no one denies, but people think that necessarily in the long run the majority is right, that it is not only the sole legal judge of its interests but also the surest and most infallible judge. The result of this idea is that enlightenment must be diffused widely among the people, that one cannot enlighten the people too much. You know how many times in France we have been anxious (we and a thousand others) to know if it is to be desirable or fearful for education to penetrate through all the ranks of society. This question, which is so difficult for France to resolve, does not even seem to present itself here. I have already posed this question a hundred times to the most reflective men; I have seen, by the way they have answered it, that it has never given them pause, and to them even stating the question had something shocking and absurd about it. Enlightenment, they say, is the sole guarantee we have against the mistakes of the multitude.

There you have, my dear friend, what I will call the *beliefs* of this country. They believe, in good faith, in the excellence of the government that rules them, they believe in the wisdom of the masses, provided that they are enlightened, and they do not seem to suspect that there is some education that can never be shared by the masses and that nonetheless can be necessary for governing a state.

As for what we generally understand by *beliefs*, ancient mores, ancient traditions, the power of memories, I have not seen any trace of these up to now. I even doubt that religious opinions have as great a power as one thinks at first sight.

The state of religion among this people is perhaps the most curious thing to examine here. I will try to tell you what I know about this when I again pick up my letter, which I now have to interrupt, perhaps for several days.

Calwell, 45 miles from New York

My mind has been so stirred up since this morning by the beginning of my letter that I feel I have to take it up again without knowing just what I am going to say to you. I was speaking to you above about religion: one is struck on arriving here by the practical exactitude that accompanies the practice of religion. Sunday is observed Judaically, and I have seen streets blocked off in front of churches during the holy services. The law commands these things imperiously, and opinion, much stronger than the law, compels everyone to appear at church and to abstain from all amusements. Nevertheless, either I am badly mistaken or there is a great store of doubt and indifference hidden underneath these external forms. Political passion is not mixed, as it is in our country, with irreligion, but even so religion does not have any more power. It is a very strong impulse that was given in days gone by and which now is expiring day by day. Faith is evidently inert; enter the churches (I mean the Protestant ones) and you hear them speak of morality; of dogma not a word, nothing that could in any way shock a neighbor, nothing that could reveal the hint of dissidence. The human spirit loves to plunge itself into abstractions of dogma, discussions which are especially appropriate to a religious doctrine, whenever a belief has seized it strongly; the Americans themselves were formerly like that. This so-called tolerance, which, in my opinion, is nothing but a huge indifference, is pushed so far that in public establishments like prisons, the homes for juvenile delinquents . . . seven or eight ministers of different sects come to preach successively to the same inmates. But, I was saying, how those men and those children who belong to one sect find themselves listening to the ministry of another. The infallible response is this: the different preachers, because they occupy themselves only with treating the platitudes of morality, cannot do harm to one another. Besides, it is evident that here, generally speaking, religion does not move people deeply; in France those who believe demonstrate their belief by sacrifices of time, effort, and wealth. One senses that they are acting under the sway of a passion that dominates them and for which they have become agents. It is true that alongside these people one finds the kinds of brutes who hold in horror the very name of religion and who do not very easily even distinguish good from evil. Neither of these groups seems to exist here among the bulk of Protestants. People follow a religion the way our fathers took a medicine in the month of May – if it does not do any good, people seem to say, at least it cannot do any harm, and, besides, it is proper to conform to the general rule. How could it be otherwise? . . . It is an incredible thing to see the infinite subdivisions into which the sects have been divided in America. One might say they are circles successively drawn around the same point; each new one is a little more distant than the last. The Catholic faith is the immobile point from which each new sect distances itself a little more, while drawing nearer to pure deism. You feel that such a spectacle cannot fail to throw the mind of a thinking Protestant into inextricable doubt, and that indeed is the sentiment I think I see visibly ruling in the depths of almost everyone's soul. It seems clear to me that the reformed religion is a kind of compromise, a sort of *representative monarchy* in matters of religion which can well fill an era, serve as the passage from one state to another, but which cannot constitute a definitive state itself and which is approaching its end. By what will it be replaced? Here is where my doubt begins: this country presents as the solution to this question, which is after all a *human* question, very precious information, because the religious and irreligious instincts which can exist in man develop here in perfect liberty. I would like to have you see this curious spectacle; you would encounter here the struggle between two principles which divide the political world elsewhere. Protestants of all persuasions – Anglicans, Lutherans, Calvinists, Presbyterians, Anabaptists, Quakers, and a hundred other Christian sects – this is the core of the population. This churchgoing and indifferent population, which lives day to day, becomes used to a *milieu* which is hardly satisfying, but which is tranquil, and in which the *proprieties* are satisfied. They live and die in compromises, without ever concerning themselves with reaching the depths of things; they no longer recruit anyone. Above them is to be found a fistful of Catholics, who are making use of the tolerance of their ancient adversaries, but who are staying basically as intolerant as they have always been, as intolerant in a word as people who *believe*. For them there is only truth in a single point; on any line one side or another of this point: eternal damnation. They live in the midst of civil society, but they forbid themselves any relationship with the religious societies that surround them. It even seems to me that their dogma on liberty of conscience is pretty much the same as in Europe, and I am not sure that they would not be persecuting if they found themselves to be the strongest. These people are in general poor, but full of zeal, their priests are completely devoted to the religion of sacrifice they have embraced; they are not in effect businessmen of religion, as are the Protestant ministers. Everything I have observed to date leads me to think that Catholics are increasing in number in a prodigious manner. Many Europeans who are arriving strengthen their ranks; but conversions are numerous. New England and the Mississippi Basin are beginning to fill up with them. It is evident that all the naturally religious minds among the Protestants, serious and complete minds, which the uncertainties of Protestantism tire and which at the same time deeply feel the need for a religion, are abandoning the despair of seeking the truth and are throwing themselves anew under the empire of *authority*. Their reason is a burden that weighs on them and which they sacrifice with joy; they become Catholics. Catholicism, moreover, seizes the senses and the soul deeply and is better suited to the people than reformed religion; thus the greatest number of converts belongs to the working classes of the society. That is one of the ends of the chain; now we will pass to the other end. On the borders of Protestantism is a sect which is Christian only in name; these are the *Unitarians*. Among the Unitarians, which is to say among those who deny the Trinity and recognize only one God, there are some who see in Jesus Christ only an angel, others a prophet, finally others a philosopher like Socrates. These are pure deists; they speak of the Bible, because they do not want to shock opinion too strongly, as it is still completely *Christian*. They have a service on Sunday; I have been to one. There they read verses of Dryden or other English poets on the existence of God and the immortality of the soul. A speech on some point of morality is made, and the service is over. This sect is gaining proselytes in almost the same proportion as Catholicism, but it recruits in the upper ranks of society. It is growing rich, like Catholicism, from the losses of Protestantism. It is evident that the Protestants, whose spirit is cold and logical, *debating* classes, men whose habits are intellectual and scientific, are seizing the opportunity to embrace a completely philosophical sect that allows them to profess, almost publicly, pure deism . . . Thus you see: Protestantism, a mixture of authority and reason, is battered at the same time by the two absolute principles of *reason* and *authority*. Anyone who wants to look for it can see this spectacle to some extent everywhere; but here it is quite striking. It is apparent here, because in America no power of fact or opinion hinders the march of human intelligence or passions on this point; they follow their natural bent. At a time that does not seem to me very far away, it seems certain that the two extremes will find themselves face to face. What will be the final result then? Here I am absolutely lost in uncertainty, and I no longer see the clear path. Can deism ever be suitable for all classes of a people? Especially for those who have the most need to have the bridle of religion? That is what I cannot convince myself of. I confess that what I see here disposes me more than I ever was before to believing that what is called natural religion could suffice for the superior classes of society, provided that the belief in the two or three great truths that it teaches is real and that something of an external religion mixes and ostensibly unites men in the public profession of these truths. By contrast, the people either will become what they once were and still are in all parts of the world, or they will see in this natural religion only the absence of any belief in the afterlife and they will fall steadily into the single doctrine of self interest.[3]

But to return to the current state of minds in America, one must not take what I have just said in too absolute a sense. I spoke to you of a *disposition* and not of accomplished facts. It is evident that there still remains here a larger foundation for Christian religion than in any other country in the world . . .

But do you not wonder at the misery of our nature? One religion works powerfully on the will, it dominates the imagination, it gives rise to real and profound beliefs; but it divides the human race into the fortunate and the damned, creates divisions on earth that should exist only in the other life, the child of intolerance and fanaticism. The other preaches tolerance, attaches itself to reason, in effect its symbol; it obtains no power, it is an inert work, without strength and almost without life. That is enough on that subject, to which my imagination is constantly dragging me back and which in the end would drive me mad if I often examined it deeply. Besides, it seems to me I still have a lot of other things to tell you.

. . .

We ourselves are moving, my dear friend, toward a democracy without limits. I am not saying that this is a good thing; what I see in this country convinces me, on the contrary, that France will come to terms with it badly; but we are being pushed toward it by an irresistible force.

. . .

In a word, from now on democracy seems to me a fact that a government can have the pretension of *regulating*, but of stopping, no. It is not without difficulty, I assure you, that I have surrendered to this idea; what I see in this country does not prove to me that, even in the most favorable circumstances, and they have existed here, the government of the multitude is an excellent thing. It is generally agreed that in the first days of the republic, the men of state, the members of the Chambers, were much more distinguished than they are today. They almost all belonged to the class of proprietors, of which I spoke to you above. Now the people no longer have *so fortunate a hand*. Their choices in general fall on those who flatter its passions and put themselves within its reach. This effect of democracy, together with the extreme instability in all things, with the absolute lack that one notices here of any spirit of continuation and duration, convinces me more every day that the most rational government is not that in which all the interested parties take part, but that which the most enlightened and most moral classes of the society direct. It cannot be concealed, however, that as a whole this country

3   For Tocqueville's treatment of religion in *Democracy in America*, including Protestant evangelicalism, see selections 3a2, 3b17, 6b1, and 6c12.

presents an admirable spectacle. It impresses me, I tell you frankly, with the superiority of free governments over all others. I feel more convinced than ever that all peoples are not made to enjoy such government to the same extent, but I am also more than ever disposed to think that it is regrettable that this is so. A universal satisfaction with the existing government prevails here, to an extent you cannot imagine. These people incontestably are situated higher on the moral scale than among us; each man has a sense of his independent position and his individual dignity that does not always make his bearing very agreeable, but which definitely leads him to respect himself and to respect others. I especially admire two things here: the first is the extreme respect people have for the law; alone and without public force, it commands in an irresistible way. I believe, in truth, that the principal cause of this is that they make it themselves and can change it. One is always seeing thieves who have violated all the laws of their countries scrupulously obeying those they make themselves. I believe that something similar is happening in the spirit of the people everywhere. The second thing that I envy in the people here is the ease with which it does without government. Every man here considers himself interested in public security and in the exercise of laws. Instead of counting on the police, he counts only on himself. It follows, in short, that without its ever appearing, public force is everywhere. It is a truly incredible thing to see, I assure you, how this people keeps itself in order by the sole sentiment that it has no safeguard against itself except within itself.

You see that I am giving you the most thorough account I can of all the impressions I am receiving. In short, they are more favorable to America than they were during the first days after my arrival. There is in the picture a throng of defective details, but the ensemble seizes the imagination. I understand especially that it acts in an irresistible way on logical and superficial minds, a combination that is not rare. The principles of government are so simple, the consequences are deduced from them with so perfect a regularity, that the mind is subjugated and carried away if it does not take care. It is necessary to take stock of oneself, to struggle against the current in order to perceive that these institutions which are so simple and so logical would not suit a great nation that needs a strong internal government and fixed foreign policy; that a government is not durable by its nature; that a government requires, within the people that confers it on itself, a long habit of liberty and of a body of *true* enlightenment which can be acquired only rarely and in the long run. And after all that is said, one comes back again to thinking that this is nonetheless a good thing and that it is regrettable that the moral and physical constitution of man prohibits him from obtaining it everywhere and forever.

. . .

Keep this letter. It will be interesting for me later on.

1c   To Tocqueville's Mother

Philadelphia, October 24, 1831

I have little new to tell you about myself, my dear mother. Alexandrine has most likely already read you my last letter. Not much has changed since. I am visiting prisons and learned societies during the day, and going to parties at night. Such is our life. I know you'll be happy to hear that I am still in good health. The Fall here is superb, with a pure and sparkling sky as in summer days. The foliage is far more varied here than at the same season in Europe. In the woods, all the shades of green and red intermingle. This is the time of the year when America appears in all its glory.

Do not believe half the negative reports about this country you have heard from S. He does not know this country himself, and what he knows of it, he got from a certain class of Frenchmen he has been mingling with here, to the exclusion of all others. In America as elsewhere these people are prone to display all that is worst in our way of thinking. Along with England, America is the most interesting and most instructive country to visit. Its superiority over England is that it has the unique privilege of being a country that is simultaneously in its childhood and maturity, which gives it the most extraordinary appearance in the world.

I must admit that not every American is pleasant to interact with. A great many smoke, chew tobacco, and spit in front of you. But Americans are nevertheless a very remarkable race of men. Furthermore, while they feel no embarrassment for their behavior, they tolerate yours just as well. It is actually the most difficult thing in the world to upset an American. Unless you hit him in the face, he has no idea that you are trying to insult him. He attributes everything to chance and nothing to your intentions. But it is precisely this kind of behavior that S. finds so shocking. S. would tolerate Americans better if they were liars, dissolute, irreligious, even thieves. But if they step on your toe without saying sorry or spit in your sight . . . these are horrible offenses which cannot be tolerated and dishonor a people. I certainly admit that Americans are not very refined. They lack grace and elegance. This is a fact. In America one constantly feels the bare beginnings of an upper class which would be able, if it existed, to set the tone for the rest of society. But these are superficial matters, and it is not reasonable to spend much time on them.

You see that all this doesn't amount to much. If I ever write a book on America, I'll work on it when I return to France with the documents I have assembled to bring back with me. When I leave America, I'll be in a position to understand these documents which I have not yet had a chance to study. This will be the clearest result of the voyage. Beyond this I only have my own notes on this country, but these are without any order or logic: disconnected ideas which only I can understand; isolated facts which remind me of many others. The most valuable documents I am returning with are two small notebooks where I have written down, word for word, the conversations I have had with the most remarkable men of this country. These scraps of rag are priceless to me, but I alone know the real value of the questions and answers they contain. Up to now I have expressed only a few general ideas on America, in the letters I have sent to the family and a few other people in France. I have written them in haste, on steamboats or in some corner where I had to use my knees as a table. Will I ever publish anything on this country? The truth is that I don't know. I think I have a few good ideas but I am not sure about what form to put them in and I am afraid of going public.

Adieu, my dear mother. The wind is blowing from the east, and I am hoping to get some news from you in a day or two. I would never have believed that I would one day like rain. But this is what has been happening since I have been in this country. Rain means an east wind here, and the east wind the liner from France.

2

Excerpts from American Notebooks: Tocqueville's Conversations with his American Informants; Travel Impressions on the Road

2a General Questions[1]: Contrast of Ancient Republics as Virtuous vs. the United States as Based on Enlightened Self-Interest

Sing-Sing, May 29, 1831

The principle of the republics of antiquity was to sacrifice private interests to the general good. In that sense one could say that they were *virtuous*. The principle of this one seems to be to make private interests harmonize with the general interest. A sort of refined and intelligent selfishness seems to be the pivot on which the whole machine turns. These people here do not trouble themselves to find out whether public virtue is good, but they do claim to prove that it is useful. If the latter point is true, as I think it is in part, this society can pass as enlightened, but not as virtuous. But up to what extent can the two principles of individual well-being and the general good in fact be merged? How far can a conscience, which one might say was based on reflection and calculation, master those political passions which are not yet born, but which certainly will be born? That is something which only the future will show.

---

1   Alphabetic notebook A.

2b   Conversation with Jared Sparks[2], on the Tyranny of the Majority

September 29, 1831[3]

Mr. Sparks said to us today: "There are general political questions concerning the whole Union, which occupy the attention of all provincial papers. They all take sides for or against the central administration. In that their collective effect is, in its lesser degree, comparable to the effect produced by the two or three great Parisian newspapers. In fact it is fairly rare for them to take sides even about the administration of a particular State. The papers are little concerned with that, and are absorbed in the petty interests of the localities where they are published. At least that is how it is in Massachusetts."

Q   "Representatives and senators are elected every year. Is there sometimes as a result a complete change of the legislative body?"

A   "No. Generally three-quarters of the members are reelected."

Q   "Does the choice of Governor give rise to a lot of intrigue and are the elections stormy?"

A   "The Governor of Massachusetts has but little power and only holds office for a year. It follows that there is no great passion in men's longing to achieve that position and they can always hope to succeed in a year's time; this moderates the heat of faction. In Pennsylvania where the Governor has a great deal of power, for instance that of *removing* as well as appointing public officials, and where he stays in office for three years, the elections are often strongly contested."

Q   "Is it essential for the President of the United States, in order to carry on the government, to have a majority in Congress?"

A   "No. The opposite has often happened. General Jackson did not have a majority in the last Congress."

Mr. Sparks added: "The political dogma of this country is that the majority is always right. By and large we are very well satisfied to have adopted it, but one cannot deny that experience often gives the lie to the principle. (He quoted several examples of this.) Sometimes the majority has wished to oppress the minority. Luckily we have in the Governor's veto, and especially in the judges' power to refuse to apply an unconstitutional law, guarantees against the passions and mistakes of democracy."

He also said: "I think our origin is the fact that best explains our

2   Unitarian minister and Harvard history professor.
3   Non-alphabetic notebooks 2 and 3.

government and our manners. When we arrived here we were enthusiastic republicans and men of religion. We found ourselves left to our own devices, forgotten in this corner of the world. Almost all societies, even in America, have begun with one place where the government was concentrated, and have then spread out around that central point. Our forefathers on the contrary founded *the locality before the State*. Plymouth, Salem, Charleston existed before one could speak of a government of Massachusetts; they only became united later and by an act of deliberate will. You can see what strength such a point of departure must have given to the *spirit of locality* which so eminently distinguishes us even among other Americans, and to republican principles. Those who would like to imitate us should remember that there are no precedents for our history."

2c   The Three Great Human Miseries

October 14, 1831[4]

If I had to class human miseries, I should put them in this order:

1st. Illnesses.
2nd. Death.
3rd. Doubt.

Life is neither a pleasure nor a grief. It is a serious duty imposed on us, to be seen through to the end to our credit.

2d   Conversation with Mr. John H. B. Latrobe, a Very Distinguished Lawyer from Baltimore, on Slavery and Sectionalism

October 30, 1831[5]

He said to us: "I think the constitution of Maryland is the most democratic in America. No property qualification is demanded for the electors. Any man who is a citizen of the United States and has been living for a year in the Republic is an elector."

4   Pocket notebook number 3.
5   Non-alphabetic notebook 2 and 3.

"Do you not find," I said, "that this universal suffrage has disadvantages?"

"There are some," said Mr. Latrobe. "The choices are not always good. It has been noticed that we have fewer able men in our Legislature than the Virginians have in theirs."

"But," I answered, "since your Legislature is so democratic, is it not true then that Maryland is the place in the United States where the spirit of aristocracy is most in evidence?"

Mr. Latrobe answered: "Our outward habits have indeed kept an aristocratic cast which is found neither in our laws nor in our political practice. So there is more luxury here than anywhere else: in the streets you see four-horse carriages, *jackets*, something like liveries; the members of different families are distinguished by names of estates."

"Formerly your laws, like your manners, were aristocratic?"

"Yes, Maryland was founded by English nobles, and moreover the first emigrants professed the Catholic religion which itself is favorable to aristocracy. So they divided the territory into great estates; but America does not at all favor the existence of great landed fortunes, and the landowners were never able to get large incomes from their lands. Up to the Revolution however Maryland had the appearance of an English county; birth was as much valued there as on the other side of the Atlantic; all the power was in the hands of the great families."

"What changed this state of affairs?"

"The law of inheritance. With equal shares, fortunes were quickly divided up. Some families, that of Charles Carroll for instance, having only one representative during several generations, kept their fortunes, but in general the great estates have been divided into a thousand fragments. With the small landowners and commercial industry, democracy was born. You see what progress it has made."

"But how have the members of the great families put up with this change? What is their position regarding the people, and what do the people think of them?"

"The people has not, as you seem to think, any hostility against the members of the old families. It shows no discrimination against them in appointments to all the offices. On their side the members of the old families do not show any hostility against the present order. This state of affairs is due to two circumstances; when war broke out with Great Britain, the great families of Maryland zealously supported the cause of independence. They shared the passion of the people and led them on the field of battle. After the War of Independence the political question dividing people was concerned with the Constitution. The nation was split between the Federalists who wanted to give the Union a very strong central power, and the Democrats or

Republicans who wanted to keep almost complete independence for the States. The latter party, which won in the end, was the most popular. Now it happened that the Maryland aristocrats, from love of power and a wish to keep their local importance, almost all supported it. So these were two great occasions on which they went with the people and won rights for them. I was speaking just now of Federalists and Republicans and told you that in the end the Republicans carried off the victory. That is to say that they came to power in the end. For the rest, once in charge of the government, they managed things in almost all respects in the same way as their adversaries would have done. They allowed a central power, a standing army, a navy . . . Oppositions never can govern with the principles that have brought them to power. Now, to put the matter truthfully, there are no parties in the United States; everything turns on questions of personalities. There are those who have got power and those who want to have it; the 'ins' and 'outs.'"

"What class is most usually elected by the people?"

"Lawyers. The United States are ruled by lawyers. It is they who hold almost all the offices. The President is a military man, but look at all his ministry; there is not one minister who is not a lawyer. The lawyers here have even more preponderance than in the rest of the Union, because here it is the custom before an election for the candidates to address the people. We often see the eloquence of one of them carry an election by surprise against an opponent whose real merit should have decided the matter."

"Is there still slavery in Maryland?"

"Yes. But we are making great efforts to get rid of it. The law allows the export of slaves and does not allow their import. Cultivating wheat we can very easily do without the blacks. It is perhaps even an economy."

"Is enfranchisement allowed?"

"Yes, but we often find that enfranchisement brings great evil in its train, and that the freed Negro finds himself more unhappy and unable to help himself than the slave. One odd thing is that west of the Chesapeake, the Negro population is increasing faster than the white, whereas to the east of that bay the opposite is true. I think the reason is that the west is divided into great estates which have no attraction for the hard working, free population."

"Baltimore which now has a population of 80,000 did not have thirty houses at the time of the Revolution."

"What then has made that city grow so fast?"

"First as a result of our Revolution; then the ruin of San Domingo which sent many French families as refugees to us and made us supply the colony, and finally the wars of the French Revolution in Europe. England was at war with the whole continent and ruled the seas; we became Europe's manufacturers."

"Is it true that there are great differences between Americans of the North and those of the South?"

"Yes, at Baltimore we think we can recognize a Yankee in the street, and even an inhabitant of New York or of Philadelphia."

"But what are the principal traits that distinguish the North from the South?"

"I would express the difference like this: what distinguishes the North is the *spirit of enterprise*; what distinguishes the South is the *spirit of chivalry*. The manners of a Southerner are frank and open; he is excitable, even irritable, and very ticklish on a point of honor. The New Englander is cold, calculating and patient. As long as you are staying with a Southerner, you are made welcome, and he shares all the pleasures of his house with you. The Northerner, when he has received you, begins to think whether he can do business with you."

(Having painted this spirited portrait, Mr. Latrobe seemed to be afraid that he had been talking too frankly to us, and he added several details to diminish the effect.)

"But your present legislation, your law of inheritance among other things, should change the look of your society?"

"Yes, we used to have a race of landowners living on their estates. In general those were the most distinguished people in the country. They had received an excellent education, and had the manners and standards of the English upper classes. We still have a certain number of these 'gentleman farmers'; but the law of inheritance and democracy are killing them. In two or three generations they will have disappeared."

"Do you not regret that it should be so?"

"Yes, from some points of view. In general that class was a seedbed of distinguished people for the legislature and the army. They were our best statesmen and our finest characters. All the great men of the Revolution came, in the South, from that class. But nonetheless I am inclined to think that, all things considered, the new order is better. Our upper classes now are less remarkable, but the people is more enlightened; there are fewer distinguished men, but more general happiness. In a word we are daily getting more like New England. Now New England, in spite of all I was saying to you about it, is well ahead of us in everything to do with the economy of society. I think that the whole American continent must model itself one day on New England. What hastens this tendency is the perpetual flow of people from the North to the South. Their will to grow rich and their spirit of enterprise are continually driving them among us. Little by little all trade and control over society is falling into their hands."

"Do you think you could do without slaves in Maryland?"

"Yes, I am convinced of it. Slavery is in general an expensive way of farming, and it is more so with certain crops. Thus wheat farming requires many laborers, but only twice in the year, at sowing time and at harvest. Slaves are useful at those two seasons. For the rest of the year they must be fed and kept without, one may say, employing them. Besides, on a farm with slaves there are always a multitude of women and children who must be fed without being employed. So generally speaking slavery is worth nothing in wheat growing country. And that applies to the greater part of Maryland. In the South where the crop from the plantations is very large, one can employ slaves."

"But if sugar and coffee are more profitable crops than corn, and if slave labor for agriculture is more expensive than free, it surely follows that the Southerners can keep their slaves, but it also follows that they would get a better return from their lands if they cultivated them themselves or employed free labor?"

"No doubt, but in the South the white man cannot, without getting ill or dying, do what the black does easily. Besides there are certain crops that are raised much more economically by slaves than by free workers. Tobacco for instance. Tobacco needs continual attention; one can employ women and children in cultivating it. In a country where labor is as expensive as it is in America, it would be difficult to grow tobacco without slaves: it is a crop admirably suited for slave labor. Tobacco is the only Southern crop grown in Maryland. People will end by giving up growing it in proportion as slavery disappears. It would be better to lose that source of income than to keep it. All that I have been telling you just now is not only my own opinion, it is an expression of public opinion. Over the last fifteen years there has been a complete revolution in people's attitude to this matter. Fifteen years ago one was not allowed to say that slavery could be abolished in Maryland; now no one disputes that."

"Do you not think that the law of inheritance should have a great influence on the existence of slavery?"

"Yes, immense. The division of properties multiplies small fortunes and quickly creates a class of white laborers who start competing with the slaves. Everywhere in Maryland where properties have been divided up, slavery has disappeared and the white population has developed extraordinarily."

"In Maryland do you have a code for the blacks?"

"No. The penal code applies to both races. There are however some offences which can only be committed by a black. A black for instance, even if free, cannot carry arms. A black slave cannot buy or sell on his own account without the written permission of his master. Free blacks cannot come together for meetings."

"Do enfranchised blacks have political rights?

"None. The law gives them political rights in Pennsylvania, but in practice they do not use them any more than with us."

"Is it true that public education in Maryland is infinitely less advanced than in New England?"

"Yes. We have only just set out on the road along which the Northerners have been going for two hundred years. We find the chief obstacle in the sentiments of the people themselves. A curious thing has long happened and still happens with us: the enlightened classes of the population feel the need for public education and work ceaselessly to spread it. But the people, who still does not see the need to give their money to attain this object, does not reelect to office those who thus work for their welfare in spite of themselves."

"Do you realize that what you are saying is a very strong argument against the principle of the sovereignty of the people?"

"No, at least not in my view. The people is often blind and falls into incredible mistakes. But I have always found that it ends up by understanding its own interests. And then it does more than the strongest power could do. So in public education it has long been impossible for us to do anything; but now public opinion begins to turn to our side. The impulse has been given and nothing will now stop it."

"How do the Catholics in America prosper?"

"They are increasing extraordinarily and are pursuing a very skillful policy. The Catholics are the only congregation that is never divided about doctrine. They march united like a single man. For the last twenty years they have very skillfully diverted all their efforts towards education. They have established seminaries and colleges. The best educational institutions in Maryland are Catholic. They have even colleges in other States. These colleges are full of Protestants. There is perhaps no young man in Maryland who has received a good education who has not been brought up by the Catholics. Although they are very careful not to speak of their beliefs to their pupils, you realize that they always exercise a certain influence. They have also very cleverly directed their chief attention to the education of women. They think that where the mother is Catholic, the children will almost always become such. Generally their bishops in America are able men."

"What are the doctrines of the American Catholics about the question of Church government?"

"They recognize the Pope's right to appoint the bishops, and the bishops' right to appoint the parish priests. As to matters of faith they think that only an Ecumenical Council presided over by the Pope has a right to pronounce."

2e   On Davy Crockett[6]

Memphis, December 20, 1831

When voting rights are universal, and deputies are paid by the State, it is a strange thing how low the people's choice can descend and how far it can be mistaken.

Two years ago the inhabitants of the district of which Memphis is the capital sent to the House of Representatives of Congress an individual called David Crockett, who had received no education, could read only with difficulty, had no property, no fixed dwelling, but spent his time hunting, selling his game for a living, and spending his whole life in the woods. His competitor, who failed, was a fairly rich and able man.

2f   Conversation[7] with Mr. Sam Houston, on Indians

December 31, 1831

This man has an extraordinary history. After a stormy and troubled youth, he finally settled in the State of Tennessee. There his natural talents and no doubt also his obscure origin won him the people's votes. He had been elected Governor of the State.

At this time he had trouble inside his own family. He complained about his wife; others say that he behaved very badly to her. What is certain is that he left Tennessee, crossed the Mississippi, and withdrew among the Creeks in the district of Arkansas. There he was adopted by one of the chiefs and, it is said, married his daughter. Since then he has lived in the midst of the wilderness, half European, half savage . . .

We asked him a great many questions about the Indians, of which these are some:

Q   "Have the Indians a religion?"

A   "Some of them have no belief in the immortality of the soul. But generally the Indians believe in a God who punishes or rewards the deeds of this life in the other world."

Q   "Have they any form of worship?"

6   Notebook E.
7   In notebook E, the conversation took place on a steamboat on the Mississippi river.

A "The Osages, who live on the frontier of Mexico, pray every morning to the rising sun. The Creeks have no worship. It is only in times of great calamity, or before undertaking some great enterprise, that they devote themselves to some public manifestations of worship."

Q "Have you often seen Indian Christians?"

A "Seldom. My view is that it is a very bad plan for civilizing the Indians to send missionaries among them. Christianity is the religion of an enlightened and intellectual people; it is above the intellectual level of a people as little advanced in civilization, and so much the slaves of mere material instincts as the Indians. In my view, one should first try to win the Indians away from their wandering life, and persuade them to cultivate the soil. The introduction of the Christian religion would follow naturally on the change that had taken place in their social condition. I have noticed that only Catholicism has been able to succeed in making a durable impression on the Indians. It strikes their senses and speaks to their imagination."

. . .

Q "Do you think that the Indians have great natural intelligence?"

A "Yes. I do not think they yield to any other race of men on that account. Besides, I am equally of the opinion that it is the same in the case of the Negroes. The difference one notices between the Indian and the Negro seems to me to result solely from the different education they have received. The Indian is born free; he makes use of this freedom from his first steps in life. He is left to look after himself as soon as he can act; even a father's power is an imperceptible bond for him. Surrounded by dangers, pressed by necessities, and unable to count on anyone, thus his mind must be ever active to find means to ward off such troubles and to maintain his existence. This necessity imposed on the Indian gives his intelligence a degree of development and ingenuity which are often wonderful. The ordinary Negro has been a slave before he was born. Without pleasures as without needs, and useless to himself, the first notions of existence which he receives, make him understand that he is the property of another, that care for his own future is no concern of his, and that the very power of thought is for him a useless gift of providence."

Q "Is it true that the valley of the Mississippi shows signs of the passage of a race of men more civilized than those who inhabit it today?"

A "Yes. I have often come across fortified works which bear evidence of the existence of a people who had reached a fairly high state of civilization. Whence did that people come? Whither did it vanish? There is a mystery there. But one cannot doubt that it existed, and nothing indicates that the Indians of our day are the remnants thereof. The most probable view seems to me that they were Mexicans who in old days came and settled in the valley of the Mississippi."

Q   "Could you give me any information about the line the American
Government takes with the Indian tribes?"

A   "Yes. Very easily. There were and there still are within the Southern
parts of the United States, several half civilized Indian nations whose position
vis-à-vis the governors of those States is equivocal, and who hold up the
development that might take place in that part of the Union. Congress
therefore, as much in the interests of the States of the South as those of the
Indians themselves, has conceived the project of transporting them, with their
consent, to country which should always remain essentially Indian land. Its
choice fell on the upper part of the district of Arkansas. The territory which
should be inhabited by the Indian nations begins at an imaginary line that you
can draw on the map from Louisiana to Missouri, and stretches right up to
the frontiers of Mexico and to the vast prairies inhabited by the wandering
hordes of the Osages. The United States have bound themselves by the most
solemn oaths never to sell the lands contained within those limits, and never
in any form to allow the introduction of a white population there. There are
already 10,000 Indians in the territory. I think that in time there will be
50,000; the country is healthy and the soil extremely fertile."

Q   "Do you think that by this means the Indian race can be saved from
the disappearance that seems to threaten it? Do you think that this arrange-
ment will not still be only provisional, and that the Indians will not soon be
forced to retreat?"

A   "No. I think that the Indian tribes of the South will find a refuge
there, and that they will civilize themselves, if the government is willing to
take trouble to encourage civilization among them. Note that the isolated
position in which the Indian tribes will be settled will make it possible
to take effective measures to prevent the introduction of strong drink
among them. Brandy is the main cause of the destruction of the natives of
America."

Q   "But do you not think that the tribes foreign to one another will carry
on continual internecine war?"

A   "The United States have among them posts to prevent it."

Q   "Do you believe in the possibility of saving the Indians?"

A   "Yes, surely. Twenty-five years of skillful handling by the government
would certainly bring this result about. Several of the tribes of the South are
already half-civilized."

Q   "What degrees of civilization do you find among these people?"

A   "At the head of all come the *Cherokees*. The *Cherokees* live entirely by
cultivating the soil. They are the only Indian tribe that has a written
language."

After the *Cherokees* come the *Creeks*. The *Creeks* subsist partly from hunting and partly from cultivating some land. They have some definite penal laws and a form of government. Next I place the *Chickasaws* and the *Choctaws*. One cannot yet say that they have begun to get civilized, but they have begun to lose many of the traits of their savage nature.

The *Osages* come last of all; they live in continually moving hordes, are almost naked, hardly use firearms at all, and know no Europeans except the fur traders.

The *Osages* are the last tribe of the South-West which has a treaty with the United States."

Q   "But that reserve in Arkansas, of which we were speaking just now, is only intended to receive the Indians of the South. What line has been taken about those of the West and North?"

A   "The Indians of the West and North do not find themselves surrounded, as do those of the South, by white populations. They border the United States, and are pushed back before them as the latter advance."

2g   On Common Law, on the Mississippi[8]

December 31, 1831

In the United States where the laws as well as mores tend towards a democracy without limits, one nevertheless still finds this tendency which the Common Law gives to the human spirit. One notices it in the unruffled state in the whole of society but it is among the men of law that one sees its evident mark. The men of law in the United States are the enemies of change, the men of precedents: that is not precisely their character in France. The mania for generalizing everything is what distinguishes our lawyers; the absence of general ideas is notable in America among the men of law.

Generally American men of law emphatically sing the praises of the Common Law. They oppose codification with all their powers, which is to be explained in this way:

1st.   If a code of laws was made, they would have to begin their studies again.

2nd.   The law becoming accessible to the common herd, they would lose a part of their importance. They would no longer be like the Egyptian priests, the sole interpreters of an occult science.

8   Notebook F.

Some distinguished men in America, even outside the bar, are opposed to codification, among others Mr. Poinsett.[9] Mr. E. Livingston[10] on the contrary is very much in favor of it. He told me straight out today that the lawyers who were of an opposite opinion had an interest in the matter.

The fact is that unwritten constitutions often give rise to less argument than those that are written down.

It is easier to prove an antecedent fact than to discern the intention of a legislator and the spirit of the written law.

9   See selection 2d.
10   Edward Livingston, an expert on the penal system in Louisiana and Andrew Jackson's secretary of state.

3

Volume One of *Democracy in America*, 1835

3a   Part I

3a1   *Introduction*

Among the novel objects that attracted my attention during my stay in the United States, nothing struck me more forcibly than the general equality of conditions among the people. I discovered without difficulty the enormous influence that this primary fact exercises on the whole course of society; it gives a certain direction to the public mind and a certain tone to the laws, new standards for the governing authorities and particular habits to the governed.

I soon perceived that the influence of this fact extends far beyond the political character and the laws of the country, and that it has no less effect on civil society than on the government; it creates opinions, gives birth to sentiments, suggests usages, and modifies whatever it does not produce. The more I advanced in the study of American society, the more I perceived that this equality of condition is the fundamental fact from which all others seem to be derived and the central point at which all my observations come to a head.

I then turned my thoughts to our own hemisphere, and it seemed to me that I discerned there something analogous to the spectacle which the New World presented to me. I observed that equality of conditions, without having attained its ultimate limits as it has in the United States, was becoming more prevalent day by day; and that the democracy which governs the American communities appeared to be rapidly advancing to prominence in Europe.

At this moment, I conceived the idea of the book that you will read.

A great democratic revolution is going on among us; all see it, without judging it the same way. Some consider it to be a new phenomenon, but taking it for an accident, still hope to put a stop to it; while others judge it to be irresistible, because it seems to them to be the most uniform, the most ancient, and the most permanent fact known to history.

I look back for a moment on the situation of France seven hundred years ago, when the territory is divided among a small number of families, who hold the land and govern the inhabitants; the right of governing descends with the family inheritance from generation to generation; men have but one means to impose their will on others – through force; and one can find but a single source of power – landed property. But then, the political power of the clergy appears, which had just been consolidated and soon begins to spread: the clergy open their ranks to all classes, to rich and poor, commoner and noble. Through the church, equality penetrates into the government, and he who as a serf must have vegetated in perpetual bondage could, as a priest, take his place in the midst of nobles, and would often sit above kings. Society becoming with time more civilized and more stable, the various relations of men with one another become more complicated and numerous. Hence the want of civil laws is felt; and the ministers of law soon rise from the obscurity of the tribunals and their dusty chambers to sit at the monarch's court, by the side of the feudal barons clothed in their ermine and armor.

The kings ruin themselves by their great enterprises; the nobles exhaust their resources by private wars; the lower orders enriching themselves by commerce. The influence of money begins to make itself felt in affairs of state. The transactions of business open a new road to power, and the financier rises to a station of political influence in which he is at once flattered and despised.

Gradually education spreads; one sees a reawakening of taste for literature and the arts; then the mind becomes an element in achieving success; knowledge becomes a tool of government, intelligence a social force; the educated take part in enterprises.

The value attached to high birth declines just as fast as new avenues to power are discovered. In the eleventh century, nobility was priceless; in the thirteenth, it could be purchased. Nobility was first conferred by gift in 1270, and equality was thus introduced into the government by the aristocracy itself.

In the course of these seven hundred years it sometimes happened that the nobles, in order to resist the authority of the crown or to diminish the power of their rivals, granted some political power to the common people.

More frequently still, we find the king permitting the lower classes to participate in the government, with the intention of humbling the aristocracy. In France the kings have always been the most active and most constant of levelers. When they were strong and ambitious, they spared no pains to elevate the people to the level of the nobles; when they were temperate and feeble, they allowed the people to rise above themselves. Some assisted democracy by their talents, others by their vices. Louis XI and Louis XIV reduced all ranks beneath the throne to the same degree of subjection; and finally Louis XV himself descended with all his court into the dust.

When citizens could begin to hold land in other ways besides feudal tenure, and when personal property could in its turn create influence and confer power, one could not make a discovery in the arts, one could not introduce an improvement in commerce and industry, without creating so many new elements of equality among men. From this moment on, every new invention, every new want which it occasioned, and every new desire that had to be satisfied were steps towards a general leveling. The taste for luxury, the love of war, the rule of fashion, and the most superficial as well as the deepest passions of the human heart seemed to co-operate to enrich the poor and to impoverish the rich.

Once the works of the mind had become sources of strength and of wealth, we must consider every addition to science, every fresh truth, and every new idea as a seed of power placed within the reach of the people. Poetry, eloquence, and memory, the graces of the mind, the fire of imagination, depth of thought, and all the gifts which Heaven scatters at random turned to the advantage of democracy; and even when these gifts were found in the possession of its adversaries, they still served the cause of democracy by throwing into bold relief the natural greatness of man. Its conquests spread, therefore, with those of civilization and knowledge; and literature became an arsenal open to all, where the poor and the weak daily resorted for arms.

In running over the pages of our history, we shall scarcely find a single great event of the last seven hundred years that has not promoted equality of condition.

The Crusades and the English wars decimated the nobles and divided their possessions: the municipal corporations introduced democratic liberty into the bosom of feudal monarchy; the invention of firearms equalized the vassal and the noble on the field of battle; the art of printing opened the same resources to the minds of all classes; the post brought knowledge to the door of the cottage and to the gate of the palace alike; and Protestantism proclaimed that all men are equally able to find the road to heaven. The discovery of America opened a thousand new paths to fortune and led obscure adventurers to wealth and power.

If, beginning with the eleventh century, we examine what has happened in France from one half-century to another, we shall not fail to perceive that at the end of each of these periods a two-fold revolution has taken place in the state of society. The noble has gone down the social ladder, and the commoner has gone up; the one descends as the other rises. Every half-century brings them nearer to each other, and they will soon meet.

Nor is this peculiar to France. Wherever we look, we perceive the same revolution going on throughout the Christian world. Everywhere one sees various incidents in the lives of peoples turning to the advantage of democracy: all men have aided it by their exertions, both those who have intentionally labored in its cause and those who have served it unwittingly; those who have fought for it and even those who have declared themselves its opponents have all been driven along in the same direction, have all labored to one end; some unknowingly and some despite themselves, all have been blind instruments in the hands of God.

The gradual development of the principle of equality is, therefore, a providential fact. It has all the chief characteristics of such a fact: it is universal, it is lasting, it constantly eludes all human interference, and all events as well as all men contribute to its progress.

Would it, then, be wise to believe that a social movement that goes so far back can be checked by one generation's efforts? Can it be believed that the democracy which has overthrown the feudal system and vanquished kings will retreat before tradesmen and capitalists? Will it stop now that it has grown so strong and its adversaries so weak?

Whither, then, are we tending? No one can say, for terms of comparison already fail us: the conditions are more equal in our day among Christian societies than at any time, or in any part of the world, so that the magnitude of what already has been done prevents us from foreseeing what is yet to be accomplished.

The whole book that you are going to read has been written under the influence of a kind of religious awe produced in the author's mind by the view of that irresistible revolution which has advanced for centuries over every obstacle and which is advancing still in the midst of the ruins it has made.

It is not necessary that God himself should speak in order that we may discover the unquestionable signs of his will. It is enough to ascertain what is the habitual course of nature and the constant tendency of events. I know, without special revelation, that the planets move in the orbits traced by the Creator's hand.

If the men of our time should be convinced, by attentive observation and sincere reflection, that the gradual and progressive development of social equality is at once the past and the future of their history, this discovery alone would confer upon the change the sacred character of a divine decree. To attempt to check democracy would be in that case to fight God himself, and it would only remain to the nations of the world to accommodate themselves to this social state which is imposed on them by Providence.

The Christian nations of our day seem to me to present a most alarming spectacle; the movement which impels them is already so strong that it cannot be stopped, but not yet so rapid that it cannot be guided. Their fate is still in their own hands; but soon it will evade them. To educate democracy, to reawaken, if possible, its religious beliefs, to purify its morals, to mold its actions, to substitute a knowledge of statecraft for its inexperience, and an awareness of its true interest for its blind instincts, to adapt its government to time and place, and to modify it according to men and to conditions: such is the first of the duties imposed in our time to those who direct society.

We need a new science of politics for a world completely new.

But this is exactly what we avoid contemplating. Placed in the middle of a rapid stream, we obstinately fix our eyes on the ruins that may still be seen on the shore we have left, while the current hurries us away and drags us backward towards the abyss.

In no country in Europe has the great social revolution that I have just described made such rapid progress as in France; but it has always advanced without guidance. The heads of the state have made no preparation for it, and it has advanced without their consent or without their knowledge. The most powerful, the most intelligent, and the most moral classes of the nation have never attempted to control it in order to guide it. Democracy has consequently been abandoned to its wild instincts, and it has grown up like those children who have no parental guidance, who receive their education in the public streets, and who are acquainted only with the vices and wretchedness of society. Its existence was seemingly unknown when suddenly it acquired supreme power. Each person then submitted himself servilely to its smallest caprices; it was worshiped as the idol of strength; and when afterwards it was enfeebled by its own excesses, the legislator conceived the rash project of destroying it, instead of instructing it and correcting its vices, and without teaching it to govern, they thought only of excluding it from government.

The result has been that the democratic revolution has taken place in the body of society without that concomitant change in the laws, ideas, customs, and morals which was necessary to render such a revolution beneficial. Thus we have a democracy without anything to lessen its vices and bring out its natural advantages; and although we already perceive the evils it brings, we are ignorant of the benefits it may confer.

While the power of the crown, supported by the aristocracy, peaceably governed the nations of Europe, society, amidst its wretchedness, had several sources of happiness which can now scarcely be conceived or appreciated. The power of a few of his subjects was an insurmountable barrier to the ruler's tyranny; and the monarch, who felt the almost divine character which he enjoyed in the eyes of the multitude, derived a motive for the just use of his power from the respect which he inspired. The nobles, placed high as they were above the people, could take that calm and benevolent interest in their fate which the shepherd feels towards his flock; and without acknowledging the poor as their equals, they watched over the destiny of those whose welfare Providence had entrusted to their care. The people, never having conceived the idea of a social condition different from their own, and never expecting to become equal to their leaders, received benefits from them without discussing their rights. They became attached to them when they were clement and just and submitted to their exactions without resistance or servility, as to the inevitable visitations of the Deity. Custom and usage, moreover, had established certain limits to oppression and founded a sort of law in the very midst of violence.

As the noble never suspected that anyone would attempt to deprive him of the privileges which he believed to be legitimate, and as the serf looked upon his own inferiority as a consequence of the immutable order of nature, it is easy to imagine that some mutual exchange of goodwill took place between two classes so differently endowed by fate. Inequality and wretchedness were then to be found in society, but the souls of neither rank of men were degraded. Men are not corrupted by the exercise of power or debased by the habit of obedience, but by the exercise of a power which they believe to be illegitimate, and by obedience to a rule which they consider to be usurped and oppressive.

On one side were wealth, strength, and leisure, accompanied by the pursuit of luxury, the refinements of taste, the pleasures of wit, and the cultivation of the arts; on the other were labor, clownishness, and ignorance. But in the midst of this coarse and ignorant multitude it was not uncommon to meet with energetic passions, generous sentiments, profound religious convictions, and wild virtues. The social state thus organized might boast of its stability, its power, and, above all, its glory.

But now the distinctions of rank are done away with; the barriers raised among men are falling; property is divided, power is shared by many, the light of knowledge spreads, and the intellectual capacities of all become more equal. Society becomes democratic, and the empire of democracy is slowly and peaceably introduced into institutions and customs.

I can conceive of a society in which all men would feel an equal love and respect for the laws of which they consider themselves the authors; in which the authority of the government would be respected as necessary, and not divine; and in which the loyalty of the subject to the chief magistrate would not be a passion, but a quiet and rational persuasion. With every individual in the possession of rights which he is sure to retain, a kind of manly confidence and reciprocal courtesy would arise between all classes, removed alike from pride and servility. The people, well acquainted with their own true interests, would understand that, in order to profit from the advantages of the state, it is necessary to satisfy its requirements. The voluntary association of citizens might then take the place of the individual authority of the nobles, and the community would be protected from tyranny and license.

I understand that, in a democratic state thus constituted, society would not be stationary, but the movements of society could be regular and progressive. If there were less splendor than in an aristocracy, misery would also be less prevalent; the pleasures of enjoyment might be less excessive, but those of comfort would be more general; the sciences might be less perfectly cultivated, but ignorance would be less common; the ardor of the feelings would be constrained, and the habits of the nation softened; there would be more vices and fewer crimes.

In the absence of enthusiasm and ardent faith, great sacrifices may be obtained from the members of a commonwealth by an appeal to their understanding and their experience; each individual will feel the same necessity of union with his fellows to protect his own weakness; and as he knows that he can obtain their help only on condition of helping them, he will readily perceive that his personal interest is identified with the interests of the whole community. The nation, taken as a whole, will be less brilliant, less glorious, and perhaps less strong; but the majority of the citizens will enjoy a greater degree of prosperity, and the people will remain peaceable, not because they despair of a change for the better, but because they are conscious that they are well off already.

If all the consequences of this state of things were not good or useful, society would at least have appropriated all such as were useful and good; and having once and forever renounced the social advantages of aristocracy, mankind would enter into possession of all the benefits that democracy can offer. But here it may be asked what we have adopted in the place of those institutions, those ideas, and those customs of our forefathers which we have abandoned.

The spell of royalty is broken, but it has not been succeeded by the majesty of the laws. The people have learned to despise all authority, but they still fear it; and fear now extorts more than was formerly paid from reverence and love. I perceive that we have destroyed those individual powers which were able, single-handed, to cope with tyranny; but it is the government alone that has inherited all the privileges of which families, guilds, and individuals have been deprived; to the power of a small number of persons, which if it was sometimes oppressive was often conservative, has succeeded the weakness of the whole community.

The division of property has lessened the distance which separated the rich from the poor; but in drawing closer to each other they seem to have found new reasons to hate each other, and, casting on one another glances full of terror and envy, they resist each other's claims to power. For the one as for the other, the idea of right does not exist, and force affords to both the only argument for the present and the only guarantee for the future.

The poor man conserves the prejudices of his forefathers without their faith, and their ignorance without their virtues; he has adopted the doctrine of self-interest as the rule of his actions without understanding the science behind it; and his selfishness is no less blind than was formerly his devotion to others.

If society is tranquil, it is not because it is conscious of its strength and its well-being, but because it fears its weakness and its infirmities; a single effort may cost it its life. Everybody feels the evil, but no one has courage or energy enough to seek the cure. The desires, the repinings, the sorrows, and the joys of the present time lead to nothing visible or permanent, like the passions of old men, which terminate in impotence. We have, then, abandoned whatever advantages the old state of things afforded, without receiving any compensation from our present condition; we have destroyed an aristocracy, and we seem inclined to survey its ruins with complacency and to accept them.

What is happening in the intellectual world is not the less deplorable. The democracy of France, hampered in its course or abandoned to its lawless passions, has overthrown whatever crossed its path and has shaken all that it has not destroyed. Its empire has not been gradually introduced or peaceably established, it has not ceased to advance amidst the disorders and agitations of a conflict. In the heat of the struggle each partisan is hurried beyond the natural limits of his opinions by the doctrines and the excesses of his opponents, until he loses sight of the end of his exertions, and holds forth in a way which does not correspond to his real sentiments or secret instincts.

Hence arises the strange confusion that we are compelled to witness.

I can recall nothing in history more worthy of sorrow and pity than the scenes which are passing before our eyes. It is as if the natural bond that unites the opinions of man to his tastes, and his actions to his principles, was now broken; the harmony that has always been observed between the feelings and the ideas of mankind appears to be dissolved and all the laws of moral analogy to be abolished. Zealous Christians are still found among us, whose minds are nurtured on the thoughts that pertain to a future life, and who readily espouse the cause of human liberty as the source of all moral greatness. Christianity, which has declared that all men are equal in the sight of God, will not refuse to acknowledge that all citizens are equal in the eye of the law. But, by a strange coincidence of events, religion has been for a time entangled with those institutions which democracy destroys; and it is not infrequently brought to reject the equality which it loves, and to curse as a foe that cause of liberty whose efforts it might hallow by its alliance.

By the side of these religious men I discern others whose thoughts are turned to earth rather than to heaven. These are the partisans of freedom, not only as the source of the noblest virtues, but more especially as the root of all solid advantages; and they sincerely desire to secure its authority, and to impart its blessings to mankind. It is natural that they should hasten to invoke the assistance of religion, for they must know that freedom cannot be established without morality, nor morality without faith. But they have seen religion in the ranks of their adversaries, and they inquire no further; some of them attack it openly, and the rest are afraid to defend it.

In former ages slavery was advocated by the venal and slavish minded, while the independent and warm-hearted were struggling without hope to save the freedoms of mankind. But men of high and generous character are now to be met with, whose opinions are directly at variance with their inclinations, and who praise that servility and meanness which they have themselves never known. Others, on the contrary, speak of freedom as if they were able to feel its sanctity and its majesty, and loudly claim for humanity those rights which they have always refused to acknowledge.

There are virtuous and peaceful individuals whose pure morality, quiet habits, comfortable life, and enlightened viewpoints fit them to be the leaders of their fellow men. Their love of country is sincere, and they are ready to make the greatest sacrifices for its welfare. But civilization often finds them among its opponents; they confound its abuses with its benefits, and the idea of evil is inseparable in their minds from that of novelty. Near these I find others whose object is to materialize mankind, to hit upon what is expedient without heeding what is just, to acquire knowledge without faith, and prosperity apart from virtue; claiming to be the champions of modern civilization, they place themselves arrogantly at its head, usurping a place which is abandoned to them, and of which they are wholly unworthy.

Where are we, then?

The religious are the enemies of freedom, and the friends of freedom attack religion; the high-minded and the noble advocate bondage, and the meanest and most servile preach independence; honest and well-educated citizens are opposed to all progress, while men without patriotism and without principle put themselves forward as the apostles of civilization and intelligence.

Has such been the fate of the centuries which preceded our own? Has man always inhabited a world like the present, where all things are not in their proper relationships, where virtue is without genius, and genius without honor; where the love of order is confused with a taste for oppression, and the holy cult of freedom with a contempt of law; where the light thrown by conscience on human actions is dim, and where nothing seems to be any longer forbidden or allowed, honorable or shameful, false or true?

I cannot believe that the Creator made man to leave him in an endless struggle with the intellectual wretchedness that surrounds us. God destines a calmer and a more certain future to the communities of Europe. I am ignorant of his designs, but I shall not cease to believe in them because I cannot fathom them, and I had rather mistrust my own capacity than his justice.

There is one country in the world where the great social revolution that I am speaking of seems to have nearly reached its natural limits. It has been effected there in a manner both simple and easy; or better yet one could say that this country realizes the benefits of the democratic revolution which we are undergoing, without having had the revolution itself.

The emigrants who colonized the shores of America at the beginning of the seventeenth century somehow separated the democratic principle from all the principles that it had to contend with in the old communities of Europe, and transplanted it alone to the New World. It has there been able to spread in perfect freedom and peaceably to determine the character of the laws by influencing the manners of the country.

It appears to me beyond a doubt that, sooner or later, we shall arrive, like the Americans, at an almost complete equality of conditions. But I do not conclude from this that we shall ever be necessarily led to draw the same political consequences which the Americans have derived from a similar social organization. I am very far from believing that they have found the only form of government that democracy could adopt, but it is sufficient that in these two countries the underlying principle generating laws and manners is the same, so that we have an immense interest in knowing what it has produced in each of them.

It is not, then, merely to satisfy a curiosity, however legitimate, that I have examined America; my wish has been to find there instruction by which we ourselves may profit. Whoever should imagine that I intended to write a panegyric would be strangely mistaken, and on reading this book he will perceive that such was not my design; nor has it been my object to advocate any form of government in particular, for I am of the opinion that absolute perfection is rarely to be found in any system of laws. I have not even pretended to judge whether the social revolution, which I believe to be irresistible, is advantageous or prejudicial to mankind. I have acknowledged this revolution as a fact already accomplished, or on the eve of its accomplishment; and I have selected the nation, from among those which have undergone it, in which its development has been the most peaceful and the most complete, in order to discern its natural consequences and to find out, if possible, the means of rendering it profitable to mankind. I confess that in America I saw more than America; I sought there the image of democracy itself, with its inclinations, its character, its prejudices, and its passions, in order to learn what we have to fear or to hope from its progress.

In the first part of this work I have attempted to show the direction that democracy, left in America to its inclinations and abandoned almost without restraint to its instincts, gave to its laws, the course it impressed on government, and in general the control which it exercised over affairs of state. I have sought to discover the evils and advantages which it brings. I have examined the safeguards used by the Americans to direct it, as well as those that they have not adopted, and I have undertaken to point out the factors which enable it to govern society.

My object was to portray, in a second part, the influence which the equality of conditions and democratic government in America exercised on civil society, on habits, ideas, and customs; but I began to feel less enthusiastic about carrying out this plan. Before I could have completed the task which I set for myself, my work would have become purposeless. Someone else would before long set forth to the public the principal traits of the American character and, delicately cloaking a serious picture, lend the truth a charm which I should not have been able to equal.

I do not know whether I have succeeded in making known what I saw in America, but I am certain that such has been my sincere desire, and that I have never, knowingly, molded facts to ideas, instead of ideas to facts.

Whenever a point could be established by the aid of written documents, I have had recourse to the original text, and to the most authentic and reputable works. I have cited my authorities in the notes, and anyone may verify them. Whenever opinions, political customs, or remarks on the manners of the country were concerned, I have endeavored to consult the most informed men I met with. If the point in question was important or doubtful, I was not satisfied with one witness, but I formed my opinion on the evidence of several witnesses. Here the reader must necessarily rely upon my word. I could frequently have cited in support of my assertions names which are either known to him or deserve to be so; but I have carefully abstained from this practice. A stranger frequently hears important truths at his host's fireside, which the latter would perhaps conceal from the ear of friendship; he consoles himself with his guest for the silence to which he is restricted, and the shortness of the traveler's stay removes all fear of indiscretion. I carefully noted every conversation of this nature as soon as it occurred, but these notes will never leave my writing-case. I had rather injure the success of my statements than add my name to the list of those strangers who repay the generous hospitality they have received by subsequent chagrin and annoyance.

I am aware that, notwithstanding my care, nothing will be easier than to criticize this book should anyone care to do so.

Those readers who may examine it closely will discover, I think, in the whole work a dominant thought that binds, so to speak, its several parts together. But the diversity of the subjects I have had to treat is exceedingly great, and it will not be difficult to oppose an isolated fact to the body of facts which I cite, or an isolated idea to the body of ideas I put forth. I hope to be read in the spirit which has guided my labors, and that my book may be judged by the general impression it leaves, as I have formed my own judgment not on any single consideration, but upon the mass of evidence.

It must not be forgotten that the author who wishes to be understood is obliged to carry all his ideas to their utmost theoretical conclusions, and often to the verge of what is false or impracticable; for if it be necessary sometimes to depart in action from the rules of logic, such is not the case in discourse, and a man finds it almost as difficult to be inconsistent in his language as to be consistent in his conduct.

I conclude by pointing out myself what many readers will consider the principal defect of the work. This book is written to favor no particular views, and in composing it I have entertained no design of serving or attacking any party. I have not undertaken to see differently from others, but to look further, and while they are busied for the morrow only, I have turned my thoughts to the whole future.

3a2   Chapter 2: "On the Point of Origin and its Importance for the Future of the Anglo-Americans"

A man is born; his early years pass obscurely among the pleasures and activities of childhood. He grows up; his manhood begins; the doors to the world finally open to receive him; he enters into contact with his fellows. He is then studied for the first time, and people think they see in him the seeds of the vices and virtues of his maturer years.

This, if I am not mistaken, is a great error.

Go back; watch the infant in his mother's arms, see the first images which the external world casts upon the dark mirror of his mind; contemplate the first occurrences he witnesses; listen to the first words which awaken the sleeping powers of thought; finally, look at his earliest struggles; and only then will you understand where the prejudices, habits, and passions which will rule his life come from. The entire man is, so to speak, to be seen in the child's cradle.

There is something analogous to this with nations. They all bear some marks of their origin. The circumstances that accompany their birth and contribute to their development influence their entire future.

If we were able to go back to the fundamental elements of states and examine the oldest records of their history, I doubt not that we should discover in them the primal cause of the prejudices, the habits, the ruling passions, and, in short, all that constitutes what is called the national character. We should there find the explanation of certain customs which now seem at variance with recognized principles; of such laws as conflict with established principles; and of such incoherent opinions as are here and there to be met with in society, like those fragments of broken chains which we sometimes see hanging from the vaults of an old edifice, supporting nothing. This might explain the destinies of certain nations which seem borne on by an unknown force to ends of which they themselves are ignorant. But hitherto facts have been lacking for such a study: the spirit of analysis has come upon nations only as they matured; and when at last they thought of contemplating their origin, time had already obscured it, or ignorance and pride had surrounded it with fables behind which the truth was hidden.

America is the only country in which it has been possible to witness the natural and tranquil growth of society, and where it is possible to trace the influence exercised by their point of origin on nations' futures.

When the peoples of Europe landed in the New World, their national characteristics were already completely formed; each of them had a physiognomy of its own; and as they had already attained that stage of civilization at which men are led to study themselves, they have transmitted to us a faithful picture of their opinions, their manners, and their laws. The men of the sixteenth century are almost as well known to us as our contemporaries. America, consequently, exhibits in broad daylight the phenomena which the ignorance or rudeness of earlier ages conceals from our research. The men of our day seem destined to see further than their predecessors into human events; they are close enough to the founding of the American settlements to know their elements in detail, and already far enough away from that time to be able to judge what these beginnings have produced. Providence has given us a torch which our forefathers did not possess, and has allowed us to discern fundamental causes in the history of the world which the obscurity of the past concealed from them.

If we carefully examine the social and political state of America, after having studied its history, we shall remain perfectly convinced that not an opinion, not a custom, not a law, I may even say not an event is upon record which the origin of that people will not explain. The readers of this book will find in the present chapter the seed of all that is to follow and the key to almost the whole work.

The emigrants who came at different periods to occupy the territory now covered by the American Union differed from each other in many respects; their aim was not the same, and they governed themselves on different principles. These men had, however, certain features in common, and they were all placed in an analogous situation.

The tie of language is, perhaps, the strongest and the most durable that can unite mankind. All the emigrants spoke the same language; they were all children of the same people. Born in a country that was agitated for centuries with the struggle of opposing parties, and where the factions had been obligated in their turn to place themselves under the protection of the law, their political education had been perfected in this rude school. They were more conversant with the notions of right and the principles of true freedom than the greater part of their European contemporaries. At the period of the first emigrations the township system, that fertile seed of free institutions, had already profoundly entered into English customs; and with it the doctrine of the sovereignty of the people insinuated itself into the very bosom of the Tudor monarchy.

The religious quarrels which have agitated the Christian world were then rife. England had plunged into the new order of things with headlong vehemence. The character of its inhabitants, which had always been sedate and reflective, became argumentative and austere. General information was increased as a result of intellectual struggles; and the mind received from this a more profound culture. While occupied in speaking of religion, morals become more pure. All these national features are more or less discoverable in the physiognomy of those Englishmen who came to seek a new home on the opposite shores of the Atlantic.

Another observation, moreover, to which we shall have occasion to return later, is applicable not only to the English, but to the French, the Spaniards, and all the Europeans who successively established themselves in the New World. All these European colonies contained the elements, if not the development, of a complete democracy. Two causes led to this result. It may be said that on leaving the mother country the emigrants had, in general, no notion of superiority over one another. The happy and the powerful do not go into exile, and there are no surer guarantees of equality among men than poverty and misfortune. It happened, however, on several occasions, that persons of rank were driven to America by political and religious quarrels. Laws were made to establish a gradation of ranks; but it was soon found that America's soil repelled an aristocracy based on land-holdings. It was realized that clearing this difficult land required nothing less than the constant and self-interested efforts of the owner himself; the ground prepared, it became evident that its products were not sufficient to enrich at the same time an owner as well as a tenant. The land was then naturally broken up into small portions, which the proprietor cultivated for himself. Land is the basis of an aristocracy, which clings to the soil that supports it; for it is not by privileges alone, nor by birth, but by landed property handed down from generation to generation that an aristocracy is constituted. A nation may present immense fortunes and extreme wretchedness; but unless those fortunes are territorial, there is no true aristocracy, but simply the class of the rich and that of the poor.

All the British colonies had striking similarities at the time of their origin. All of them, from their beginning, seemed destined to present the development of freedom, not the aristocratic freedom of their mother country, but the bourgeois and democratic freedom as yet never fully displayed in the history of the world.

Within this general uniformity, however, several marked divergences could be observed, which it is necessary to point out. Two branches may be distinguished in the great Anglo-American family, which have hitherto grown up without entirely commingling; one in the South, the other in the North.

Virginia received the first English colony; the immigrants took possession of it in 1607. The idea that gold and silver mines are the sources of national wealth was at that time singularly prevalent in Europe, a fatal delusion, which has done more to impoverish the European nations who adopted it – and has cost more lives in America – than the united influence of war and bad laws. The men sent to Virginia were seekers of gold, adventurers without resources and without character, whose turbulent and restless spirit endangered the infant colony and made its progress uncertain. Artisans and agriculturists arrived afterwards; and although they were a more moral and orderly race of men, they were hardly in any respect above the level of the inferior classes in England. No lofty views, no spiritual conception, presided over the foundation of these new settlements. The colony was scarcely established when slavery was introduced; this was the capital fact which was to exercise an immense influence on the character, the laws, and the whole future of the South. Slavery, as I shall afterwards show, dishonors labor; it introduces idleness into society, and with idleness, ignorance and pride, luxury and distress. It enervates the powers of the mind and benumbs the activity of man. The influence of slavery, united to the English character, explains the manners and the social state of the Southern states.

On this same English foundation very different characteristics developed in the North. Here I may be allowed to enter into some details. In the English colonies of the North, more generally known as the New England states, the two or three main ideas that now constitute the basis of the social theory of the United States were first combined. The principles of New England spread at first to the neighboring states; they then passed successively to the more distant ones; and at last, if I may so speak, they interpenetrated the whole confederation. They now extend their influence beyond its limits, over the whole American world. The civilization of New England has been like a beacon lit upon a hill, which, after it has diffused its warmth immediately around it, also tinges the distant horizon with its glow.

The foundation of New England was a novel spectacle, and all the circumstances attending it were singular and original. Nearly all colonies have had for their first inhabitants men without education and without resources that misery and misconduct drove from the land which gave them birth, or greedy speculators and industrial adventurers. Some settlements cannot even boast so honorable an origin; Santo Domingo was founded by pirates; and at the present day the criminal courts of England supply the population of Australia.

The settlers who established themselves on the shores of New England all belonged to the more independent classes of their native country. Their union on the soil of America at once presented the singular phenomenon of a society containing neither lords nor common people, and we may almost say neither rich nor poor. These men possessed, in proportion to their number, a greater mass of intelligence than is to be found in any European nation of our own time. All, perhaps without a single exception, had received a good education, and many of them were known in Europe for their talents and acquirements. The other colonies had been founded by adventurers without families; the immigrants of New England brought with them the best elements of order and morality; they landed on the desert coast accompanied by their wives and children. But what especially distinguished them from all others was the aim of their undertaking. They had not been obliged by necessity to leave their country; the social position they abandoned was one to be regretted, and their means of subsistence were certain. Nor did they cross the Atlantic to improve their situation or increase their wealth; it was a purely intellectual craving that called them from the comforts of their former homes; in facing the inevitable sufferings of exile their object was the triumph of an idea.

The immigrants, or, as they deservedly styled themselves, the Pilgrims, belonged to that English sect whose austere principle had given them the name of Puritans. Puritanism was not merely a religious doctrine, but corresponded in many points with the most absolute democratic and republican theories. It was this tendency that had aroused its most dangerous adversaries. Persecuted by the government of their mother country, and offended amidst the rigor of their principles by the daily habits of the society in which they lived, the Puritans went forth to seek some rude and unfrequented part of the world where they could live according to their own opinions and worship God in freedom.

. . .

In New England, townships were completely and definitely constituted as early as 1650. Interests, passions, duties, and rights came to be grouped around the township's individual identity and were firmly attached to it. At the heart of the township, one could see a real, active, completely democratic and republican political life reigning. The colonies still recognized the supremacy of the mother country; monarchy was still the law of the state, but the republic was already established in every township.

The towns named their own magistrates of every kind, assessed themselves, and levied their own taxes. In the New England town the law of representation was not adopted; the affairs of the community were discussed, as at Athens, in the marketplace, by a general assembly of the citizens.

In studying the laws that were promulgated at this early era of the American republics, it is impossible not to be struck by the legislator's knowledge of government and advanced theories.

It is clear that he has made the duties of society towards its members more elevated and more all-encompassing than the European legislators of the time, and that he imposed on society obligations that it still evaded elsewhere. In the states of New England, from the first, the condition of the poor is provided for; strict measures are taken for the maintenance of roads, and surveyors are appointed to attend to them; records are established in every town, in which the results of public deliberations and the births, deaths, and marriages of the citizens are entered; clerks are directed to keep these records; officers are appointed to administer properties having no claimants, and others to determine the boundaries of inherited lands, many others have for their principal function the maintenance of public order in the community. The law enters into a thousand various details to anticipate and satisfy a crowd of social wants that even now are very inadequately felt in France.

But it is by the mandates relating to public education that the original character of American civilization is at once placed in the clearest light. "Whereas," says the law, "Satan, the enemy of mankind, finds his strongest weapons in the ignorance of men, and whereas it is important that the wisdom of our fathers shall not remain buried in their tombs, and whereas the education of children is one of the prime concerns of the state, with the aid of the Lord . . ." Here follow clauses establishing schools in every township and obliging the inhabitants, under pain of heavy fines, to support them.

Schools of a superior kind were founded in the same manner in the more populous districts. The municipal authorities must see to it that parents send their children to school; they have the right to inflict fines upon all who refuse compliance; and in cases of continued resistance, society assumes the place of the parent, takes possession of the child, and deprives the father of those natural rights which he used to such poor purpose. The reader will undoubtedly have noted the preamble of these enactments: in America religion is the road to knowledge, and the observance of the divine laws leads man to civil freedom.

If, after having cast a rapid glance over the state of American society in 1650, we turn to the condition of Europe, and more especially to that of the Continent, at the same period, we cannot fail to be infused with a profound astonishment. On the continent of Europe, at the beginning of the seventeenth century absolute monarchy had everywhere triumphed over the ruins of the oligarchical and feudal liberties of the Middle Ages. Never perhaps were the ideas of right more completely overlooked than in the midst of the splendor and literature of Europe; never was there less political activity among the people; never were the principles of true freedom less widely circulated; and at that very time those principles which were scorned or unknown by the nations of Europe were proclaimed in the deserts of the New World and were accepted as the future creed of a great people. The boldest theories of the human spirit were put into practice in a society so humble in appearance that it could not attract the attention of a single statesman; and an unprecedented system of legislation was produced offhand by the natural originality of men's imaginations. In the bosom of this obscure democracy, which had as yet brought forth neither generals nor philosophers nor authors, a man might stand up in the face of a free people, and pronounce with general applause the following fine definition of liberty: ". . . there is a Civil, a Moral, a Federal *liberty*, which is the proper End and Object of *Authority*; it is a *Liberty* for that only which is *just* and *good*; for this *Liberty* you are to stand with the hazard of your very *Lives*."[1]

I have said enough to put the character of Anglo-American civilization in its true light. It is the result (and this should be constantly kept in mind) of two distinct elements, which in other places have been in frequent disagreement, but which the Americans have succeeded in incorporating to some extent one with the other and combining admirably. I allude to the *spirit of religion* and the *spirit of liberty*.

The settlers of New England were at the same time ardent sectarians and

---

1   Cotton Mather, quoting John Winthrop, in *Magnalia Christi Americana* 1702, book II, paragraph 9, line 41–44.

daring innovators. Narrow as the limits of some of their religious opinions were, they were free from all political prejudices. Hence arose two tendencies, distinct but not opposite, which are everywhere discernible in the manners as well as the laws of the country.

Men sacrifice for a religious opinion their friends, their family, and their country; one can consider them devoted to the pursuit of intellectual goals they purchased at so high a price. One sees them, however, seeking with almost equal eagerness material wealth and moral satisfaction; heaven in the world to come, and material well-being and freedom in this one.

Under their hand, political principles, laws, and human institutions seem malleable, capable of being shaped and combined at will. As they go forward, the barriers which imprisoned society and behind which they were born are lowered; old opinions, which for centuries had controlled the world, vanish; a course almost without limits, a field without horizon, is revealed: the human mind rushes forward and traverses it in every direction. But having reached the limits of the political world, the human mind stops of itself; in fear it relinquishes the need of exploration; it even abstains from lifting the veil of the sanctuary; it bows with respect before truths which it accepts without discussion.

Thus in the moral world everything is classified, systematized, foreseen, and decided beforehand; in the political world everything is agitated, disputed, and uncertain. In the one is a passive though a voluntary obedience; in the other, an independence scornful of experience, and jealous of all authority. These two tendencies, apparently so discrepant, are far from conflicting; they advance together and support each other.

Religion perceives that civil liberty affords a noble exercise to the faculties of man and that the political world is a field prepared by the Creator for the efforts of mind. Free and powerful in its own sphere, satisfied with the place reserved for it, religion never more surely establishes its empire than when it reigns in the hearts of men on its own strength without outside support.

Freedom regards religion as its companion in all its battles and its triumphs, as the cradle of its infancy and the divine source of its claims. It considers religion the safeguard of morality, and morality the best security of law and the surest pledge of the duration of freedom.

Reasons for certain anomalies which the laws and customs of the
Anglo-Americans present

The reader is cautioned not to draw too general or too absolute an inference from what has been said. The social condition, the religion, and the customs of the first immigrants undoubtedly exercised an immense influence on the destiny of their new country. Nevertheless, they could not found a state of things originating solely in themselves: no man can entirely shake off the influence of the past; and the settlers, intentionally or not, mingled habits and notions derived from their education and the traditions of their country with those habits and notions that were exclusively their own. To know and judge the Anglo-Americans of the present day, it is therefore necessary to distinguish what is of Puritan and what of English origin.

Laws and customs are frequently to be met with in the United States which contrast strongly with all that surrounds them. These laws seem to be drawn up in a spirit contrary to the prevailing tenor of American legislation; and these customs are no less opposed to the general tone of society. If the English colonies had been founded in an age of darkness, or if their origin was already lost in the lapse of years, the problem would be insoluble.

I shall cite a single example to illustrate my meaning. The civil and criminal procedure of the Americans has only two means of action, committal or bail. The first act of the magistrate is to exact security from the defendant or, in case of refusal, to incarcerate him; the ground of the accusation and the importance of the charges against him are then discussed. It is evident that such a legislation is hostile to the poor and favorable only to the rich. The poor man cannot always secure collateral, even in a civil case; and if he is obliged to wait for justice in prison, he is speedily reduced to distress. A wealthy person, on the contrary, always escapes imprisonment in civil cases; nay, more, if he has committed a crime, he may readily elude punishment by breaking his bail. Thus all the penalties of the law are, for him, reduced to fines. Nothing can be more aristocratic than this system of legislation. Yet in America it is the poor who make the law, and they usually reserve the greatest advantages of society to themselves. The explanation of the phenomenon is to be found in England; the laws of which I speak are English, and the Americans have retained them, although repugnant to the general tenor of their legislation and the mass of their ideas.

Next to its habits the thing which a nation is least apt to change is its civil legislation. Civil laws are familiarly known only to lawyers, whose direct interest it is to maintain them as they are, whether good or bad, simply because they themselves are conversant with them. The bulk of the nation is scarcely acquainted with them; it sees their action only in particular cases, can with difficulty detect their tendency, and obeys them without thought.

I have quoted one instance where it would have been easy to adduce many others. The picture of American society has, if I may so speak, a democratic coat of paint, beneath which the old aristocratic colors sometimes peep out.

3a3   Chapter 3: "Social Condition of the Anglo-Americans"

Social condition is commonly the result of circumstances, sometimes of laws, more often still of these two causes united; but when once established, it may justly be considered as itself the first cause of almost all the laws, usages, and ideas which regulate the conduct of nations: whatever it does not produce, it modifies. If we would become acquainted with the legislation and the manners of a nation, therefore, we must begin by the study of its social condition.

The striking characteristic of the social condition of the Anglo-Americans is its essential democracy

One could make many important remarks about the social condition of the Anglo-Americans; but there is one that dominates all the rest. The social condition of the Americans is eminently democratic; this was its character at the foundation of the colonies, and it is still more strongly marked at the present day.

I stated in the preceding chapter that great equality existed among the immigrants who settled on the shores of New England. Even the seeds of aristocracy were never planted in that part of the Union. The only influence which obtained there was that of intellect; the people became accustomed to revere certain names as representatives of knowledge and virtue. Some of their fellow citizens acquired a power over the others that might truly have been called aristocratic if it had been capable of transmission from father to son.

This was the state of things to the east of the Hudson: to the southwest of that river, and as far as the Floridas, the case was different. In most of the states situated southwest of the Hudson some great English proprietors had settled who had imported with them aristocratic principles and the English law of inheritance. I have explained the reasons why it was impossible ever to establish a powerful aristocracy in America; these reasons existed with less force southwest of the Hudson. In the South one man, aided by slaves, could cultivate a great extent of country; it was therefore common to see rich landed proprietors. But their influence was not altogether aristocratic, as that term is understood in Europe, since they possessed no privileges; and the cultivation of their estates being carried on by slaves, they had no tenants depending on them, and consequently no patronage. Still, the great proprietors south of the Hudson constituted a superior class, having ideas and tastes of its own and forming the center of political action. This kind of aristocracy sympathized with the body of the people, whose passions and interests it easily embraced;

but it was too weak and too short-lived to excite either love or hatred. This was the class which headed the insurrection in the South and furnished the best leaders of the American Revolution.

At this period society was shaken to its center. The people, in whose name the struggle had taken place, conceived the desire of exercising the authority that it had acquired; its democratic tendencies were awakened; and having thrown off the yoke of the mother country, it aspired to independence of every kind. The influence of individuals gradually ceased to be felt, and custom and law united to produce the same result.

But it was the law of inheritance that stimulated the final step toward equality.

. . .

When the equal partition of property is established by law, the intimate connection is destroyed between family feeling and the preservation of the paternal estate; the property ceases to represent the family; for, as it must inevitably be divided after one or two generations, it has evidently a constant tendency to diminish and must in the end be completely dispersed. The sons of the great landed proprietor, if they are few in number, or if fortune befriends them, may indeed entertain the hope of being as wealthy as their father, but not of possessing the same property that he did; their riches must be composed of other elements than his.

Now, as soon as you divest the landowner of that interest in the preservation of his estate which he derives from association, from tradition, and from family pride, you may be certain that, sooner or later, he will dispose of it; for there is a strong pecuniary interest in favor of selling, as liquid assets produce higher interest than real property and are more readily available to gratify the passions of the moment. Great landed estates which have once been divided never come together again; for the small proprietor draws from his land a better revenue, in proportion, than the large owner does from his; and of course he sells it at a higher rate. The reasons of economy, therefore, which have led the rich man to sell vast estates will prevent him all the more from buying little ones in order to form a large one.

What is called family pride is often founded upon an illusion of self-love. A man wishes to perpetuate and immortalize himself, as it were, in his great-grandchildren. At the point at which family pride ends, individual egoism comes into play. When the idea of family becomes vague, indeterminate, and uncertain, a man thinks of his present convenience; he provides for the establishment of his next succeeding generation and no more. Either a man gives up the idea of perpetuating his family, or at any rate he seeks to accomplish it by other means than by a landed estate.

Thus, not only does the law of succession render it difficult for families to preserve their ancestral domains entire, but it deprives them of the inclination to attempt it and compels them in some measure to co-operate with the law in their own extinction. The law of equal distribution proceeds by two methods: by acting upon things, it acts upon persons; by influencing persons, it affects things. By both these means the law succeeds in striking at the root of landed property, and dispersing rapidly both families and fortunes.

Most certainly it is not for us, Frenchmen of the nineteenth century, who daily witness the political and social changes that the law of partition is bringing to pass, to question its influence. It is perpetually conspicuous in our country, overthrowing the walls of our dwellings, and removing the landmarks of our fields. But although it has produced great effects in France, much still remains for it to do. Our recollections, opinions, and habits present powerful obstacles to its progress.

In the United States it has nearly completed its work of destruction, and there we can best study its results. The English laws concerning the transmission of property were abolished in almost all the states at the time of the Revolution. The law of entail was so modified as not materially to interrupt the free circulation of property.

The first generation having passed away, estates began to be parceled out; and the change became more and more rapid with the progress of time. And now, after a lapse of a little more than sixty years, the aspect of society is totally altered; the families of the great landed proprietors are almost all mingled with the general mass. In the state of New York, which formerly contained many of these, there are but two who still keep their heads above the stream; and they must shortly disappear. The sons of these opulent citizens have become merchants, lawyers, or physicians. Most of them have lapsed into obscurity. The last trace of hereditary ranks and distinctions is destroyed; the law of partition has reduced all to one level.

I do not mean that there is any lack of wealthy individuals in the United States; I know of no country, indeed, where the love of money has taken stronger hold on the affections of men and where a more profound contempt is expressed for the theory of the permanent equality of property. But wealth circulates with inconceivable rapidity, and experience shows that it is rare to find two succeeding generations in the full enjoyment of it.

This picture, colored as one may suppose it to be, still gives a very imperfect idea of what is taking place in the new states of the West and Southwest. At the end of the last century a few bold adventurers began to penetrate into the valley of the Mississippi, and the mass of the population very soon began to move in that direction: communities unheard of till then suddenly appeared in the desert. States whose names did not even exist a few years earlier claimed their place in the American Union; and in the Western settlements we may behold democracy reaching its utmost limits. In these states, founded offhand and as it were by chance, the inhabitants arrived just yesterday on the soil that they currently occupy. Scarcely known to one another, the nearest neighbors are ignorant of each other's history. In this part of the American continent, therefore, the population has escaped the influence not only of great names and great wealth, but even of the natural aristocracy of knowledge and virtue. None is there able to wield that respectable power which men willingly grant to the remembrance of a life spent in doing good before their eyes. The new states of the West are already inhabited, but society does not yet exist there.

It is not only the fortunes of men that are equal in America; even their accomplishments partake in some degree of the same uniformity. I do not believe that there is a country in the world where, in proportion to the population, there are so few ignorant and at the same time so few learned individuals. Primary instruction is within the reach of everybody; superior instruction is scarcely to be obtained by any. This is not surprising; it is, in fact, the necessary consequence of what I have advanced above. Almost all Americans are in easy circumstances and can therefore obtain the first elements of human knowledge.

In America there are but few wealthy persons; nearly all Americans have to take a profession. Now, every profession requires an apprenticeship. The Americans can devote to general education only the early years of life. At fifteen they enter upon their calling, and thus their education generally ends at the age when ours begins. If it is continued beyond that point, it aims only towards a particular specialized and profitable purpose; one studies science as one takes up a business; and one takes up only those applications whose immediate practicality is recognized.

In America most of the rich men were formerly poor; most of those who now enjoy leisure were absorbed in business during their youth; the consequence of this is that when they might have had a taste for study, they had no time for it, and when the time is at their disposal, they have no longer the inclination. There is no class, then, in America, in which the taste for intellectual pleasures is transmitted with hereditary fortune and leisure and by which the labors of the intellect are held in honor. In addition, the will as well as the power to take up such labors is lacking.

A middling standard is fixed in America for human knowledge. All approach as near to it as they can; some as they rise, others as they descend. Of course, a multitude of persons are to be found who entertain the same number of ideas on religion, history, science, political economy, legislation, and government. The gifts of intellect proceed directly from God, and man cannot prevent their unequal distribution. But it is at least a consequence of what I have just said that although the capacities of men are different, as the Creator intended they should be, the means that Americans find for putting them to use are equal.

In America the aristocratic element has always been feeble from its birth; and if at the present day it is not actually destroyed, it is at any rate so completely disabled that we can scarcely assign to it any degree of influence on the course of affairs. The democratic principle, on the contrary, has gained so much strength by time, by events, and by legislation, as to have become not only predominant, but all-powerful. No family or corporate authority can be perceived; very often one cannot even discover in it any very lasting individual influence.

America, then, exhibits in her social state an extraordinary phenomenon. Men are there seen on a greater equality in point of fortune and intellect, or, in other words, more equal in their strength, than in any other country of the world, or in any age of which history has preserved the remembrance.

Political consequences of the social condition of the Anglo-Americans

The political consequences of such a social condition are easily deducible. It is impossible to believe that equality will not eventually find its way into the political world, as it does everywhere else. To conceive of men remaining forever unequal upon a single point, yet equal on all others, is impossible; they must come in the end to be equal upon all.

Now, I know of only two methods of establishing equality in the political world; rights must be given to every citizen, or none at all to anyone. For nations which are arrived at the same stage of social existence as the Anglo-Americans, it is, therefore, very difficult to discover a middle position between the sovereignty of all and the absolute power of one man: and it would be vain to deny that the social condition which I have been describing is just as liable to one of these consequences as to the other.

There is, in fact, a manly and lawful passion for equality that incites men to wish all to be powerful and honored. This passion tends to elevate the humble to the rank of the great; but there exists also in the human heart a depraved taste for equality, which impels the weak to attempt to lower the powerful to their own level and reduces men to prefer equality in slavery to inequality with freedom. Not that those nations whose social condition is democratic naturally despise liberty; on the contrary, they have an instinctive love of it. But liberty is not the chief and constant object of their desires; equality is their idol: they make rapid and sudden efforts to obtain liberty and, if they miss their aim, resign themselves to their disappointment; but nothing can satisfy them without equality, and they would rather perish than lose it.

On the other hand, in a state where the citizens are all practically equal, it becomes difficult for them to preserve their independence against the aggressions of power. No one among them being strong enough to engage in the struggle alone with advantage, nothing but a general combination can protect their liberty. Now, such a union is not always possible. From the same social position, then, nations may derive one or the other of two great political results; these results are extremely different from each other, but they both proceed from the same cause. The Anglo-Americans are the first nation who, having been exposed to this formidable alternative, have been happy enough to escape the dominion of absolute power. They have been allowed by their circumstances, their origin, their intelligence, and especially by their morals to establish and maintain the sovereignty of the people.

3a5   Chapter 5: "Necessity of Examining the Condition of the States Before that of the Union at Large"

Political effects of administrative decentralization in the United States

"Centralization" is a word that is constantly repeated today, yet in general no one seeks to understand its meaning. Nevertheless, there exist two very distinct kinds of centralization, which need to be well understood. Certain interests are common to all parts of a nation, such as the enactment of its general laws and the maintenance of its foreign relations. Other interests are peculiar to certain parts of the nation, such, for instance, as the business of the several townships.

To concentrate in the same place or in the same hand the power to direct the first set of interests, that is the basis for what I will call governmental centralization. To concentrate in the same manner the power to direct the second set of interests, that is the basis for what I will call administrative centralization. Upon some points these two kinds of centralization coincide, but by classifying the objects which fall more particularly within the province of each, they may easily be distinguished.

It is evident that governmental centralization acquires immense power when united to administrative centralization. Thus combined, it accustoms men to set their own will habitually and completely aside; to submit, not only for once, or upon one point, but in every respect, and at all times. Not only, therefore, does this union of power subdue them by force but it captures them by their ordinary habits; it isolates them and then ties them up one after the other in the common mass.

These two kinds of centralization assist and attract each other, but they must not be supposed to be inseparable. It is impossible to imagine greater governmental centralization than that which existed in France under Louis XIV; when the same individual was the author and the interpreter of the laws and the representative of France at home and abroad, he was justified in asserting that he constituted the state. Nevertheless, under Louis XIV there was much less administrative centralization than in our day.

In our time, we see one power, England, in which governmental centralization is carried to a very high degree; the state has the compact vigor of one man, and it puts in motion at its will immense masses and gathers and brings to bear where it will the whole force of its power. But England, which has done such great things for the last fifty years, lacks administrative centralization. Indeed, I cannot conceive that a nation can live and prosper without strong governmental centralization. But I am of the opinion that administrative centralization is fit only to enervate the nations in which it exists, by incessantly diminishing their local spirit. Although administrative centralization can bring together at a given moment, on a given point, all the disposable resources of a people, it injures the renewal of those resources. It may ensure a victory in the hour of strife, but it gradually relaxes the sinews of strength. It may help admirably the transient greatness of a man, but not the durable prosperity of a nation.

One can be sure that when one says that a state cannot act because it lacks centralization, one speaks almost always, unconsciously, of governmental centralization. It is frequently asserted, and I assent to the proposition, that the German Empire has never been able to bring all its powers into action. But the reason is that the state has never been able to enforce obedience to its general laws; the several members of that great body always claimed the right, or found the means, of refusing their co-operation to the representatives of the common authority, even in the affairs that concerned the mass of the people; in other words, there was no centralization of government. The same remark is applicable to the Middle Ages; the cause of all the miseries of feudal society was that the control, not only of administration, but of government, was divided among a thousand hands and broken up in a thousand different ways. The want of all governmental centralization prevented the nations of Europe from advancing with energy toward a single end.

I have shown that in the United States there is no administrative centralization. One hardly finds there a trace of hierarchy. Local authority has been carried farther than any European nation could endure without great inconvenience, and it has even produced some disadvantageous consequences in

America. But in the United States governmental centralization is perfect; and it would be easy to prove that the national power is more concentrated there than it has ever been in the old nations of Europe. Not only is there but one legislative body in each state, not only does there exist but one source of political authority, but numerous assemblies in districts or counties have not, in general, been multiplied lest they should be tempted to leave their administrative duties and interfere with the government. In America the legislature of each state is supreme; nothing can impede its authority, neither privileges, nor local immunities, nor personal influence, nor even the empire of reason, since it represents that majority which claims to be the sole organ of reason. Its own determination is therefore the only limit to its action. In juxtaposition with it, and under its immediate control, is the representative of the executive power, whose duty it is to constrain malcontents to submit by superior force. The only symptom of weakness lies in certain details of the action of the government. The American republics have no standing armies to intimidate a discontented minority; but as no minority has as yet been reduced to declare open war, the necessity of an army has not been felt. The state usually employs the officers of the township or the county to deal with the citizens. Thus, for instance, in New England the town assessor fixes the tax-rate; the town collector receives them; the town treasurer transmits the amount to the public treasury; and the disputes that may arise are brought before the ordinary courts of justice. This method of collecting taxes is slow as well as inconvenient, and it would prove a perpetual hindrance to a government whose pecuniary demands were large. It is desirable that, in whatever materially affects its existence, the government should be served by officers of its own, appointed by itself, removable at its pleasure, and accustomed to rapid methods of proceeding. But it will always be easy for the central government, organized as it is in America, to introduce more energetic and efficacious modes of action according to its wants.

It is not, then, as it is often repeated, because there is no centralization in the United States that the republics of the New World will perish; far from not being sufficiently centralized, one could assert that the American governments are too centralized, as I shall prove later. The legislative bodies daily absorb bits and pieces of governmental power, and their tendency, like that of the French Convention, is to appropriate it entirely to themselves. The social power thus centralized is constantly changing hands, because it is subordinate to the power of the people. It often happens to lack wisdom and foresight in the consciousness of its strength. Hence arises its danger. Its vigor, and not its impotence, will probably be the cause of its ultimate destruction.

Administrative decentralization produces several different effects in America. The Americans seem to me to have overstepped the limits of sound policy in isolating the administration of the government; for order, even in secondary affairs, is a matter of national importance. As the state has no administrative functionaries of its own, stationed on different points of its territory, to whom it can give a common impulse, the consequence is that it rarely attempts to issue any general police regulations. The want of these regulations is severely felt and is frequently observed by Europeans. The appearance of disorder which prevails on the surface leads one at first to imagine that society is in a state of anarchy; nor does one perceive one's mistake till one has gone deeper into the subject. Certain undertakings are of importance to the whole state; but they cannot be executed, because there is no state administration to direct them. Abandoned to the exertions of the towns or counties, under the care of elected and temporary agents, they lead to no result, or at least to no durable benefit.

The partisans of centralization in Europe are wont to maintain that the government can administer the affairs of each locality better than the citizens can do it for themselves. This may be true when the central power is enlightened and the local authorities are ignorant; when it is alert and they are slow; when it is accustomed to act and they to obey. Indeed, it is evident that this double tendency must augment with the increase of centralization, and that the readiness of the one and the incapacity of the others must become more and more prominent. But I deny that it is so when the people are as enlightened, as awake to their interests, and as accustomed to reflect on them as the Americans are.

I am persuaded, on the contrary, that in this case the collective strength of the citizens will always be more able to produce social well-being than the authority of the government.

I know it is difficult to point out with certainty the means of arousing a sleeping population and of giving it passions and knowledge which it does not possess; it is, I am well aware, an arduous task to persuade men to busy themselves about their own affairs. It would often be less arduous to interest them in the details of court etiquette than in the repairs of their public buildings.

But I also think that whenever a central administration attempts completely to replace the free concourse among the interested parties, it misleads itself or hopes to mislead you. However enlightened and skillful a central power may be, it cannot of itself embrace all the details of the life of a great nation. Such vigilance exceeds the powers of man. And when it attempts unaided to create and set in motion so many complicated springs, it must submit to a very imperfect result or exhaust itself in bootless efforts.

Centralization easily succeeds, indeed, in subjecting the external actions of men to a certain uniformity, which we come at last to love for its own sake, independently of the objects to which it is applied, like those devotees who worship the statue and forget the deity it represents. Centralization imparts without difficulty an admirable regularity to the routine of business; provides skillfully for the details of the social police; represses small disorders and petty misdemeanors; maintains society in a status quo equally secure from improvement and decline; and perpetuates a drowsy regularity in the conduct of affairs which the heads of the administration are wont to call good order and public tranquillity; in short, it excels in prevention, but not in action. When it is a question of significantly moving society or of stimulating it to a rapid pace, its force abandons it. To the extent that its measures require the co-operation of individuals, one is very surprised by the weakness of this immense machine; it finds itself reduced all of a sudden to impotence.

Even while the centralized power, in its despair, invokes the assistance of the citizens, it says to them: "You shall act just as I please, as much as I please, and in the direction which I please. You are to take charge of the details without aspiring to guide the system; you are to work in darkness; and afterwards you may judge my work by its results." These are not the conditions on which the alliance of the human will is to be obtained; it must be free in its gait and responsible for its acts, or (such is the constitution of man) the citizen had rather remain a passive spectator than a dependent actor in schemes with which he is unacquainted.

It is undeniable that the want of those uniform regulations which control the conduct of every inhabitant of France is not infrequently felt in the United States. Gross instances of social indifference and neglect are to be met with; and from time to time disgraceful blemishes are seen, in complete contrast with the surrounding civilization. Useful undertakings which cannot succeed without perpetual attention and rigorous exactitude are frequently abandoned; for in America, as well as in other countries, the people proceed by sudden impulses and momentary exertions.

The European, accustomed to find a functionary always at hand to interfere with all he undertakes, reconciles himself with difficulty to the complex mechanism of the administration of the townships. In general it may be affirmed that the small details of order that make life easy and comfortable are neglected in America, but that the essential guarantees of man in society are as strong there as elsewhere. In America the power that conducts the administration is far less regular, less enlightened, and less skillful, but a hundredfold greater than in Europe. In no country in the world do the citizens make such exertions for the common weal. I know of no people who have established schools so numerous and efficacious, places of public worship better suited to the wants of the inhabitants, or roads kept in better repair. It is not necessary to seek in the United States uniformity and permanence of

point of view, minute care over details, perfection in administrative procedures; what one finds there is the very image of force, a little wild it is true,
but full of power, the image of life, accompanied by accidents, but also by
energy and effort.

Granting, for an instant, that the villages and counties of the United States
would be more usefully governed by a central authority placed far from them
than by functionaries chosen from among them; admitting, for the sake of
argument, that there would be more security in America, and the resources of
society would be better employed there, if the whole administration centered
in a single arm – still the *political* advantages which the Americans derive from
their decentralized system would induce me to prefer it to the contrary plan.
It profits me but little, after all, that a vigilant authority always protects the
tranquillity of my pleasures and constantly averts all dangers from my path,
without my care or concern, if this same authority is the absolute master of
my freedom and my life, and if it so monopolizes movement and life that
when it languishes everything languishes around it, that when it sleeps
everything must sleep, and that when it dies the state itself must perish.

There are countries in Europe where the native considers himself a kind of
settler, indifferent to the fate of the spot which he inhabits. The greatest
changes occur in his country without his involvement; he doesn't even know
what precisely happened; he wonders if he has heard the event talked about
by chance. Furthermore, the condition of his village, the policing of his street,
the repairs of the church or the parsonage, do not concern him; for he looks
upon all these things as unconnected with himself and as the property of a
powerful stranger whom he calls the government. He has only a life interest
in these possessions, without the spirit of ownership or any ideas of improvement. This want of interest in his own affairs goes so far that if his own safety
or that of his children is at last endangered, instead of trying to avert the peril,
he will fold his arms and wait till the whole nation comes to his aid. This
man who has so completely sacrificed his own free will does not, more than
any other person, love obedience; he cowers, it is true, before the pettiest
officer, but he braves the law with the spirit of a conquered foe as soon as its
superior force is withdrawn; he perpetually oscillates between servitude and
license.

When a nation has arrived at this state, it must either change its customs
and its laws, or perish; for the source of public virtues is dried up; and though
it may contain subjects, it has no citizens. Such communities are a natural
prey to foreign conquests; and if they do not wholly disappear from the scene,
it is only because they are surrounded by other nations similar or inferior to
themselves; it is because they still have an indefinable instinct of patriotism;

and an involuntary pride in the name of their country, or a vague reminiscence of its bygone fame, which suffices to give them an impulse of self-preservation.

Nor can the prodigious exertions made by certain nations to defend a country in which they had lived, so to speak, as strangers be adduced in favor of such a system; for it will be found that in these cases their main incitement was religion. The permanence, the glory, or the prosperity of the nation had become parts of their faith, and in defending their country, they defended also that Holy City of which they were all citizens. The Turkish tribes have never taken an active share in the conduct of their affairs, but they accomplished stupendous enterprises as long as the victories of the Sultan were triumphs of the Mohammedan faith. In the present age they are in rapid decay because their religion is departing and only despotism remains. Montesquieu, who attributed to absolute power an authority peculiar to itself, did it, as I conceive, an undeserved honor; for despotism, taken by itself, can maintain nothing durable. On close inspection we shall find that religion, and not fear, has ever been the cause of the long-lived prosperity of an absolute government. Do what you may, there is no true power among men except in the free union of their will; and patriotism and religion are the only two motives in the world that can long urge all the people towards the same end.

Laws cannot rekindle an extinguished faith, but men may be interested by the laws in the fate of their country. It depends upon the laws to awaken and direct the vague impulse of patriotism, which never abandons the human heart; and if it be connected with the thoughts, the passions, and the daily habits of life, it may be consolidated into a durable and rational sentiment. Let it not be said that it is too late to make the experiment; for nations do not grow old as men do, and every fresh generation is a new people ready for the legislator's care.

What I admire the most in America is not the *administrative* effects of decentralization; rather it is the *political* effects. In the United States the interests of the country are everywhere kept in view; they are an object of solicitude to the people of the whole Union, and every citizen is as warmly attached to them as if they were his own. He takes pride in the glory of his nation; he boasts of its success, to which he conceives himself to have contributed; and he rejoices in the general prosperity by which he profits. The feeling he entertains towards the state is analogous to that which unites him to his family, and it is by a kind of egoism that he interests himself in the welfare of his country.

To the European, a public officer represents a superior force; to an American, he represents a right. In America, then, it may be said that no one renders obedience to man, but to justice and to law. If the opinion that the citizen entertains of himself is exaggerated, it is at least salutary; he unhesitatingly confides in his own powers, which appear to him to be all-sufficient. When a private individual meditates an undertaking, however directly connected it may be with the welfare of society, he never thinks of soliciting the government's co-operation; instead he publishes his plan, offers to execute it, courts the assistance of other individuals, and struggles manfully against all obstacles. Undoubtedly he is often less successful than the state might have been in his position; but in the end the sum of these private undertakings far exceeds all that the government could have done.

As the administrative authority is within the reach of the citizens, whom in some degree it represents, it excites neither their jealousy nor hatred; as its resources are limited, everyone feels that he must not rely solely on its aid. Thus when the administration thinks fit to act within its own limits, it is not abandoned to itself, as in Europe; the duties of private citizens are not supposed to have lapsed because the state has come into action, but everyone is ready, on the contrary, to guide and support it.

With the action of individual forces joined to that of social forces, one can often achieve what the most concentrated and energetic administration could not accomplish. It would be easy to adduce several facts in proof of what I advance, but I had rather give only one, with which I am best acquainted. In America the means that the authorities have at their disposal for the discovery of crimes and the arrest of criminals are few. A state police does not exist, and passports are unknown. The criminal police of the United States cannot be compared with that of France; the magistrates and public agents are not numerous; they do not always initiate the measures for arresting the guilty; and the examinations of prisoners are rapid and oral. Yet I believe that in no country does crime more rarely elude punishment. The reason is that everyone conceives himself to be interested in furnishing evidence of the crime and in seizing the delinquent. During my stay in the United States I witnessed the spontaneous formation of committees in a county for the pursuit and prosecution of a man who had committed a great crime. In Europe a criminal is an unhappy man who is struggling for his life against the agents of power, while the people are merely a spectator of the conflict; in America he is looked upon as an enemy of the human race, and the whole of mankind is against him.

I believe provincial institutions to be useful to all peoples, but nowhere do they appear to me to be more necessary than among a democratic people. In an aristocracy order can always be maintained in the midst of freedom; and as the rulers have a great deal to lose, order is to them a matter of great interest. In like manner an aristocracy protects the people from the excesses of despotism, because it always possesses an organized power ready to resist a despot. But a democracy without provincial institutions has no security against these evils. How can a populace unaccustomed to freedom in small concerns learn to use it temperately in great affairs? What resistance can be offered to tyranny in a country where each individual is weak and where the citizens are not united by any common interest? Those who dread the license of the mob and those who fear absolute power ought alike to desire the gradual development of provincial freedoms.

I am also convinced that there are no nations more exposed to falling under the yoke of administrative centralization than those whose social state is democratic. Several causes come together to produce this result, but among others the following:

The constant tendency of these nations is to concentrate all the strength of the government in the hands of the only power that directly represents the people; because beyond the people nothing is to be perceived but a mass of equal individuals. But when the same power already has all the attributes of government, it can scarcely refrain from penetrating into the details of administration, and an opportunity of doing so is sure to present itself in the long run, as was the case in France. In the French Revolution there were two impulses in opposite directions, which must never be confounded; the one was favorable to freedom, the other to despotism. Under the old monarchy the king was the sole author of the laws; and below the power of the sovereign certain vestiges of provincial institutions, half destroyed, were still distinguishable. These provincial institutions were incoherent, ill arranged, and frequently absurd; in the hands of the aristocracy they had sometimes been converted into instruments of oppression. The Revolution declared itself the enemy at once of royalty and of provincial institutions; it confounded in indiscriminate hatred all that had preceded it, despotic power and the checks to its abuses; and its tendency was at once to republicanize and to centralize.

This double character of the French Revolution is a fact which has been adroitly handled by the friends of absolute power. Can they be accused of laboring in the cause of despotism when they are defending that administrative centralization that was one of the Revolution's great innovations? In this manner popularity may be united with hostility to the rights of the people, and the secret slave of tyranny may be the professed lover of freedom.

I have visited the two nations in which the system of provincial freedom has been most perfectly established, and I have listened to the opinions of different parties in those countries. In America I met with men who secretly aspired to destroy the democratic institutions of the Union; in England I found others who openly attacked the aristocracy; but I found no one who did not regard provincial independence as a great good. In both countries I heard a thousand different causes assigned for the evils of the state, but the local system was never mentioned among them. I heard citizens attribute the power and prosperity of their country to a multitude of reasons, but they all placed the advantages of local institutions in the foremost rank.

Am I to suppose that when men who are naturally so divided on religious opinions and on political theories agree on one point (and that one which they can best judge, as it is one of which they have daily experience) they are all in error? The only nations which deny the utility of provincial freedoms are those which have fewest of them; in other words, only those who do not know it censure the institution.

3b   Part II

3b7   Chapter 7: "Unlimited Power of the Majority in the United States, and Its Consequences"

The very essence of democratic government consists in the absolute sovereignty of the majority; for there is nothing in democratic states capable of resisting it. Most of the American constitutions have sought to increase this natural strength of the majority by artificial means.

Of all political institutions, the legislature is the one that is most easily swayed by the will of the majority. The Americans determined that the members of the legislature should be elected by the people directly, and for a very brief term, in order to subject them, not only to the general views, but also to the everyday passions of their constituents. The members of both houses are taken from the same classes in society and nominated in the same manner; so that the movements of the legislative bodies are almost as rapid, and quite as irresistible, as those of a single assembly. It is to a legislature thus constituted that almost all the authority of the government has been entrusted.

At the same time as the law increased the strength of those authorities which were naturally strong, it enfeebled more and more those which were naturally weak. It accorded to representatives of the executive power neither stability nor independence; and by subjecting them completely to the caprices of the legislature, it robbed them of the slender influence that the nature of a democratic government might have allowed them to exercise.

In several states the judicial power was also submitted to the election of the majority and in all of them its existence was made to depend on the pleasure of the legislative authority, since the representatives were empowered annually to regulate the stipend of the judges.

Custom has done even more than law.

A proceeding is becoming more and more general in the United States which will, in the end, do away with the guarantees of representative government: it frequently happens that the voters, in electing a delegate, point out a certain line of conduct to him and impose upon him certain positive obligations that he is pledged to fulfill. The tumult excepted, it is as if the majority itself were deliberating in the market place.

Several particular circumstances combine to render the power of the majority in America not only preponderant, but irresistible. The moral authority of the majority is partly based upon the notion that there is more intelligence and wisdom in a number of men united than in a single individual, and that the number of the legislators is more important than their quality. The theory of equality is thus applied to human intellects. This doctrine assails the pride of man in its last refuge, so the minority admits it under duress and only becomes accustomed to it over the long term. Like all other powers, and perhaps more than any other, the authority of the many requires the sanction of time in order to appear legitimate. At first it enforces obedience by constraint; and its laws are not respected until they have been long maintained.

The idea that the majority has the right to govern society according to its lights was brought to the soil of the United States by their first inhabitants. This idea, which of itself would be sufficient to create a free nation, has now been amalgamated with the customs of the people and the minor incidents of social life.

The French under the old monarchy held it for a maxim that the king could do no wrong; and if he did do wrong, the blame was imputed to his advisers. This notion made obedience very easy; it enabled the subject to complain of the law without ceasing to love and honor the lawgiver. The Americans entertain the same opinion with respect to the majority.

The moral power of the majority is founded upon yet another principle, which is that the interests of the many are to be preferred to those of the few. Now, one readily understands that the respect that is professed for the right of the greatest number naturally increases or diminishes according to the condition of the respective parties. When a nation is divided into several great irreconcilable interests, the privilege of the majority is often overlooked, because it becomes too objectionable to comply with its demands.

If there existed in America a certain class of citizens whom the legislator sought to deprive of the exclusive privileges they had possessed for ages and to bring them down from an elevated station to the level of the multitude, it is probable that the minority would be less ready to submit to its laws.

But as the United States was colonized by men holding equal rank, there is as yet no natural or permanent disagreement between the interests of its different inhabitants.

There are communities in which the members of the minority can never hope to draw the majority over to their side, because they must then give up the very point that is at issue between them. Thus an aristocracy can never become a majority while it retains its exclusive privileges, and it cannot cede its privileges without ceasing to be an aristocracy. In the United States, political questions cannot be taken up in so general and absolute a manner; and all parties are willing to recognize the rights of the majority, because they all hope at some time to be able to exercise them to their own advantage.

The majority in the United States wields immense physical power and a power of persuasion that is nearly as great; no obstacles exist which can impede or even retard its progress, so as to make it heed the complaints of those whom it crushes upon its path. This state of things is harmful in itself and dangerous for the future.

How the omnipotence of the majority increases, in America, the legislative and administrative instability that is natural to democracies

I spoke previously of the vices that are normal to the government of democracy; there is not one of them that doesn't grow in proportion to the power of the majority. To begin with the most evident of them all:

Legislative inconsistency is an evil inherent to democratic government, because it is in the nature of democracies to raise new men to power. But this evil is more or less perceptible in proportion to the authority and the means of action which the legislature possesses.

In America the authority exercised by the legislatures is supreme; nothing prevents them from accomplishing their wishes with speed and irresistible power, and they are supplied with new representatives every year. That is to say, they have adopted precisely the combination that most favors democratic instability and that permits democracy to subject its most important ends to its changing wishes. Hence America is, at the present day, the country beyond all others where laws last the shortest time. Almost all the American constitutions have been amended within thirty years; there is not one American state which has not modified the principles of its legislation in that time. As for the laws themselves, a single glance at the archives of the different states of the Union suffices to convince one that in America the activity of the legislator never slackens. Not that the American democracy is naturally less stable than any other, but it is allowed to follow, in the formation of the laws, the natural instability of its desires.

The omnipotence of the majority and the rapid as well as absolute manner in which its decisions are executed in the United States not only render the law unstable, but exercise the same influence upon the execution of the law and the conduct of the administration. As the majority is the only power that it is important to court, all its projects are taken up with the greatest ardor; but the moment its attention is distracted, all this ardor ceases; while in the free states of Europe, where the administration is at once independent and secure, the projects of the legislature continue to be executed even when its attention is directed to other objects.

In America certain improvements are prosecuted with much more zeal and activity than elsewhere; in Europe the same ends are promoted by much less social effort more continuously applied.

Some years ago several pious individuals undertook to improve the condition of the prisons. The public were moved by their statements, and the reform of criminals became a popular undertaking. New prisons were built; and for the first time the idea of reforming as well as punishing the delinquent formed a part of prison discipline.

But this happy change, in which the public had taken so hearty an interest and which the simultaneous exertions of the citizens rendered irresistible, could not be completed in a moment. While the new penitentiaries were being erected and the will of the majority was hastening the work, the old prisons still existed and contained a great number of offenders. These jails became more unwholesome and corrupt in proportion as the new establishments were reformed and improved. This contrast can be easily understood. The majority was so eagerly employed in founding the new prisons that those which already existed were forgotten; and as the general attention was diverted to a novel object, the care which had hitherto been bestowed upon the others ceased. The salutary regulations of discipline were first relaxed and afterwards broken; so that in the immediate neighborhood of a prison that bore witness to the mild and enlightened spirit of our times, dungeons existed that reminded one of the barbarism of the Middle Ages.

Tyranny of the majority

I hold it to be an impious and detestable maxim that, politically speaking, the people have a right to do anything; and yet I have asserted that all authority originates in the will of the majority. Am I, then, in contradiction with myself?

A general law, which bears the name of justice, has been made and sanctioned, not only by a majority of this or that people, but by a majority of mankind. The rights of every people are therefore confined within the limits of what is just. A nation may be considered as a jury which is empowered to represent society at large and to apply justice, which is its law. Ought such a jury, which represents society, to have more power than the society itself whose laws it executes?

When I refuse to obey an unjust law, I do not contest the right of the majority to command, but I simply appeal from the sovereignty of the people to the sovereignty of mankind.

There are those people who do not hesitate to say that a people, when concerned with affairs that interest it alone, cannot possibly step beyond the bounds of justice and reason and that one must not fear to give all power to the majority that represents it. But this is the language of a slave.

A majority taken collectively is only an individual, whose opinions, and frequently whose interests, are opposed to those of another individual, who is called a minority. If it be admitted that a man possessing absolute power may misuse that power by wronging his adversaries, why should not a majority be liable to the same reproach? Men do not change their characters by uniting with one another; nor does their patience in the presence of obstacles increase with their strength. For my own part, I cannot believe it; the power to do everything, which I should refuse to one of my equals, I will never grant to any number of them.

I do not think that, for the sake of preserving liberty, it is possible to combine several principles in the same government so as really to oppose them to one another. The form of government that is usually called mixed has always appeared to me a mere chimera. Accurately speaking, there is no such thing as a mixed government in the sense usually given to that word, because in all communities some one principle of action may be discovered which preponderates over the others. England in the last century, which has been especially cited as an example of this sort of government, was essentially an aristocratic state, although it comprised some great elements of democracy; for the laws and customs of the country were such that the aristocracy could not but preponderate in the long run and direct public affairs according to its own will. The error arose from seeing the interests of the nobles perpetually contending with those of the people, without considering the issue of the contest, which was really the important point. When a community actually has a mixed government – that is to say, when it is equally divided between adverse principles – it must either experience a revolution or fall into anarchy.

I think, therefore, that one must always preserve somewhere social power superior to all others, but I believe at the same time that liberty is endangered when this power finds no obstacle which can retard its course and allow it to moderate its own vehemence.

Unlimited power is in itself a bad and dangerous thing. Human beings are not competent to exercise it with discretion. God alone can be omnipotent, because his wisdom and his justice are always equal to his power. There is no power on earth so worthy of honor in itself or clothed with rights so sacred that I would admit its uncontrolled and all-powerful authority. When I see that the right and means of absolute command are conferred on any power whatever, be it called a people or a king, an aristocracy or a democracy, a monarchy or a republic, I say there is the seed of tyranny, and I seek to live elsewhere, under other laws.

What I reproach most in democratic government, such as it is organized in the United States, is not its weakness, as many people proclaim in Europe, but its irresistible force. And what repulses me most in America is not the extreme freedom that prevails but the few safeguards to be found against tyranny.

When an individual or a party is wronged in the United States, to whom can he apply for redress? If to public opinion, public opinion constitutes the majority; if to the legislature, it represents the majority and implicitly obeys it; if to the executive power, it is appointed by the majority and serves as a passive tool in its hands. The public force consists of the majority under arms; the jury is the majority invested with the right of hearing judicial cases; and in certain states even the judges are elected by the majority. However iniquitous or absurd the measure of which you complain, you must submit to it as well as you can.

If, on the other hand, a legislative power could be so constituted as to represent the majority without necessarily being the slave of its passions, an executive so as to retain a proper share of authority, and a judiciary so as to remain independent of the other two powers, a government would be formed which would still be democratic while incurring scarcely any risk of tyranny.

I do not say that there is a frequent use of tyranny in America at the present day; but I maintain that there is no sure barrier against it, and that the causes which mitigate the government there are to be found in the circumstances and manners of the country more than in its laws.

Effects of the omnipotence of the majority upon the arbitrary authority
of American officials

A distinction must be drawn between tyranny and arbitrary power. Tyranny may be exercised by means of the law itself, and in that case it is not arbitrary; arbitrary power may be exercised for the public good, in which case it is not tyrannical. Tyranny usually employs arbitrary means, but if necessary it can do without them.

In the United States the omnipotence of the majority, which is favorable to the legal despotism of the legislature, likewise favors the arbitrary authority of the magistrate. The majority, being the absolute master in making the law and in overseeing its enactment, having equal control over the government as well as the governed, considers public officials to be its passive agents and readily confides to them the task of carrying out its designs. The majority does not involve itself in the detail of their duties nor hardly takes the trouble to define their rights. It treats them as a master does his servants, since they are always at work in his sight and he can direct or reprimand them at any instant.

In general, American functionaries are far more independent within the sphere that is prescribed to them than French civil officials. Sometimes, even, they are allowed by popular authority to exceed those bounds; and as they are protected by the opinion and backed by the power of the majority, they dare do things that even a European, accustomed as he is to arbitrary power, is astonished at. By this means habits are formed in the heart of a free country which may some day prove fatal to its liberties.

Power exercised by the majority in America upon opinion

It is only when one comes to consider the role of free thinking in the United States that one truly perceives to what extent the power of the majority surpasses all powers that we recognize in Europe. Free thought is an invisible and almost unknowable power that makes sport of all tyrannies. At present the most absolute monarchs in Europe cannot prevent certain opinions hostile to their authority from circulating in secret through their dominions and even in their courts. It is not so in America; as long as the majority is still undecided, discussion is carried on; but as soon as its decision is irrevocably pronounced, everyone is silent, and the friends as well as the opponents of the measure unite in assenting to its propriety. The reason for this is perfectly clear: no monarch is so absolute as to combine all the powers of society in his own hands and to conquer all opposition, as a majority is able to do, which has the right both of making and of executing the laws.

The authority of a king is physical and controls the actions of men without subduing their will. But the majority possesses a power that is physical and moral at the same time, which acts upon the will as much as upon the actions and represses not only all contest, but all controversy. I know of no country in which there is so little independence of mind and real freedom of discussion as in America. In any constitutional state in Europe every sort of religious and political theory may be freely preached and disseminated; for there is no country in Europe so subdued by single authority that he who wants to speak the truth there does not find some support capable of protecting him against the consequence of his boldness. If he is unfortunate enough to live under an absolute government, the people are often on his side; if he inhabits a free country, he can, if necessary, find shelter behind the throne. The aristocratic part of society supports him in some countries, and the democracy in others. But in a nation where democratic institutions exist, organized like those of the United States, there is but one authority, one element of strength and success, with nothing beyond it.

In America the majority draws an imposing circle around free thought; within these barriers an author may write what he pleases, but woe to him if he goes beyond them. Not that he is in danger of an *auto-da-fé*, but he is the daily butt of all manner of scorn and persecution. His political career is closed forever, since he has offended the only authority that is able to open it. Every sort of compensation, even that of celebrity, is refused to him. Before making public his opinions he thought he had sympathizers; now it seems to him that he has none any more since he has revealed himself to everyone; for those who blame him criticize loudly and those who think as he does, but without having his courage, keep quiet and move away. He yields, he finally gives in under the effort of each day and retreats into silence, as if he felt remorse for having spoken the truth.

Fetters and executioners, these are the coarse instruments that tyranny used to employ; but in our days civilization has taken despotism itself to a new level, although it had seemed to have nothing left to learn. Rulers had, so to speak, materialized oppression; the democratic republics of the present day have rendered oppression as intellectual as the will they want to constrain. Under the absolute sway of one man the body was attacked in order to subdue the soul; but the soul escaped the blows which were directed against it and rose proudly superior. Such is not the course adopted by tyranny in democratic republics; there the body is left free and the soul is enslaved. The master no longer says: "You shall think as I do or you shall die"; but he says: "You are free to think differently from me and to retain your life, your property, and all that you possess; but you are henceforth a stranger among your people. You may retain your civil rights, but they will be useless to you, for you will never be chosen by your fellow citizens if you solicit their votes; and they will scorn you if you ask for their esteem. You will remain among men, but you will be deprived of the rights of mankind. Your fellow creatures will shun you like an impure being; and even those who believe in your innocence will abandon you, lest they should be shunned in their turn. Go in peace! I have given you your life, but it is an existence worse than death."

Absolute monarchies had dishonored despotism; let us beware lest democratic republics should rehabilitate it and that in rendering despotism more oppressive for some, they do not reduce its odious aspect and degrading character in the eyes of the many.

Works have been published in the proudest nations of the Old World expressly intended to censure the vices and the follies of the times: La Bruyère lived in Louis XV's palace when he composed his chapter on the great, and Molière criticized the courtiers in plays that he presented before the court. But the ruling power in the United States is not to be made game of. The smallest reproach irritates its sensibility, and the slightest joke that has any foundation in truth renders it indignant, from the forms of its language up to the solid virtues of its character, everything must be made the subject of praise. No writer, whatever his eminence, can escape paying this tribute of adulation to his fellow citizens. The majority lives in the perpetual utterance of self-applause, and there are certain truths which the Americans can learn only from strangers or from experience.

If America has not as yet had any great writers, the reason is given in these facts; there can be no literary genius without freedom of opinion, and freedom of opinion does not exist in America. The Inquisition has never been able to prevent a vast number of anti-religious books from circulating in Spain. The empire of the majority succeeds much better in the United States, since it actually removes any wish to publish them. Unbelievers are to be met with in America, but there is no public organ of infidelity. Attempts have been made by some governments to protect morality by prohibiting licentious books. In the United States no one is punished for this sort of books, but no one is induced to write them; not because all the citizens are immaculate in conduct, but because the majority of the community is decent and orderly.

In this case the use of the power is unquestionably good; and I am discussing the nature of the power itself. This irresistible authority is a constant fact, and its judicious exercise is only an accident.

Effects of the tyranny of the majority upon the national character of the Americans – the courtier spirit in the United States

The tendencies that I have just mentioned are as yet but slightly perceptible in political society, but they already exercise an unfavorable influence upon the national character of the Americans. I attribute the small number of distinguished men in political life to the ever increasing despotism of the majority in the United States.

When the American Revolution broke out, eminent men arose in great numbers; for public opinion then served, not to tyrannize over, but to direct the exertions of individuals. Those celebrated men, sharing the agitation of mind common at that period, had a grandeur peculiar to themselves, which was reflected back upon the nation, but was by no means borrowed from it.

In absolute governments the great nobles who are nearest the throne flatter the passions of the sovereign and voluntarily truckle to his caprices. But the mass of the nation does not degrade itself by servitude; it often submits from weakness, from habit, or from ignorance, and sometimes from loyalty. Some nations have been known to sacrifice their own desires to those of the sovereign with pleasure and pride, thus exhibiting a sort of independence of mind in the very act of submission. These nations are miserable, but they are not degraded. There is a great difference between doing what one does not approve, and pretending to approve what one does; the one is the weakness of a feeble person, the other suits the temper of a servant.

In free countries, where everyone is more or less called upon to give his opinion on affairs of state, in democratic republics, where public life is constantly mingled with domestic affairs, where the sovereign authority is accessible on every side, and where one has only to raise one's voice to reach its ear, one meets many more people who seek to speculate on the basis of its weakness and to take advantage of its passions than in absolute monarchies. It is not that men are worse there than elsewhere, but that temptation is stronger there and, at the same time, available to people. The result is a more extensive debasement of character.

Democratic republics extend the practice of currying favor with the many and introduce it into all classes at once; this is the most serious reproach that can be addressed to them. This is especially true in democratic states organized like the American republics, where the power of the majority is so absolute and irresistible that one must give up one's rights as a citizen and almost abjure one's qualities as a man if one intends to stray from the track the majority prescribes.

In that immense crowd which throngs the avenues to power in the United States, I found very few men who displayed that manly candor and masculine independence of opinion which frequently distinguished the Americans in former times, and which constitutes the leading feature in distinguished characters wherever they may be found. It seems at first sight as if all American minds were formed upon one model, so accurately do they follow the same route. A stranger does, indeed, sometimes meet with Americans who dissent from the rigor of these formulas, with men who deplore the defects of the laws, the mutability and ignorance of democracy, who even go so far as to observe the evil tendencies that impair the national character, and to point out such remedies as it might be possible to apply; but no one is there to hear them except yourself, and you to whom these secret reflections are confided are a stranger and a bird of passage. They are very ready to communicate truths which are useless to you, but they use a different language in public.

If these lines are ever read in America, I am well assured of two things: in the first place, that all who see them will raise their voices to condemn me; and, in the second place, that many of them will absolve me at the bottom of their conscience.

I have heard patriotism spoken of in the United States, and I have found true patriotism among the people, but never among the leaders of the people. This may be explained by analogy: despotism debases the oppressed much more than the oppressor: in absolute monarchies the king often has great virtues, but the courtiers are invariably servile. It is true that American courtiers do not say "Sire," or "Your Majesty," a distinction without a difference. They are forever talking of the natural intelligence of the people whom they serve; they do not debate the question which of the virtues of their master is pre-eminently worthy of admiration, for they assure him that he possesses all the virtues without having acquired them, or without caring to acquire them; they do not give him their daughters and their wives to be raised at his pleasure to the rank of his concubines; but by sacrificing their opinions they prostitute themselves. Moralists and philosophers in America are not obliged to conceal their opinions under the veil of allegory; but before they venture upon a harsh truth, they say: "We are aware that the people whom we are addressing are too superior to the weaknesses of human nature to lose the command of their temper for an instant. We should not hold this language if we were not speaking to men whom their virtues and their intelligence render more worthy of freedom than all the rest of the world." The sycophants of Louis XIV could not flatter more dexterously.

For my part, I am persuaded that in all governments, whatever their nature may be, servility will cower to force, and adulation will follow power. The only means of preventing men from degrading themselves is to invest no one with that unlimited authority which is the sure method of debasing them.

That the greatest dangers of the American republics come from the omnipotence of the majority

Governments usually perish from impotence or tyranny. In the former case, their power escapes from them; it is wrested from their grasp in the latter. Many observers who have witnessed the anarchy of democratic states have imagined that the government of those states was naturally weak and impotent. The truth is that from the moment that conflict begins among the parties, the government loses its control over society. But I do not think that a democratic power is naturally without force or resources; say, rather, that it is almost always by the abuse of its force and the misemployment of its resources that it becomes a failure. Anarchy is almost always produced by its tyranny or its mistakes, but not by its want of strength.

It is important not to confuse stability with force, or the greatness of a thing with its duration. In democratic republics the power that directs society is not stable, for it often changes hands and assumes a new direction. But whichever way it turns, its force is almost irresistible. The governments of the American republics appear to me to be as much centralized as those of the absolute monarchies of Europe, and more energetic than they are. I do not, therefore, imagine that they will perish from weakness.

If ever the free institutions of America are destroyed, that event may be attributed to the omnipotence of the majority, which may at some future time push the minorities to desperation and oblige them to have recourse to physical force. Anarchy will then be the result, but it will have been brought about by despotism.

Mr. Madison expresses the same opinion in *The Federalist*, No. 51. "It is of great importance in a republic, not only to guard the society against the oppression of its rulers, but to guard one part of the society against the injustice of the other part . . ."

Jefferson also said: "The executive in our governments is not the sole, it is scarcely the principal object of my jealousy. The tyranny of the legislatures is the most formidable dread at present, and will be for long years. That of the executive will come in its turn, but it will be at a remote period."

I am glad to cite the opinion of Jefferson upon this subject rather than that of any other, because I consider him the most powerful advocate democracy has ever had.

3b8   Chapter 8: "That Which Tempers the Tyranny of the Majority in the United States"

Absence of centralized administration

I have previously distinguished two types of centralization: I have called one governmental and the other administrative. The former exists in America, but the latter is nearly unknown there. If the directing power of the American communities had both these instruments of government at its disposal and united the habit of executing its commands to the right of commanding; if, after having established the general principles of government, it descended to the details of their application; and if, having regulated the great interests of the country, it could descend to the circle of individual interests, freedom would soon be banished from the New World. But in the United States the majority, which so frequently displays the tastes and propensities of a despot, is still destitute of the most perfect instruments of tyranny.

In the American republics the central government has never as yet busied itself except with a small number of objects sufficiently prominent to attract its attention. It has not tried to regulate the secondary affairs of society. There is no sign that it has even conceived the desire to do so. The majority has become more and more absolute, but has not increased the prerogatives of the central government; those great prerogatives have been confined to a certain sphere. Although despotism can be felt very heavily at a single point, it cannot be applied generally. However the predominant party in the nation may be carried away by its passions, however ardent it may be in pursuit of its projects, it cannot oblige all the citizens to comply with its desires in the same manner and at the same time throughout the country. When the central government which represents that majority has issued a decree, it must entrust the execution of its will to agents over whom it frequently has no control and whom it cannot perpetually direct. The townships, municipal bodies, and counties form so many concealed breakwaters, which check or part the tide of popular determination. If an oppressive law were passed, liberty would still be protected by the mode of executing that law; the majority cannot descend to the details and what may be called the puerilities of administrative tyranny. It does not even imagine that it can do so, for it has not a full consciousness of its authority. It knows only the extent of its natural powers, but is unacquainted with the art of increasing them.

This point deserves attention; for if a democratic republic, similar to that of the United States, were ever founded in a country where the power of one man had previously established a centralized administration and had sunk it deep into the habits and the laws of the people, I do not hesitate to assert that in such a republic a more insufferable despotism would prevail than in any of the absolute monarchies of Europe; or, indeed, than any that could be found on this side of Asia.

3b9   Chapter 9: "Principal Causes Which Tend to Maintain the Democratic Republic in the United States"

Religion considered as a political institution which powerfully contributes to the maintenance of a democratic republic among the Americans

Alongside every religion is to be found a political opinion with which it has an affinity. If the human mind is left to follow its own bent, it will regulate the temporal and spiritual institutions of society in a uniform manner, and man will endeavor, if I may so speak, to harmonize earth with heaven.

The greatest part of British America was peopled by men who, after having shaken off the Pope's authority, acknowledged no other religious supremacy: they brought with them into the New World a form of Christianity which I cannot better describe than by styling it a democratic and republican religion. This contributed powerfully to the establishment of a republic and a democracy in public affairs; and from the beginning, politics and religion found themselves in accord, and since that time have never ceased to be in agreement.

About fifty years ago Ireland began to pour a Catholic population into the United States; and on their part, the Catholics of America made proselytes, so that at the present moment more than a million Christians professing the truths of the Church of Rome are to be found in the Union. These Catholics are faithful to the observances of their religion; they are fervent and zealous in the belief of their doctrines. Yet they constitute the most republican and most democratic class in the United States. This fact may surprise the observer at first, but the causes of it may easily be discovered upon reflection.

I think that the Catholic religion has erroneously been regarded as the natural enemy of democracy. Among the various sects of Christians, Catholicism seems to me, on the contrary, to be one of the most favorable to equality of condition among men. In the Catholic Church the religious community is composed of only two elements: the priest and the people. The priest alone rises above the rank of his flock, and all below him are equal.

On doctrinal points the Catholic faith places all human capacities upon the same level; it subjects the wise and ignorant, the man of genius and the vulgar crowd, to the details of the same creed; it imposes the same observances upon the rich and the needy, it inflicts the same austerities upon the strong and the weak; it makes no compromises with any mortal man, but, applying to each person the same measure, it likes to mix all the classes of society at the foot of the same altar, just as they are united in the sight of God. If Catholicism predisposes the faithful to obedience, it certainly does not prepare them for inequality; but the contrary may be said of Protestantism, which generally brings men less toward equality than toward independence. Catholicism is like an absolute monarchy; if the sovereign be removed, all the other classes of society are more equal than in republics.

It has not infrequently occurred that the Catholic priest has left the service of the altar to mix with the governing powers of society and take his place among the civil ranks of men. This religious influence has sometimes been used to secure the duration of that political state of things to which he belonged. Thus we have seen Catholics taking the side of aristocracy from a religious motive. But no sooner is the priesthood entirely separated from government, as is the case in the United States, than it is found that no class of men is more naturally disposed than the Catholics to transfer the doctrine of the equality of condition into the political world.

If, then, the Catholic citizens of the United States are not forcibly led by the nature of their tenets to adopt democratic and republican principles, at least they are not necessarily opposed to them; and their social position, as well as their limited number, obliges them to adopt these opinions. Most of the Catholics are poor, and they have no chance of taking part in government unless it is open to all the citizens. They constitute a minority, and all rights must be respected in order to ensure to them the free exercise of their own privileges. These two causes induce them, even unconsciously, to adopt political doctrines which they would perhaps support with less zeal if they were rich and in the majority.

The Catholic clergy of the United States have never attempted to oppose this political tendency; they seek rather to justify it. The Catholic priests in America have divided the intellectual world into two parts: in the one they place the doctrines of revealed religion, which they assent to without discussion, in the other they leave those political truths which they believe the Deity has left open to free inquiry. Thus the Catholics of the United States are at the same time the most submissive believers and the most independent citizens.

It may be asserted, then, that in the United States no religious doctrine displays the slightest hostility to democratic and republican institutions. The clergy of all the different sects there hold the same language; their opinions are in agreement with the laws, and the human mind flows onwards, so to speak, in one undivided current.

I happened to be staying in one of the largest cities in the Union when I was invited to attend a public meeting in favor of the Poles and of sending them supplies of arms and money. I found two or three thousand persons collected in a vast hall which had been prepared to receive them. In a short time a priest in his ecclesiastical robes advanced to the front of the platform. The spectators rose and stood uncovered in silence while he spoke in the following terms:

"Almighty God! Lord of hosts! Thou who didst strengthen the hearts and guide the arms of our fathers when they were fighting for the sacred rights of their national independence! Thou who didst make them triumph over a hateful oppression, and hast granted to our people the benefits of liberty and peace! Turn, O Lord, a favorable eye upon the other hemisphere; look down with pity upon an heroic nation which is even now struggling as we did in the former time, and for the same rights. Thou, who didst create man in the same image, let not tyranny mar thy work and establish inequality upon the earth. Almighty God! Watch over the destiny of the Poles, and make them worthy to be free. May thy wisdom direct their councils, may thy strength sustain their arms! Shed forth thy terror over their enemies; scatter the powers which take counsel against them; and permit not the injustice which the world has witnessed for fifty years to be consummated in our time. O Lord, who holdest the hearts of nations and men alike in thy powerful hand, raise up allies to the sacred cause of right; arouse the French nation from the apathy in which its rulers retain it, that it may go forth again to fight for the liberties of the world."

"Lord, turn not thou thy face from us, and grant that we may always be the most religious, as well as the freest, people of the earth. Almighty God, hear our supplications this day. Save the Poles, we beseech thee, in the name of thy well-beloved Son, our Lord Jesus Christ, who died upon the cross for the salvation of all men. Amen."

The whole meeting responded: "Amen!" with devotion.

Indirect influence of religious opinions upon political society in the United States

I have just shown what the direct influence of religion upon politics is in the United States. Its indirect influence seems to me to be even more powerful, and it is precisely when it does not speak of freedom that it teaches Americans most about the art of being free.

The sects that exist in the United States are innumerable. They all differ in respect to the worship which is due to the Creator; but they all agree in respect to the duties which are due from man to man. Each sect adores the Deity in its own peculiar manner, but all sects preach the same moral law in the name of God. If it is of the highest importance to man, as an individual, that his religion should be true, it is not so to society. Society has no future life to hope for or to fear; and provided the citizens profess a religion, the particular tenets of that religion are of little importance to its interests. Moreover, all the sects of the United States are comprised within the great unity of Christianity, and Christian morality is everywhere the same.

It may fairly be believed that a certain number of Americans pursue a particular form of worship more from habit than from conviction. In the United States the sovereign authority is religious, and consequently hypocrisy must be common; but there is no country in the world where the Christian religion retains greater influence over the souls of men than in America; and there can be no greater proof of its utility and its conformity to human nature than that its influence is powerfully felt over the most enlightened and free nation of the earth.

I have remarked that the American clergy in general, without even excepting those who do not admit religious liberty, are all in favor of civil freedom; but they do not support any particular political system. They keep aloof from parties and from public affairs. In the United States religion exercises but little influence upon the laws and the details of public opinion; but it directs the customs of the community, and, by regulating domestic life, it regulates the state.

I do not question that the great austerity of manners that is observable in the United States arises, in the first instance, from religious faith. Religion is often unable to restrain man from the numberless temptations which chance offers; nor can it check that passion for gain which everything contributes to arouse; but its influence over the mind of woman is supreme, and women are the protectors of morals. There is certainly no country in the world where the tie of marriage is more respected than in America or where conjugal happiness is more highly or worthily appreciated.

In Europe almost all the disturbances of society arise from the irregularities of domestic life. To despise the natural bonds and legitimate pleasures of home is to contract a taste for excesses, a restlessness of heart, and fluctuating desires. Agitated by the tumultuous passions that frequently disturb his dwelling, the European is galled by the obedience which the legislative powers of the state exact.

. . .

Religion in America takes no direct part in the government of society, but it must be regarded as the first of their political institutions; for if it does not impart a taste for freedom, it facilitates the use of it. Indeed, it is from this same point of view that the inhabitants of the United States themselves look upon religious belief. I do not know whether all Americans have a sincere faith in their religion – for who can search the human heart? – but I am certain that they hold it to be indispensable to the maintenance of republican institutions This opinion is not peculiar to a class of citizens or to a party, but it belongs to the whole nation and to every rank of society.

3b10   Chapter 10: "The Present and Probable Future Condition of the Three Races that Inhabit the Territory of the United States"

The present and probable future condition of the Indian tribes that inhabit the territory possessed by the Union

There is less greed and violence in the manner in which the Union acts toward the Indians than in the policies the individual states pursue, but the two governments are alike deficient in good faith. The states extend what they call the benefits of their laws to the Indians, believing that the tribes will recede rather than submit to them; and the central government, which promises a permanent refuge to these unhappy beings in the West, understands that it cannot guarantee it to them. Thus the tyranny of the states obliges the savages to retire; the Union, by its promises and resources, facilitates their retreat; and these measures tend to precisely the same end.

"By the will of our Father in heaven, the Governor of the whole world," said the Cherokees in their petition to Congress, "the red man of America has become small, and the white man great and renowned. When the ancestors of the people of these United States first came to the shores of America, they found the red man strong: though he was ignorant and savage, yet he received them kindly, and gave them dry land to rest their weary feet. They met in peace and shook hands in token of friendship. Whatever the white man wanted and asked of the Indian, the latter willingly gave. At that time the Indian was the lord, and the white man the suppliant. But now the scene has changed. The strength of the red man has become weakness. As his neighbors increased in numbers, his power became less and less; and now, of the many and powerful tribes who once covered these United States, only a few are to be seen – a few whom a sweeping pestilence has left. The Northern tribes, who were once so numerous and powerful, are now nearly extinct. Thus it has happened to the red man in America. Shall we, who are remnants, share the same fate?"

"The land on which we stand we have received as an inheritance from our fathers, who possessed it from time immemorial, as a gift from our common Father in heaven . . . They bequeathed it to us as their children, and we have sacredly kept it, as containing the remains of our beloved men. This right of inheritance we have never ceded nor ever forfeited. Permit us to ask, what better right can the people have to a country than the right of inheritance and immemorial peaceable possession?"

. . .

Such is the language of the Indians: what they say is true; what they foresee seems inevitable. From whichever side we consider the destinies of the aborigines of North America, their calamities appear irremediable: if they remain savages, they will continually be pushed back as civilization marches forward; if they attempt to civilize themselves, the contact with more sophisticated men will deliver them to oppression and poverty. They perish if they continue to wander from waste to waste, and if they attempt to settle they still must perish. The assistance of Europeans is necessary to instruct them, but the approach of Europeans corrupts and repels them into savage life. They refuse to change their habits as long as their solitudes are their own, and it is too late to change them when at last they are forced to submit.

The Spaniards pursued the Indians with bloodhounds, like wild beasts; they sacked the New World like a city taken by storm, with no discernment or compassion; but destruction must cease at last and frenzy has a limit: the remnant of the Indian population which had escaped the massacre mixed with its conquerors and adopted in the end their religion and their manners. The conduct of the Americans of the United States towards the aborigines is characterized, on the other hand, by a singular attachment to the formalities of law. Provided that the Indians retain their barbarous condition, the Americans take no part in their affairs; they treat them as independent nations and do not possess themselves of their hunting-grounds without a treaty of purchase; and if an Indian nation happens to be so encroached upon as to be unable to subsist upon their territory, they kindly take them by the hand and transport them to a grave far from the land of their fathers.

The Spaniards were unable to exterminate the Indian race by those unparalleled atrocities which brand them with indelible shame, nor did they succeed even in wholly depriving it of its rights; but the Americans of the United States have accomplished this double purpose with singular felicity, tranquilly, legally, philanthropically, without shedding blood, and without violating a single great principle of morality in the eyes of the world. It is impossible to destroy men with more respect for the laws of humanity.

The position that the Black race occupies in the United States; dangers that Whites run from its presence

The Indians will perish in the same isolated condition in which they have lived, but the destiny of the Negroes is in some measure interwoven with that of the Europeans. These two races are fastened to each other without intermingling; and they are equally unable to separate entirely or to combine. The most formidable of all the ills that threaten the future of the Union arises from the presence of a black population upon its territory. When one seeks the cause of the current difficulties and future dangers facing the Union, one almost always returns to this primary consideration from whatever point one started out.

Generally speaking, men must make great and unceasing efforts before permanent evils are created; but there is one calamity which penetrated furtively into the world. At first, one hardly notices it in the midst of the ordinary abuses of power; it begins with an individual whose name history has not preserved; it is deposited like some cursed seed, it nurtures itself afterward, spreading without effort and growing naturally with the society that has received it: this calamity is slavery. Christianity suppressed slavery, but the Christians of the sixteenth century re-established it, as an exception, indeed, to their social system, and restricted to one of the races of mankind; but the wound thus inflicted upon humanity, though less extensive, was far more difficult to cure.

It is important to make an accurate distinction between slavery itself and its consequences. The immediate evils produced by slavery were very nearly the same in antiquity as they are among the moderns, but the consequences of these evils were different. The slave among the ancients belonged to the same race as his master, and was often the superior of the two in education and intelligence. Freedom was the only distinction between them; and when freedom was conferred, they were easily joined together. The ancients, then, had a very simple means of ridding themselves of slavery and its consequences: that of enfranchisement; and they succeeded as soon as they adopted this measure generally. It is not that in antiquity the traces of servitude did not last for some time after slavery was destroyed. There is a natural prejudice that prompts men to despise whoever has been their inferior long after he has become their equal; and the real inequality that is produced by fortune or by law is always succeeded by an imaginary inequality that is implanted in the manners of the people. But among the ancients this secondary consequence of slavery had a natural limit; for the freedman bore so complete a resemblance to those born free that it soon became impossible to distinguish him from them.

The greatest difficulty in antiquity was that of altering the law; among the moderns it is that of altering customs, and as far as we are concerned, the real obstacles begin where those of the ancients left off. This arises from the circumstance that among the moderns the abstract and transient fact of slavery is fatally united with the physical and permanent fact of color. The tradition of slavery dishonors the race, and the peculiarity of the race perpetuates the tradition of slavery. No African has ever voluntarily emigrated to the shores of the New World, whence it follows that all the blacks who are now found there are either slaves or freedmen. Thus the Negro transmits the eternal mark of his ignominy to all his descendants; and although the law may abolish slavery, God alone can obliterate the traces of its existence.

The modern slave differs from his master not only in his condition but in his origin. You may set the Negro free, but you cannot make him otherwise than an alien to the European. Nor is this all: we scarcely acknowledge the common features of humanity in this stranger whom slavery has brought among us. His physiognomy is to our eyes hideous, his understanding weak, his tastes low; and we are almost inclined to look upon him as a being intermediate between man and the brutes. The moderns, then, after they have abolished slavery, have three prejudices to contend against, which are less easy to attack and far less easy to conquer than the mere fact of servitude: the prejudice of the master, the prejudice of the race, and the prejudice of the White.

It is difficult for us, who have had the good fortune to be born among men like ourselves by nature and our equals by law, to conceive the irreconcilable differences that separate the Negro from the European in America. But we may derive some faint notion of them from analogy. Formerly, we witnessed among us great inequalities that had their source only in laws. What can be more flimsy than a purely legal inferiority? What more contrary to the instinct of man than these permanent differences established between people so evidently similar? Yet these divisions existed for ages; they still exist in many places and everywhere they have left imaginary vestiges, which time alone can efface. If it is so difficult to root out an inequality that originates solely in law, how are those distinctions to be destroyed which seem to be based on the immutable laws of nature herself? When I remember the extreme difficulty with which aristocratic bodies, of whatever nature they may be, are joined with the mass of the people, and the exceeding care which they take to preserve inviolate for ages the ideal boundaries of their caste, I despair of seeing an aristocracy disappear which is founded upon visible and indelible signs. Those who hope that the Europeans will ever be amalgamated with the Negroes appear to me to delude themselves. I am not led to any such conclusion by my reason or by the evidence of facts. Hitherto wherever the whites have been the most powerful, they have held the blacks in degradation or in slavery; wherever the Negroes have been strongest, they have destroyed the whites: this has been the only balance that has ever taken place between the two races.

I see that in a certain portion of the territory of the United States at the present day the legal barrier which separated the two races is falling away, but not that which exists in the manners of the country. Slavery recedes, but the prejudice to which it has given birth is immovable. Whoever has inhabited the United States must have perceived that in those parts of the Union in which the Negroes are no longer slaves they have in no way drawn nearer the whites. On the contrary, the prejudice of race appears to be stronger in the states that have abolished slavery than in those where it still exists; and nowhere is it so intolerant as in those states where servitude has never been known.

It is true that in the North of the Union marriages may be legally contracted between Negroes and whites; but public opinion would stigmatize as infamous a man who should connect himself with a Negress, and it would be difficult to cite a single instance of such a union. The electoral franchise has been conferred upon the Negroes in almost all the states in which slavery has been abolished, but if they come forward to vote, their lives are in danger. If oppressed, they may bring an action at law, but they will find none but whites among their judges; and although they may legally serve as jurors, prejudice repels them from that office. The same schools do not receive the children of the black and of the European. In the theaters gold cannot procure a seat for the servile race beside their former masters; in the hospitals they lie apart; and although they are allowed to invoke the same God as the whites, it must be at a different altar and in their own churches, with their own clergy. The gates of heaven are not closed against them, but their inferiority is continued to the very confines of the other world. When the Negro dies, his bones are cast aside, and the distinction of condition prevails even in the equality of death. Thus the Negro is free, but he can share neither the rights, nor the pleasures, nor the labor, nor the afflictions, nor the tomb of him whose equal he has been declared to be; and he cannot meet him upon fair terms in life or in death.

In the South, where slavery still exists, the Negroes are less carefully kept apart; they sometimes share the labors and recreations of the whites; the whites consent to intermix with them to a certain extent, and although legislation treats them more harshly, the habits of the people are more tolerant and compassionate. In the South the master is not afraid to raise his slave to his own standing, because he knows that he can in a moment reduce him to the dust at pleasure. In the North the white no longer distinctly perceives the barrier that separates him from the degraded race, and he shuns the Negro all the more tenaciously since he fears lest they should some day be confounded together.

Among the Americans of the South, nature sometimes reasserts her rights and restores a transient equality between blacks and whites; but in the North pride restrains the most imperious of human passions. The American of the Northern states would perhaps allow the Negress to share his licentious pleasures if the laws of his country did not declare that she may aspire to be the legitimate partner of his bed, but he recoils with horror from her who might become his wife.

. . . In general, the colonies in which there were no slaves became more populous and more prosperous than those in which slavery flourished. The farther they went, the more was it shown that slavery, which is so cruel to the slave, is prejudicial to the master.

But this truth was most satisfactorily demonstrated when civilization reached the banks of the Ohio. The stream that the Indians had distinguished by the name of Ohio, or the Beautiful River, waters one of the most magnificent valleys which have ever been made the abode of man. Undulating lands extend upon both shores of the Ohio, whose soil affords inexhaustible treasures to the laborer; on either bank the air is equally wholesome and the climate mild, and each of them forms the extreme frontier of a vast state: that which follows the numerous windings of the Ohio upon the left is called Kentucky; that upon the right bears the name of the river. These two states differ only in a single respect: Kentucky has admitted slavery, but the state of Ohio has prohibited the existence of slaves within its borders. Thus the traveler who floats down the current of the Ohio to the spot where that river falls into the Mississippi may be said to sail between freedom and servitude; and a transient inspection of surrounding objects will convince him which of the two is more favorable to humanity.

Upon the left bank of the stream the population is sparse; from time to time one descries a troop of slaves loitering in the half-desert fields; the primeval forest reappears at every turn; society seems to be asleep, man to be idle, and nature alone offers a scene of activity and life.

From the right bank, on the contrary, a confused hum is heard, which proclaims afar the presence of industry; the fields are covered with abundant harvests; the elegance of the dwellings announces the taste and activity of the laborers; and man appears to be in the enjoyment of that wealth and contentment which is the reward of labor.

The state of Kentucky was founded in 1775, the state of Ohio only twelve years later; but twelve years are more in America than half a century in Europe; and at the present day the population of Ohio exceeds that of Kentucky by two hundred and fifty thousand souls. These different effects of slavery and freedom may readily be understood; and they suffice to explain many of the differences which we notice between the civilization of antiquity and that of our own time.

Upon the left bank of the Ohio labor is confounded with the idea of slavery, while upon the right bank it is identified with that of prosperity and improvement; on the one side it is degraded, on the other it is honored. On the former territory no white laborers can be found, for they would be afraid of assimilating themselves to the Negroes; all the work is done by slaves; on the latter no one is idle, for the white population extend their activity and intelligence to every kind of employment. Thus the men whose task it is to cultivate the rich soil of Kentucky are ignorant and apathetic, while those who are active and enlightened either do nothing or pass over into Ohio, where they may work without shame.

It is true that in Kentucky the planters are not obliged to pay the slaves whom they employ, but they derive small profits from their labor, while the wages paid to free workmen would be returned with interest in the value of their services. The free workman is paid, but he does his work quicker than the slave; and rapidity of execution is one of the great elements of economy. The white sells his services, but they are purchased only when they may be useful; the black can claim no remuneration for his toil, but the expense of his maintenance is perpetual; he must be supported in his old age as well as in manhood, in his profitless infancy as well as in the productive years of youth, in sickness as well as in health. Payment must equally be made in order to obtain the services of either class of men: the free workman receives his wages in money; the slave in education, in food, in care, and in clothing. The money which a master spends in the maintenance of his slaves goes gradually and in detail, so that it is scarcely perceived; the salary of the free workman is paid in a round sum and appears to enrich only him who receives it; but in the end the slave has cost more than the free servant, and his labor is less productive.

The influence of slavery extends still further: it affects the character of the master and imparts a peculiar tendency to his ideas and tastes. Upon both banks of the Ohio the character of the inhabitants is enterprising and energetic, but this vigor is very differently exercised in the two states. The white on the right bank, obliged to live by his own labor, has made material well-being the principal purpose of his existence; and as the country which he occupies presents inexhaustible resources to his industry and ever varying inducements to his activity, his acquisitive ardor surpasses the ordinary limits of human cupidity: he is tormented by the desire of wealth, and he boldly enters upon every path that fortune opens to him; he becomes a sailor, a pioneer, an artisan, or a cultivator with the same indifference, and supports with equal constancy the fatigues and the dangers incidental to these various professions; the resources of his intelligence are astonishing, and his avidity in the pursuit of gain amounts to a species of heroism.

But the Kentuckian scorns not only labor but all the undertakings that labor promotes; as he lives in idle independence, his tastes are those of an idle man; money has lost a portion of its value in his eyes; he covets wealth much less than pleasure and excitement; and the energy which his neighbor devotes to gain turns with him to a passionate love of field sports and military exercises; he delights in violent bodily exertion, he is familiar with the use of arms, and is accustomed from a very early age to expose his life in single combat. Thus slavery prevents the whites not only from becoming opulent, but even from desiring to become so.

As the same causes have been continually producing opposite effects for the last two centuries in the British colonies of North America, they have at last established a striking difference between the commercial capacity of the inhabitants of the South and those of the North. At the present day it is only the Northern states that are in possession of shipping, manufactures, railroads, and canals. This difference is perceptible not only in comparing the North with the South, but in comparing the several Southern states. Almost all those who carry on commercial operations or endeavor to turn slave labor to account in the most southern districts of the Union have emigrated from the North. The natives of the Northern states are constantly spreading over that portion of the American territory where they have less to fear from competition; they discover resources there which escaped the notice of the inhabitants; and as they comply with a system which they do not approve, they succeed in turning it to better advantage than those who first founded and who still maintain it.

. . .

Servitude had begun in the South and had thence spread towards the North, but it now retires again. Freedom, which started from the North, now descends uninterruptedly towards the South. Among the great states, Pennsylvania now constitutes the farthest boundary of slavery to the North; but even within those limits the slave system is shaken: Maryland, which is immediately below Pennsylvania, is preparing for its abolition; and Virginia, which comes next to Maryland, is already discussing its utility and its dangers.

No great change takes place in human institutions without involving among its causes the law of inheritance.

When the law of primogeniture obtained in the South, each family was represented by a wealthy individual, who was neither compelled nor induced to labor; and he was surrounded, as by parasitic plants, by the other members of his family, who were then excluded by law from sharing the common inheritance, and who led the same kind of life as himself. The same thing then occurred in all the families of the South which still happens in the noble families of some countries in Europe: namely, that the younger sons remain in the same state of idleness as their elder brother, without being as rich as he is. This identical result seems to be produced in Europe and in America by wholly analogous causes. In the South of the United States the whole race of whites formed an aristocratic body, headed by a certain number of privileged individuals, whose wealth was permanent and whose leisure was hereditary. These leaders of the American nobility kept alive the traditional prejudices of the white race, in the body of which they were the representatives, and maintained idleness in honor. This aristocracy contained many who were poor, but none who would work; its members preferred want to labor; consequently Negro laborers and slaves met with no competition; and, whatever opinion might be entertained as to the utility of their industry, it was necessary to employ them, since there was no one else to work.

No sooner was the law of primogeniture abolished than fortunes began to diminish and all the families of the country were simultaneously reduced to a state in which labor became necessary to existence; several of them have since entirely disappeared, and all of them learned to look forward to the time when it would be necessary for everyone to provide for his own wants. Wealthy individuals are still to be met with, but they no longer constitute a compact and hereditary body, nor have they been able to adopt a line of conduct in which they could persevere and which they could infuse into all ranks of society. The prejudice that stigmatized labor was, in the first place, abandoned by common consent, the number of needy men was increased, and the needy were allowed to gain a subsistence by labor without blushing for their toil. Thus one of the most immediate consequences of the equal division of estates has been to create a class of free laborers. As soon as competition began between the free laborer and the slave, the inferiority of the latter became manifest, and slavery was attacked in its fundamental principle, which is the interest of the master.

As slavery recedes, the black population follows its retrograde course and returns with it towards those tropical regions whence it originally came. However singular this fact may at first appear to be, it may readily be explained. Although the Americans abolish the principle of slavery, they do not set their slaves free. To illustrate this remark, I will quote the example of the state of New York. In 1788 this state prohibited the sale of slaves within its limits, which was an indirect method of prohibiting the importation of them. Thenceforward the number of Negroes could only increase according to the ratio of the natural increase of population. But eight years later, a more decisive measure was taken, and it was enacted that all children born of slave parents after the 4th of July 1799 should be free. No increase could then take place, and although slaves still existed, slavery might be said to be abolished.

As soon as a Northern state thus prohibited the importation, no slaves were brought from the South to be sold in its markets. On the other hand, as the sale of slaves was forbidden in that state, an owner could no longer get rid of his slave (who thus became a burdensome possession) otherwise than by transporting him to the South. The day when a Northern state declares that a slave's son is born free, the slave loses a great deal of his monetary value. Because his posterity can no longer be put on the market, there is now an even greater reason to transport him South. Thus the same law prevents the slaves of the South from coming North and drives those of the North to the South. But there is another cause more powerful than any that I have described. The want of free hands is felt in a state in proportion as the number of slaves decreases. But in proportion as labor is performed by free hands, slave labor becomes less productive; and the slave is then a useless or onerous possession, whom it is important to export to the South, where the same competition is not to be feared. Thus the abolition of slavery does not set the slave free, but merely transfers him to another master, and from the North to the South.

. . .

The emancipated Negroes and those born after the abolition of slavery do not, indeed, migrate from the North to the South; but their situation with regard to the Europeans is not unlike that of the Indians; they remain half civilized and deprived of their rights in the midst of a population that is far superior to them in wealth and knowledge, where they are exposed to the tyranny of the laws and the intolerance of the people. On some accounts they are still more to be pitied than the Indians, since they are haunted by the reminiscence of slavery, and they cannot claim possession of any part of the soil. Many of them perish miserably, and the rest congregate in the great towns, where they perform the meanest offices and lead a wretched and precarious existence.

If, moreover, the number of Negroes were to continue to grow in the same proportion during the period when they did not have their liberty, yet, with the number of the whites increasing at a double rate after the abolition of slavery, the Negroes would soon be swallowed up in the midst of an alien population.

A district which is cultivated by slaves is in general less populous than a district cultivated by free labor; moreover, America is still a new country, and a state is therefore not half peopled when it abolishes slavery. No sooner is an end put to slavery than the want of free labor is felt, and a crowd of enterprising adventurers immediately arrives from all parts of the country, who hasten to profit by the fresh resources which are then opened to industry. The soil is soon divided among them, and a family of white settlers takes possession of each portion. Besides, European immigration is exclusively directed to the free states; for what would a poor immigrant do who crosses the Atlantic in search of ease and happiness if he were to land in a country where labor is stigmatized as degrading?

Thus the white population grows by its natural increase, and at the same time by the immense influx of immigrants; while the black population receives no immigrants and is upon its decline. The proportion that existed between the two races is soon inverted. The Negroes constitute a scanty remnant, a poor tribe of vagrants, lost in the midst of an immense people who own the land; and the presence of the blacks is only marked by the injustice and the hardships of which they are the victims.

In several of the Western states the Negro race never made its appearance, and in all the Northern states it is rapidly declining. Thus the great question of its future condition is confined within a narrow circle, where it becomes less formidable, though not more easy of solution. The more we descend towards the South, the more difficult it becomes to abolish slavery with advantage; and this arises from several physical causes which it is important to point out.

The first of these causes is the climate: it is an axiom that the closer Europeans approach the tropics the more labor becomes difficult for them. Many of the Americans even assert that within a certain latitude it is fatal to them, while the Negroes can work there without danger; but I do not think that this opinion, which is so favorable to the indolence of the inhabitants of the South, is confirmed by experience. The southern parts of the Union are not hotter than the south of Italy and of Spain; and it may be asked why the European cannot work as well there as in the latter two countries. If slavery has been abolished in Italy and in Spain without causing the destruction of the masters, why should not the same thing take place in the Union? I cannot believe that nature has prohibited the Europeans in Georgia and the Floridas, under pain of death, from raising the means of subsistence from the soil; but their labor would unquestionably be more irksome and less productive to them than to the inhabitants of New England. To the degree that free workers lose some of their superiority over the slave in the Southern states, there are fewer inducements to abolish slavery.

All the plants of Europe grow in the northern parts of the Union; the South has special products of its own. It has been observed that slave labor is a very expensive method of cultivating cereal grain. The farmer of grainland in a country where slavery is unknown habitually retains only a small number of laborers in his service, and at seedtime and harvest he hires additional hands, who live at his cost for only a short period. To replenish his granaries or sow his fields, the farmer who lives in a slave state is obliged to maintain a great number of field hands during the entire year, although they are only necessary for a period of several days. In contrast to free laborers, slaves cannot wait and work for themselves until the moment when someone has a pressing reason to hire them for a task. It is necessary to buy them to have their services. Slavery, independently of its general disadvantages, is therefore still more inapplicable to countries in which grain is cultivated than to those which produce crops of a different kind. The cultivation of tobacco, of cotton, and especially of sugarcane demands, on the other hand, unremitting attention; and women and children are employed in it, whose services are of little use in the cultivation of wheat. Thus slavery is naturally more fitted to the countries from which these productions are derived.

Tobacco, cotton, and sugarcane are exclusively grown in the South, and they form the principal sources of the wealth of those states. If slavery were abolished, the inhabitants of the South would be driven to this alternative:

they must either change their system of cultivation, and then they would come into competition with the more active and more experienced inhabitants of the North; or, if they continued to cultivate the same produce without slave labor, they would have to support the competition of the other states of the South, which might still retain their slaves. Thus peculiar reasons for maintaining slavery exist in the South which do not operate in the North.

But there is yet another motive, which is more cogent than all the others: the South might, indeed, rigorously speaking, abolish slavery; but how should it rid its territory of the black population? Slaves and slavery are driven from the North by the same law; but this twofold result cannot be hoped for in the South.

In proving that slavery is more natural and more advantageous in the South than in the North, I have shown that the number of slaves must be far greater in the former. It was to the Southern settlements that the first Africans were brought, and it is there that the greatest number of them have always been imported. As we advance towards the South, the prejudice that sanctions idleness increases in power. In the states nearest to the tropics there is not a single white laborer; the Negroes are consequently much more numerous in the South than in the North. And, as I have already observed, this disproportion increases daily, since the Negroes are transferred to one part of the Union as soon as slavery is abolished in the other. Thus the black population augments in the South, not only by its natural fecundity, but by the compulsory emigration of the Negroes from the North; and the African race has causes of increase in the South very analogous to those which accelerate the growth of the European race in the North.

In the state of Maine there is one Negro in three hundred inhabitants; in Massachusetts, one in one hundred; in New York, two in one hundred; in Pennsylvania, three in the same number; in Maryland, thirty-four; in Virginia, forty-two; and lastly, in South Carolina, fifty-five percent of the inhabitants are black. Such was the proportion of the black population to the whites in the year 1830. But this proportion is perpetually changing, as it constantly decreases in the North and augments in the South.

It is evident that the most southern states of the Union cannot abolish slavery without incurring great dangers which the North had no reason to apprehend when it emancipated its black population. I have already shown how the Northern states made the transition from slavery to freedom, by keeping the present generation in chains and setting their descendants free; by this means the Negroes are only gradually introduced into society; and while the men who might abuse their freedom are kept in servitude, those who are emancipated may learn the art of being free before they become their own masters. But it would be difficult to apply this method in the South. To declare that all the Negroes born after a certain period shall be free is to introduce the principle and the notion of liberty into the heart of slavery; the blacks whom the law thus maintains in a state of slavery from which their children are delivered are astonished at so unequal a fate, and their astonishment is only the prelude to their impatience and irritation. Thenceforward slavery loses, in their eyes, that kind of moral power which it derived from time and habit; it is reduced to a mere palpable abuse of force. The Northern states had nothing to fear from the contrast, because in them the blacks were few in number, and the white population was very considerable. But if this faint dawn of freedom were to show two millions of men their true position, the oppressors would have reason to tremble. After having enfranchised the children of their slaves, the Europeans of the Southern states would very shortly be obliged to extend the same benefit to the whole black population.

In the North, as I have already remarked, a twofold migration ensues upon the abolition of slavery, or even precedes that event when circumstances have rendered it probable: the slaves quit the country to be transported southwards; and the whites of the Northern states, as well as the immigrants from Europe, hasten to fill their place. But these two causes cannot operate in the same manner in the Southern states. On the one hand, the mass of slaves is too great to allow any expectation of their being removed from the country; and on the other hand, the Europeans and Anglo-Americans of the North are afraid to come to inhabit a country in which labor has not yet been reinstated in its rightful honors. Besides, they very justly look upon the states in which the number of the Negroes equals or exceeds that of the whites as exposed to very great dangers; and they refrain from turning their activity in that direction.

Thus the inhabitants of the South, while abolishing slavery, would not be able, like their Northern countrymen, to initiate the slaves gradually into a state of freedom; they would not sensibly diminish the number of Blacks, and they would be helpless to contain them. Thus in the course of a few years a great people of free Negroes would exist in the heart of a white nation of equal size.

The same abuses of power that now maintain slavery would then become the source of the most alarming perils to the white population of the South. At the present time the descendants of the Europeans are the sole owners of the land and the absolute masters of all labor; they alone possess wealth, knowledge, and arms. The black is destitute of all these advantages, but can subsist without them because he is a slave. Having become free and responsible for his own lot, could he allow himself to be deprived of all these things without dying? Or would not the very instruments that give the white power while slavery exists expose him to a thousand perils after slavery is abolished?

As long as the Negro remains a slave, he may be kept in a condition not far removed from that of the brutes; but with his liberty he cannot but acquire a degree of instruction that will enable him to appreciate his misfortunes and discern a remedy for them. Moreover, there exists a singular principle of relative justice which is firmly implanted in the human heart. Men are much more forcibly struck by those inequalities which exist within the same class than by those which may be noted between different classes. One comprehends slavery, but how does one conceive of the existence of several million true citizens eternally bent under the weight of infamy and delivered to hereditary wretchedness? In the North the population of freed Negroes feels these hardships and indignities, but its numbers and powers are small, while in the South it would be numerous and strong.

As soon as it is admitted that the whites and the emancipated blacks are placed upon the same territory in the situation of two foreign communities, it will readily be understood that there are but two chances for the future: the Negroes and the whites must either wholly part or wholly mingle. I have already expressed my conviction as to the latter event. I do not believe that the white and black races will ever live in any country upon an equal footing. But I believe the difficulty to be still greater in the United States than elsewhere. An isolated individual may surmount the prejudices of religion, of his country, or of his race; and if this individual is a king, he may effect surprising changes in society; but a whole people cannot rise, as it were, above itself. A despot who should subject the Americans and their former slaves to the same yoke might perhaps succeed in mingling their races; but as long as the American democracy remains at the head of affairs, no one will undertake so difficult a task; and it may be foreseen that the freer the white population of the United States becomes, the more isolated will it remain.

I have previously observed that the mixed race is the true bond of union between Europeans and Indians; just so, the mulattos are the true means of transition between the white and the Negro; so that wherever mulattos abound, the intermixture of the two races is not impossible. In some parts of America the European and the Negro races are so crossed with one another that it is rare to meet with a man who is entirely black or entirely white; when they have arrived at this point, the two races may really be said to be combined, or, rather, to have been absorbed in a third race, which is connected with both without being identical with either.

Of all Europeans, the English are those who have mixed least with the Negroes. More mulattos are to be seen in the South of the Union than in the North, but infinitely fewer than in any other European colony. Mulattos are by no means numerous in the United States; they have no force peculiar to themselves, and when quarrels originating in differences of color take place, they generally side with the whites, just as the servants of the great in Europe assume the contemptuous airs of nobility towards the lower orders.

The pride of origin, which is natural to the English, is singularly augmented by the personal pride that democratic freedom fosters among the Americans: the white citizen of the United States is proud of his race and proud of himself. But if the whites and the Negroes do not intermingle in the North of the Union, how should they mix in the South? Can it be supposed for an instant that an American of the Southern states, placed, as he must forever be, between the white man, with all his physical and moral superiority, and the Negro, will ever think of being joined with the latter? The American of the South has two overriding passions that will always tend to isolate him: he fears resembling the Negro, his former slave, and descending below his White neighbor.

If I were called upon to predict the future, I should say that the abolition of slavery in the South will in the common course of things increase the repugnance of the white population for the blacks. I base this opinion upon the analogous observation I have already made in the North. I have remarked that the white inhabitants of the North take increasing care to avoid Negroes in proportion to efforts by the legislature to remove the legal barriers that separate them; and why should not the same result take place in the South? In the North whites are deterred from intermingling with blacks by an imaginary danger; in the South, where the danger would be real, I cannot believe that the fear would be less.

If, on the one hand, it be admitted (and the fact is unquestionable) that the colored population perpetually accumulate in the extreme South and increase more rapidly than the whites; and if, on the other hand, it be allowed that it is impossible to foresee a time when the whites and the blacks will be so intermingled as to derive the same benefits from society, must it not be inferred that the blacks and whites will, sooner or later, come to open strife in the Southern states? But if it be asked what the issue of the struggle is likely to be, it will readily be understood that we are here left to vague conjectures. The human mind may succeed in tracing a wide circle, as it were, which includes the future; but within that circle chance rules, and eludes all our foresight. In every picture of the future there is a dim spot which the eye of the understanding cannot penetrate. It appears, however, extremely probable that in the West Indies islands the white race is destined to be subdued, and upon the continent the blacks.

In the West Indies the white planters are isolated amid an immense black population; on the continent the blacks are placed between the ocean and an innumerable people, who already extend above them, in a compact mass, from the icy confines of Canada to the frontiers of Virginia, and from the banks of the Missouri to the shores of the Atlantic. If the white citizens of North America remain united, it is difficult to believe that the Negroes will escape the destruction which menaces them; they must be subdued by want or by the sword. But the black population accumulated along the coast of the Gulf of Mexico has a chance of success if the American Union should be dissolved when the struggle between the two races begins. The Federal tie once broken, the people of the South could not rely upon any lasting succor from their Northern countrymen. The latter are well aware that the danger can never reach them; and if a clear-cut obligation does not arise to induce them to march to the relief of the South, one can foresee that racial sympathies will not prove sufficient motivation.

Yet, at whatever period the strife may break out, the whites of the South, even if they are abandoned to their own resources, will enter the lists with an immense superiority of knowledge and the means of warfare; but the blacks will have numerical strength and the energy of despair upon their side, and these are powerful resources to men who have taken up arms. The fate of the white population of the Southern states will perhaps be similar to that of the Moors in Spain. After having occupied the land for centuries, it will perhaps retire by degrees to the country whence its ancestors came and abandon to the Negroes the possession of a territory which Providence seems to have destined for them, since they can subsist and labor in it more easily than the whites.

The danger of a conflict between the white and the black inhabitants of the Southern states of the Union (a danger which, however remote it may be, is inevitable) perpetually haunts the imagination of the Americans, like a painful dream. The inhabitants of the North make it a common topic of conversation, although directly they have nothing to fear from it; but they vainly endeavor to devise some means of obviating the misfortunes which they foresee. In the Southern states the subject is not discussed: the planter does not allude to the future in conversing with strangers; he does not communicate his apprehensions to his friends; he seeks to conceal them from himself. But there is something more alarming in the tacit forebodings of the South than in the clamorous fears of the North.

This all-pervading disquiet has given birth to an undertaking as yet but little known, which, however, may change the fate of a portion of the human race. From apprehension of the dangers that I have just described, some American citizens have formed a society for the purpose of exporting to the coast of Guinea, at their own expense, such free Negroes as may be willing to escape from the oppression to which they are subject.

In 1820 the society to which I allude formed a settlement in Africa, on the seventh degree of north latitude, which bears the name of Liberia. The most recent intelligence informs us that two thousand five hundred Negroes are collected there. They have introduced the democratic institutions of America into the country of their forefathers. Liberia has a representative system of government, Negro jurymen, Negro magistrates, and Negro priests; churches have been built, newspapers established, and, by a singular turn in the vicissitudes of the world, white men are prohibited from establishing themselves within the settlement.

This is indeed a strange caprice of fortune. Two hundred years have now elapsed since the inhabitants of Europe undertook to tear the Negro from his family and his home in order to transport him to the shores of North America. Now the European settlers are engaged in sending back the descendants of those very Negroes to the continent whence they were originally taken: the barbarous Africans have learned civilization in the midst of bondage and have become acquainted with free political institutions in slavery. Up to the present time Africa has been closed against the arts and sciences of the whites, but the inventions of Europe will perhaps penetrate into those regions now that they are introduced by Africans themselves. The settlement of Liberia is founded upon a lofty and fruitful idea; but, whatever may be its results with regard to Africa, it can afford no remedy to the New World.

In twelve years the Colonization Society has transported two thousand five hundred Negroes to Africa; in the same space of time about seven hundred thousand blacks were born in the United States. If the colony of Liberia were able to receive thousands of new inhabitants every year, and if the Negroes were in a state to be sent thither with advantage; if the Union were to supply the society with annual subsidies, and to transport the Negroes to Africa in government vessels, it would still be unable to counterpoise the natural increase of population among the blacks; and as it could not remove as many men in a year as are born upon its territory within that time, it could not prevent the growth of the evil which is daily increasing in the states. The Negro race will never leave those shores of the American continent to which it was brought by the passions and the vices of Europeans; and it will not disappear from the New World as long as it continues to exist. The inhabitants of the United States may retard the calamities which they apprehend, but they cannot now destroy their cause.

I am obliged to confess that I do not regard the abolition of slavery as a means of warding off the struggle of the two races in the Southern states. The Negroes may long remain slaves without complaining; but if they are once raised to the level of freemen, they will soon revolt at being deprived of almost all their civil rights; and as they cannot become the equals of the whites, they will speedily show themselves as enemies. In the North, people had every benefit from freeing the slaves; one thus delivered them from slavery without having strengthened the free Negroes. These were too small in number to ever reclaim their rights. But such is not the case in the South. The question of slavery was a commercial and manufacturing question for the slaveowners in the North; for those of the South it is a question of life and death. God forbid that I should seek to justify the principle of Negro slavery, as has been done by some American writers! I say only that all the countries which formerly adopted that execrable principle are not equally able to abandon it at the present time.

When I contemplate the condition of the South, I can discover only two modes of action for the white inhabitants of those States: namely, either to emancipate the Negroes and to intermingle with them, or, remaining isolated from them, to keep them in slavery as long as possible. All intermediate measures seem to me likely to terminate, and that shortly, in the most horrible of civil wars and perhaps in the extirpation of one or the other of the two races. Such is the view that the Americans of the South take of the question, and they act consistently with it. As they are determined not to mingle with the Negroes, they refuse to emancipate them.

Not that the inhabitants of the South regard slavery as necessary to the wealth of the planter; on this point many of them agree with their Northern countrymen in freely admitting that slavery is prejudicial to their interests; but they are convinced that the removal of this evil would imperil their own existence. The instruction which is now diffused in the South has convinced the inhabitants that slavery is injurious to the slaveowner, but it has also shown them, more clearly than before, the virtual impossibility of destroying it. Hence arises a singular contrast: the more the utility of slavery is contested, the more firmly is it established in the laws; and while its principle is gradually abolished in the North, that selfsame principle gives rise to more and more rigorous consequences in the South.

The legislation of the Southern states with regard to slaves presents at the present day such unparalleled atrocities as suffice to show that the laws of humanity have been totally perverted, and to betray the desperate position of the community in which that legislation has been promulgated. The Americans of this portion of the Union have not, indeed, augmented the hardships of slavery; on the contrary, they have bettered the physical condition of the slaves. The only means by which the ancients maintained slavery were fetters and death; the Americans of the South of the Union have discovered more intellectual securities for the duration of their power. They have employed their despotism and their violence against the human mind. In antiquity precautions were taken to prevent the slave from breaking his chains; at the present day measures are adopted to deprive him even of the desire for freedom. The ancients kept the bodies of their slaves in bondage, but placed no restraint upon the mind and no check upon education; and they acted consistently with their established principle, since a natural termination of slavery then existed, and one day or other the slave might be set free and become the equal of his master. But the Americans of the South, who do not admit that the Negroes can ever be commingled with themselves, have forbidden them, under severe penalties, to be taught to read or write; and as they will not raise them to their own level, they sink them as nearly as possible to that of the brutes.

The hope of liberty had always been allowed to the slave, to cheer the hardships of his condition. But the Americans of the South are well aware that emancipation cannot but be dangerous when the freed man can never be assimilated to his former master. To give a single man his freedom, yet to leave him in misery and ignominy, what is that, in effect, but to furnish a future leader for a slave revolt? Moreover, it has long been remarked that the presence of a free Negro vaguely agitates the minds of his less fortunate brethren, and conveys to them a dim notion of their rights. The Americans of the South have consequently taken away from slaveowners the right of emancipating their slaves in most cases.

I happened to meet an old man, in the South of the Union, who had lived in illicit intercourse with one of his Negresses and had had several children by her, who were born the slaves of their father. He had, indeed, frequently thought of bequeathing to them at least their liberty; but years had elapsed before he could surmount the legal obstacles to their emancipation, and meanwhile his old age had come and he was about to die. He pictured to himself his sons dragged from market to market and passing from the authority of a parent to the rod of the stranger, until these horrid anticipations worked his expiring imagination into frenzy. When I saw him, he was prey to all the anguish of despair; and I then understood that nature knows how to revenge itself for the injuries committed under the guise of law.

These evils are unquestionably great, but they are the necessary and foreseen consequences of the very principle of modern slavery. When the Europeans chose their slaves from a race differing from their own, which many considered inferior to the other human races and with which all viewed the idea assimilation with horror, they must have believed that slavery would last forever, since there is no intermediate state that can be durable between the excessive inequality produced by servitude and the complete equality that originates in independence.

The Europeans did imperfectly feel this truth, but without acknowledging it even to themselves. Whenever they have had to do with Negroes, their conduct has been dictated either by their interest and their pride or by their compassion. They first violated every right of humanity by their treatment of the Negro, and they afterwards informed him that those rights were precious and inviolable. They opened their ranks to their slaves, and when the latter tried to come in, they drove them forth in scorn. Desiring slavery, they have allowed themselves unconsciously to be swayed in spite of themselves towards freedom, without having the courage to be either completely iniquitous or completely just.

If it is impossible to anticipate a period at which the Americans of the South will mingle their blood with that of the Negroes, can they allow their slaves to become free without compromising their own security? And if they are obliged to keep that race in bondage in order to save their own families, may they not be excused for availing themselves of the means best adapted to that end? The events that are taking place in the Southern states appear to me to be at once the most horrible and the most natural results of slavery. When I see the order of nature overthrown, and when I hear the cry of humanity in its vain struggle against the laws, my indignation does not light upon the men of our own time who are the instruments of these outrages; but I reserve my execration for those who, after a thousand years of freedom, brought back slavery into the world once more.

Whatever may be the efforts of the Americans of the South to maintain slavery, they will not always succeed. Slavery, now confined to a single tract of the civilized earth, attacked by Christianity as unjust and by political economy as prejudicial, and now contrasted with democratic liberty and the intelligence of our age, cannot survive. By the act of the master, or by the will of the slave, it will cease; and in either case great calamities may be expected to ensue. If liberty be refused to the Negroes of the South, they will in the end forcibly seize it for themselves; if it be given, they will before long abuse it.

Conclusion

. . . The Middle Ages were a period when everything was broken up, when each people, each province, each city, and each family tended strongly to maintain its distinct individuality. At the present time an opposite tendency seems to prevail, and the nations seem to be advancing to unity. Intellectual ties bring together the remotest parts of the earth; and men cannot remain strangers to one another or be ignorant of what is taking place in any corner of the globe. The consequence is that there is less difference at the present day between the Europeans and their descendants in the New World, in spite of the ocean that divides them, than there was in the thirteenth century between certain towns that were separated only by a river. If this tendency to assimilation brings foreign nations closer to each other, it must a *fortiori* prevent the descendants of the same people from becoming aliens to one another.

The time will therefore come when one hundred and fifty million men will be living in North America, equal in condition, all belonging to one family, owing their origin to the same cause, and preserving the same civilization, the same language, the same religion, the same habits, the same manners, and imbued with the same opinions, propagated under the same forms. The rest is uncertain, but this is certain; and it is a fact new to the world, a fact that the imagination strives in vain to grasp.

There are at the present time two great nations in the world, which started from different points, but seem to tend towards the same end. I allude to the Russians and the Americans. Both of them have grown up unnoticed; and while the attention of mankind was directed elsewhere, they have suddenly placed themselves in the front rank among the nations, and the world learned their existence and their greatness at almost the same time. All other nations seem to have nearly reached their natural limits, and they have only to maintain their power; but these are still in the act of growth. All the others have stopped, or continue to advance with extreme difficulty; these alone are proceeding with ease and celerity along a path to which no limit can be perceived. The American struggles against the obstacles that nature opposes to him; the adversaries of the Russian are men. The former combats the wilderness and savage life; the latter, civilization with all its arms. The conquests of the American are therefore gained by the plowshare; those of the Russian by the sword. The Anglo-American relies upon personal interest to accomplish his ends and gives free scope to the unguided strength and common sense of the people; the Russian centers all the authority of society in a single arm. The principal instrument of the former is freedom; of the latter, servitude. Their starting point is different and their courses are not the same; yet each of them seems marked out by the will of Heaven to sway the destinies of half the globe.

3c   To Francisque de Corcelle[2], Reactions to Corcelle's Review of Volume One of Democracy in America

Paris, April 12, 1835

Dear Mr. de Corcelle,

In asking my opinion of the work that you have asked me to read, you have imposed conditions that I don't know how to fulfill.[3] After allowing me to see the flattering ways in which you speak of me, you forbid me to express my gratitude. These two things cannot be reconciled, and since you have allowed me to see in what terms you express yourself, you must permit me to express my thanks. I shall say that I have been extremely touched by and very proud of your words. I would be happy to hear such praise from anybody; but it is especially precious coming from you.

I have examined your criticisms with as much detachment as an author is capable of. Some of them are very justified. All are made in such a generous spirit that they might even contribute to the success of the book. In short, sir, I am being totally frank when I say that I would not want to see them cut back. They hide your extreme generosity under an air of rigorous impartiality which adds new weight to your judgments.

I will say only one thing. Here it is: I think you make my views about the future of democracy a little too gloomy. If I were as negative as you think, you would be right in thinking that there were contradictions in my conclusions, which tend definitely towards the progressive organization of Democracy. I have sought, it is true, to uncover the natural tendencies a democratic social state gives to human thought and institutions. I have highlighted the dangers awaiting humanity on the way to democracy. But I have not suggested that one cannot fight against these dangers and combat them if diagnosed in time. One can avert them if they are properly anticipated.

I am under the impression that Democrats (in the good sense of the word), yes, that Democrats nowadays do not see clearly either the advantages or the dangers of the social and political state towards which they are trying to direct society. Therefore they are likely to be mistaken as to the means they should use to maximize the former and minimize the latter. I have thus tried to highlight both as clearly and as firmly as I am capable of, so that we can face

2   Francisque de Corcelle later served as ambassador to the Vatican when Tocqueville was minister of foreign affairs in 1849.

3   Corcelle's review of *Democracy in America*, volume one, in *La Revue des Mondes*, June 15, 1835.

our enemies and know what we are fighting against. This is what puts me in a category altogether different from Mr. Jouffroy.[4] Mr. Jouffroy notes the perils of democracy and sees them as inevitable. For him, it is a question of putting them off as long as possible. When they finally come, the only option is to cover one's head and submit to destiny. But I would like to see society aware of the dangers of democracy like a strong man who knows that perils exist and that he has to confront them to reach his goal. Such a man exposes himself to dangers without regret and without misgivings, as the necessary requirement of his undertaking. He is fearful only when he cannot see them fully.

I apologize for going on about this point at such length. But it is no mere detail. It is my premise, the fundamental idea of my book, and I think it is very important that the public not err in such a case.

I do not want to end, my dear Monsieur de Corcelle, without expressing again my deep gratitude and without saying that I hope that after having lauded the book altogether too much, you will agree to become one of the author's friends.

---

4   Théodore Jouffroy, *Mélanges philosophiques*, 1833.

Part II
Great Britain, France, and the United States

Preliminary Note

In this section, we cover the years 1835–40, separating the publication of the two volumes of *Democracy*. They are important in capturing Tocqueville as an emerging social reformer, an apprentice politician, and a self-described "liberal of a new kind." The essays on pauperism and poverty in England and Ireland, and on savings accounts for French industrial workers show Tocqueville thinking seriously about social policy (4a–c). This is a significant, albeit neglected, aspect of his career, and had been ever since he and Beaumont embarked on the American prison investigation in 1831.

We read Tocqueville confiding to his future wife not only his love for her but his political ambitions (5a), and working out in letters to his old friends Stoffels and Kergorlay the liberal ideology he stands for, especially his desire to see "the taste for freedom" take root in French institutions (5b–d). Once established as a politician, however, we find Tocqueville impatient with the political process and torn between action and reflection (5f).

The bulk of this section is naturally devoted to volume two of *Democracy*. This is the most theoretically ambitious part of the American work, where Tocqueville presents a sustained comparison of aristocratic and democratic societies (6a–d). At the end of the previous section, the reader found a letter to Francisque de Corcelle, where Tocqueville clarified his intent for volume one (3c). Here, Tocqueville does the same for volume two in his correspondence with his British translator Henry Reeve (5e), but engages in self-criticism when responding to a glowing review by another British friend, the young philosopher John Stuart Mill (6e).

4

Discovery of England, Poverty, Pauperism, and Social Policy, 1835–1837

4a First Memoir on Pauperism, 1835[1]

There are two kinds of welfare. One leads each individual, according to his means, to alleviate the evils he sees around him. This type is as old as the world; it began with human misfortune. Christianity made a divine virtue of it and called it charity. The other, less instinctive, more reasoned, less emotional, and often more powerful, leads society to concern itself with the misfortunes of its members and is ready systematically to alleviate their sufferings. This type is born of Protestantism and has developed only in modern societies. The first type is a private virtue; it escapes social action; the second, on the contrary, is produced and regulated by society. It is therefore with the second that we must be especially concerned.

At first glance there is no idea that seems more beautiful and grander than that of public charity. Society is continually examining itself, probing its wounds, and undertaking to cure them. At the same time that it assures the rich the enjoyment of their wealth, society guarantees the poor against excessive misery. It asks some to give of their surplus in order to allow others the basic necessities. This is certainly a moving and elevating sight.

How does it happen that experience destroys some of these beautiful illusions? The only country in Europe which has systematized and applied the theories of public charity on a grand scale is England.

. . .

Almost two and a half centuries have passed since the principle of legal

---

1   Delivered before the Royal Academic Society of Cherbourg in 1835, and printed in the Society's proceedings of that year.

charity was fully embraced by our neighbors, and one may now judge the fatal consequences that flowed from the adoption of this principle. Let us examine them successively.

Since the poor have an absolute right to the help of society, and have a public administration organized to provide it everywhere, one can observe in a Protestant country the immediate rebirth and generalization of all the abuses with which its reformers rightly reproached some Catholic countries. Man, like all socially organized beings, has a natural passion for idleness. There are, however, two incentives to work: the need to live and the desire to improve the conditions of life. Experience has proven that the majority of men can be sufficiently motivated to work only by the first of these incentives. The second is effective only with a small minority. Well, a charitable institution indiscriminately open to all those in need, or a law that gives all the poor a right to public aid, whatever the origin of their poverty, weakens or destroys the first stimulant and leaves only the second intact. The English peasant, like the Spanish peasant, if he does not feel the deep desire to better the position into which he has been born, and to raise himself out of his misery (a feeble desire which is easily crushed in the majority of men) the peasant of both countries, I maintain, has no interest in working, or, if he works, has no interest in saving. He therefore remains idle or thoughtlessly squanders the fruits of his labors. Both these countries, by different causal patterns, arrive at the same result; the most generous, the most active, the most industrious part of the nation devotes its resources to furnishing the means of existence for those who do nothing or who make bad use of their labor.

. . .

Nothing is as difficult to distinguish as the nuances that separate unmerited misfortune from an adversity produced by vice. How many miseries are simultaneously the result of both these causes! What profound knowledge must be presumed about the character of each man and of the circumstances in which he has lived, what knowledge, what sharp discernment, what cold and inexorable reason! Where will you find the magistrate who will have the conscience, the time, the talent, the means of devoting himself to such an examination? Who would dare to let a poor man die of hunger because it's his own fault that he is dying? Who will hear his cries and reason about his vices? Even personal interest is restrained when confronted by the sight of other men's misery. Would the interest of the public treasury really prove to be successful? And if the overseer's heart were unconcerned with such emotions, which are appealing even when misguided, would he remain indifferent to fear? Who, being judge of the joy or suffering, life or death, of a large segment of his fellow men, of its most dissolute, its most turbulent, its crudest segment, who would not shrink before the exercise of such terrible power? And if any of these intrepid beings can be found, how many will there be? In any event, such functions can only be exercised with a restricted territory. A large number must be delegated to do so. The English have been obliged to put overseers in every parish. What inevitably follows from all this? Poverty is verified, the causes of poverty remain uncertain: the first is a patent fact, the second is proved by an always debatable process of reasoning. Since public aid is only indirectly harmful to society, while the refusal of aid instantly hurts the poor and the overseer himself, the overseer's choice cannot be in doubt. The laws may declare that only innocent poverty will be relieved; practice will alleviate all poverty. I will present plausible arguments for the second point, equally based on experience.

We would like work to be the price of relief. But, first, is there always public work to be done? Is it equally spread over the whole country in such a way that you never see a good deal of work to be done with few people to do it in one district and in another many indigents to be helped but little work to be undertaken? If this difficulty is present at all times, doesn't it become insurmountable when, as a consequence of the progressive development of civilization, of population growth, of the effect of the Poor Law itself, the proportion of indigents, as in England, reaches a sixth, some say a quarter, of the total population?

But even supposing that there would always be work to do, who will take responsibility for determining its urgency, supervising its execution, setting the price? That man, the overseer, aside from the qualities of a great magistrate, will therefore also possess the talents, the energy, the special knowledge of a good industrial entrepreneur. He will find in the feeling of duty alone what self interest itself would be powerless to create – the courage to force the most inactive and vicious part of the population into sustained and productive effort. Would it be wise to delude ourselves? Pressured by the needs of the poor, the overseer will impose make–work, or even – as is almost always the case in England – pay wages without demanding labor. Laws must be made for men and not in terms of a perfect world which cannot be sustained by human nature, nor of models which it offers only very occasionally.

Any measure that establishes legal charity on a permanent basis and gives it an administrative form thereby creates an idle and lazy class, living at the expense of the industrial and working class. This, at least, is its inevitable consequence, if not the immediate result. It reproduces all the vices of the monastic system, minus the high ideals of morality and religion that often went along with it. Such a law is a bad seed planted in the legal structure. Circumstances, as in America, can prevent the seed from developing rapidly, but they can not destroy it, and if the present generation escapes its influence, it will devour the well being of generations to come.

If you closely observe the condition of populations among whom such legislation has long been in force, you will easily discover that the effects are not less unfortunate for morality than for public prosperity, and that it depraves men even more than it impoverishes them.

There is nothing which, generally speaking, elevates and sustains the human spirit more than the idea of rights. There is something great and virile in the idea of right which removes from any request its suppliant character, and places the one who claims it on the same level as the one who grants it. But the right of the poor to obtain society's help is unique in that instead of elevating the heart of the man who exercises it, it lowers him. In countries where legislation does not allow for such an opportunity, the poor man, while turning to individual charity, recognizes, it is true, his condition of inferiority in relation to the rest of his fellow men; but he recognizes it secretly and temporarily. From the moment that an indigent is inscribed on the poor list of his parish, he can certainly demand relief, but what is the achievement of this right if not a notarized manifestation of misery, of weakness, of misconduct on the part of its recipient? Ordinary rights are conferred on men by reason of some personal advantage acquired by them over their fellow men. This other kind is accorded by reason of a recognized inferiority. The first is a clear statement of superiority; the second publicizes inferiority and legalizes it. The more extensive and the more secure ordinary rights are, the more honor they confer; the more permanent and extended the right to relief is, the more it degrades.

The poor man who demands alms in the name of the law is, therefore, in a still more humiliating position than the indigent who asks pity of his fellow men in the name of He who regards all men from the same point of view and who subjects rich and poor to equal laws.

But this is still not all: individual almsgiving established valuable ties between the rich and the poor. The deed itself involves the giver in the fate of the one whose poverty he has undertaken to alleviate. The latter, supported by aid which he had no right to demand and which he may have had no hope of getting, feels inspired by gratitude. A moral tie is established between those two classes whose interests and passions so often conspire to separate them from each other, and although divided by circumstance they are willingly reconciled. This is not the case with legal charity The latter allows the alms to persist but removes its morality. The law strips the man of wealth of a part of his surplus without consulting him, and he sees the poor man only as a greedy stranger invited by the legislator to share his wealth. The poor man, on the other hand, feels no gratitude for a benefit that no one can refuse him and that could not satisfy him in any case. Public alms guarantee life but do not make it happier or more comfortable than individual almsgiving; legal charity does not thereby eliminate wealth or poverty in society. One class still views the world with fear and loathing while the other regards its misfortune with despair and envy. Far from uniting these two rival nations, who have existed since the beginning of the world and who are called the rich and the poor, into a single people, it breaks the only link which could be established between them. It ranges each one under a banner, tallies them, and, bringing them face to face, prepares them for combat.

I have said that the inevitable result of public charity was to perpetuate idleness among the majority of the poor and to provide for their leisure at the expense of those who work.

If the idleness of the rich, an hereditary idleness, merited by work or by services, an idleness immersed in public consideration, supported by psychological complacency, inspired by intellectual pleasures, moralized by mental exercise – if this idleness, I say, has produced so many vices, what will come of a degraded idleness obtained by baseness, merited by misconduct, enjoyed in ignominy? It becomes tolerable only in proportion to the extent that the soul subjects itself to all this corruption and degradation.

What can be expected from a man whose position cannot improve, since he has lost the respect of his fellow men which is the precondition of all progress, whose lot could not become worse, since, being reduced to the satisfaction of his most pressing needs, he is assured that they will always be satisfied? What course of action is left to the conscience or to human activity in a being so limited, who lives without hope and without fear? He looks at the future as an animal does. Absorbed in the present and the ignoble and transient pleasures it affords, his brutalized nature is unaware of the determinants of its destiny.

Read all the books on pauperism written in England, study the inquiries ordered by the British Parliament, look at the discussions that have taken place in the Lords and Commons on this difficult question. They boil down to a single deafening cry – the degraded condition into which the lower classes have fallen! The number of illegitimate children and criminals grows rapidly and continuously, the indigent population is limitless, the spirit of foresight and of saving becomes more and more alien to the poor. While throughout the rest of the nation education spreads, morals improve, tastes become more refined, manners more polished the indigent remains motionless, or rather he goes backward. He could be described as reverting to barbarism. Amidst the marvels of civilization, he seems to emulate savage man in his ideas and his inclinations.

Legal charity affects the pauper's freedom as much as his morality. This is easily proved. When local governments are rigorously obligated to aid the indigent, they necessarily owe relief only to the poor who reside in their jurisdiction. This is the only fair way of equalizing the public burden which results from the law, and of proportioning it to the means of those who must bear it. Since individual charity is almost unknown in a country of organized public charity, anyone whose misfortunes or vices have made him incapable of earning a living is condemned, under pain of death, to remain in the place of his birth. If he leaves, he moves through enemy country. The private interest within the parish, infinitely more active and powerful than the best organized national police could be, notes his arrival, dogs his every step, and, if he wants to establish a new residence, informs the public authority who takes him to the boundary line. Through their Poor Laws, the English have immobilized a sixth of their population. They have bound it to the earth like the medieval peasantry. Then, man was forced against his will to stay on the land where he was born. Legal charity keeps him from even wishing to move. That is the only difference between the systems. The English have gone further. They have reaped even more disastrous consequences from the principle of public welfare. The English parishes are so dominated by the fear that an indigent person might be placed on their rolls and acquire residency, that when a stranger whose clothes do not clearly indicate wealth temporarily settles among them, or when an unexpected misfortune suddenly strikes him, the municipal authorities immediately ask him to post bond against possible indigence, and if the stranger cannot furnish this security, he must leave.

Thus legal charity has not only taken freedom of movement from the English poor but also from those who are threatened by poverty.

. . .

I am certainly far from wanting to put the most natural, the most beautiful, and the most holy of virtues on trial. But I think there is no principle, however good, whose every consequence can be regarded as good. I think that beneficence must be a manly and reasoned virtue, not a weak and unreflecting inclination. It is necessary to do what is most useful to the receiver, not what pleases the giver, to do what best serves the welfare of the majority, not what rescues the few. I can conceive of beneficence only in this way. Any other way it is still a sublime instinct, but it no longer seems to me worthy of the name of virtue.

I recognize that individual charity almost always produces useful results. It devotes itself to the greatest miseries, it seeks out misfortune without publicity, and it silently and spontaneously repairs the damage. It can be observed wherever there are unfortunates to be helped. It grows with suffering. And yet, it cannot be unthinkingly relied on, because a thousand accidents can delay or halt its operation. One cannot be sure of finding it, and it is not aroused by every cry of pain.

I admit that by regulating relief, charitable persons in association could infuse individual philanthropy with more activity and power. I recognize not only the utility but the necessity of public charity applied to inevitable evils such as the helplessness of infancy, the decrepitude of old age, sickness, insanity. I even admit its temporary usefulness in times of public calamities which God sometimes allows to slip from his hand, proclaiming his anger to the nation. State alms are then as spontaneous as unforeseen, as temporary as the evil itself.

I even understand that public charity which opens free schools for the children of the poor and gives intelligence the means of acquiring the basic physical necessities through labor.

But I am deeply convinced that any permanent, regular administrative system whose aim will be to provide for the needs of the poor will breed more miseries than it can cure, will deprave the population that it wants to help and comfort, will in time reduce the rich to being no more than the tenant farmers of the poor, will dry up the sources of savings, will stop the accumulation of capital, will retard the development of trade, will benumb human industry and activity, and will culminate by bringing about a violent revolution in the State, when the number of those who receive alms will have become as large as those who give it, and the indigent, no longer being able to take from the impoverished rich the means of providing for his needs, will find it easier to plunder them of all their property at one stroke than to ask for their help.

4b   Journey in Ireland, July–August, 1835

Visit to the Poorhouse and the University, July 9, 1835

A vast edifice sustained annually by voluntary gifts. 1,800 to 2,000 paupers are received there during the day; they receive food, lodging, and when they are capable of it, work. They go to sleep where they can.

The sight inside. The most hideous and disgusting aspect of destitution. A very long room full of women and children whose infirmities or age prevent them from working. On the floor the paupers are lying down pell-mell like pigs in the mud of their sty. One has difficulty not to step on a half-naked body.

In the left wing, a smaller room, full of old or crippled men. They are seated on wooden benches, all turned in the same direction, crowded together as in the pit of a theatre. They do not talk at all, they do not move, they look at nothing, they do not appear to be thinking. They neither expect, fear, nor hope for anything from life. I am mistaken, they are waiting for dinner, which is due in three hours. It is the only pleasure that is left to them, after which they will have nothing more than to die.

Further on are those who are able to work. They are seated on the damp earth. They have small mallets in their hands and are breaking stones. At the end of the day they receive a penny (two sous in France). They are the lucky ones.

On leaving there we came upon a small covered wheelbarrow pushed by two paupers. This wheelbarrow goes to the door of the houses of the rich; into it is thrown the remains of the meals, and this debris is brought to the poorhouse to make the soup.

From the poorhouse they took us to the university. An immense and magnificent garden kept up like that of a nobleman. A palace of granite, a superb church, a wonderful library. Lackeys in livery, 14 fellows, 70 [scholars]. Enormous revenues. Men of all religions are educated there. But only members of the Church of England can administer the establishment and receive its revenues.

This university was founded by Elizabeth with the estates confiscated from Catholics, the fathers of those whom we had just seen wallowing in their mud at the poorhouse! This establishment contains 1500 students. Very few belong to rich Irish families. Not only do the Irish nobility live abroad; not only do they spend abroad the money Ireland produces, [but] they rear their children in England, for fear undoubtedly that the vague instinct of patriotism and youthful memories might bind them one day to Ireland.

If you wish to know what the spirit of conquest, religious hatred, combined with all the abuses of aristocracy without any of its advantages, can produce, come to Ireland.

Dinner with the Bishop of Kilkenny, July 26, 1835

Go to Mayo, you will encounter thousands of men literally nearly dead of hunger. The marquis of Sligo has, in the same province, seventy thousand acres of land, the revenue of which he consumes in England. And should not the law force this man to give his fellows some part of his surplus? Why are so many people dying of hunger in Mayo? Because the landlords find it in their interest to increase their grasslands, and if they can make a little more money, they laugh at us besides. At the present time, gentlemen, it is the interest of the landlords of Ireland to render the people as wretched as possible, for the more the cultivator is threatened by starvation, the readier he will be to submit to every condition they wish to impose on him. Let us give the landlords an interest in making the poor comfortable.[2]

This long democratic tirade was listened to with enthusiasm and interrupted several time by cries of "*Hear!*" from the guests.

4c   Second Memoir on Pauperism, 1837

I will content myself with saying briefly that these plans have always encountered one of two obstacles to their success: On the one hand, almost all the capitalist industrial entrepreneurs have shown themselves little inclined to give their workers a proportional share of the profits, or to invest in their businesses the small sums with which their workers could entrust them. I think that in their own interest they are very wrong not to do this, but it would be neither just nor useful to force them.

On the other hand, when workers have tried to dispense with capitalists, to associate themselves, to combine their money and manage their work themselves with the aid of a union, they have been unable to succeed. It is not long before disorder introduces itself into their association, its agents are not faithful, its capital insufficient or badly assured, its credit almost nil, its commercial relationships very limited. Soon a ruinous competition forces the association to dissolve itself. We have seen these attempts frequently repeated, particularly in the last seven years, but always in vain.

I am led to believe, however, that a time is approaching when it will be possible to manage many industries in this manner. As our workers acquire a broader education, and the art of association for honest and peaceful purposes makes progress among us, when politics will not be mingled in the slightest with industrial associations, when the government, reassured as to their purpose, will not refuse such associations its goodwill and support, we will see such associations multiply and prosper. I think that in democratic centuries like ours, association in all things must gradually replace the dominant action of a few powerful individuals. It thus seems to me that the idea of industrial associations will be fruitful, but I do not believe it is ripe. For the present, therefore, we must look elsewhere for solutions.

Since we cannot give workers an ownership interest in the factory, we can at least help them use the salary they receive from the factory to create an independent property.

---

2   Tocqueville relates here the Bishop's speech.

5

Ambitions, Marriage, and Tocqueville's Views of his Own Brand of Liberalism, 1833–1840

5a To Marie Mottley, on his Ambitions and his Love for his Future Wife

Cherbourg, August 2, 1833

My travels in the countryside have proven very profitable. First of all I have fully acquainted myself with my affairs and proven to all concerned that I understand them. Second, I have met people who can be helpful to me in the long run. I have convinced myself that it would be a lot less difficult than I had initially thought to become known around here. Our family is held in high esteem, and given the moderate opinions you know I have, I might even some day become influential. It gives me pleasure to contemplate the prospect of an honorable position in my region earned by honest means. Marie, I cannot tell you how much I feel determined to pursue this high goal, which is what I always have been striving for. Why would I not share with you, who know me so well, what I truly think? I don't really know in truth what the range of my intelligence is, and I would be tempted to judge my intelligence very ordinary. But I believe I feel, deep inside me, a soul more elevated than that of most men. What most men so often display superficially, I think I really feel at the bottom of my heart. It seems to me that when I say I love my country, that I detest tyranny regardless of who the ruler is, that I love freedom with all the sacred rights that it consecrates, when I say all of this, it seems to me when I say this that I am only voicing my true feelings. I express feelings which profoundly stir every fiber of my heart. When I add that to satisfy these elevated passions, I would be ready to risk my life and fortune, I once again feel sure that I am only speaking the literal truth. This is what I think of myself, I confess. Is it wrong? I would be very unhappy if it were. My own ambition, and I admit that it often stirs my blood, is that my country should judge me as I judge myself on this point. Truly I do not ask of the world either money or power, but only esteem. I want the world to believe that I am really led by the motivations which are and will always be the rule of my conduct. I believe that these motivations are high and noble. I would like everybody to do me justice in appreciating them as such. To fail on this point would sadden me deeply; to succeed would satisfy all my desires.

Oh, Marie, what makes the feelings we have for each other more valuable than anything else in the world, in my eyes, is that I can tell you these things. It is to find in you a soul that can understand me, and a heart into which I can pour out all the conceit of my own. What alone is worth all the treasures of the universe to me is to have met one person in the world who knows me well enough to interpret all the nuances of my thought, to judge all my actions, regardless of appearances, and whom I can count on to treat me fairly even when nobody else in the world would.

5b   To Eugène Stoffels, on His Love of Freedom and New Kind of Liberalism[1]

July 24, 1836

What has always struck me about my country, but chiefly in the last few years, has been to see lined up on one side the men who prize morality, religion, order, and on the other those who love freedom and the equality of men before the law. This sight has struck me as the most extraordinary and most deplorable ever offered a man's view; for all these things which we separate are, I am certain, indissolubly united in the eyes of God. They are all *holy* things, if I can express myself so, because the greatness and happiness of man in this world can come only from the simultaneous combination of them all. Since then I have realized that one of the most beautiful enterprises of our times would be to show that all these things are not at all incompatible; that on the contrary they are necessarily linked to one another, so that each of them is weakened by being separated from the others. This is my general idea. You understand it very well; you share it. There is however a difference between you and me. I love freedom more strongly, more sincerely than you do. You want it, if it can be obtained without difficulty, but you are ready to do without it. It's the same way with a multitude of good people in France.

1   A friend from the years in the lycée at Metz.

This is not my feeling. I have always loved freedom instinctively, and all my reflections lead me to believe that no moral and political greatness is possible for long without it. I am therefore as strongly attached to freedom as to morality, and I am ready to lose some of my tranquillity to achieve it.

With this difference, we are in agreement about the ends. But you claim that we differ enormously as to the means: I think that here, in truth, you only partly understand me.

You think that I am going to put forward radical and almost revolutionary theories. In this you are wrong. I have shown and I will continue to show a strong and reasoned preference for freedom, and that for two reasons: first, because it is my profound opinion; second, because I don't want to be confused with those friends of order who would sell free choice and the laws cheaply in order to sleep quietly in their beds. There are already enough of those kind of people, and I dare predict that they will never achieve anything great and lasting. I will therefore show frankly the taste for freedom, and the general desire to see it develop in all the political institutions of my country; but at the same time I will profess such a great respect for justice and religious beliefs, that I can't believe people won't clearly recognize me for a liberal of a new kind, and that they will confuse me with most of the dirty democrats of our days.

5c   To Louis de Kergorlay,[2] on Pleasure and Materialism

Baden, August 5, 1836

I write you, my dear friend, from the little town of Baden, where I didn't plan to come but where the following circumstances led me. Since her earliest youth Marie has experienced nervous pains in her uterus which make her suffer greatly once a month. While we were at Bern, several women of her acquaintance assured us that the waters of Baden were extremely useful in such cases. The best doctors of the town said the same thing. As a result, I decided to spend the month of August here, and we will continue our trip afterwards, while prolonging it a little. So you should write me here at Baden, Canton of Aargau, Switzerland. You don't need to mention our stay here to the people you know.

At Bern I received your letter of 20 July. It was very interesting and you didn't have to tell me to keep it. This letter leads me to think more and more what I have already told you, that you need to be careful not to hurt your

2   A distant cousin, best friend since childhood.

writing style by trying to polish it too much. What you write carefully gives the impression, it is true, of a page torn from a writer of the seventeenth century, but not from a first-rate writer; your relaxed style, amidst its flaws, on the contrary often has great qualities and the outstanding points lead me to prefer it, despite its blemishes. For the rest, we need to talk about this again.

What you say to me about material pleasures has always seemed to me very true and seems to me still more so at the moment, when I am reading Plato. The philosophers of this school hardly appear to make the strong distinction among the pleasures of the senses about which you complain. Seeing women and delivering oneself to the pleasures of luxury seem to be in their eyes if not similar, at least analogous, and they tolerate them both equally. They even show for what we now exclusively call pleasures of the senses a leniency that is striking and in my opinion badly placed. I think, further, that you are mistaken when you say that it was Christianity which drew the dividing line which you complain about. Christianity forbade chiefly the pleasures produced by sex, and that is easily understood: but I think that Jesus Christ and in general the Church protested very strongly against the kind of materialism you are talking about. The tendency of which we speak is more recent. I consider it as the beginning of a reaction of materialism against spiritualism which at first reigned unopposed, or of *the flesh against the spirit*, as the clergy would say. This tendency began to be *legitimized* by the Reformation. Everywhere the indirect effect of the Reformation has been to lead men to improve their material conditions without nevertheless losing the next world entirely from sight. In order to satisfy this double goal, it was necessary to make a classification among material things; to reject those which were most obviously condemnable; to accept the others as more or less permitted, and to slide over as gently as possible among the pleasures of this world into the ineffable joys of the other. The good Catholics, the sight of whom is shocking, fundamentally have become true Protestants; nothing more. The ideas which you express are very *original*, in their form; as to the substance, they are only *recent*. The Platonists and the Church Fathers said, I think, similar things. Only I do not remember ever having seen anyone make, with the clarity and strength you do, the analogy among all material pleasures whatsoever. People limited themselves to condemning them all.

Now I come to what I think myself. Whatever one does it is impossible to prevent men from having a body as well as a soul: that the angel not be shut up with the beast, "as Janvier says."[3] Any philosophy or any religion which

---

3   Eugène Janvier, lawyer and deputy for Montauban 1834–48, a friend of Tocqueville and Beaumont.

wants to entirely ignore one of these two things will produce some extraordinary examples, but it will never effect humanity overall. This is what I believe and what makes me lament; for you know that without being more detached from the beast than others, I worship the angel and at all cost I would like to see it dominate. I therefore constantly work my brain to discover if there isn't, between these two extremes, a middle path which humanity can keep to and which leads neither to Heliogabalus nor to St. Jerome; for I consider it certain that you will never make the mass of people into either the one or the other, and still less into St. Jerome than Heliogabalus. I am therefore not as shocked as you by this *honest materialism* of which you complain so bitterly. Not that it doesn't excite my contempt as much as it does yours. But I look at it practically and ask myself if something at least analogous is not still the best that it is permissible to ask for, not from such a man in particular, but from our poor species in general. Think about these ideas and respond. Now I am changing subjects, because I don't have much to do here and just writing to you is a great pleasure for me.

I brought with me Machiavelli's *History of Florence* and I have just read it very carefully. This reading has given birth to a few ideas which I want to share with you following our old method of constantly philosophizing with each other. I will speak to you first of the writer. The Machiavelli of the *History of Florence* is for me the Machiavelli of *The Prince*. I do not understand how the reading of the first work has ever allowed the least doubt about the purpose of the author in writing the second. In his history Machiavelli doubtless sometimes praises great and good actions; but one sees that with him this is an exercise of the imagination. The basis of his thought is that all actions are indifferent in themselves and that they must all be judged by the ability that they show and by the success which they achieve. For him the world is a great arena from which God is absent, where conscience is of no use and where everyone takes care of himself as best he can. Machiavelli is Mr. Thiers' grandfather. That's saying everything.

As to the things he tells about, I confess to you that I am frightened by the idea of the centuries whose portrait he paints and that I feel a little reconciled to our own and disposed to believe that we judge it too severely. In those medieval Italian republics, there was a sort of rude energy, it is true. But how little we see real virtues. Nothing but brutal violence, alongside extraordinary refinements of vice! What egotism! What contempt for law! What skepticism among the upper classes and what superstitions among the lower! What a society deeply corrupted without yet being generally enlightened!

I know for the rest that what was true of the Italians of the sixteenth century was not accurate of the other peoples of Europe. I imagine however that the times which immediately preceded the Reformation were centuries of great corruption everywhere. Ignorance and badly-understood religion among the lower classes; doubt or unbelief among the upper classes. In a word the evils of barbarism and of great civilization combined together. This leads me more and more to think that once religious beliefs are shaken among a people, one cannot hesitate, and that one must at all costs push them towards education. For if a skeptical and enlightened people presents a sad sight, there is nothing more frightful than the sight presented by a nation simultaneously ignorant, rude and unbelieving.

But I am beginning to get tired of writing. Adieu. Respond quickly. Your letters are always a real pleasure for me; here still more than elsewhere. Furthermore, I am eager to know what the situation is with the marriage. I embrace you with all my heart. Marie sends you a thousand greetings. We often speak together about you. I wish you could hear us.

5d   To Eugène Stoffels,[4] on Revolution and Order

Tocqueville, October 5, 1836

I found your letter of August 18th on passing through Geneva . . . Nothing you tell me makes me change my mind, because I agree with it all. It is obvious that we are fighting each other in the dark without seeing each other clearly. I was rather heated in the reasoning of my discussions with you, and you took that for the sign that I was impetuously carried away by my own ideas toward immediate action: nothing of the kind is true. You represent to me with good reason that revolutions are great evils and rarely serve in the education of a people, that a prolonged agitation is indeed regrettable and that respect for law arises only from stability of the laws.

. . .

All things that I believe deeply. I do not think that in France there is a man who is less revolutionary than I, nor one who has a more profound hatred for what is called the revolutionary spirit (a spirit which, parenthetically, is very easily combined with the love of an absolute government). What am I then? And what do I want? Let us distinguish, in order to understand each other better, between the end and the means. What is the end? What I want is not a republic, but a hereditary monarchy. I would even prefer it to be legitimate rather than elected like the one we have, because it would be stronger, especially externally. What I want is a central government energetic in its own sphere of action. Energy from the central government is even more

---

4   A friend from the years in the lycée at Metz.

necessary among a democratic people in whom the social force is more diffused than in an aristocracy. Besides our situation in Europe lays down an imperative law for us in what should be a thing of choice. But I wish that this central power had a clearly delineated sphere, that it were involved with what is a necessary part of its functions and not with everything in general, and that it were forever subordinated, in its tendency, to public opinion and to the legislative power that represents this public opinion. I believe that the central power can be invested with very great prerogatives, can be energetic and powerful in its sphere, and that at the same time provincial liberties can be well developed. I think that a government of this kind can exist, and that at the same time the majority of the nation itself can be involved with its own affairs, that political life can be spread almost everywhere, the direct or indirect exercise of political rights can be quite extensive. I wish that the general principles of government were liberal, that the largest possible part were left to the action of individuals, to personal initiative. I believe that all these things are compatible; even more, I am profoundly convinced that there will never be order and tranquility except when they are successfully combined.

As for the means: with all those who admit that we must make our way gradually toward this goal, I am very much in accord. I am the first to admit that it is necessary to proceed slowly, with precaution, with legality. My conviction is that our current institutions are sufficient for reaching the result I have in view. Far, then, from wanting people to violate the laws, I profess an almost superstitious respect for the laws. But I wish that the laws would tend little and gradually toward the goal I have just indicated, instead of making powerless and dangerous efforts to turn back. I wish that the government would itself prepare mores and practices so that people would do without it in many cases in which its intervention is still necessary or invoked without necessity. I wish that citizens were introduced into public life to the extent that they are believed capable of being useful in it, instead of seeking to keep them away from it at all costs. I wish finally that people knew where they wanted to go, and that they advanced toward it prudently instead of proceeding aimlessly as they have been doing almost constantly for twenty years. What else will I tell you, my dear friend? One could speak all day on the text without doing anything else but enlarging upon it. You must understand my thought without my having to dilute it or to explain it by a thousand examples.

. . .

In short, I conceive clearly the ideal of a government that is not at all revolutionary or agitated beyond measure, and one which I believe possible to give to our country. But on the other hand, I understand as well as anyone that such a government (which is moreover only the extension of the one we have), in order to become established, requires mores, habits, laws that do not yet exist, and which can only be introduced slowly and with great precautions.

5e   To Henry Reeve,[5] on the Parts and the Whole

Paris, February 3, 1840

My dear friend, I am disheartened and humiliated by my behavior towards your friend Mr. Chorley.[6] He must think I am a boor. He has come to my house twice and written me once. I did not answer his letter and, when I went to the Canterbury hotel yesterday around 4 p.m, he had just left to take the stagecoach. Would you please express my apologies to him and make sure that he accepts them? I hope he will not keep the bad opinion of me that he has surely acquired during this trip, and that he will give me the opportunity to prove to him that, although a democrat, I am no hick. The truth is that I am so overworked with all sorts of tasks that I am rude with everybody.

I have been amused by your difficulties with regard to general ideas. I am sure that, whatever you say, you will very easily solve the problems you mention.[7] But you are basically wrong on the issue. I think that the realists are mistaken. Above all, I am sure that the political consequences of their philosophy, dangerous in all periods, are especially pernicious in ours. You can be certain that the great danger of democratic ages is the destruction or excessive weakening of *the parts* of society against the *whole*. Everything which nowadays strengthens the idea of the individual is healthy. Everything which gives the species a life of its own and aggrandizes the concept of the genre is dangerous. Our contemporaries are naturally inclined to go in that direction. The realists' doctrine, when used in politics, leads to all the abuses of Democracy. It facilitates despotism, centralization, contempt for particular rights, the doctrine of necessity. It favors all the institutions and all the doctrines which make it possible for society to crush people, which turn the nation into everything, and the citizens into nothing.

This is one of my *central* opinions; many of my ideas converge towards it. I have reached complete conviction on this point, and the main object of my book has been to convey this conviction to the reader.

Adieu, with my most sincere friendship.

---

5   Tocqueville's English translator.
6   Henry Fothergill Chorley, with whom Reeve shared an apartment in 1838.
7   Although volume two of *Democracy* appears in France only in April 1840, Reeve is already translating it from the page proofs.

5f   To Pierre-Paul Royer-Collard,[8] on Life in Politics

Tocqueville, September 27, 1841

You indicated, Monsieur, that you wanted some news from me. I will be careful not to let this chance to write you escape, and, since you permit it, I will in fact start by telling you about myself. My health has recovered, without being completely restored. Mental work always tires me, although I hardly devote myself to it, and I fear that I will ultimately lose the habit of mental work and acquire the habit of idle musing, that is to say *touching* subjects without embracing them. It seems to me that I used to be capable of more penetrating and more sustained attention. I imagine that this energetic mental gait will return with my physical strength.

. . .

When I attentively consider our miserable political world and those who compose it, I do not see where I will find my place. To want to form a government or an opposition apart from both M. Thiers and M. Guizot seems to me an impossibility of the first order, for a thousand reasons that are either general or particular to those two men. Those who attempt it seem to me to give themselves over to a fruitless endeavor. There is today no power in parliament except in joining these two men or at least in using one of them. Now, I do not want to, nor can I, join with the one any more than with the other. Both are fundamentally antipathetical to my way of feeling and thinking. I despise them. Apart from them, however, there is nothing that can bring about anything noteworthy in our country's affairs; there is no action. And what is politics without action? To live in a public assembly and not to work effectively for public concerns, not to act and not to join with those who alone have the power to act, is that not manifestly absurd? Is that not to miss the principal character of what one has undertaken to do and what one claims to be doing? Does it not in the end amount to transferring one kind of life into another, theoretical observation into the life of action, to the great detriment of both? That is, Monsieur, what I say sorrowfully to myself when I am not in the Chamber and with impatience and irritation when the session is open. I go around hitting myself in turn against these two obstacles: what is painful and almost untenable in isolation and inaction in a political assembly induces me to try something, and before long the impossibility of my acting in common with these men who alone can make action

8   A leader of the "Doctrinaires," who had reconciled the principles of 1789 with the legitimacy of the monarchy, and influential statesman of the Bourbon restauration.

effective throws me back into immobility and nails me to my seat. These tugs in contrary directions fatigue and exhaust me, even more than would energetic and continuous action. I compare myself to a wheel that goes around very quickly, but which, having missed its gear, does nothing and is useful for nothing. It seems to me, however, that in other times and with other men, I could have done better. But will the times improve?

I feel an almost invincible repugnance to associating myself in a permanent manner with any of the political men of our times and, among all the parties that divide our country, I do not see a single one to which I would want to be tied. I do not find in any of them, I do not say *everything* that I would want to see in political associates, but even the principal things for which I would willingly give up the lesser (because I know that one can only join at this price). Some seem to me to have an exaggerated, pusillanimous and soft yearning for peace, and their love of order is most often only fear. The others mix with their national pride and their taste for liberty (two things I value highly in themselves) crass and anarchistic passions that repel me. The *liberal but not revolutionary* party, which alone suits me, does not exist, and certainly it is not given to me to create it. So I am almost alone and it only remains to me to express my individual opinion as well as possible on the events and on the laws as they are presented, without having any hope of modifying them. That is an honorable role, but sterile. Often I instinctively revolt against it, because my nature is to be active and, I must admit, ambitious. I would like power if it could be honorably acquired and kept.

I will stop here.

. . .

PS My wife wishes to be expressly and particularly remembered to you. Since I have made one postscript for her, I want to add one for me. My inkwell has just fallen and made spots on my paper, for which I ask your pardon as well as for the numerous erasures that this letter contains.

6

Volume Two of *Democracy in America*, 1840

6a   Author's Preface to the Second Part

The Americans live in a democratic state of society, which has naturally tended to give them certain laws and a certain political character. This same state of society has, moreover, created among them a multitude of feelings and opinions which were unknown among the older aristocratic communities of Europe: it has destroyed or modified all the relations which before existed, and established others of a new kind. The appearance of civil society has been no less affected by these changes than the face of the political world. The former subject has been treated in the work on American democracy, which I published five years ago; to examine the latter is the object of the present book; but these two parts complete each other, and form one work.

I must at once warn the reader against an error which would be extremely prejudicial to me. When he finds that I attribute so many different consequences to the principle of equality, he may thence infer that I consider that principle to be the sole cause of all that takes place in the present age: but this would be to impute to me a very narrow view. A multitude of opinions, feelings, and propensities are now in existence, which owe their origin to circumstances unconnected with or even contrary to the principle of equality. Thus if I were to select the United States as an example, I could easily prove that the nature of the country, the origin of its inhabitants, the religion of its founders, their acquired knowledge, and their former habits, have exercised, and still exercise, independently of democracy, a vast influence upon the thoughts and feelings of that people. Different causes, but no less distinct from the circumstance of the equality of conditions, might be traced in Europe, and would explain a great portion of the occurrences taking place amongst us.

I acknowledge the existence of all these different causes, and their power, but my subject does not lead me to speak of them. I have not undertaken to unfold the reason of all our inclinations and all our ideas; I have wanted only to make clear the degree to which equality has altered both of them.

One might be astonished that, while being firmly of the opinion that the democratic revolution that we are witnessing is an irresistible fact against which it would be neither wise nor desirable to struggle, I have often, in this book, severely criticized the democratic societies that this revolution has created.

I respond simply that it is because I am not an adversary of democracy that I wanted to be honest about it.

Men will not accept truth at the hands of their enemies, and truth is seldom offered them by their friends; for this reason I have spoken it. I was persuaded that many would take it upon themselves to announce the new blessings which the principle of equality promises to mankind, but that few would dare to point out from afar the dangers with which it threatens them. It is therefore principally toward these perils that I direct my regard and, believing that I had described them clearly, I had not the timidity to hush them up.

I trust that my readers will find in this Second Part that impartiality which seems to have been remarked in the former work. Placed as I am in the midst of the conflicting opinions between which we are divided, I have tried to suppress within me for a time the favorable sympathies or the adverse emotions with which each of them inspires me. If those who read this book can find a single sentence intended to flatter any of the great parties which have agitated my country, or any of those petty factions which now harass and weaken it, let such readers raise their voices to accuse me.

The subject I have sought to embrace is immense, for it includes the greater part of the feelings and opinions to which the new state of society has given birth. Such a subject is doubtless beyond my strength, and in treating it I have not succeeded in satisfying myself. But, if I have not been able to reach the goal which I had in view, my readers will at least do me the justice to acknowledge that I have conceived and followed up my undertaking in a spirit not unworthy of success.

March, 1840

6b   Part I: "Influence of Democracy on the Action of Intellect in the United States"

6b1   Chapter 1: "Philosophical Method of the Americans"

I think that in no country in the civilized world is less attention paid to philosophy than in the United States. The Americans have no philosophical school of their own, and they care very little about all those that divide Europe; they don't even know their names.

Yet it is easy to perceive that almost all the inhabitants of the United States use their minds in the same manner, and direct them according to the same rules; that is to say, without ever having taken the trouble to define the rules, they have a philosophical method common to the whole people.

To evade the bondage of system and habit, of family maxims, class opinions, and, in some degree, of national prejudices; to accept tradition only as a means of information, and existing facts only as a lesson to be used in doing otherwise and doing better; to seek the reason of things for oneself and in oneself alone; to strive for results without being bound to means, and to strike through the form to the substance – such are the principal characteristics of what I shall call the philosophical method of the Americans. But if I go further and seek among these characteristics the principal one, which includes almost all the rest, I discover that in most of the operations of the mind each American appeals only to the individual effort of his own understanding.

America is therefore one of the countries where the precepts of Descartes are least studied and are best applied. Nor is this surprising. The Americans do not read the works of Descartes, because their social condition deters them from speculative studies; but they follow his maxims, because this same social condition naturally disposes their minds to adopt them.

In the midst of the continual movement that agitates a democratic community, the tie that unites one generation to another is relaxed or broken; every man there readily loses all trace of the ideas of his forefathers or takes no care about them. Men living in this state of society cannot derive their belief from the opinions of the class to which they belong; for, so to speak, there are no longer any classes, or those which still exist are composed of such mobile elements that the body can never exercise any real control over its members.

As to the influence which the intellect of one man may have on that of another, it must necessarily be very limited in a country where the citizens, placed on an equal footing, are all closely seen by one another; and where, as no signs of incontestable greatness or superiority are perceived in any one of them, they are constantly brought back to their own reason as the most obvious and proximate source of truth. It is not only confidence in this or that man which is destroyed, but the disposition to trust the authority of any man whatsoever. Everyone shuts himself up tightly within himself and insists upon judging the world from there.

Americans' habit of setting their standard of judgment for themselves leads their minds to other habits. As they perceive that they succeed in resolving without assistance all the little difficulties which their practical life presents, they readily conclude that everything in the world may be explained, and that nothing in it transcends the limits of the understanding. Thus they fall to denying what they cannot comprehend; which leaves them but little faith for whatever is extraordinary and an almost insurmountable distaste for whatever is supernatural. As it is on their own testimony that they are accustomed to rely, they like to discern the object which engages their attention with extreme clearness; they therefore strip off as much as possible all that covers it; they rid themselves of whatever separates them from it, they remove whatever conceals it from sight, in order to view it more closely and in broad daylight. This disposition of mind soon leads them to condemn forms, which they regard as useless and inconvenient veils placed between them and the truth.

The Americans, then, have found no need of drawing philosophical method out of books; they have found it in themselves. The same thing may be remarked in what has taken place in Europe. This same method has only been established and made popular in Europe in proportion as the condition of society has become more equal and men have grown more like one another. Let us consider for a moment the course of history.

In the sixteenth century the reformers subject some of the dogmas of the ancient faith to the scrutiny of private judgment; but they continue to exclude from discussion all the others. In the seventeenth century Bacon in the natural sciences and Descartes in philosophy proper abolish received formulas, destroy the empire of tradition, and overthrow the authority of the schools. The philosophers of the eighteenth century, generalizing at length on the same principle, undertake to submit to the private judgment of each man all the objects of his belief.

Who does not see that Luther, Descartes, and Voltaire employed the same method, and that they differed only in the greater or less use which they professed should be made of it? Why did the reformers confine themselves so strictly within the circle of religious ideas? Why did Descartes, choosing to apply his method only to certain matters, though he had made it fit to be applied to all, declare that men might judge for themselves in matters philosophical, but not in matters political? How did it happen that in the eighteenth century those general applications were all at once drawn from this same method, which Descartes and his predecessors either had not perceived or had rejected? To what, lastly, is the fact to be attributed that at this period the method we are speaking of suddenly emerged from the schools, to penetrate into society and become the common standard of intelligence; and that after it had become popular among the French, it was openly adopted or secretly followed by all the nations of Europe?

The philosophical method here designated may have been born in the sixteenth century; it may have been more accurately defined and more extensively applied in the seventeenth; but neither in the one nor in the other could it be commonly adopted. Political laws, the condition of society, and the habits of mind that are derived from these causes were as yet opposed to it. It was discovered at a time when men were beginning to become equal and to resemble each other. It could be generally followed only in ages when conditions had finally become nearly equal and men nearly alike.

The philosophical method of the eighteenth century, then, is not only French, but democratic; and this explains why it was so readily admitted throughout Europe, where it has contributed so powerfully to change the face of society. It is not because the French have changed their former opinions and altered their former manners that they have convulsed the world, but because they were the first to elaborate and shed light on a philosophical method with which one could easily attack all that was old and open a path to all that was new.

If it be asked why at the present day this same method is more rigorously followed and more frequently applied by the French than by the Americans, although the principle of equality is no less complete and of more ancient date among the latter people, the fact may be attributed to two circumstances, which it is first essential to have clearly understood.

It must never be forgotten that religion gave birth to Anglo-American society. In the United States, religion is therefore mingled with all the nation's habits and all the feelings of patriotism, whence it derives a peculiar force. To this reason another of no less force may be added: in America religion has, as it were, laid down its own limits. The religious order has remained entirely distinct from the political order, in such a manner that one could easily modify well-established laws without changing well-established beliefs. Christianity has therefore retained a strong hold on the public mind in America; and I would more particularly remark that it reigns not only as a philosophical doctrine that has been adopted upon inquiry, but as a religion that is believed without discussion. In the United States, Christian sects are infinitely diversified and perpetually modified; but Christianity itself is an established and irresistible fact, which no one undertakes either to attack or defend. The

Americans, having admitted the principal doctrines of the Christian religion without inquiry, are obliged to accept in like manner a great number of moral truths originating in it and connected with it. This restricts the power of individual analysis within narrow limits; it excludes some of the most important human opinions.

The second circumstance to which I have alluded is that the social condition and the Constitution of the Americans are democratic, but they have not had a democratic revolution. They arrived on the soil they occupy in nearly the condition in which we see them at the present day; and this is of considerable importance.

There are no revolutions that do not shake existing belief, enervate authority, and throw doubts on commonly received ideas. Every revolution has more or less the effect of releasing men to their own conduct and of opening before the mind of each of them an almost limitless perspective. When equality of conditions succeeds a protracted conflict between the different classes of which the old society was composed, envy, hatred, and uncharitableness, pride and exaggerated self-confidence seize upon the human heart, and plant their sway in it for a time. This, independently of equality itself, tends powerfully to divide men, to lead them to mistrust one another's judgement, and to seek the light of truth nowhere but in themselves. Everyone then attempts to be his own sufficient guide and makes it his boast to form his own opinions on all subjects. Men are no longer bound together by ideas, but by interests; and it would seem as if human opinions were reduced to a sort of intellectual dust, scattered on every side, unable to collect, unable to cohere.

Thus, the independence of mind inherent in equality is never so great and never appears so excessive as during the hard work of its establishment and during the initial period of its spread. That sort of intellectual freedom which equality may give ought, therefore, to be very carefully distinguished from the anarchy which revolution brings. Each of these two things must be separately considered in order not to conceive exaggerated hopes or fears of the future.

I believe that the men who will live under the new forms of society will make frequent use of their private judgment, but I am far from thinking that they will often abuse it. This is attributable to a cause which is more generally applicable to democratic countries, and which, in the long run, must restrain, within fixed and sometimes narrow limits, individual freedom of thought. I shall proceed to point out this cause in the next chapter.

6b7   Chapter 7: "What Causes Democratic Nations to Incline Towards Pantheism"

I shall show hereafter how the preponderant taste of a democratic people for very general ideas manifests itself in politics, but I wish to point out at present its principal effect on philosophy.

It cannot be denied that pantheism has made great progress in our age. The writings of part of Europe bear visible marks of it: the Germans introduce it into philosophy, and the French into literature. Most of the works of imagination published in France contain some opinions or some tinge caught from pantheistic doctrines or they disclose some tendency to such doctrines in their authors. This appears to me not to proceed only from an accidental, but from a permanent cause.

When the conditions of society are becoming more equal and each individual man becomes more like all the rest, more weak and insignificant, a habit grows up of ceasing to notice the citizens and considering only the people, of overlooking individuals to think only of their kind. At such times the human mind seeks to embrace a multitude of different objects at once, and it constantly strives to connect a variety of consequences with a single cause. The idea of unity so possesses man and is sought by him so generally that if he thinks he has found it, he readily yields himself to repose in that belief. Not only does he discover that there is nothing in the world but a creation and a Creator, but he is bothered by this primary division of things and seeks to expand and simplify his conception by including God and the universe in one great whole.

If there is a philosophical system which teaches that all things material and immaterial, visible and invisible, which the world contains are to be considered only as the several parts of an immense Being, who alone remains eternal amidst the continual change and ceaseless transformation of all that constitutes him, we may readily infer that such a system, although it destroys the individuality of man, or rather because it destroys that individuality, will have secret charms for men living in democracies. All their habits of thought prepare them to conceive it and predispose them to adopt it. It naturally attracts and fixes their imagination; it fosters the pride while it fosters slothful thinking.

Among the different systems by whose aid philosophy endeavors to explain the universe I believe pantheism to be one of those most fitted to seduce the human mind in democratic times. Against it all who abide in their attachment to the true greatness of man should combine and struggle.

6b8   Chapter 8: "How Equality Suggests to the Americans the Idea of the Indefinite Perfectibility of Man"

Equality suggests to the human mind several ideas that would not have originated from any other source, and it modifies almost all those previously entertained. I take as an example the idea of human perfectibility, because it is one of the principal notions that the intellect can conceive and because it constitutes in itself a great philosophical theory, which is everywhere to be traced by its consequences in the conduct of human affairs.

Although man has many points of resemblance with the brutes, one trait is peculiar to himself: he improves; they are incapable of improvement. Mankind could not fail to discover this difference from the beginning. The idea of perfectibility is therefore as old as the world; equality did not give birth to it, but has imparted to it a new character.

When the citizens of a community are classed according to rank, profession, or birth and when all men are forced to follow the career which chance has opened before them, each person believes he has perceived the farthest boundaries of human power lying close by, and no one seeks any longer to resist what is felt to be an inevitable destiny. Not, indeed, that an aristocratic people absolutely deny man's faculty of self-improvement, but they do not hold it to be indefinite; they can conceive improvement, but not change: they imagine that the future condition of society may be better, but not essentially different; and, while they admit that humanity has made progress and may still have some to make, they assign to it beforehand certain impassable limits.

Thus they do not presume that they have arrived at the supreme good or at absolute truth (what people or what man was ever wild enough to imagine it?), but they cherish an opinion that they have pretty nearly reached that degree of greatness and knowledge which our imperfect nature admits of; and as nothing is stirring around them, they are willing to fancy that everything is in its fit place. Then it is that the legislator appears to lay down eternal laws; that kings and nations will raise none but imperishable monuments; and that the present generation undertakes to spare generations to come the trouble of regulating their destinies.

In proportion as castes disappear and the classes of society draw together, as manners, customs, and laws vary, because of the tumultuous intercourse of men, as new facts arise, as new truths are brought to light, as ancient opinions are dissipated and others take their place, the image of an ideal but always fugitive perfection presents itself to the human mind. Continual changes are then every instant occurring under the observation of every man; the position of some is rendered worse, and he learns but too well that no people and no individual, however enlightened they may be, can lay claim to infallibility; the condition of others is improved, whence he infers that man is endowed with an indefinite faculty for improvement. His reverses teach him that none have discovered absolute good; his success stimulates him to the never ending pursuit of it. Thus, forever seeking, forever falling to rise again, often disappointed, but not discouraged, he tends unceasingly towards that unmeasured greatness so indistinctly visible at the end of the long track which humanity has yet to tread.

It can hardly be believed how many facts naturally flow from the philosophical theory of the indefinite perfectibility of man or how strong an influence it exercises even on those who, living entirely for the purposes of action and not thought, seem to conform their actions to it without knowing anything about it. I accost an American sailor and inquire why the ships of his country are built so as to last for only a short time, he answers without hesitation that the art of navigation is every day making such rapid progress that the finest vessel would become almost useless if it lasted beyond a few years. In these words, which fell accidentally, and on a particular subject, from an uninstructed man, I recognize the general and systematic idea upon which a great people direct all their concerns. Aristocratic nations are naturally too inclined to narrow the scope of human perfectibility; democratic nations, to expand it beyond reason.

6b20   Chapter 20: "Some Characteristics of Historians in Democratic Times"

Historians who write in aristocratic ages are inclined to refer all occurrences to the particular will and character of certain individuals; and they are apt to attribute the most important revolutions to slight accidents. They trace out the smallest causes with sagacity, and frequently leave the greatest unperceived.

Historians who live in democratic ages exhibit precisely opposite characteristics. Most of them attribute hardly any influence to the individual over the destiny of the race, or to citizens over the fate of a people; but, on the other hand, they assign great general causes to all petty incidents. These contrary tendencies explain each other.

When the historian of aristocratic ages surveys the theater of the world, he at once perceives a very small number of prominent actors who manage the whole piece. These great personages, who occupy the front of the stage, arrest attention and fix it on themselves; and while the historian is bent on penetrating the secret motives which make these persons speak and act, the others escape his memory. The importance of the things that some men are seen to do gives him an exaggerated estimate of the influence that one man may possess, and naturally leads him to think that in order to explain the impulses of the multitude, it is necessary to refer them to the particular influence of some one individual.

When, on the contrary, all the citizens are independent of one another, and each of them is individually weak, no one is seen to exert a great or still less a lasting power over the community. At first sight individuals appear to be absolutely devoid of any influence over it, and society would seem to advance solely by the free and voluntary action of all the men who compose it. This naturally prompts the mind to search for that general reason which operates upon so many men's faculties at once and turns them simultaneously in the same direction.

I am very well convinced that even among democratic nations the genius, the vices, or the virtues of certain individuals retard or accelerate the natural current of a people's history; but causes of this secondary and accidental nature are infinitely more various, more concealed, more complex, less powerful, and consequently less easy to trace in periods of equality than in ages of aristocracy, when the task of the historian is simply to detach from the mass of general events the particular influence of one man or of a few men. In the former case the historian is soon wearied by the toil, his mind loses itself in this labyrinth, and, in his inability clearly to discern or conspicuously to point out the influence of individuals, he denies that they have any. He prefers talking about the characteristics of race, the physical conformation of the country, or the genius of civilization, and thus abridges his own labors and satisfies his reader better at less cost.

M. de Lafayette says somewhere in his Memoirs that the exaggerated system of general causes affords surprising consolations to second-rate statesmen. I will add that its effects are not less consoling to second-rate historians; it can always furnish a few mighty reasons to extricate them from the most difficult part of their work, and it indulges the indolence or incapacity of their minds while it confers upon them the honors of deep thinking.

For myself, I am of the opinion that, at all times, one great portion of the events of this world are attributable to very general facts and another to special influences. These two kinds of cause are always in operation; only their proportion varies. General facts serve to explain more things in democratic than in aristocratic ages, and fewer things are then assignable to individual influences. During periods of aristocracy the reverse takes place: special influences are stronger, general causes weaker; unless, indeed, we consider as a general cause the fact itself of the inequality of condition, which allows some individuals to baffle the natural tendencies of all the rest.

The historians who seek to describe what occurs in democratic societies are right, therefore, in assigning much to general causes and in devoting their chief attention to discover them; but they are wrong in wholly denying the special influence of individuals because they cannot easily trace or follow it. Historians who live in democratic ages not only are prone to assign a great cause to every incident, but they are also given to connecting incidents together so as to deduce a system from them. In aristocratic ages, as the attention of historians is constantly drawn to individuals, the connection of events escapes them; or rather they do not believe in any such connection. To them, the thread of history seems constantly to be broken by the course of one man's life. In democratic ages, on the contrary, as the historian sees much more of actions than of actors, he may easily establish some kind of sequence and methodical order among the former.

Ancient literature, which is so rich in fine historical compositions, does not contain a single great historical system, while the poorest of modern literatures abound with them. It would appear that the ancient historians did not make sufficient use of those general theories which our historical writers are ever ready to carry to excess.

Those who write in democratic ages have another more dangerous tendency. When the traces of individual action upon nations are lost, it often happens that you see the world move without the impelling force being evident. As it becomes extremely difficult to discern and analyze the reasons that, acting separately on the will of each member of the community, concur in the end to produce movement in the whole mass, men are led to believe that this movement is involuntary and that societies unconsciously obey some superior force ruling over them. But even when the general fact that governs the private volition of all individuals is supposed to be discovered upon the earth, the principle of human free-will is not made certain. A cause sufficiently extensive to affect millions of men at once and sufficiently strong to bend them all together in the same direction may well seem irresistible, having seen that mankind do yield to it, the mind is close to the inference that mankind cannot resist it.

Historians who live in democratic ages, then, not only deny that the few have any power of acting upon the destiny of a people, but deprive the people themselves of the power of modifying their own condition, and they subject them either to an inflexible Providence or to some blind necessity. According to them, each nation is indissolubly bound by its position, its origin, its antecedents, and its character to a certain lot that no efforts can ever change. They involve one generation with another, and thus, going back from age to age, and from necessity to necessity, back to the origin of the world, they forge a tight and enormous chain, which girds and binds the human race. To their minds it is not enough to show what events have occurred: they wish to show that events could not have occurred otherwise. They take a nation arrived at a certain stage of its history and affirm that it could not but follow the track that brought it there. It is easier to make such an assertion than to show how the nation might have adopted a better course.

In reading the historians of aristocratic ages, and especially those of antiquity, it would seem that, to be master of his lot and to govern his fellow creatures, man requires only to be master of himself. In perusing the historical volumes which our age has produced, it would seem that man is utterly powerless over himself and over all around him. The historians of antiquity taught how to command; those of our time teach only how to obey; in their writings the author often appears great, but humanity is always tiny.

If this doctrine of necessity, which is so attractive to those who write history in democratic ages, passes from authors to their readers till it infects the whole mass of the community and gets possession of the public mind, it will soon paralyze the activity of modern society and reduce Christians to the level of the Turks.

Moreover, I would observe that such doctrines are peculiarly dangerous at the period at which we have arrived. Our contemporaries are only too prone to doubt human free will, because each of them feels himself confined on every side by his own weakness; but they are still willing to acknowledge the strength and independence of men united in society. This principle must not be lost sight of, for it is a question of uplifting men's souls, not of completing their prostration.

6c   Part II: "Influence of Democracy on the Feelings of the Americans"

6c1   Chapter 1: "Why Democratic Nations Show a More Ardent and Enduring Love of Equality Than of Liberty"

The first and most intense passion that is produced by equality of condition is, I need hardly say, the love of that equality. My readers will therefore not be surprised that I speak of this feeling before all others.

Everybody has remarked that in our time, and especially in France, this passion for equality is gaining ground daily in the human heart. It has been said a hundred times that our contemporaries are far more ardently and tenaciously attached to equality than to freedom; but as I do not find that the causes of the fact have been sufficiently analyzed, I shall try to point them out.

It is possible to imagine an extreme point at which freedom and equality would meet and blend. Let us suppose that all the people take a part in the government, and that each one of them has an equal right to take a part in it. As no one is different from his fellows, none can exercise a tyrannical power; men will be perfectly free because they are all entirely equal; and they will all be perfectly equal because they are entirely free. To this ideal state democratic nations tend. This is the most perfect form that equality can take on earth, but there are a thousand others that, without being so perfect, can be scarcely less precious to its peoples.

The principle of equality may be established in civil society without prevailing in the political world. There may be equal rights of indulging in the same pleasures, of entering the same professions, of frequenting the same places; in a word, of living in the same manner and seeking wealth by the same means, although all men do not take an equal share in the government. A kind of equality may even be established in the political world though there should be no political freedom there. A man may be the equal of all his countrymen save one, who is the master of all without distinction and who selects equally from among them all the agents of his power. Several other combinations might be easily imagined by which very great equality would be united to institutions more or less free or even to institutions wholly without freedom.

Although men cannot become absolutely equal unless they are entirely free, and consequently equality, pushed to its furthest extent, may be confused with freedom, yet there is good reason for distinguishing the one from the other. The taste which men have for freedom and that which they feel for equality are, in fact, two different things; and I am not afraid to add that among democratic nations they are two disparate things.

Upon close inspection it will be seen that there is in every age some peculiar and preponderant fact with which all others are connected; this fact almost always gives birth to some pregnant idea or some ruling passion, which attracts to itself and bears away in its course all the feelings and opinions of the time; it is like a great stream towards which each of the neighboring rivulets seems to flow.

Freedom has appeared in the world at different times and under various forms; it has not been exclusively bound to any social condition, and it is not confined to democracies. Freedom cannot, therefore, form the distinguishing characteristic of democratic ages. The peculiar and preponderant fact that marks those ages as its own is the equality of conditions; the ruling passion of men in those periods is the love of this equality. Do not ask what singular charm the men of democratic ages find in being equal, or what special reasons they may have for clinging so tenaciously to equality rather than to the other advantages that society holds out to them: equality is the distinguishing characteristic of the age they live in; that of itself is enough to explain that they prefer it to all the rest.

But independently of this reason there are several others which will at all times habitually lead men to prefer equality to freedom. If a people could ever succeed in destroying, or even in diminishing, the equality that prevails in its own body, they could do so only by long and laborious efforts. Their social condition must be modified, their laws abolished, their opinions superseded, their habits changed, their manners corrupted. But political liberty is more easily lost; to neglect to hold it fast is to allow it to escape. Therefore not only do men cling to equality because it is dear to them; they also adhere to it because they think it will last forever.

That political freedom in its excesses may compromise the tranquillity, the property, the lives of individuals is obvious even to narrow and unthinking minds. On the contrary, none but attentive and clear-sighted men perceive the perils with which equality threatens us, and they commonly avoid pointing them out. They know that the calamities they apprehend are remote and flatter themselves that they will fall only upon future generations, for which the present generation takes but little thought. The evils that freedom sometimes brings with it are immediate; they are apparent to all, and all are more or less affected by them. The evils that extreme equality may produce are slowly disclosed; they creep gradually into the social frame; they are seen only at intervals; and at the moment at which they become most violent, habit already causes them to be no longer felt.

The advantages that freedom brings are shown only by the lapse of time, and it is always easy to mistake the cause in which they originate. The advantages of equality are immediate, and they may always be traced from their source.

Political freedom bestows exalted pleasures from time to time upon a certain number of citizens. Equality every day confers a number of small enjoyments on every man. The charms of equality are felt every instant and are within the reach of all; the noblest hearts are not insensible to them, and the most vulgar souls exult in them. The passion that equality creates must therefore be at once strong and general. Men cannot enjoy political liberty unpurchased by some sacrifices, and they never obtain it without great exertions. But the pleasures of equality are self-proffered; each of the petty incidents of life seems to occasion them, and in order to taste them, nothing is required but to live.

Democratic nations are at all times fond of equality, but there are certain epochs at which the passion they entertain for it swells to the height of fury. This occurs at the moment when the old social system, long menaced, is overthrown after a severe internal struggle, and the barriers of rank are at length thrown down. At such times men pounce upon equality as their booty, and they cling to it as to some precious treasure which they fear to lose. The passion for equality penetrates on every side into men's hearts, expands there, and fills them entirely. Tell them not that by this blind surrender of themselves to an exclusive passion they risk their dearest interests; they are deaf. Show them not freedom escaping from their grasp while they are looking another way; they are blind, or rather they can discern but one object to be desired in the universe.

What I have said is applicable to all democratic nations; what I am about to say concerns the French alone. Among most modern nations, and especially among all those of the continent of Europe, the taste and the idea of freedom began to exist and to be developed only at the time when social conditions were tending to equality and as a consequence of that very equality. Absolute kings were the most efficient levelers of ranks among their subjects. Among these nations equality preceded freedom; equality was therefore a fact of some standing when freedom was still a novelty; the one had already created customs, opinions, and laws belonging to it when the other, alone and for the first time, came into actual existence. Thus the latter was still only a matter of opinion and taste while the former had already crept into the people's habits, possessed itself of their manners, and given a particular turn to the smallest actions in their lives. Can it be wondered at that the men of our own time prefer the one to the other?

I think that democratic communities have a natural taste for freedom; left to themselves, they will seek it, cherish it, and view any privation of it with regret. But for equality their passion is ardent, insatiable, incessant, invincible; they call for equality in freedom; and if they cannot obtain that, they still call for equality in slavery. They will endure poverty, servitude, barbarism, but they will not endure aristocracy.

This is true at all times, and especially in our own day. All men and all powers seeking to cope with this irresistible passion will be overthrown and destroyed by it. In our age freedom cannot be established without it, and despotism itself cannot reign without its support.

6c2   Chapter 2: "Of Individualism in Democratic Countries"

I have shown how it is that in ages of equality every man seeks for his opinions within himself; I will now show how it is that in the same ages all his feelings are turned towards himself alone. Individualism is a novel expression, to which a novel idea has given birth. Our fathers were only acquainted with egoism. Egoism is a passionate and exaggerated love of self, which leads a man to connect everything with himself and to prefer himself to everything in the world. Individualism is a mature and calm feeling, which disposes each member of the community to sever himself from the mass of his fellows and to draw apart with his family and his friends, so that after he has thus formed a little circle of his own, he willingly leaves society at large to itself. Egoism originates in blind instinct; individualism proceeds from erroneous judgment more than from depraved feelings; it originates as much in deficiencies of mind as in perversity of heart.

Egoism blights the germ of all virtue; individualism, at first, only saps the virtues of public life; but in the long run it attacks and destroys all others and is at length absorbed in downright egoism. Egoism is a vice as old as the world, which does not belong to one form of society more than to another; individualism is of democratic origin, and it threatens to spread in the same ratio as the equality of condition.

Among aristocratic nations, as families remain for centuries in the same condition, often on the same spot, all generations become, as it were, contemporaneous. A man almost always knows his forefathers and respects them; he thinks he already sees his remote descendants and he loves them. He willingly imposes duties on himself towards the former and the latter, and he will frequently sacrifice his personal gratifications to those who went before and to those who will come after him. Aristocratic institutions, moreover, have the effect of closely binding every man to several of his fellow citizens. As the classes of an aristocratic people are strongly marked and permanent, each of them is regarded by its own members as a sort of lesser country, more tangible and more cherished than the country at large. As in aristocratic communities all the citizens occupy fixed positions, one above another, the result is that each of them always sees a man above himself whose patronage is necessary to him, and below himself another man whose co-operation he may claim. Men living in aristocratic ages are therefore almost always closely tied to things outside their own position, and they are often disposed to forget themselves. It is true that in these ages the notion of human fellowship is faint and that men seldom think of sacrificing themselves for mankind; but they often sacrifice themselves for other men. In democratic times, on the contrary, when the duties of each individual to the race are much more clear, devoted service to any one man becomes more rare; the bond of human affection is extended, but it is relaxed.

Among democratic nations new families are constantly springing up, others are constantly falling away, and all that remain change their condition; the web of time is every instant broken and the track of generations effaced. Those who went before are soon forgotten; of those who will come after, no one has any idea: the interest of man is confined to those in close propinquity to himself. As each class gradually approaches others and mingles with them, its members become undifferentiated and lose their class identity for each other. Aristocracy had made a chain of all the members of the community, from the peasant to the king; democracy breaks that chain and severs every link of it.

As social conditions become more equal, the number of persons increases who, although they are neither rich nor powerful enough to exercise any great influence over their fellows, have nevertheless acquired or retained sufficient education and fortune to satisfy their own wants. They owe nothing to any man, they expect nothing from any man; they acquire the habit of always considering themselves as standing alone, and they are apt to imagine that their whole destiny is in their own hands.

Thus not only does democracy make every man forget his ancestors, but it hides his descendants and separates his contemporaries from him; it throws him back forever upon himself alone and threatens in the end to confine him entirely within the solitude of his own heart.

6c4   Chapter 4: "That the Americans Combat the Effects of Individualism with Free Institutions"

Despotism which by its nature is suspicious, sees in the separation among men the surest guarantee of its continuance, and it usually makes every effort to keep them separate. No vice of the human heart is so acceptable to it as egoism: a despot easily forgives his subjects for not loving him, provided they do not love one another. He does not ask them to assist him in governing the state; it is enough that they do not aspire to govern it themselves. He stigmatizes as turbulent and unruly spirits those who would combine their exertions to promote the prosperity of the community; and, perverting the natural meaning of words, he applauds as good citizens those who have no sympathy for any but themselves.

Thus the vices which despotism produces are precisely those which equality fosters. These two things perniciously complete and assist each other. Equality places men side by side, unconnected by any common tie; despotism raises barriers to keep them asunder; the former predisposes them not to consider their fellow creatures, the latter makes general indifference a sort of public virtue.

Despotism, then, which is at all times dangerous, is more particularly to be feared in democratic ages. It is easy to see that in those same ages men stand most in need of freedom. When the members of a community are forced to attend to public affairs, they are necessarily drawn from the circle of their own interests and snatched at times from self-observation. As soon as a man begins to treat of public affairs, he begins to perceive that he is not so independent of his fellow men as he had at first imagined, and that in order to obtain their support he must often lend them his co-operation.

When the public governs, there is no man who does not feel the value of public goodwill or who does not endeavor to court it by drawing to himself the esteem and affection of those among whom he is to live. Many of the passions which freeze arts and separate them are then obliged to retire to the bottom of the soul and hide there. Pride must be dissembled; disdain dares not break out; egoism fears its own self. Under a free government, as most public offices are elective, the men whose lofty souls and restless desires make private life too confining, feel daily that they cannot do without the people who surround them. Men learn at such times to think of their fellow men from ambitious motives; and they frequently find it, in a way, in their interest to forget themselves.

I may here be met by an objection derived from electioneering, intrigues, the meanness of candidates, and the calumnies of their opponents. These are indeed shameful occasions, and they occur all the more often as elections become more frequent. Such evils are doubtless great, but they are transient; whereas the benefits that attend them remain. The desire of being elected may lead some men for a time to violent hostility; but this same desire leads all men in the long run to support each other; and if it happens that an election accidentally severs two friends, the electoral system brings a multitude of citizens permanently together who would otherwise always have remained unknown to one another. Freedom produces private animosities, but despotism gives birth to general indifference.

The Americans have used freedom to fight the individualism that arises from equality, and they have beaten it. The legislators of America did not believe that in order to cure this malady so natural to democratic society and so deadly, it was enough to extend to the entire nation the opportunity for representation. They thought that, in addition, it was appropriate to give political life to each portion of territory and thus to multiply infinitely the opportunities for citizens to work together and to make them feel every day that they depend on each other.

The plan was a wise one. The general affairs of a country engage the attention only of leading politicians, who assemble from time to time in the same places; and as they often lose sight of each other afterwards, no lasting ties are established between them. But if the object is to have the local affairs of a district conducted by the men who reside there, the same persons are always in contact, and they are, in a way, forced to be acquainted with and to adapt themselves to one another.

It is difficult to draw a man out of his own circle to interest him in the destiny of the state, because he does not clearly understand what influence the destiny of the state can have upon his own lot. But if it is proposed to make a road cross the end of his land, he will see at a glance that there is a connection between this small public affair and his greatest private affairs; and he will discover, without its being shown to him, the close tie that unites private to general interest. Thus far more may be done by entrusting to the citizens the administration of minor affairs than by surrendering to them the control of important ones, towards interesting them in the public welfare and convincing them that they constantly stand in need of one another in order to provide for it. A brilliant achievement may win for you the favor of a people at one stroke; but to earn the love and respect of the population that surrounds you, a long succession of little services rendered and of obscure good deeds, a constant habit of kindness, and an established reputation for disinterestedness will be required. Local freedom, then, which leads a great number of citizens to value the affection of their neighbors and of their kindred, perpetually brings men together and forces them to help one another in spite of the propensities that sever them.

In the United States the wealthier citizens take great care not to stand aloof from the people; on the contrary, they constantly keep on easy terms with the lower classes: they listen to them, they speak to them every day. They know that the rich in democracies always stand in need of the poor, and that in democratic times you attach a poor man to you more by your manner than by benefits conferred. The magnitude of such benefits, which sets off the difference of condition, causes a secret irritation to those who reap advantage from them, but the charm of simplicity of manners is almost irresistible; affability carries men away, and even want of polish is not always displeasing. This truth does not take root at once in the minds of the rich. They generally resist it as long as the democratic revolution lasts, and they do not acknowledge it immediately after that revolution is accomplished. They are very ready to do good to the people, but they still choose to keep them at arm's length; they think that is sufficient, but they are mistaken. They might spend fortunes thus without warming the hearts of the population around them; that population does not ask them for the sacrifice of their money, but of their pride.

It would seem as if every imagination in the United States is stretched to invent means of increasing the wealth and satisfying the wants of the public. The best-informed inhabitants of each district constantly use their information to discover new truths that may augment the general prosperity; and if they have made any such discoveries, they eagerly surrender them to the mass of the people.

When the vices and weaknesses frequently exhibited by those who govern in America are closely examined, the prosperity of the people occasions, but improperly occasions, surprise. Elected magistrates do not make the American democracy flourish; it flourishes because the magistrates are elective.

It would be unjust to suppose that the patriotism and zeal that every American displays for the welfare of his fellow citizens are wholly insincere. Although private interest directs the greater part of human actions in the United States as well as elsewhere, it does not regulate them all. I must say that I have often seen Americans make great and real sacrifices to the public welfare; and I have noticed a hundred instances in which they hardly ever failed to lend faithful support to one another. The free institutions which the inhabitants of the United States possess, and the political rights of which they make so much use, remind every citizen, in a thousand ways, that he lives in society. They every instant impress upon his mind the notion that it is the duty as well as the interest of men to make themselves useful to their fellow creatures; and as he sees no particular ground of animosity to them, since he is never either their master or their slave, his heart readily leans to the side of kindness. Men attend to the interests of the public, first by necessity, afterwards by choice; what was intentional becomes an instinct, and by dint of working for the good of one's fellow citizens, the habit and the taste for serving them are at length acquired.

Many people in France consider equality of conditions as one evil and political freedom as a second. When they are obliged to yield to the former, they strive at least to escape from the latter. But I contend that in order to combat the evils which equality may produce, there is only one effectual remedy: namely, political freedom.

6c5   Chapter 5: "Of the Use Which the Americans Make of Public Associations in Civil Life"

I do not propose to speak of those political associations by the aid of which men endeavor to defend themselves against the despotic action of a majority or against the aggressions of regal power. That subject I have already treated. If each citizen did not learn, in proportion as he individually becomes more feeble and consequently more incapable of preserving his freedom single-handed, to combine with his fellow citizens for the purpose of defending it, it is clear that tyranny would unavoidably increase together with equality.

Only those associations that are formed in civil life without reference to political objects are here referred to. The political associations that exist in the United States are only a single feature in the midst of the immense assemblage of associations in that country. Americans of all ages, all conditions, and all dispositions constantly form associations. They have not only commercial and manufacturing companies, in which all take part, but associations of a thousand other kinds, religious, moral, serious, futile, general or restricted, enormous or tiny. The Americans make associations to give entertainments, to found seminaries, to build inns, to construct churches, to distribute books, to send missionaries to the poles; in this manner they found hospitals, prisons, and schools. If it is proposed to inculcate some truth or to foster some feeling by the encouragement of a great example, they form a society. Wherever at the head of some new undertaking you see the government in France, or a man of rank in England, in the United States you will be sure to find an association.

I met with several kinds of associations in America of which I confess I had no previous notion; and I have often admired the extreme skill with which the inhabitants of the United States succeed in proposing a common object for the exertions of a great many men and in inducing them to pursue it voluntarily.

I have since traveled over England, from which the Americans have taken some of their laws and many of their customs; and it seemed to me that the principle of association was by no means so constantly or adroitly used in that country. The English often perform great things singly, whereas the Americans form associations for the smallest undertakings. It is evident that the former people consider association as a powerful means of action, but the latter seem to regard it as the only means they have of acting.

Thus the most democratic country on the face of the earth is that in which men have, in our time, carried to the highest perfection the art of pursuing in common the object of their common desires and have applied this new science to the greatest number of purposes. Is this the result of accident, or is there in reality any necessary connection between the principle of association and that of equality?

Aristocratic communities always contain, among a multitude of persons who by themselves are powerless, a small number of powerful and wealthy citizens, each of whom can achieve great undertakings single-handed. In aristocratic societies men do not need to combine in order to act, because they are strongly held together. Every wealthy and powerful citizen constitutes the head of a permanent and compulsory association, composed of all those who are dependent upon him or whom he makes subservient to the execution of his designs.

Among democratic nations, on the contrary, all the citizens are independent and feeble; they can do hardly anything by themselves, and none of them can oblige his fellow men to lend him their assistance. They all, therefore, become powerless if they do not learn to help one another voluntarily. If men living in democratic countries had no right and no inclination to associate for political purposes, their independence would be in great jeopardy, but they might long preserve their wealth and their cultivation: whereas if they never acquired the habit of forming associations in ordinary life, civilization itself would be endangered. A people among whom individuals lost the power of achieving great things single-handed, without acquiring the means of producing them by united exertions, would soon relapse into barbarism.

Unhappily, the same social condition that renders associations so necessary to democratic nations renders their formation more difficult among those nations than among all others. When several members of an aristocracy agree to combine, they easily succeed in doing so; as each of them brings great strength to the partnership, the number of its members may be very limited; and when the members of an association are limited in number, they may easily become mutually acquainted, understand each other, and establish fixed regulations. The same opportunities do not occur among democratic nations, where the associated members must always be very numerous for their association to have any power.

I am aware that many of my countrymen are not in the least embarrassed by this difficulty. They contend that the more enfeebled and incompetent the citizens become, the more able and active the government ought to be made in order that society at large may execute what individuals can no longer accomplish. They believe this answers the whole difficulty, but I think they are mistaken.

A government could take the place of some of the largest American associations, and several states, members of the Union, have already attempted it; but what political power could ever carry on the vast multitude of lesser undertakings which the American citizens perform every day, with the assistance of the principle of association? It is easy to foresee that the time is drawing near when man will be less and less able to produce, by himself alone, the commonest necessaries of life.

The task of the governing power will therefore perpetually increase, and its very efforts will extend it every day. The more it stands in the place of associations, the more will individuals, losing the notion of combining together, require its assistance: these are causes and effects that unceasingly create each other. Will the administration of the country ultimately assume the management of all the manufactures which no single citizen is able to carry on? And if a time at length arrives when, in consequence of the extreme subdivision of landed property, the soil is split into an infinite number of parcels, so that it can be cultivated only by companies of tillers, will it be necessary that the head of the government should leave the helm of state to follow the plow? The morals and intelligence of a democratic people would be as much endangered as its business and manufactures if the government ever wholly usurped the place of private companies. Feelings and opinions are recruited, the heart is enlarged, and the human mind is developed only by the reciprocal influence of men upon one another. I have shown that these influences are almost null in democratic countries; they must therefore be artificially created, and this can only be accomplished by associations.

When the members of an aristocratic community adopt a new opinion or conceive a new sentiment, they give it a station, as it were, beside themselves, upon the lofty platform where they stand; and opinions or sentiments so conspicuous to the eyes of the multitude are easily introduced into the minds or hearts of all around. In democratic countries the governing power alone is naturally in a condition to act in this manner, but it is easy to see that its action is always inadequate, and often dangerous. A government can no more be competent to keep alive and to renew the circulation of opinions and feelings among a great people than to manage all the speculations of productive industry. No sooner does a government attempt to go beyond its political sphere and to enter upon this new track than it exercises, even unintentionally, an insupportable tyranny; for a government can only dictate strict rules, the opinions which it favors are rigidly enforced, and it is never easy to discriminate between its advice and its commands. Worse still will be the case if the government really believes itself interested in preventing all circulation of ideas; it will then stand motionless and oppressed by the heaviness of voluntary torpor. Governments, therefore, should not be the only active powers; associations ought, in democratic nations, to stand in lieu of those powerful private individuals whom the equality of conditions has swept away.

As soon as several of the inhabitants of the United States have taken up an opinion or a feeling which they wish to promote in the world, they look out for mutual assistance; and as soon as they have found one another out, they combine. From that moment they are no longer isolated men, but a power seen from afar, whose actions serve for an example and whose language is listened to. The first time I heard in the United States that a hundred thousand men had bound themselves publicly to abstain from spirituous liquors, it appeared to me more like a joke than a serious engagement, and I did not at once see why these temperate citizens could not content themselves with drinking water by their own firesides. I at last understood that these hundred thousand Americans, alarmed by the progress of drunkenness around them, had made up their minds to patronize temperance.

They acted in just the same way as a man of high rank who should dress very plainly in order to inspire the humbler orders with a contempt of luxury. It is probable that if these hundred thousand men had lived in France, each of them would individually have written the government to ask it to oversee the bars throughout the kingdom.

Nothing, in my opinion, is more deserving of our attention than the intellectual and moral associations of America. The political and industrial associations of that country strike us forcibly; but the others elude our observation, or if we discover them, we understand them imperfectly because we have hardly ever seen anything of the kind. It must be acknowledged, however, that they are as necessary to the American people as the former, and perhaps more so. In democratic countries the science of association is the mother of science; the progress of all the rest depends upon the progress it has made.

Among the laws that rule human societies there is one which seems to be more precise and clear than all others. If men are to remain civilized or become so, the art of associating together must grow and improve in the same ratio in which the equality of conditions is increased.

6c6   Chapter 6: "Of the Relation Between Public Associations and the Newspapers"

When men are no longer united among themselves by firm and lasting ties, it is impossible to obtain the co-operation of any great number of them unless you can persuade every man whose help you require that his private interest obliges him to voluntarily unite his exertions to the exertions of all the others. This can be habitually and conveniently effected only by means of a newspaper; nothing but a newspaper can drop the same thought into a thousand minds at the same moment. A newspaper is an adviser that does not require to be sought, but that comes of its own accord and talks to you briefly every day about public affairs, without distracting you from your private business.

Newspapers therefore become more necessary in proportion as men become more equal and individualism more to be feared. To suppose that they only serve to protect freedom would be to diminish their importance: they maintain civilization. I shall not deny that in democratic countries newspapers frequently lead the citizens to launch together into very ill-digested schemes; but if there were no newspapers there would be no common activity. The evil which they produce is therefore much less than that which they cure.

The effect of a newspaper is not only to suggest the same purpose to a great number of persons, but to furnish means for executing together the plans which they may have conceived individually. The principal citizens who inhabit an aristocratic country discern each other from afar; and if they wish to unite their forces, they move towards each other, drawing a multitude of men after them. In democratic countries, on the contrary, it frequently happens that a great number of men who wish or who want to combine cannot accomplish it because as they are very insignificant and lost amid the crowd, they cannot see and do not know where to find one another. A newspaper then takes up the notion or the feeling that had occurred simultaneously, but individually, to each of them. All are then immediately guided towards this beacon; and these wandering minds, which had long sought each other in darkness, at length meet and unite. The newspaper brought them together, and the newspaper is still necessary to keep them united.

In order that an association among a democratic people should have any power, it must be a numerous body. The persons of whom it is composed are therefore scattered over a wide extent, and each of them is detained in the place he lives by the narrowness of his income or by the small unremitting exertions by which he earns it. Means must then be found to converse every day without seeing one another, and to take steps in common without having met. Thus hardly any democratic association can do without newspapers.

Consequently, there is a necessary connection between public associations and newspapers: newspapers make associations, and associations make newspapers; and if it has been correctly suggested that associations will increase in number as the conditions of men become more equal, it is not less certain that the number of newspapers increases in proportion to that of associations. Thus it is in America that we find at the same time the greatest number of associations and of newspapers.

This connection between the number of newspapers and that of associations leads us to the discovery of a further connection between the state of the periodical press and the form of the administration in a country, and shows that the number of newspapers must diminish or increase among a democratic people in proportion as its administration is more or less centralized. For among democratic nations the exercise of local powers cannot be entrusted to the principal members of the community as in aristocracies. Those powers must be either abolished or placed in the hands of very large numbers of men, who then in fact constitute an association permanently established by law for the purpose of administering the affairs of a certain extent of territory; and they require a journal to bring to them every day, in the midst of their own minor concerns, some intelligence of the state of their public affairs. The more numerous local powers are, the greater is the number of men in whom they are vested by law; and as this want is hourly felt, the more profusely do newspapers abound.

The extraordinary subdivision of administrative power has much more to do with the enormous number of American newspapers than the great political freedom of the country and the absolute liberty of the press. If all the inhabitants of the Union had the suffrage, but a suffrage which should extend only to the choice of their legislators in Congress, they would require but few newspapers, because they would have to act together only on very important, but very rare, occasions. But within the great national association lesser associations have been established by law in every county, every city, and indeed in every village, for the purposes of local administration. The laws of the country thus compel every American to co-operate every day of his life with some of his fellow citizens for a common purpose, and each one of them requires a newspaper to inform him what all the others are doing.

I am of the opinion that a democratic people without any national representative assemblies but with a great number of small local powers would have in the end more newspapers than another people governed by a centralized administration and an elective legislature. What best explains to me the enormous circulation of the daily press in the United States is that among the Americans I find the utmost national freedom combined with local freedom of every kind.

There is a prevailing opinion in France and England that the circulation of newspapers would be indefinitely increased by removing the taxes which have been laid upon the press. This is a very exaggerated estimate of the effects of such a reform. Newspapers increase in numbers, not according to their cheapness, but according to the more or less frequent want which a great number of men may feel for intercommunication and combination.

In like manner I should attribute the increasing influence of the daily press to causes more general than those by which it is commonly explained. A newspaper can survive only on the condition of publishing sentiments or principles common to a large number of men. A newspaper, therefore, always represents an association that is composed of its habitual readers. This association may be more or less defined, more or less restricted, more or less numerous.

This leads me to a last reflection, with which I shall conclude this chapter. The more equal the conditions of men become and the less strong men individually are, the more easily they give way to the current of the multitude and the more difficult it is for them to adhere by themselves to an opinion which the multitude discard. A newspaper represents an association; it may be said to address each of its readers in the name of all the others and to exert its influence over them in proportion to their individual weakness. The power of the newspaper press must therefore increase as the social conditions of men become more equal.

6c7   Chapter 7: "Relation of Civil to Political Associations"

There is only one country on the face of the earth where the citizens enjoy unlimited freedom of association for political purposes. This same country is the only one in the world where the citizens have conceived of making the right of association an integral part of civil life and where they have come to procure in this manner all the goods that civilization can offer.

In all the countries where political associations are prohibited, civil associations are rare. It is hardly probable that this is the result of accident, but the inference should rather be that there is a natural and perhaps a necessary connection between these two kinds of associations. A group of men have by chance a common interest in some enterprise; either a commercial undertaking is to be managed, or an industrial project to be completed: they meet, they combine, and thus, by degrees, they become familiar with the principle of association. The greater the multiplicity of small affairs, the more do men, even without knowing it, acquire facility in prosecuting great undertakings in common.

Civil associations, therefore, facilitate political association; but, on the other hand, political association singularly strengthens and improves associations for civil purposes. In civil life every man may, strictly speaking, fancy that he can provide for his own wants; in politics he can fancy no such thing. When a people, then, have any knowledge of public life, the notion of association and the wish to coalesce present themselves every day to the minds of the whole community; whatever natural distaste may restrain men from acting in concert, they will always be ready to combine for the sake of a unifying cause. Thus political life makes the love and practice of association more general; it imparts a desire of union and teaches the means of combination to numbers of men who otherwise would have always lived apart.

Politics give birth not only to numerous associations, but to associations of great extent. In civil life it seldom happens that any one interest draws a very large number of men to act in concert; much skill is required to bring such an interest into existence; but in politics opportunities present themselves every day. For it is solely in great associations that the general value of the principle of association is displayed. Citizens who are individually powerless do not very clearly anticipate the strength they may acquire by uniting together; it must be shown to them in order to be understood. Hence it is often easier to collect a multitude for a public purpose than a few individuals;

a thousand citizens do not see what interest they have in combining together; ten thousand will be perfectly aware of it. In politics men combine for great undertakings, and the use they make of the principle of association in important affairs teaches them from practice that it is in their interest to help one another in those of less importance. A political association draws a number of individuals at the same time out of their own circle; however they may naturally be kept apart by age, mind, and fortune, it places them nearer together and brings them into contact. Once met, they can always meet again.

Men can embark in few civil partnerships without risking a portion of their possessions; this is the case with all manufacturing and trading companies. When men are still poorly versed in the art of associating and when they are ignorant of its principle rules, they worry, when associating for the first time, that they will pay dearly for their experience. They therefore prefer depriving themselves of a powerful instrument of success to running the risks that attend the use of it. They are less reluctant, however, to join political associations, which appear to them to be without danger because they risk no money in them. But they cannot belong to these associations for any length of time without finding out how order is maintained among a large number of men and by what contrivance they are made to advance, harmoniously and methodically, to the same object. Thus they learn to surrender their own will to that of all the rest and to make their own exertions subordinate to the common impulse, all guiding principles that are not less applicable to civil than to political associations. Political associations may therefore be considered as large free schools, where all the members of the community go to learn the general theory of association. But even if political association did not directly contribute to the progress of civil association, to destroy the former would be to impair the latter. When citizens can meet in public only for certain purposes, they regard such meetings as a strange proceeding of rare occurrence, and they rarely think at all about it. When they are allowed to meet freely for all purposes, they ultimately look upon public association as the universal, that is to say, the unique, means that men can employ to accomplish the different purposes they may have in view. Every new want instantly revives the notion. The art of association then becomes, as I have said before, the mother of action, studied and applied by all.

When some kinds of associations are prohibited and others allowed, it is difficult to distinguish the former from the latter beforehand. In this state of doubt men abstain from them altogether, and a sort of public opinion gains currency which tends to consider any association whatsoever as an exceptionally bold and almost illicit enterprise. It is therefore wishful thinking to suppose that the spirit of association, when it is repressed on some one point, will nevertheless display the same vigor on all others; and that simply permitting men to pursue certain enterprises together is enough to induce them to attempt them. When the members of a community are allowed and accustomed to combine for all purposes, they will combine as readily for the lesser as for the more important ones; but if they are allowed to combine only for small affairs, they will be neither inclined nor able to effect it. In vain will you give them complete freedom to work together on business ventures: they will hardly care to avail themselves of the rights you have granted them; and after having exhausted your strength in vain efforts to put down prohibited associations, you will be surprised that you cannot persuade men to form the associations you encourage.

I do not say that there can be no civil associations in a country where political association is prohibited, for men can never live in society without embarking in some common undertakings; but I maintain that in such a country civil associations will always be few in number, feebly planned, and unskillfully managed. They will never take up any vast projects, or, if doing so, will fail in the execution of them.

This naturally leads me to think that freedom of association in political matters is not so dangerous to public tranquillity as is supposed, and that possibly, after having agitated society for some time, it may in the end strengthen the state. In democratic countries political associations are, so to speak, the only powerful individual entities that aspire to rule the state. Accordingly, the governments of our time look upon associations of this kind just as sovereigns in the Middle Ages regarded the great vassals of the crown: they entertain a sort of instinctive abhorrence of them and combat them on all occasions. They bear a natural goodwill to civil associations, on the contrary, because they readily discover that instead of directing the minds of the community to public affairs these institutions serve to divert them from such reflections, and that, by engaging them more and more in the pursuit of objects which cannot be attained without public tranquillity, they deter them from revolutions. But these governments do not pay attention to the fact that political associations tend amazingly to multiply and facilitate those of a civil character, and that in avoiding a dangerous evil they deprive themselves of an efficacious remedy.

When you see the Americans freely and constantly forming associations for the purpose of promoting some political principle, of raising one man to the head of affairs, or of wresting power from another, you have some difficulty in understanding how men so independent do not constantly fall into the abuse of freedom. If, on the other hand, you survey the infinite number of trading companies in operation in the United States, and perceive that the Americans are on every side unceasingly engaged in the execution of important and difficult plans, which the slightest revolution would throw into confusion, you will readily comprehend why people so well employed are by no means tempted to perturb the state or to destroy that public tranquillity by which they all profit. Is it enough to observe these things separately, or should we not discover the hidden tie that connects them? In their political associations the Americans, of all conditions, minds, and ages, daily acquire a general taste for association and grow accustomed to the use of it. There they meet together in large numbers, they converse, they listen to one another, and they are mutually stimulated to all sorts of undertakings. They afterwards transfer to civil life the notions they have thus acquired and make them serve a thousand purposes. Thus it is by the enjoyment of a dangerous freedom that the Americans learn the art of rendering the dangers of freedom less formidable.

If a certain moment in the existence of a nation is selected, it is easy to prove that political associations perturb the state and paralyze productive industry; but take the whole life of a people, and it may perhaps be easy to demonstrate that freedom of association in political matters is favorable to the prosperity and even to the tranquillity of the community. I said in the former part of this work: "The unrestrained liberty of political association cannot be entirely assimilated to the liberty of the press. The one is at the same time less necessary and more dangerous than the other. A nation may confine it within certain limits without ceasing to be mistress of itself, and it may sometimes be obliged to do so in order to maintain its own authority." And further on I added: "It cannot be denied that the unrestrained freedom of association for political purposes is the last degree of liberty which a people is fit for. If it does not throw them into anarchy, it perpetually brings them, as it were, to the verge of it."[1] Thus I do not think that a nation is always at liberty to invest its citizens with an absolute right of association for political purposes; and I doubt whether, in any country or in any age, it is wise to set no limits to freedom of association.

A certain nation, it is said, could not maintain tranquillity in the community, cause the laws to be respected, or establish a lasting government if the right of association were not confined within narrow limits. These blessings are doubtless invaluable, and I can imagine that to acquire or to preserve them a nation may impose upon itself severe temporary restrictions: but still it is well that the nation should know at what price these blessings are purchased. I can understand that it may be advisable to cut off a man's arm in order to save his life, but it would be ridiculous to assert that he will be as dexterous as he was before he lost it.

---

1   *Volume one*, part two, chapter four.

6c8   Chapter 8: "How the Americans Combat Individualism by the Principle of Self-Interest Rightly Understood"

When the world was managed by a few rich and powerful individuals, these persons loved to entertain a lofty idea of the duties of man. They were fond of professing that it is praiseworthy to forget oneself and that good should be done without hope of reward, as it is by the Deity himself. Such were the standard opinions of that time in morals.

I doubt whether men were more virtuous in aristocratic ages than in others, but they were incessantly talking of the beauties of virtue, and its utility was only studied in secret. But since the imagination takes less lofty flights, and every man's thoughts are centered in himself, moralists are alarmed by this idea of self-sacrifice and they no longer venture to present it to the human mind. They therefore content themselves with inquiring whether the personal advantage of each member of the community does not consist in working for the good of all; and when they have hit upon some point on which private interest and public interest meet and amalgamate, they are eager to bring it into notice. Observations of this kind are gradually multiplied; what was only a single remark becomes a general principle, and it is held as a truth that man serves himself in serving his fellow creatures and that his private interest is to do good.

I have already shown, in several parts of this work, by what means the inhabitants of the United States almost always manage to combine their own advantage with that of their fellow citizens; my present purpose is to point out the general rule that enables them to do so. In the United States hardly anybody talks of the beauty of virtue, but they maintain that virtue is useful and prove it every day. The American moralists do not profess that men ought to sacrifice themselves for their fellow creatures because it is noble to make such sacrifices, but they assert frankly that such sacrifices are as necessary to the one who makes them as to the one who profits from them.

They have found out that, in their country and their age, man is returned to consideration of his own interests by an irresistible force; and, losing all hope of stopping that force, they turn all their thoughts to the direction of it. They therefore do not deny that every man may follow his own interest, but they endeavor to prove that it is the interest of every man to be virtuous. I shall not here enter into the reasons they allege, which would divert me from my subject; suffice it to say that they have convinced their fellow countrymen.

Montaigne said long ago: "Were I not to follow the straight road for its straightness, I should follow it for having found by experience that in the end it is commonly the happiest and most useful track." The doctrine of interest rightly understood is not then new, but among the Americans of our time it finds universal acceptance; it has become popular there; you may trace it at the bottom of all their actions, you will remark it in all they say. It is as often asserted by the poor man as by the rich. In Europe the doctrine of self-interest is much coarser than in America, and at the same time it is less widespread and less evident, and people still claim a sense of devotion to others that they no longer have.

The Americans, on the other hand, are fond of explaining almost all the actions of their lives by the principle of self-interest rightly understood; they show complacently how an enlightened regard for themselves constantly prompts them to assist one another and inclines them willingly to sacrifice a portion of their time and property to the welfare of the state. In this respect I think they frequently fail to do themselves justice, for in the United States as well as elsewhere people are sometimes seen to give way to those disinterested and spontaneous impulses that are natural to man; but the Americans seldom admit that they yield to emotions of this kind; they are more anxious to do honor to their philosophy than to themselves.

I might here pause without attempting to pass a judgment on what I have described. The extreme difficulty of the subject would be my excuse, but I shall not avail myself of it; and I had rather that my readers, clearly perceiving my object, would refuse to follow me than that I should leave them in suspense.

The principle of self-interest rightly understood is not a lofty one, but it is clear and sure. It does not aim at mighty objects, but it attains without excessive exertion all those at which it aims. As it lies within the reach of all capacities, everyone can without difficulty learn and retain it. By its admirable conformity to human weaknesses it easily obtains great dominion; nor is that dominion precarious, since the principle checks one personal interest by another, and uses, to direct the passions, the very same instrument that excites them.

The principle of self-interest rightly understood produces no great acts of self-sacrifice, but it suggests daily small acts of self-denial. By itself it cannot suffice to make a man virtuous; but it disciplines a number of persons in habits of regularity, temperance, moderation, foresight, self-command; and if it does not lead men straight to virtue by the will, it gradually draws them in that direction by their habits. If the principle of interest rightly understood were to sway the whole moral world, extraordinary virtues would doubtless be more rare; but I think that gross depravity would then also be less common. The principle of interest rightly understood perhaps prevents men from rising far above the level of mankind, but a great number of other men, who were falling far below it, are caught and restrained by it. Observe some few individuals, they are lowered by it; survey mankind, they are raised.

I am not afraid to say that the principle of self-interest rightly understood appears to me the best suited of all philosophical theories to the wants of the men of our time, and that I regard it as their chief remaining security against themselves. Towards it, therefore, the minds of the moralists of our age should turn; even should they judge it to be incomplete, it must nevertheless be adopted as necessary.

I do not think, on the whole, that there is more selfishness among us than in America; the only difference is that there it is enlightened, here it is not. Each American knows when to sacrifice some of his private interests to save the rest; we want to save everything, and often we lose it all. Everybody I see about me seems bent on teaching his contemporaries, by precept and example, that what is useful is never wrong. Will nobody undertake to make them understand how what is right may be useful?

No power on earth can prevent the increasing equality of conditions from inclining the human mind to seek out what is useful or from leading every member of the community to be wrapped up in himself. It must therefore be expected that personal interest will become more than ever the principal if not the sole spring of men's actions; but it remains to be seen how each man will understand his personal interest. If the members of a community, as they become more equal, become more ignorant and coarse, it is difficult to foresee to what pitch of stupid excesses their selfishness may lead them; and no one can foretell into what disgrace and wretchedness they would plunge themselves lest they should have to sacrifice something of their own well-being to the prosperity of their fellow creatures.

I do not think that the system of self-interest as it is professed in America is in all its parts self-evident, but it contains a great number of truths so evident that men, if they are only educated, cannot fail to see them. Educate them then, in any case, for the age of implicit self-sacrifice and instinctive virtues is already flitting far away from us, and the time is fast approaching when freedom, public peace, and social order itself will not be able to exist without education.

6c10   Chapter 10: "Of the Taste for Material Well-Being in America"

In America the passion for material well-being does not always exclude other passions, but it is general; and if all do not feel it in the same manner, yet it is felt by all. The effort to satisfy even the least wants of the body and to provide the little conveniences of life is uppermost in every mind. Something of an analogous character is more and more apparent in Europe. Among the causes that produce these similar consequences in both hemispheres, several are so connected with my subject as to deserve notice.

When riches are hereditarily fixed in families, a great number of men enjoy the comforts of life without feeling an overwhelming craving for those comforts. What draws the human heart most compellingly is not the peaceful possession of a precious object, but an imperfectly satisfied desire to possess it and a constant fear of losing it. In aristocratic communities the wealthy, never having experienced a condition different from their own, entertain no fear of changing it; the existence of such conditions hardly occurs to them. The comforts of life are not to them the end of life, but simply a way of living; they regard them like existence itself, enjoyed but scarcely thought of. As the natural and instinctive taste that all men feel for being well off is thus satisfied without trouble and without apprehension, their faculties are turned elsewhere and applied to more arduous and lofty undertakings, which excite and engross their minds. Hence it is that in the very midst of physical gratifications the members of an aristocracy often display a haughty contempt of these very enjoyments and exhibit singular powers of endurance under the privation of them. All the revolutions which have ever shaken or destroyed aristocracies have shown how easily men accustomed to superfluous luxuries can do without the necessaries of life; whereas men who have toiled to acquire a fortune can hardly live after they have lost it.

If I turn my observation from the upper to the lower classes, I find analogous effects produced by opposite causes. Among a nation where aristocracy predominates in society and keeps it stationary, the people in the end get as much accustomed to poverty as the rich to their wealth. The latter bestow no anxiety on their physical comforts because they enjoy them without effort; the former do not think of things which they despair of obtaining and which they hardly know enough about to desire. In communities of this kind the imagination of the poor is driven to seek another world; the miseries of real life enclose it, but it escapes from their control and flies to seek its pleasures far beyond.

When, on the contrary, distinctions of ranks are obliterated and privileges are destroyed, when hereditary property is subdivided and education and freedom are widely diffused, the desire of acquiring the comforts of the world haunts the imagination of the poor, and the dread of losing them that of the rich. Many scanty fortunes spring up; those who possess them have a sufficient share of physical gratifications to conceive a taste for these pleasures, not enough to satisfy it. They never procure them without exertion, and they never indulge in them without apprehension. They are therefore always straining to pursue or to retain gratifications so delightful, so imperfect, so fugitive.

If I were to inquire what passion is most natural to men who are stimulated and circumscribed by the obscurity of their birth or the mediocrity of their fortune, I could discover none more peculiarly appropriate to their condition than this love of material prosperity. The passion for material comforts is essentially a passion of the middle classes; with those classes it grows and spreads, with them it is preponderant. From them it mounts into the higher orders of society and descends into the mass of the lower classes.

I never met in America any citizen so poor as not to cast a glance of hope and envy at the enjoyments of the rich or whose imagination did not possess itself by anticipation of those good things that fate still obstinately withheld from him. On the other hand, I never perceived among the wealthier inhabitants of the United States that proud contempt for material well-being which is sometimes found even in the most opulent and dissolute aristocracies. Most of these wealthy persons were once poor; they have felt the sting of want; they were long a prey to adverse fortunes; and now that the victory is won, the passions which accompanied the contest have survived it; their minds are, as it were, intoxicated by the small enjoyments which they have pursued for forty years.

Not but that in the United States, as elsewhere, there is a certain number of wealthy persons who, having come into their property by inheritance, possess without exertion an opulence they have not earned. But even these men are not less devotedly attached to the pleasures of material life. The love of well-being has now become the predominant taste of the nation; the great current of human passions runs in that channel and sweeps everything along in its course.

6c12   Chapter 12: "Why some Americans Manifest a Sort of Fanatical Spiritualism"

Although the desire of acquiring the good things of this world is the prevailing passion of the American people, certain momentary outbreaks occur when their souls seem suddenly to burst the bonds of matter by which they are restrained and to soar impetuously towards heaven. In all the states of the Union, but especially in the half-peopled country of the Far West, there are itinerant preachers who peddle the divine word from place to place. Whole families, old men, women, and children, cross rough passes and untrodden wilds, coming from a great distance, to join a camp-meeting, where, in listening to these discourses, they totally forget for several days and nights the cares of business and even the most urgent wants of the body.

Here and there in the midst of American society you meet with men full of a fanatical and almost wild spiritualism, which hardly exists in Europe. From time to time strange sects arise which endeavor to strike out extraordinary paths to eternal happiness. Religious insanity is very common in the United States.

Nor ought these facts to surprise us. It was not man who implanted in himself the taste for what is infinite and the love of what is immortal; these lofty instincts are not the offspring of his capricious will; their steadfast foundation is fixed in human nature, and they exist in spite of his efforts. He may cross and distort them; destroy them he cannot.

The soul has wants which must be satisfied; and whatever pains are taken to divert it from itself, it soon grows weary, restless, and disquieted amid the enjoyments of sense. If ever the faculties of the great majority of mankind were exclusively bent upon the pursuit of material objects, it might be anticipated that an amazing reaction would take place in the souls of some men. They would drift at large in the world of spirits, for fear of remaining shackled by the close bondage of the body.

It is not, then, wonderful if in the midst of a community whose thoughts tend earthward a small number of individuals are to be found who turn their looks to heaven. I should be surprised if mysticism did not soon make some advance among a people solely engaged in promoting their own worldly welfare. It is said that the deserts of the Thebaid[2] were peopled by the persecutions of the emperors and the massacres of the Circus; I should rather say that it was by the luxuries of Rome and the Epicurean philosophy of Greece. If their social condition, their present circumstances, and their laws did not confine the minds of the Americans so closely to the pursuit of worldly welfare, it is probable that they would display more reserve and more experience whenever their attention is turned to things immaterial, and that they would check themselves without difficulty. But they feel imprisoned within bounds, which they will apparently never be allowed to pass. As soon as they have passed these bounds, their minds do not know where to fix themselves and they often rush unrestrained beyond the range of common sense.

2 In Egypt.

6d   Part IV: "Influence of Democratic Ideas and Feelings on Political Society"

I should imperfectly fulfill the purpose of this book if, after having shown what ideas and feelings are suggested by the principle of equality, I did not point out, before I conclude, the general influence that these same ideas and feelings may exercise upon the government of human societies. To succeed in this object I shall frequently have to retrace my steps, but I trust the reader will not refuse to follow me along paths already known to him, which may lead to some new truth.

6d1   Chapter 1: "Equality Naturally Gives Men a Taste for Free Institutions"

The principle of equality, which makes men independent of each other, gives them a habit and taste for following in their private actions no other guide than their own will. This complete independence, which they constantly enjoy in regard to their equals and in the intercourse of private life, tends to make them look on all authority with a jealous eye, and speedily suggests to them the notion and the love of political freedom. Men living at such times have a natural bias towards free institutions. Take any one of them at a venture and search if you can his most deep-seated instincts, and you will find that, of all governments, he will soonest conceive and most highly value that government whose head he has himself elected and whose administration he may control.

Of all the political effects produced by the equality of conditions, this love of independence is the first to strike the observing and alarm the timid; nor can it be said that their alarm is wholly misplaced, for anarchy has a more formidable aspect in democratic countries than elsewhere. As the citizens have no direct influence on each other, as soon as the supreme power of the nation, which kept them all in their various places, fails, it would seem that disorder must instantly reach its utmost pitch and that, every man going in a different direction, the fabric of society must at once crumble away. I am convinced, however, that anarchy is not the principal evil that democratic ages have to fear, but the least. For the principle of equality begets two tendencies: one leads men straight to independence and may suddenly drive them into anarchy; the other conducts them by a longer, less obvious, but more certain road to servitude. Nations readily perceive the former tendency and are prepared to resist it; they are led away by the latter without seeing its drift; hence it is especially important to point it out. Personally, far from finding fault with equality because it inspires a spirit of independence, I praise it primarily for that very reason. I admire it because it lodges in the very depths of each man's mind and heart that indefinable feeling, the instinctive inclination for political independence, and thus prepares the remedy for the ill which it engenders. It is precisely for this reason that I cling to it.

6d2   Chapter 2: "That the Opinions of Democratic Nations about Government are Naturally Favorable to the Concentration of Power"

The notion of secondary powers placed between the sovereign and his subjects occurred naturally to the imagination of aristocratic nations, because those communities contained individuals or families raised above the common level and apparently destined to command by their birth, education, and wealth. This same notion is naturally missing from the minds of men in democratic ages, for the opposite reasons. It can only be introduced artificially, it can only be retained with difficulty, because they conceive, as it were without thinking about the subject, the notion of a single and central power which governs the whole community by its direct influence. Moreover, in politics as well as in philosophy and religion the intellect of democratic nations welcomes simple and general ideas with delight. Complicated systems are repugnant to it, and its favorite conception is that of a great nation composed of citizens all formed according to one pattern and all governed by a single power.

The next idea alongside that of a single and central power which presents itself to the minds of men in ages of equality is the notion of uniform legislation. As every man sees that he differs little from those about him, he cannot understand why a rule that is applicable to one man should not be equally applicable to all others. Hence the slightest privileges are repugnant to his reason; the slightest dissimilarities in the political institutions that affect the same people offend him, and uniform legislation appears to him to be the first condition of good government. I find, by contrast, that this notion of a uniform rule equally binding on all members of the community was almost unknown to the human mind in aristocratic ages; either it was never broached, or it was rejected.

These opposing intellectual tendencies, on both sides, ultimately end up becoming instincts so blind and habits so entrenched that they still shape actions despite individual facts to the contrary. Notwithstanding the immense variety of conditions in the Middle Ages, a certain number of persons existed at that period in precisely similar circumstances; but this did not prevent the legislator from assigning to them diverse duties and different rights. On the contrary, at the present time all the powers of government are exerted to impose the same customs and the same laws on populations which have as yet but few points of resemblance.

As the conditions of men become equal among a people, individuals seem less and society more important; or rather every citizen, having come to resemble all the others, is lost in the crowd, and nothing stands conspicuous but the great and imposing image of the people at large. This naturally gives people of democratic periods a lofty opinion of the privileges of society and a very humble notion of the rights of individuals; they freely admit that the interests of the former are everything and those of the latter nothing. They are willing to acknowledge that the power which represents the community has far more information and wisdom than any of the members of that community; and that it is the duty, as well as the right, of that power to guide as well as govern each private citizen.

If we closely scrutinize our contemporaries and penetrate to the root of their political opinions, we shall detect some of the notions that I have just pointed out, and we shall perhaps be surprised to find so much agreement among men who are so often at odds.

The Americans hold that in every state the supreme power ought to emanate from the people; but that once that power is constituted, they can conceive, as it were, no limits to it, and they are ready to admit that it has the right to do whatever it pleases. They have not the slightest notion of special privileges granted to cities, families, or persons; their minds appear never to have foreseen that it might be possible not to apply with strict uniformity the same laws to every part of the state and to all its inhabitants.

These same opinions are spreading more and more in Europe; they even insinuate themselves among those nations that most vehemently reject the principle of the sovereignty of the people. Such nations assign a different origin to the supreme power, but they ascribe to that power the same characteristics. Among all of them the idea of intermediate powers is weakened and obliterated; the idea of rights inherent in certain individuals is rapidly disappearing from the men's minds; the idea of the omnipotence and sole authority of society at large rises to fill its place. These ideas take root and spread in proportion as social conditions become more equal and men more alike. They are produced by equality, and in turn they hasten the progress of equality.

In France, where the revolution of which I am speaking has gone further than in any other European country, these opinions have got complete hold of the public mind. If we listen attentively to the language of the various parties in France, we find that there is not one which has not adopted them. Most of these parties censure the conduct of the government, but they all hold that the government ought perpetually to act and interfere in everything that is done. Even those which disagree most with each other are nevertheless agreed on this head. The unity, the ubiquity, the omnipotence of the supreme power, and the uniformity of its rules constitute the principal characteristics of all the political systems that have been put forward in our age. One finds them at the heart of the most bizarre utopias. The human mind still pursues these images even when it dreams. If these notions spontaneously arise in the minds of private individuals, they suggest themselves still more forcibly to the minds of rulers.

While the ancient fabric of European society is altered and dissolved, sovereigns acquire new conceptions of their opportunities and their duties; they learn for the first time that the central power which they represent may and ought to administer, by its own agency and on a uniform plan, all the concerns of the whole community. This opinion, which, I will venture to say, was never held before our time by the monarchs of Europe, now profoundly penetrates these rulers' minds; they hold on to it firmly amid the hubbub of conflicting opinion.

Our contemporaries are therefore much less divided than is commonly supposed; they are constantly disputing as to the hands in which supremacy is to be vested, but they readily agree on the duties and the rights of that supremacy. The notion they all form of government is that of a sole, simple, providential, and creative power. All secondary opinions in politics are mutable; this one remains fixed, invariable, and consistent. It is adopted by statesmen and political philosophers; it is eagerly laid hold of by the multitude; those who govern and those who are governed agree to pursue it with equal ardor; it is the earliest notion of their minds, it seems innate. It originates, therefore, in no caprice of the human intellect, but is a necessary condition of the present state of mankind.

6d4   Chapter 4: "Of Certain Peculiar and Accidental Causes Which Either Lead a People to Complete the Centralization of Government or Divert Them From it"

If, during centuries of equality, men readily perceive the idea of a great central power, it is evident that their habits and their sentiments will predispose them to recognize and to foster it. The demonstration of this idea can be accomplished with few words, the majority of reasons having already been given elsewhere.

Among men who have lived free long before they became equal, the tendencies derived from free institutions combat, to a certain extent, the propensities suggested by the principle of equality; and although the central power may increase its privileges among such a people, the private members of such a community will never entirely forfeit their independence. But when equality of conditions grows up among a people who have never known or have long ceased to know what freedom is (and such is the case on the continent of Europe), as the former habits of the nation are suddenly combined, by some sort of natural attraction, with the new habits and principles engendered by the state of society, all powers seem to spontaneously rush towards the center. These powers accumulate there with astonishing rapidity, and the state instantly attains the utmost limits of its strength, while private persons allow themselves to sink as suddenly to the lowest degree of weakness.

The English who emigrated three hundred years ago to found a democratic commonwealth on the shores of the New World had all learned to take a part in public affairs in their mother country; they were conversant with trial by jury; they were accustomed to freedom of speech and of the press, to personal freedom, to the notion of rights and the practice of asserting them. They carried with them to America these free institutions and manly customs, and these institutions preserved them against the state's encroachments. Thus among the Americans it is freedom that is old; equality is of comparatively modern date. The reverse is occurring in Europe, where equality, introduced by absolute power and under the rule of kings, was already infused into the habits of nations long before freedom had entered their thoughts.

I have said that among democratic nations the notion of government naturally presents itself to the mind under the form of a sole and central power, and that the notion of intermediate powers is not familiar to them. This is peculiarly applicable to democratic nations which have witnessed the triumph of the principle of equality by means of a violent revolution. As the classes that managed local affairs have been suddenly swept away by the storm, and as the confused mass that remains has as yet neither the organization nor the habits which fit it to assume the administration of these affairs, the state alone seems capable of taking upon itself all the details of government, and centralization becomes, as it were, the unavoidable state of the country.

Napoleon deserves neither praise nor blame for having centered in his own hands almost all the administrative power of France; for after the abrupt disappearance of the nobility and the higher rank of the middle classes, these powers devolved on him as a matter of course: it would have been almost as difficult for him to reject as to assume them. But a similar necessity has never been felt by the Americans, who, having passed through no revolution, and having governed themselves from the first, never had to call upon the state to act for a time as their guardian. Thus the progress of centralization among a democratic people depends not only on the progress of equality, but on the manner in which this equality has been established.

At the commencement of a great democratic revolution, when hostilities have but just broken out between the different classes of society, the lower classes try to centralize the public administration in the hands of the government, in order to wrest the management of local affairs from the aristocracy. Towards the close of such a revolution, on the contrary, it is usually the conquered aristocracy that endeavors to make over the management of all affairs to the state, because such an aristocracy dreads the tyranny of a people that has become its equal and not infrequently its master.

Thus it is not always the same class of the community that strives to increase the prerogative of the government; but as long as the democratic revolution lasts, there is always one class in the nation, powerful in numbers or wealth, which is induced, by special passions or interests, to centralize public administration, independently of that hatred of being governed by one's neighbor which is a general and permanent feeling among democratic nations. It may be remarked that at the present day the lower orders in England are striving with all their might to destroy local independence and to transfer administration from all the points of the circumference to the center; whereas the higher classes try to keep this administration within its ancient boundaries. I venture to predict that a time will come when the very reverse will happen.

These observations explain why the supreme power is always stronger, and private individuals weaker, among a democratic people that has passed through a long and arduous struggle to reach a state of equality than among a democratic community in which the citizens have been equal from the first. The example of the Americans completely demonstrates the fact. The inhabitants of the United States were never divided by any privileges; they have never known the mutual relation of master and inferior; and as they neither dread nor hate each other, they have never known the necessity of calling in the supreme power to manage their affairs. The Americans' lot is unique: they have derived from the aristocracy of England the notion of private rights and the taste for local freedom; and they have been able to retain both because they have had no aristocracy to fight.

If education enables men at all times to defend their independence, this is most especially true in democratic times. When all men are alike, it is easy to found a sole and all-powerful government by the aid of mere instinct. But men require much intelligence, knowledge, and art to organize and maintain secondary powers under similar circumstances and to create, amid the independence and individual weakness of the citizens, such free associations as may be able to struggle against tyranny without destroying public order.

Hence the concentration of power and the subjection of individuals will increase among democratic nations, not only in the same proportion as their equality, but in the same proportion as their ignorance. It is true that in ages of imperfect civilization the government is frequently as wanting in the knowledge required to impose a despotism upon the people as the people are wanting in the knowledge required to shake it off; but the effect is not the same on both sides. However rude a democratic people may be, the central power that rules them is never completely devoid of cultivation, because it readily draws to its own uses what little cultivation is to be found in the country, and if necessary may seek assistance elsewhere. Hence among a nation which is ignorant as well as democratic an amazing difference cannot fail to speedily arise between the intellectual capacity of the ruler and that of each of his subjects. This completes the easy concentration of all power in his hands: the administrative function of the state is perpetually extended because the state alone is competent to administer the affairs of the country.

Aristocratic nations, however unenlightened they may be, never afford the same spectacle, because in them instruction is nearly equally shared between the monarch and the leading members of the community. The Pasha who now rules in Egypt found the population of that country composed of men exceedingly ignorant and equal, and he has borrowed the science and ability of Europe to govern that people. As the personal attainments of the sovereign are thus combined with the ignorance and democratic weakness of his subjects, the utmost centralization has been established without impediment, and the Pasha has made the country his factory, and the inhabitants his workmen. I think that extreme centralization of government ultimately enervates society and thus, after a length of time, weakens the government itself; but I do not deny that a centralized social power may be able to execute great undertakings with facility in a given time and on a particular point. This is more especially true of war, in which success depends much more on the means of transferring all the resources of a nation to one single point than on the extent of those resources. Hence it is chiefly in war that nations desire, and frequently need, to increase the powers of the central government. All men of military genius are fond of centralization, which increases their strength; and all men of centralizing genius are fond of war, which compels nations to combine all their powers in the hands of the government. Thus the democratic tendency that leads men unceasingly to multiply the privileges of the state and to circumscribe the rights of private persons is much more rapid and constant among those democratic nations that are exposed by their position to great and frequent wars than among all others.

I have shown how the dread of disturbance and the love of material well-being gradually lead democratic nations to increase the functions of the central government as the only power which appears to be intrinsically sufficiently strong, enlightened, and secure to protect them from anarchy. I would now add that all the particular circumstances which tend to make the state of a democratic community agitated and precarious enhance this general propensity and lead private persons more and more to sacrifice their rights to their tranquillity.

A people is therefore never so disposed to increase the functions of central government as at the close of a long and bloody revolution, which, after having wrested property from the hands of its former possessors, has shaken all belief and filled the nation with fierce hatreds, conflicting interests, and contending factions. At such times the love of public tranquillity becomes an indiscriminate passion, and the members of the community are apt to conceive a most inordinate devotion to order.

I have already examined several of the incidents that may concur to promote the centralization of power, but the principal cause still remains to be noticed. The leading incidental cause which may draw the management of all affairs into the ruler's hands in democratic countries is the origin of that ruler himself and his own propensities. Men who live in ages of equality are naturally fond of central power and are willing to extend its privileges; but if it happens that this same power faithfully represents their own interests and exactly copies their own inclinations, the confidence they place in it knows no bounds, and they think that whatever they bestow upon it is bestowed upon themselves.

The attraction of administrative powers to the center will always be less easy and less rapid under the reign of kings who are still in some way connected with the old aristocratic order than under new princes, the children of their own achievements, whose birth, prejudices, propensities, and habits appear to bind them indissolubly to the cause of equality. I do not mean that princes of aristocratic origin who live in democratic ages do not attempt to centralize; I believe they apply themselves as diligently as any others to that object. For them the sole advantages of equality lie in that direction; but their opportunities are less great, because the community, instead of volunteering compliance with their desires, frequently obeys them with reluctance. In democratic communities the rule is that centralization must increase in proportion as the sovereign is less aristocratic.

When an ancient race of kings stands at the head of an aristocracy, as the natural prejudices of the sovereign perfectly accord with the natural prejudices of the nobility, the vices inherent in aristocratic communities have a free course and meet with no corrective. The reverse is the case when the scion of a feudal stock is placed at the head of a democratic people. The sovereign is constantly led, by his education, habits, and associations to adopt sentiments suggested by the inequality of conditions, and the people tend as constantly, by their social condition, to those manners which are created by equality. At such times it often happens that the citizens seek to limit the central power far less as a tyrannical than as an aristocratic power, and that they persist in the firm defense of their independence, not only because they want to remain free, but especially because they are determined to remain equal.

A revolution that overthrows an ancient regal family in order to place new men at the head of a democratic people may temporarily weaken the central power; but however anarchical such a revolution may appear at first, we need not hesitate to predict that its final and certain result will be to extend and to secure the prerogatives of that power.

The foremost or indeed the sole condition required in order to succeed in centralizing the supreme power in a democratic community is to love equality, or to get men to believe you love it. Thus the science of despotism, which was once so complex, is simplified, and reduced, as it were, to a single principle.

6d6   Chapter 6: "What Sort of Despotism Democratic Nations Have to Fear"

I noticed during my stay in the United States that a democratic state of society, similar to that of the Americans, might offer singular facilities for the establishment of despotism; and I perceived, upon my return to Europe, how much use had already been made, by most of our rulers, of the notions, sentiments, and desires created by this same social condition, for the purpose of extending the circle of their power. This led me to think that the nations of Christendom would perhaps eventually undergo some oppression like that which hung over several of the nations of the ancient world. A more accurate examination of the subject, and five years of further meditation, have not diminished my fears, but have changed their object.

No sovereign who ever lived, in former ages, was so absolute or so powerful as to undertake to administer by his own agency, and without the assistance of intermediate powers, all the parts of a great empire; none ever attempted to subject all his subjects indiscriminately to strictly uniform regulations and to personally tutor and direct every member of the community. The notion of such an undertaking never occurred to the human mind; and if any man had conceived it, the lack of information, the imperfection of the administrative system, and above all the natural obstacles caused by the inequality of conditions would speedily have checked the execution of so vast a design.

When the Roman emperors were at the height of their power, the different nations of the empire still preserved usages and customs of great diversity; although they were subject to the same monarch most of the provinces were separately administered; they abounded in powerful and active municipalities; and although the whole government of the empire was centered in the hands of the Emperor alone and he always remained, in case of need, the supreme arbiter in all matters, yet the details of social life and private occupations lay for the most part beyond his control. The emperors possessed, it is true, an immense and unchecked power, which allowed them to gratify all their whimsical tastes and to use for that purpose the whole strength of the state. They frequently abused that power arbitrarily to deprive their subjects of property or of life; their tyranny was extremely onerous to the few, but it did not reach the many; it was confined to some few main objects and neglected the rest; it was violent, but its range was limited.

It would seem that if despotism were to be established among the democratic nations of our days, it might assume a different character; it would be more extensive and more mild; it would degrade men without tormenting them. I do not question that, in an age of instruction and equality like our own, sovereigns might more easily succeed in collecting all political power into their own hands and might interfere more habitually and decidedly with the circle of private interests than any sovereign of antiquity could ever do. But this same principle of equality which facilitates despotism tempers its rigor. We have seen how the customs of society become more humane and gentle in proportion as men become more equal and alike. When no member of the community has much power or wealth, tyranny is, as it were, without opportunities and a field of action. As all fortunes are scanty, men's passions are naturally bounded, their imagination limited, their pleasures simple. This universal moderation moderates the sovereign himself and checks within certain limits the inordinate stretch of his desires.

Independently of these reasons, drawn from the nature of the state of society itself, I might add many others arising from causes beyond my subject; but I shall keep within the limits I have laid down.

Democratic governments may become violent and even cruel at certain periods of extreme effervescence or great danger, but these crises will be rare and brief. When I consider the petty passions of our contemporaries, the mildness of their manners, the extent of their education, the purity of their religion, the gentleness of their morality, their regular and industrious habits, and the restraint which they almost all observe in their vices no less than in their virtues, I have no fear that they will meet with tyrants in their rulers, but rather with guardians.

I think, then, that the species of oppression by which democratic nations are menaced is unlike anything that ever before existed in the world; our contemporaries will find no prototype of it in their memories. I seek in vain for an expression that will accurately convey the whole idea I have formed of it; the old words despotism and tyranny are inappropriate: the thing itself is new, and since I cannot name it, I must attempt to define it.

I seek to trace the novel features under which despotism may appear in the world. The first thing that strikes the observation is an innumerable multitude of men, all equal and alike, incessantly endeavoring to procure the petty and paltry pleasures with which they glut their lives. Each of them, living apart, is as a stranger to the fate of all the rest; his children and his private friends constitute for him the whole of mankind. As for the rest of his fellow citizens, he is close to them, but he does not see them; he touches them, but he does not feel them; he exists only in himself and for himself alone; and if his kindred still remain to him, he may be said at any rate to have lost his country.

Above this race of men stands an immense and tutelary power, which takes upon itself alone to secure their gratifications and to watch over their fate. This power is absolute, minute, regular, provident, and mild. It would be like the authority of a parent if, like that authority, its object was to prepare men for manhood; but it seeks, on the contrary, to keep them in perpetual childhood: it is well content that the people should rejoice, provided they think of nothing but rejoicing. Such a government willingly labors for their happiness, but it chooses to be the sole agent and the only arbiter of that happiness; it provides for their security, foresees and supplies their necessities, facilitates their pleasures, manages their principal concerns, directs their industry, regulates the descent of property, and subdivides their inheritances: what remains, but to spare them all the care of thinking and all the trouble of living?

Thus it every day renders the exercise of man's free agency less useful and less frequent; it circumscribes the will within a narrower range and gradually robs a man of all the uses of himself. The principle of equality has prepared men for these things; it has predisposed men to endure them and often to look on them as benefits.

After having thus successively taken each member of the community in its powerful grasp and fashioned him at will, the supreme power then extends its arm over the whole community. It covers the surface of society with a network of small complicated rules, minute and uniform, which the most original minds and the most energetic souls cannot surmount. Man's will is not shattered, but softened, bent, and guided; men are seldom forced to act, but they are constantly restrained from acting. Such a power does not destroy, but it prevents existence; it does not tyrannize, but it compresses, enervates, extinguishes, and stupefies a people, till each nation is reduced to nothing better than a flock of timid and industrious animals, of which the government is the shepherd.

I have always thought that servitude of the regular, quiet, and gentle kind which I have just described might be combined more easily than is commonly believed with some of the outward forms of freedom, and that it might even establish itself under the wing of the sovereignty of the people.

Our contemporaries are constantly excited by two conflicting passions: they want to be led, and they wish to remain free. As they cannot destroy either the one or the other of these contrary propensities, they strive to satisfy them both at once. They devise a sole, tutelary, and all-powerful form of government, but elected by the people. They combine the principle of centralization and that of popular sovereignty; this gives them a respite: they console themselves for being in tutelage by the reflection that they have chosen their own guardians. Every man allows himself to be put in leading-strings, because he sees that it is not a person or a class of persons but the people at large who hold the end of his chain.

By this system the people shake off their state of dependence just long enough to select their master and then relapse into it again. A great many persons at the present day are quite contented with this sort of compromise between administrative despotism and the sovereignty of the people; and they think they have done enough for the protection of individual freedom when they have surrendered it to the power of the nation at large. This does not satisfy me: the nature of him I am to obey signifies less to me than the fact of extorted obedience. I do not deny, however, that a constitution of this kind appears to me to be infinitely preferable to one which, after having concentrated all the powers of government, should vest them in the hands of an irresponsible person or body of persons. Of all the forms that democratic despotism could assume, the latter would assuredly be the worst.

When the sovereign is elected or watched closely by a legislature that is freely elected and independent, the oppression that he exercises over individuals is sometimes greater, but it is always less degrading; because every man, when he is oppressed and disarmed, may still imagine that, while he yields obedience, it is to himself he yields it, and that it is to one of his own inclinations that all the rest give way. In like manner, I can understand that when the sovereign represents the nation and is dependent upon the people, the rights and power of which every citizen is deprived serve not only the head of state, but the state itself; and that private persons derive some return from the sacrifice of their independence which they have made to the public. To create a representation of the people in every centralized country is, therefore, to diminish the evil that extreme centralization may produce, but not to get rid of it.

I admit that, by this means, room is left for the intervention of individuals in the more important affairs; but it is not the less suppressed in the smaller and more privates ones. It must not be forgotten that it is especially dangerous to enslave men in the minor details of life. For my own part, I should be inclined to think freedom less necessary in great things than in little ones, if it were possible to be secure of the one without possessing the other.

Subjection in minor affairs breaks out every day and is felt by the whole community indiscriminately. It does not drive men to resistance, but it crosses them at every turn, till they are led to surrender the exercise of their own will. Thus their spirit is gradually broken and their character enervated; whereas that obedience which is exacted on a few important but rare occasions only exhibits servitude at certain intervals and throws the burden of it upon a small number of men. It is in vain to summon a people who have been rendered so dependent on the central power to choose from time to time the representatives of that power; this rare and brief exercise of their free choice, however important it may be, will not prevent them from gradually losing the faculties of thinking, feeling, and acting for themselves, and thus gradually falling below the level of humanity.

I add that they will soon become incapable of exercising the great and only privilege which remains to them. Democratic nations that introduced freedom into their political constitution at the very time when they were augmenting the despotism of their administrative constitution have been led into strange paradoxes. The people are held to be unequal to the task of managing those minor affairs in which good sense is all that is wanted; but when the government of the country is at stake, the people are invested with immense powers; they are alternately made the playthings of their ruler, and his masters, more than kings and less than men. After having exhausted all the different modes of election without finding one to suit their purpose, they are confounded and look further, as if the evil they see doesn't stem from the constitution of the country much more than from the electorate.

It is indeed difficult to conceive how men who have entirely given up the habit of self-government should succeed in making a proper choice of those by whom they are to be governed; and no one will ever believe that a liberal, wise, and energetic government can spring from the suffrages of a subservient people.

A constitution republican in its head and ultra-monarchical in all its other parts has always appeared to me to be a short-lived monster. The vices of rulers and the ineptitude of the people would speedily bring about its ruin; and the nation, weary of its representatives and of itself, would create freer institutions or soon return to lay down at the feet of a single master.

6d7   Chapter 7: "Continuation of the Preceding Chapters"

I believe that it is easier to establish an absolute and despotic government among a people in which the conditions of society are equal than among any other; and I think that if such a government were once established among such a people, it not only would oppress men, but would eventually strip each of them of several of the highest qualities of humanity. Despotism, therefore, appears to me peculiarly to be dreaded in democratic times. I should have loved freedom, I believe, at all times, but in the time in which we live I am ready to worship it. On the other hand, I am persuaded that all who attempt, in the ages upon which we are entering, to base freedom upon aristocratic privilege will fail; that all who attempt to attract and retain authority within a single class will fail. At the present day no ruler is skillful or strong enough to found a despotism by re-establishing permanent distinctions of rank among his subjects; no legislator is wise or powerful enough to preserve free institutions if he does not take equality for his first principle and his watchword. All of our contemporaries who would establish or secure the independence and the dignity of their fellow men must show themselves the friends of equality; and the only worthy means of showing themselves as such is to be so: upon this depends the success of their holy enterprise. Thus the question is not how to reconstruct aristocratic society, but how to make freedom in that democratic state of society in which God has placed us.

These two truths appear to me simple, clear, and fertile in consequences; and they naturally lead me to consider what kind of free government can be established among a people in which social conditions are equal.

6d8   Chapter 8: "General Survey of the Subject"

Before finally closing the subject that I have now discussed, I should like to take a parting survey of all the different characteristics of modern society and appreciate at last the general influence to be exercised by the principle of equality upon the fate of mankind; but I am stopped by the difficulty of the task, and in presence of so great a theme my sight is troubled and my reason fails.

The society of the modern world, which I have sought to delineate and which I seek to judge, has just come into existence. Time has not yet shaped it into perfect form; the great revolution by which it has been created is not yet over; and amid the occurrences of our time it is almost impossible to discern what will pass away with the revolution itself and what will survive its close. The world that is rising into existence is still half encumbered by the remains of the world that is falling into decay; and amid the vast perplexity of human affairs no one can say how much of ancient institutions and former customs will remain or how much will completely disappear.

Although the revolution that is taking place in the social condition, the laws, the opinions, and the feelings of men is still very far from being terminated, its results already admit of no comparison with anything the world has ever before witnessed. I go back from age to age to the remotest antiquity, but I find no parallel to what is occurring before my eyes; since the past has ceased to throw its light upon the future, the mind of man wanders in obscurity.

. . .

If I endeavor to find out the most general and most prominent of all these different characteristics, I perceive that what is taking place in men's fortunes manifests itself in a thousand different forms. Almost all extremes are softened or blunted: all that was most prominent is superseded by some middle term, at once less lofty and less low, less brilliant and less obscure, than what existed in the world before.

When I survey this countless multitude of beings, shaped in each other's likeness, amid whom nothing rises and nothing falls, the sight of such universal uniformity saddens and chills me and I am tempted to regret that state of society which has ceased to be. When the world was full of men of great importance and extreme insignificance, of great wealth and extreme poverty, of great learning and extreme ignorance, I turned aside from the latter to fix my observation on the former alone, who gratified my sympathies. But I admit that this gratification arose from my own weakness; it is because I am unable to see at once all that is around me that I am allowed thus to select and separate the objects of my predilection from among so many others. Such is not the case with that Almighty and Eternal Being whose gaze necessarily includes the whole of created things and who surveys distinctly, though all at once, mankind and man.

We may naturally believe that it is not the singular prosperity of the few, but the greater well-being of all that is most pleasing in the sight of the Creator and Preserver of men. What appears to me to be man's decline is, to His eye, advancement; what afflicts me is acceptable to Him. A state of equality is perhaps less elevated, but it is more just: and its justice constitutes its greatness and its beauty. I would strive, then, to raise myself to this point of divine contemplation and thence to view and to judge the concerns of men. No man on the earth can as yet affirm, absolutely and generally, that the new state of the world is better than its former one; but it is already easy to perceive that this state is different. Some vices and virtues were so inherent in the constitution of an aristocratic nation and are so opposite to the character of a modern people that they can never be infused into it; some good tendencies and some bad propensities which were unknown to the former are natural to the latter; some ideas suggest themselves spontaneously to the imagination of the one which are utterly repugnant to the mind of the other. They are like two distinct orders of human beings, each of which has its own merits and defects, its own advantages and its own evils. Care must therefore be taken not to judge the state of society that is now coming into existence by notions derived from a state of society that no longer exists; for as these states of society are exceedingly different in their structure, they cannot be submitted to a just or fair comparison. It would be scarcely more reasonable to require of our contemporaries the peculiar virtues which originated in the social condition of their forefathers, since that social condition is itself fallen and has drawn into one common ruin the good and evil that belonged to it.

But as yet these things are imperfectly understood. I find that a great number of my contemporaries attempt to make a selection from among the institutions, the opinions, and the ideas that originated in the aristocratic constitution of society as it was; a portion of these elements they would willingly give up, but they would keep the remainder and transplant them into their new world. I fear that such men are wasting their time and their strength in virtuous but unprofitable efforts. The object is not to retain the peculiar advantages which the inequality of conditions bestows upon mankind, but to secure the new benefits which equality may supply. We should not seek to make ourselves like our ancestors, but strive to work out that species of greatness and happiness which is our own. For myself, who now look back from this extreme limit of my task and discover from afar, but all at once, the various objects which have attracted my more attentive investigation upon my way, I am full of fears and hopes. I perceive mighty dangers which it is possible to ward off, mighty evils which may be avoided or alleviated; and I cling with a firmer hold to the belief that for democratic nations to be virtuous and prosperous, they need only will it.

I am aware that many of my contemporaries maintain that nations are never their own masters here below, and that they necessarily obey some insurmountable and unintelligent power, arising from previous events, from their race, or from the soil and climate of their country. Such principles are false and cowardly; such principles can never produce anything but feeble men and pusillanimous nations. Providence has not created mankind entirely independent or entirely free. Providence traces, it is true, a circle of fate around each man that he cannot escape; but within the wide boundary of that circle he is powerful and free; as it is with man, so with communities. The nations of our time cannot prevent the conditions of men from becoming equal, but it depends upon themselves whether the principle of equality is to lead them to servitude or freedom, to knowledge or barbarism, to prosperity or wretchedness.

6e   To John Stuart Mill,[3] Appreciation of his British Friend's Review of Volume Two of *Democracy in America*

December 30, 1840

I am feeling quite guilty, my dear friend, for not having written you sooner. I hope you will forgive me when you consider the enormous pressure of public affairs under which I have been living in the last two months. Nothing else would have prevented me from writing you immediately after reading your article in the *Edinburgh Review*. I cannot adequately express all the various thoughts that your remarkable piece has provoked in me: It would be too long for a letter, especially with the limited opportunities I have now for writing letters. But there are things I should have long ago found the time to tell you and among others this: Of all the articles written on my book, yours is *the only one* where the author truly masters my thoughts and knows how to express them. I therefore do not need to tell you the extreme pleasure I have felt in reading it. I was at long last being judged by a very superior mind who had taken the trouble of understanding my ideas and submitting them to a rigorous analysis. You *alone*, I repeat, have given me this pleasure. All the people who have dispensed praise or blame to me, except you, have seemed to me insufficiently intelligent or else not paying enough attention. I am having your article bound with a copy of my book. These two items belong together and I want to always have them at hand together. A thousand thanks, my dear Mill, for what you have written. You have given me one of the greatest pleasures I have had in a long time.

In France the success of the second part of *Democracy* has been less widespread than that of part one. I do not believe nowadays in the literary misconception of public opinion. I am therefore actively trying to figure out for myself where I have gone wrong. For it is likely there is a considerable flaw in the book. I believe the defect lies in the book's own premise, which contains something obscure and problematical not grasped by the masses. When I was speaking only about the democratic society of the United States, that was readily understandable. If I had spoken of our democratic society in France, as it exists today, I would also have been understood. But starting

---

3   Nineteenth-century England's famous philosopher and radical reformer.

from ideas about American and French society, I meant to depict the general features of democratic societies, for which there is not yet a complete model. This is where I lose the ordinary reader. Only men very accustomed to looking for general and speculative truths like to follow me in this direction. I think the comparatively lesser impact of my book comes from this original sin of the subject matter much more than from the ways in which I have dealt with this or that part of the topic.

. . .

Adieu, will you ever come to France? I would have so much to talk to you about. Meanwhile let me express my sincere and keen affection.

Part III

The Years in Politics

Preliminary Note

This section differs from the others in that it consists almost entirely of writings not intended for the public, or else intended for publication only after Tocqueville's death (Tocqueville's *Recollections*). They show a less formal but no less insightful Tocqueville. They have been chosen for what they reveal of Tocqueville's character, his attitude towards French politics, and for the light they shed on his broader thought. Especially noteworthy are several brief selections which contain essential elements of Tocqueville's beliefs. Selection 7b shows a Tocqueville conscious of his own aristocratic feelings, yet rejecting them on the basis of a rational preference for equality. He loves freedom, but not equality. Selections 7d, 7e, and 9d show his continued concern with divisions between rich and poor and their political effects. Selection 10f is taken from a series of letters to Gobineau in which Tocqueville made clear his utter rejection of racism (cf. selection 3b on the three American races). Selection 7a shows Tocqueville talking to his constituents in Normandy while 8a and 8b present Tocqueville the colonialist.

The vividness of Tocqueville's often vitriolic depictions of individuals during the revolutions of 1848 (selection 9b) is remarkable. The reader can thus appreciate another dimension of Tocqueville's writing style only occasionally found in the more problem-oriented texts of *Democracy in America* and *The Old Regime and the Revolution*.

Tocqueville's five-month tenure as Minister for Foreign Affairs in 1849 has often been discounted as an incident of no importance, but his remarks on Germany (selections 9f and 10g in this section, and see also selection 13c in part IV) show him to have been an acute analyst of European nations as well as of America. Taken as a whole, this section presents a picture of Tocqueville the political actor, striving to find a means of putting his principles into practice, and not always being satisfied with the results.

7

Tocqueville's Political Philosophy

7a   To Odilon Barrot,[1] the French Fear Freedom

September 16, 1842

It is furthermore one of our country's mistakes to believe that an opposition can only survive on condition that it wants to make very large changes in the existing laws.

The parliamentary history of England and America clearly shows the contrary. In those countries there have been very powerful and brilliant oppositions who were only distinguished from the majorities by the manner in which they understood the practice of existing laws and the government's daily actions. The same legislation can sometimes be good or bad depending on the spirit in which it is applied, and this sole question of conduct is enough to profoundly divide politicians and create very visible differences among them. If the opposition, while adopting, or at least renouncing the overthrow of most existing laws, did nothing but show that it would interpret them differently than the majority, and that it would apply them in a more national sense, the opposition would still have a great role, more liberal than the majority, a role more effective certainly than if it showed itself inclined to change the legislation itself. Don't you think as I do that what slows the development of free institutions in France most is the fear inspired by those who anticipate them?

The nation loves freedom more than people think, but it is afraid of the

---

1   Leader in the Chamber of Deputies of the pro-monarchical opposition.

party that speaks of it. This is a prejudice and a weakness that needs to be managed in the interest of our principles themselves.

What has for my part always hurt me deeply about the left, I have told you many times and you have agreed, is the little real liberalism that is found there. The left is still much more revolutionary than liberal. To love freedom for itself, to sincerely respect the independence and the rights of your neighbor even when the exercise of those rights does not please, to keep the power of the government in check and to limit its actions, even when that power acts in agreement with our desires; to gradually and reasonably decentralize the administration, these are ideas which are found in your head, my dear Barrot, but there is no trace of them in the brains of most of those who follow you, less because of real sympathy for you than because of the impossibility of doing without you; as long as the opposition has not changed its instincts on these crucial points, it will only be good for announcing new Revolutions or for preparing the way for despotism.

I know that it is a very difficult undertaking to transform most of our men of the left into moderate, reasonable and liberal men. I know this and yet I believe that you can attempt it and succeed. Look at what is going on among our neighbors, I don't think that there is a man more different from the bulk of his party than Sir Robert Peel,[2] nor one who encounters a more grumbling obedience. And yet he leads them where he wants. Why? Because he is necessary to them, because he alone can powerfully represent them on the tribune, because he knows how to connect himself with the most intelligent part of that party, and with the help of this small group he dominates all the rest. People shout, they complain and they follow him. What he can do, I am convinced you can do.

7b   My Instincts, My Opinions, *circa* 1841

Experience has proved to me that with almost all men, but certainly with me, one always returns more or less to one's fundamental instincts, and people never do well anything but what is in accord with their instincts. Let us therefore sincerely look for *my fundamental instincts* and *my serious principles.*

I have an intellectual preference for democratic institutions, but I am aristocratic by instinct, that is I despise and fear the crowd.

I passionately love freedom, legality, the respect for rights, but not democracy. This is the base of my soul.

I hate demagogy, the disorderly action of the masses, their violent and

2   English statesman and head of the conservative party.

uneducated participation in affairs, the lower classes' envious passions, the irreligious tendencies. This is the base of my soul.

I belong neither to the revolutionary party nor the conservative party. But in the end I hold more to the latter than to the former. For I differ from the second more by the means than by the end, while I differ from the former by both means and end.

Freedom is the first of my passions. This is what is true.

7c On the Strategic, Commercial, and Military Importance of Cherbourg, 1846

Cherbourg today is of greater importance than would ever formerly have been supposed . . . I will remind you of only two incontrovertible facts – both direct results of either nature, or the general progress of human industry in the world. In these days of mobile wealth, great knowledge, and unlimited competition, Gentlemen, do you not see that it is imperative to raise huge amounts of capital in order to be competitive? To realize relative economies in the general costs of production in order to deliver the final product at a lower price? You have only to look around, in France and especially in England, to observe that the greater the competition, the lower the price of manufactured goods and the larger the industrial plant. In the near future, only huge factories will return a sufficient profit. What is happening, Gentlemen, in cotton manufacture for example, is happening more or less everywhere for the same reasons – in the naval field too. It is becoming more and more obvious that only very large vessels can transport cargo at reduced cost. This is so true that the inferiority into which our merchant marine has fallen can be blamed chiefly on the fact that the tonnage of our vessels is on average much smaller than that of American or English ships. Sooner or later, long distance navigation will be the exclusive province of very large vessels. So much for the first fact.

Now the second: Follow carefully the French coast along the Channel. You will find along this vast stretch of coastal land only one port, I repeat, only one port, whether made by nature or which can be adapted by art, to receive conveniently and in all weathers vessels of this kind. This port is Cherbourg.

I will not, Gentlemen, demonstrate again in any detail the great military significance of Cherbourg even though this is the main reason why our interests are so closely tied to those of all France.

I won't talk either about this recent and considerable innovation which is further turning Cherbourg into such a danger for the British and such a precious resource for us: the use of the steam engine in the Navy. I have already said all this, and many others have proven it.

I have to say, Gentlemen, that, above and beyond the minor reasons mentioned above, no matter their relevance, there is a more powerful, although less specific reason which I have always thought would make a strong impression on the government and the Chambers. This is a point drawn from history.

All the great men who, in the last century and a half, have concerned themselves with French power and glory on the seas, Vauban first among them, have had Cherbourg in mind. Vauban described Cherbourg in 1684 in the simple and vigorous language which only he knew how to use. I am happy to repeat it, for you will enjoy it. Vauban painted Cherbourg in one stroke as a *bold site*; he meant that all dangerous and difficult enterprises attempted against England should gather in Cherbourg and start from here.

All the governments who have seriously and energetically meant to fight for domination of the seas, or at least freedom of the seas, have ardently desired to create a military position at Cherbourg. On the contrary, all the pusillanimous governments, who have been frightened by possible difficulties on the seas have neglected Cherbourg. This is a true gauge of where they really stand.

7d   On the Middle Class and the People, 1847

People complain about the sterility of parliamentary life, the limited significance of the questions usually discussed in the Chambers, and the lack of virility in the political parties. Whether or not these criticisms are justified, it is obvious that the overwhelming majority of the country is rarely and then only minimally interested in our debates. The nation seems to be divided into two unequal portions: a tiny portion of the population which acts and speaks in the Chambers; a huge population that looks at this very small number of actors without really understanding the meaning of the play and without attaching any real significance to the different incidents of the parliamentary drama.

In observing closely the leaders of the two parties which divide the Chamber of Deputies, the conservative majority and the dynastic opposition, we see very different tendencies and tastes among them. But when it comes to figuring out how they would take radically different measures, one cannot think of anything. It becomes clear that they would take similar measures in different spirits, not different measures.

I very sincerely believe that the reason for the nation's general indifference towards what is taking place in the Chambers derives from this cause.

Why does the nation see the parliamentary world in this light? Is it the nation's fault or the politicians' fault? Is there a more profound and general cause which may explain in part this situation?

It may come in part from lack of political education. People are tired of revolutions and distracted by their material concerns. Institutions are flawed. But, in my view, the deeper and more general cause is the destruction of all classes in the nation and the very structure of the new society.

Very different political parties can emerge only from very distinct or even opposite interests. Parties are tenacious, animated, and loud only in proportion to the distinct and contrary interests that sustain them. For such conditions to materialize, the social circumstances of the citizens have to be varied. Some citizens must hold permanent rights, influence, and superiority; others not. If there was so much activity in political life throughout the first Revolution, it was because conflicts of interests were born out of differences in conditions, which produced the great political parties. The active and fertile awakening of public spirit during the Restoration of the monarchy must be attributed to similar causes. Seen from afar, the time span from 1789 to 1830 will appear as a single and unique drama in several acts. When we examine the Restoration, after we have set aside all secondary facts, we will realize that the final struggle of the middle classes against the aristocracy proper was its cardinal and leading event. If the elder branch of the monarchy had been able, from the beginning, to sever its ties from all the aristocratic classes of old and, instead of trying to reanimate them, achieved their diffusion into the middle class, it is likely that political passions, in the official sphere of the main powers, would have abated, just as we see today. The elder branch would not have faced any more obstacles to governing than the younger one now. But circumstances did not lend themselves to such a course of action. Moreover a government which called itself a restoration could not repudiate in such a way former allies in both governing and suffering.

The revolution of 1830 has done what the Restoration could not or did not want to do: it has completed, in the social sphere, the revolution of 1789. The revolution of 1830 has forever destroyed all the classes which divided the country. It has formed, above the lower classes, only one almost homogenous social class. Within this class interests are almost identical. It is therefore practically impossible to generate from within it, and keep alive, great parties, that is great political associations with very different interests and wanting very different things. The peculiar homogeneity which all men above the lower classes now possess strikes me as the first cause of the suddenly tepid and indolent public life of this country; for the real emptiness of parliamentary debates, and the insignificance of politicians. Altogether, there has perhaps never before been, in any country, save for the Constituent Assembly of 1789, a parliament with such diverse and brilliant talents as ours today. The orators' talent is great, the impact of their speeches small. Why is that? Because at bottom they differ more by their words than by their ideas. When they display their enmity and divisions, they are not showing clearly how they would act differently from one another. Their struggle looks more like an internal family quarrel than permanent war between two great parties with very different interests and therefore very different doctrines and courses of action.

There may one day be a time when the nation will again be divided between two real parties. We were saying earlier that the Revolution had abolished all privileges and destroyed all exclusive rights. But there is one left, that of owning property.

Men of property should not entertain any illusion about the strength of their situation. They should not imagine that property rights are an unconquerable fortress because it has not yet been breached. Our times are unprecedented. When property rights were the source of so many other rights, they were not at risk, not even challenged. Property rights were then guaranteed and so to speak protected. But now, on the contrary, property rights appear to be only the last vestige of a destroyed aristocratic world. They stand alone and isolated. They have to withstand the shock of democratic opinions alone. For the first time, people are arguing about them and attacking them.

There is little doubt that, one day, the political struggle will be between the haves and the have nots. Property will be the great battlefield, and the great political questions will be about how to change property rights and to what extent.

How is it that the early signs of this future are not obvious to all? Are we to believe that it is by chance, or just a caprice of the human mind, that we are seeing appearing everywhere doctrines which, under various labels, all have the same principal characteristic – either to destroy, to challenge, or at least to limit and weaken property rights?

No, all these doctrines are only the various symptoms of the natural state of our times. They are the symptoms of this great democratic disease which in the last sixty years has often changed its appearance, but never its nature.

7e Fragments For a Social Policy, *circa* 1847

To tell the truth, complete equality is a chimera, for there is no way of organizing a tax system so that it weighs only on the rich, and the moment taxation, whatever it is and however well-established it is, bears on both the rich and the poor, it will be easier for the rich man to pay than the poor man.

But this inevitable evil can be considerably aggravated or diminished according to what method is followed. It is impossible that inequality of fortunes not be felt in taxation as in everything.

What we at least ought to tend towards, is that it be felt as little as possible. We can arrive at this result by adopting these two [*sic*] rules.

1. Exempt the poorest people from taxation, that is those for whom the burden is heaviest.
2. Do not tax necessities, because then everyone is obliged to pay and the poor are burdened.
3. When taxes bear on things that are necessary or very useful, make them very low for everyone so that they are almost as indifferent for poor people as for rich people.
4. When the tax is high, try to make it proportional to the wealth of the taxpayer.

There are many taxes which by their nature are not proportionable. All indirect taxes are in this category.

1. Customs-duties. Their effect is to make everything they strike more expensive within the kingdom. This effect is felt by all citizens, and necessarily unequally.
2. Within the kingdom, indirect taxes proper: it is the consumer who pays them and they bear on him, not because of his wealth, but because of his consumption.

Here, it is true, one can say that consumption itself being proportionate to wealth, the standard we are looking for is found again.

Yes, at least when it is not a question of necessary commodities whose consumption is more or less equal for everyone. If one could put a tax on breathing air, for example, it is clear that the poor man like the rich man would be obliged to pay and that the one, regardless of his wealth, being unable to consume more of the taxed commodity than the other, would never have to bear heavier taxes. This example can serve as the ideal of a bad tax.

It is in this regard that court expenses paid by the parties are a bad tax. A trial is often as necessary a commodity for the poor man as for the rich.

What could be done for the lower class may be divided into several categories: *A decrease of public burdens for the poor* including all recruitment, court costs . . . here the tariff system perhaps requires most change, but for the moment that is the holy ark. It is this with which I concern myself, this is a lot, but not enough; this is an indirect way of coming to the aid of the poor. Let us see what direct means would be.

- By establishing institutions which were intended particularly for use by the poor man, which he could use to educate himself, to enrich himself, such as savings banks, credit institutions, free schools, restrictive laws about the duration of work, asylums, workshops, mutual aid societies.
- Finally by coming directly to his aid and comforting his poverty, with the resources from taxation: hospitals, charity bureaus, poor-taxes, distribution of commodities, of work, of money.

Finally, three means of coming to the aid of the lower classes:

1. Exempt him from part of the public burdens or at least only burden him proportionately.
2. Put within his reach the institutions which will let him get by and help him.
3. Come to his aid and assist him directly with his needs.

. . . that the true meaning of the revolution is equality, the more equal distribution of the goods of this world.

That the new governments or the classes newly brought to power cannot maintain themselves except by doing all that is possible in this sense.

People claim that the new government and the middle class which remains the governing class will not fulfill its duty in this. Is this true?

Complaints of the lower class or made in the name of the lower classes . . .

Suggested remedies: communism, organization of work, phalanstery[3] . . .

---

3 "Phalansteries" were the communities created by the followers of the French socialist Fourier.

These remedies all tend to make a new social order, without precedent in the world.

. . .

The middle classes have drawn from the Revolution all the profit they could expect. But have the lower classes drawn from the Revolution the profits to which they could legitimately aspire?

Has the old principle that the chief social burdens should weigh on the lower classes been really and effectively destroyed?

Does the government of the middle classes really do for the lower classes all that they have a legitimate right to expect?

Paint the state of the parties, the nation's indifference, explain it by the small difference that exists between the parliamentary parties, their common indifference to the lower classes . . .

Sinister picture that people draw of the future, imminent perils . . . I don't believe any of it. What is serious is distant, but no less serious.

8

Tocqueville the Colonialist

8a On Algeria, 1837, 1840, 1841, 1843

Second Letter on Algeria, August 22, 1837[1]

I beg you, sir, to try to envision these agile and indomitable children of the desert locked into the thousand formalities of our bureaucracy and forced to submit to the sluggishness, the uniformity, the regulations and minutiae of our centralized government. We preserved nothing from the old government of the country but the employment of the yataghan and the baton as police equipment. Everything else became French.

This applied to the towns and the nearby tribes. As for the rest of the regency's inhabitants, we didn't even try to govern them. After having destroyed their government, we did not give them any other.

Tocqueville's Notes Before his First Trip to Algeria, 1840

Why there is no priesthood among Muslims

Priest, worship, and priesthood in Mohammadanism   Mohammed preached his religion to uneducated people, nomads and warriors; this religion had war as its purpose; hence the small number of rites and the simplicity of worship. A complicated and ritualistic cult requires temples, a sedentary population, and relatively peaceful habits.

---

1   First appeared unsigned in the newspaper *La Presse Seine et Oise*.

Ritual being almost non-existent, there was little need for priests. But there is a more powerful reason to explain the almost complete lack of a distinctive clergy among the Muslims.

This appears quite odd at first glance, for all religions, especially those which have had a strong influence on men's imagination, have acquired or kept their influence with the help of a strongly constituted body of priests, firmly separated from the rest of the nation.

Mohammadanism is the religion which has most completely combined and mixed the two powers. The high priest is necessarily the ruler, and the ruler the high priest. All the acts of civil and political life are more or less regulated by religious law. Thus a separate body, directing religious life independently from political and civil society, as in Catholicism for example, cannot exist.

This has been a good thing amidst all the wrongs caused by the Muslim religion. The existence of a body of priests is often in itself the source of many social problems. When religion can be strong without it, it should be praised.

But even though the concentration and combination of the two powers established by Mohammed has produced this particular good, it has been the first cause of the despotism and social immobility which almost always characterized Muslim nations. This is also why Muslim nations are defeated in the end by those who have embraced the contrary system.

As the Koran is the common source for religious and civil law, and even lay science, the same education is required of those who want to become ministers of the cult, legal authorities, judges, and even scientists. The monarch does not discriminate among people in this educated class to nominate ministers of the cult (imams), legal authorities (muftis), and judges (cadis). Practitioners of these different professions are interchangeable. This is a situation where there is a religion but no priesthood.

Essay on Algeria, October 1841

I do not think France can think seriously about leaving Algeria. In the eyes of the world, such an abandonment would be the clear indication of our decline.

The great things we have already done in Algeria, the example set by our arts, our ideas, our power, have had a powerful effect on the spirit of the very populations that fight us with the greatest ardor and reject our yoke with the greatest energy. If we abandoned Algiers, the country would probably pass directly under the rule of another Christian nation. But even if Algiers were to fall back into the hands of the Muslims, which is possible, we can be sure that the Muslim power that would take our place would be very different from the one we have destroyed. It would aim higher, it would have other means of action, it would enter into regular contact with the Christian nations and would usually be controlled by one of them. In a word, it is clear to me that whatever happens, Africa has henceforth entered into the movement of the civilized world and will never leave it.

Letter to Arthur de Gobineau, October 22, 1843

You seem to be questioning even the political utility of religions . . .

I studied the Koran a great deal, mainly because of our position vis-à-vis the Muslim population of Algeria and throughout the Near East. I must tell you that I came away from that study with the conviction that by and large, there have been few religions in the world as deadly to men as that of Mohammed. As far as I can see, it is the principal cause of the decadence so visible today in the Muslim world, and, though it is less absurd than the polytheism of ancient times, its social and political tendencies are in my opinion infinitely more to be feared, and I therefore regard it as a form of decadence rather than a form of progress in relation to paganism itself. This is what I think I would be able to show you clearly, should the bad idea of getting circumcised ever occur to you.

8b Sketches of a Work on India, 1843

The immense British empire in India was established so suddenly and so recently that Europe, astonished by such an unusual revolution, has not yet had time to study its causes or effects. This great revolution has been seen, and is still being seen, only as an inexplicable and amazing *event*. The truth is that even if you look at the phenomenon only superficially, there has never been anything more extraordinary.

A country almost as vast as Europe has been conquered in a span of sixty years by a few thousand Europeans who landed on its shores as merchants. One hundred million people have been subjected and are governed by *thirty* thousand foreigners. The latter, totally foreign by law, religion, language, and customs, leave nothing of the direction of affairs to the former.

Not satisfied with the conquest of so many, the victors have attempted two daring and singular innovations:

They have attempted to abolish in one stroke the entire judicial system of the vanquished. This, I believe, is without historical precedent. The invaders who have taken the most away from defeated peoples have at least let them administer their own civil law.

There is more. They have redistributed the land (note: especially in Bengal), thus combining the difficulty of a great social revolution with that of a political revolution.

They have not accomplished all this by following a clever and uniform plan decided on in advance and executed by some great genius. Instead they have proceeded gradually, depending on people and circumstances, without premeditation, by trial and error, with many hesitations. Ordinary men have led this strange revolution. They have used only common sense and determination.

Finally, to show just how unique this event was, two thirds of an Empire as vast as that of Alexander has been conquered against the formal orders of the people who are now its masters. The British government and the [East India] Company have been led without their knowledge, or even against their will, to make these conquests. Several times they have disavowed their own generals. What seems to me incompatible with the normal tendency of human passions is that their desires have always been less substantial than their gains.

. . .

There are a great many castes in India; there is no nation. Rather each caste is a small separate nation of its own. It is the caste system that has kept alive the national spirit of the Hindus. The homeland, to them, is the caste. No need to look for the nation elsewhere than in the caste, where it is alive.

All conquerors have easily overturned political regimes in India and dethroned monarchs. They have overturned kingdoms, but each time they have turned their attention to the caste system, they have met with insurmountable resistance.

Thus a conqueror is never faced directly with a great people but a multitude of poorly connected small populations.

The immense majority of Hindus belong to the lower castes. Whatever happens later in life, their birth has placed them forever on the lowest step of the social ladder, where they have little to hope, or to fear, from government. One comes out of the Brahma's foot and not the head; the damage cannot be repaired. It does not matter to the lower castes who rules! The only people really interested in revolutions come from the higher ones, which comprise only a very small number of men. In the end, the power which governs millions of subject people is supported only by the interests and efforts of a few individuals.

A religion with the kind of power over the human soul needed to create and maintain a social state so contrary to nature must inspire in its devotees the kind of fanatical intolerance that takes the place of patriotism in so many barbarous nations. But this is not the case. Brahmanism is at once the most demanding and the most tolerant of religions. This is easily understood when one realizes this is a religion based on privilege. One joins by birth. There is no way to convert if not born to it. Therefore one cannot develop hatred of the people Brahma has left out. It is the idea of a common origin of the human species, of the similarity of all men, and their obligation to recognize and pray to the same god which has introduced proselytizing and persecution into the world.

9

Tocqueville in 1848

Recollections of the 1848 Revolution

*9a   Part I Section 1,[1] Origins and character of these recollections –
General aspects of the period preceding the Revolution of 1848 –
First symptoms of the Revolution*

Now that for the moment I am out of the stream of public life, and the uncertain state of my health does not even allow me to follow any consecutive study, I have in my solitude for a time turned my thoughts to myself, or rather to those events of the recent past in which I played a part or stood as witness. The best use for my leisure seems to be to go back over these events, to describe the men I saw taking part in them, and in this way, if I can, to catch and engrave on my memory those confused features that make up the uncertain physiognomy of my time.

Along with this decision of mine goes another to which I shall be equally faithful: these recollections are to be a mental relaxation for myself and not a work of literature. They are written for myself alone. These pages are to be a mirror, in which I can enjoy seeing my contemporaries and myself, not a painting for the public to view. My best friends are not to know about them, for I wish to keep my freedom to describe myself and them without flattery. I want to uncover the secret motives that made us act, them and myself as well as other men, and, when I have understood these, to state them. In a word, I want to express myself honestly in these memoirs, and it is therefore necessary that they be completely secret.

1   Written in 1850 at Tocqueville.

I do not intend to start my recollections further back than the Revolution of 1848, nor to carry them beyond the date when I left office, that is, 30 October 1849. It is only within this span that the events I want to describe had something of greatness in them, or that my position enabled me to see them clearly.

Although I was somewhat out of the stream of events, I did live in the parliamentary world of the last years of the July Monarchy, but I would find it difficult to give a clear account of that time, which is so close, but which has left so confused an impression on my memory. I lose the thread of my recollections amid the labyrinth of petty incidents, petty ideas, petty passions, personal viewpoints and contradictory projects in which the life of public men in that period was frittered away. Only the general physiognomy of that time comes readily to my mind. For that was something I often contemplated with mingled curiosity and fear, and I clearly discerned the particular features that gave it its character.

Seen as a whole from a distance, our history from 1789 to 1830 appears to be forty-one years of deadly struggle between the Ancien Régime with its traditions, memories, hopes and men (i.e. the aristocrats), and the new France led by the middle class. 1830 would seem to have ended the first period of our revolutions, or rather, of our revolution, for it was always one and the same, through its various fortunes and passions, whose beginning our fathers saw and whose end we shall in all probability not see. All that remained of the Ancien Régime was destroyed forever. In 1830 the triumph of the middle class was decisive and so complete that the narrow limits of the bourgeoisie encompassed all political powers, franchises, prerogatives, indeed the whole government, to the exclusion, in law, of all beneath it and, in fact, of all that had once been above it. Thus the bourgeoisie became not only the sole director of society, but also, one might say, its cultivator. It settled into every office, prodigiously increased the number of offices, and made a habit of living off the public Treasury almost as much as from its own industry.

No sooner had this occurred than a marked lull ensued in every political passion, a sort of universal shrinkage, and at the same time a rapid growth in public wealth. The spirit peculiar to the middle class became the general spirit of the government; it dominated foreign policy as well as home affairs. This spirit was active and industrious, often dishonest, generally orderly, but sometimes rash because of vanity and selfishness, timid by temperament, moderate in all things except a taste for well-being, and mediocre; a spirit that, combined with that of the people or of the aristocracy, could work wonders, but that by itself never produces anything but a government without either virtues or greatness. Mistress of all, as no aristocracy ever has been or perhaps ever will be, the middle class, which must be called the ruling class, entrenched in its power and, shortly afterwards, in its selfishness, treated government like a private business, each member thinking of public affairs only in so far as they could be turned to his private profit, and in his petty prosperity easily forgetting the people.

Posterity, which sees only striking crimes and generally fails to notice smaller vices, will perhaps never know how far the government of that time towards the end took on the features of a trading company whose every operation is directed to the benefit that its members may derive therefrom. These vices were linked to the natural instincts of the dominant class, to its absolute power, and to the enervation and corruption of the age. King Louis-Philippe did much to make them grow. He was the accident that made the illness fatal.

Although this prince sprang from the noblest family in Europe and had, buried in the depths of his soul, a full measure of hereditary pride, certainly not considering himself like any other man, he nevertheless shared most of the good and bad qualities associated primarily with the lower ranks of society. He had regular mores and wanted those around him to have the same. He was orderly in his behavior, simple in his habits, and moderate in his tastes; he was naturally on the side of law and hostile to any excess; sober in all his acts if not in his desires; kind, although without sensitivity; greedy and soft. He had no raging passions, or ruinous weaknesses, or striking vices, and only one kingly virtue, courage. His politeness was extreme, but without discrimination or dignity, the politeness of a tradesman rather than of a prince. He had no taste for letters or the fine arts, but cared passionately for business. He had a prodigious memory which was capable of relentlessly recalling the smallest details. His conversation was prolix, diffuse, original, anecdotal, full of little facts and wit and meaning, in short of all the pleasures of the mind that are possible in the absence of delicacy and elevation of spirit. His mind was distinguished, but restricted and clogged by the meanness and narrowness of his soul. He was enlightened, subtle and tenacious, but all his thoughts turned to the useful, and he was filled with such a deep contempt for truth and such a profound disbelief in virtue that they clouded his vision, not only making it impossible for him to see the beauty that always goes with truth and honesty, but also preventing him from understanding their frequent usefulness. He had a profound understanding of men, but only in respect to their vices; in matters of religion he had the disbelief of the eighteenth century, and in politics, the skepticism of the nineteenth. Having no belief himself, he had no faith in the belief of others. He was by nature fond of power and of dishonest courtiers, as if he really had been born on a throne. His ambition, which was limited only by prudence, never either satisfied or carried him away, but always remained close to the ground.

There have been many princes who resemble this portrait, but what was peculiar to Louis-Philippe was the analogy, or rather the kinship and consanguinity between his defects and those of his age; it was this that made him an attractive prince, but one who was singularly dangerous and corrupting for his contemporaries, and particularly for the class that held the power. Placed at the head of an aristocracy, he might perhaps have had a happy influence on it. At the head of the bourgeoisie, he pushed it down the slope that it was by nature only too inclined to go. It was a marriage of vices, and this union, which first provided the strength of the one and then brought about the demoralization of the other, ended by bringing both to destruction.

Though I was never admitted to that prince's councils, I had occasion to approach him fairly frequently. The last time I saw him at close quarters was shortly before the February catastrophe. At that time I was director of the French Academy and I had to bring to the King's notice some matter or other concerning that body. Having dealt with the question that brought me, I was about to withdraw, but the King detained me, taking a chair and motioning me to another, saying affably, "As you are here, Monsieur de Tocqueville, let us chat; I would like you to tell me a little about America." I knew him well enough to realize what that meant: I want to talk about America. And so he talked tellingly at great length, without my having a chance or even the desire to put in a word, for he really did interest me. He described places as if he could see them; he recalled the distinguished men he had met forty years before as if he had left them yesterday; he remembered their names and Christian names; mentioned their age at that time; and recounted their life stories, genealogies and descent with wonderful accuracy and infinite detail and without ever becoming boring. Without taking breath he came back from America to Europe and talked about all our affairs, foreign and domestic, with an incredible lack of restraint (for I had no right to his confidence), telling me much ill about the Emperor of Russia, whom he called Monsieur Nicolas, mentioning Lord Palmerston in passing as a scapegrace, and finally talking at length about the Spanish marriages, which had just taken place, and the trouble they had caused him from the point of view of England: "The Queen is at me about it," he said, "and gets very upset. But after all," he added, "all their outcry won't stop me *driving my own cab*." Although that turn of phrase dated back to the Ancien Régime, I thought it was doubtful that Louis XIV had ever used it after he accepted the Spanish succession. I think too that Louis-Philippe was mistaken, and, to borrow his language, the Spanish marriages played an important part in upsetting his cab.

After three quarters of an hour the King got up, thanked me for the pleasure our conversation had given him (I had not said four words) and

dismissed me, clearly delighted with me, as one usually is by anyone in whose presence one feels one has talked well. This was the last time he received me.
. . .

There I clearly noted the appearance of several of the signs that usually announce the approach of revolutions. And I began to think that in 1830 I had mistaken the end of an act for the end of the play.

A short piece I wrote then, which has remained unpublished, and a speech I made at the beginning of 1848 bear witness to these preoccupations.

Several of my parliamentary friends had met in October 1847 to try to come to an agreement about the line to take during the next legislative session. We decided that we should publish a programme in the form of a manifesto, and this task was entrusted to me. Afterwards, the idea of such a publication was abandoned, but I had composed the required piece. I have found it among my papers, and I quote the following sentences. After describing the languor of parliamentary life, I add:
. . .

Soon the political struggle will be between the Haves and the Have-nots; property will be the great battlefield; and the main political questions will turn on the more or less profound modifications of the rights of property owners that are to be made. Then we shall again see great public agitations and great political parties.[2]

. . .

I was even more explicit and urgent in the speech I made to the Chamber of Deputies on 29 January 1848, which can be read in the *Moniteur* for the 30th. Here are the main passages:

It is said that there is no danger because there is no riot, and that because there is no visible disorder on the surface of society, we are far from revolution.

Gentlemen, allow me to say that I think you are mistaken. True, there is no actual disorder, but disorder has penetrated far into men's minds. See what is happening among the working classes who are, I realize, quiet now. It is true that they are not now tormented by what may properly be called political passions to the extent they once were; but do you not see that their passions have changed from political to social? Do you not see that opinions and ideas are gradually spreading among them that tend not simply to the overthrow of such and such laws, such and such a minister, or even such and such a government, but rather to the overthrow of society, breaking down the bases

2   See the last five paragraphs of selection 7d for the full text of this excerpt.

on which it now rests? Do you not hear what is being said every day among them? Do you not hear them constantly repeating that all the people above them are incapable and unworthy to rule them? That the division of property in the world up to now is unjust? That property rests on bases of inequity? And do you not realize that when such opinions take root and spread, sinking deeply into the masses, they must sooner or later (I do not know when, I do not know how) bring in their train the most terrifying of revolutions?

Gentlemen, my profound conviction is that we are lulling ourselves to sleep over an active volcano . . .

. . . I was saying just now that sooner or later (I do not know when or whence) this ill will bring into the land revolutions of the utmost seriousness: be assured that that is so.

When I come to study what has been, at different times and epochs of history among different peoples, the effective reason why ruling classes have been ruined, I note the various events and men and accidental or superficial causes, but believe me, the real cause, the effective one, that makes men lose power is that they have become unworthy to exercise it.

Consider the old Monarchy, gentlemen. It was stronger than you, stronger because of its origin; it was better supported than you are by ancient customs, old mores and old beliefs; it was stronger than you, and yet it has fallen in the dust. And why did it fall? Do you think that it was because of some particular accident? Do you think it was due to one particular man, the deficit, the Tennis Court Oath, La Fayette or Mirabeau? No, gentlemen, there is another cause: the class that was ruling then had, through its indifference, selfishness and vices, become incapable and unworthy of ruling.

That is the real reason.

Gentlemen, feelings of patriotism should preoccupy us at all times, but now more than ever. Have you no intuitive instinct, incapable of being analyzed but certain, that tells you the ground is trembling once more in Europe? Do you not feel – how should I say it – a revolutionary wind in the air? We do not know whence it comes, or whither it goes, or what it will carry away; and at such a time you remain calm in face of the degradation of public mores for the expression is not too strong.

I am speaking here without bitterness, and I even trust that I am speaking without party feeling; I am attacking men against whom I feel no anger, but I am bound to disclose to my country my deep and firm conviction. And that profound and fixed conviction is that public mores are becoming degraded, and that this degradation will lead you shortly, very shortly perhaps, into new revolutions. Are the lives of kings supported by stronger threads, which are harder to snap, than the lives of other men? Have you at this very moment any certainty of the morrow? Do you know what may happen in France a year, a month, or perhaps a day from now? You do not know that, but you do know there is a tempest on the horizon, and it is moving towards you. Will you let it take you by surprise?

Gentlemen I implore you not to do so; I do not ask, I implore. I would gladly go down on my knees before you, so real and serious do I think the danger, and so persuaded am I that it is no idle rhetorical flourish to point it out. Yes, the danger is great. Avert it while there is yet time; cure the ill with effective remedies, attacking the thing itself and not its symptoms.

There has been talk of legislative changes. I am very much inclined to believe that such changes are not only useful, but necessary: hence I consider electoral reform useful, and parliamentary reform necessary; but, gentlemen, I am not so mad as to be unaware that the destinies of people are not shaped by laws alone. No, gentlemen, great events do not spring from the mechanism of the laws, but from the very spirit of the government. Keep those laws if you like – keep them, though I think you would be making a great mistake – even keep the same men if that gives you any pleasure; but for God's sake change the spirit of the government, for, I repeat, it is the spirit that is leading you to the abyss.

These somber prophecies were received with insulting laughter by the majority. The opposition applauded energetically, but from party spirit rather than conviction. The truth is that no one yet seriously believed in the danger I foretold, although we were so near the brink. Every politician had, during the long parliamentary comedy, contracted an inveterate habit of coloring the expression of his feelings outrageously and exaggerating his thoughts out of all proportion, and in this way they had become unable to appreciate the real and the true. For several years the majority had been saying that the opposition was endangering society, and the opposition had been constantly repeating that the Ministers were ruining the Monarchy. Both sides had asserted these things so often, without believing them very much, that in the end they came not to believe them at all, just at the moment when events were about to prove them both right. Even my personal friends thought that a bit of rhetoric was mixed with my facts.

I recall that as I came down from the tribune, Dufaure took me to one side and said with the parliamentary intuition that was his sole claim to genius: "You succeeded. But you would have succeeded even better if you had not overshot the feeling of the Assembly so much and tried to make us so frightened." And now that I am here face to face with myself and inquisitively searching my memory to see if I was as afraid as I seemed to be, I find that I was not; and I clearly see that the event justified me more promptly and completely than I had foreseen. No, I did not expect such a revolution as we were going to have; who could have expected it? I think I did see clearer than the next man the general causes that tilted the July Monarchy towards its ruin. But I did not see the accidents that were to topple it over. However, the days that still separated us from the catastrophe slipped away fast.

9b   Part II

9b1   Section 1, "My View of the Reasons for the Events of the 24th February, and my Thoughts Concerning its Effects for the Future"[3]

So the July Monarchy had fallen, fallen without a struggle, not under the victors' blows, but before they were struck; and the victors were as astonished at their success as the losers at their defeat. After the February Revolution I often heard M. Guizot and even M. Molé and M. Thiers say that it was all due to surprise and should be considered pure accident, a lucky stroke and nothing more. I have always felt tempted to answer them as Molière's Misanthrope answers Oronte: "Pour en juger ainsi, vous avez vos raisons,"[4] since for eighteen years those three men had directed the affairs of France under Louis-Philippe, and it was hard for them to admit that the prince's bad government had prepared the way for the catastrophe that threw him from the throne.

Obviously I, not having the same reasons to believe it, was not quite of their opinion. I am not asserting that accidents played no part in the February Revolution, for they played a very great one; but they were not the only thing.

In my life I have come across literary men who wrote histories without taking part in public affairs, and politicians whose only concern was to control events without a thought of describing them. And I have invariably noticed that the former see general causes everywhere, whereas the latter, spending their lives amid the disconnected events of each day, freely attribute everything to particular incidents and think that all the little strings their hands are busy pulling daily are those that control the world's destiny. Probably both of them are mistaken.

For my part I hate all those absolute systems that make all the events of history depend on great first causes linked together by the chain of fate and thus succeed, so to speak, in banishing men from the history of the human race. Their boasted breadth seems to me narrow, and their mathematical exactness false. I believe, *pace* the writers who find these sublime theories to feed their vanity and lighten their labors, that many important historical facts can be explained only by accidental circumstances, while many others are inexplicable. Finally, that chance, or rather the concatenation of secondary causes, which we call by that name because we can't sort them all out, is a

3   Written in Sorrento (Southern Italy) between November 1850 and March 1851. See selection 10a.
4   "You have your reasons for such a view."

very important element in all that we see taking place in the world's theater. But I am firmly convinced that chance can do nothing unless the ground has been prepared in advance. Antecedent facts, the nature of institutions, turns of mind and the state of mores are the materials from which chance composes those impromptu events that surprise and terrify us.

In common with all other great events of this sort, the February Revolution was born of general causes fertilized, if I may put it so, by accidents. And to make the whole thing depend on the former is as superficial as attributing it solely to the latter.

The industrial revolution, which for thirty years had been making Paris the leading manufacturing city in France, attracting a whole new population of workmen, not to mention the work on the fortifications, which had brought in a flood of laborers now out of work; the passion for material pleasures, which, spurred on by the government, was getting a firmer and firmer hold over the whole of this multitude, the democratic disease of envy silently at work; economic and political theories, which were beginning to attract notice and which tended to encourage the belief that human wretchedness was due to the laws and not to providence and that poverty could be abolished by changing the system of society; the contempt felt for the ruling class, especially its leaders, a contempt so deep and general that it paralyzed the resistance even of those who stood to lose most by the overthrow of authority; the centralization, thanks to which control of Paris and of the whole machinery of government was kept in working order, was all that was needed to complete a revolution; and lastly, the mobility of everything – institutions, ideas, mores and men in a society on the move, which had lived through seven great revolutions within sixty years, not to mention numerous small secondary upheavals: such were the general causes without which the February Revolution would have been impossible. The main accidents that brought it on were the clumsy passions of the dynastic opposition, which prepared the ground for a riot when it wanted a reform; the attempts to suppress that riot, excessive at first, then abandoned; the sudden disappearance of the former ministers, which snapped the threads of power, threads that the new ministers, in their confusion, could neither pick up nor retie; the mistakes and mental disorientation of these ministers who were so inadequate in rebuilding what they had been strong enough to throw down; the vacillation of the generals; the absence of the only members of the royal family who had either popularity or energy; and above all the senile imbecility of King Louis-Philippe, a weakness nobody could have foreseen, and which even now after the event seems almost incredible.

I sometimes wonder what in the King's soul could have produced this unanticipated sudden collapse. Louis-Philippe's life had been passed amid revolutions, and he certainly lacked neither experience, nor courage, nor intelligence, although all those qualities deserted him on that day. I think his weakness was due to the intensity of his astonishment; he was knocked flat, unaware of what had hit him. The February Revolution was *unforeseen* by everybody, but by him most of all; no warning from the outside had prepared him for it, for his mind had retreated long ago into the sort of haughty loneliness inhabited by almost all kings whose long reigns have been prosperous, who mistake luck for genius, and who do not want to listen to anybody, because they think they have no more to learn. Besides, Louis-Philippe, like his ministers, had been misled, as mentioned before, by the will-o'-the-wisp light past history cast on the present. One could make a weird collection of all the utterly dissimilar mistakes that have been fathered one by the other. There is Charles I, being driven into arbitrary behavior and violence by seeing how the spirit of opposition flourished under the kindly rule of his father; Louis XVI, determined to put up with everything because Charles I had perished unwilling to put up with anything; then Charles X provoking a revolution because he had witnessed Louis XVI's weakness; and finally Louis-Philippe, the most perspicacious of them all, who imagined that all he had to do to remain on the throne was, without violating the law, to pervert it, and that provided he himself observed the letter of the Charter, the nation would never go beyond it. To corrupt the people without defying them and to twist the spirit of the Constitution without changing the letter; to play off the country's vices one against the other; and gently to drown revolutionary passion in the love of material pleasures; this had been his idea throughout his life, and it gradually became, not just his main, but his only thought. He shut himself up in it; he lived inside it; and when he suddenly saw that it was wrong, he was like a man awakened at night by an earthquake, who, seeing his house falling down in the darkness and even the ground giving way under his feet, remains distracted and lost amid the universal unforeseen ruin.

I now sit back very comfortably to argue about the causes leading up to the 24th February, but on the afternoon of that day I had quite other thoughts in my head; the event itself filled my thoughts, and I was more concerned with what would follow than with what had produced it.

This was the second revolution within the space of seventeen years that I had seen accomplished before my eyes.

Both pained me; but how much more bitter were the impressions left by the second! Right up to the end I had felt some remnants of hereditary affection for Charles X, but that king fell because he had violated rights that were dear to me, and I was able to hope that my country's freedom would be revived rather than extinguished by his fall. Today that freedom seemed dead to me; the fugitive royal family meant nothing to me, but I felt that my own cause was lost.

I had spent the best years of my youth in a society that seemed to be regaining prosperity and grandeur as it regained freedom; I had conceived the idea of a regulated and orderly freedom, controlled by religious belief, mores and laws; I was touched by the joys of such a freedom, and it had become my whole life's passion; I had felt that I could never be consoled for its loss, and now I clearly saw that I must give it up forever.

I had had too much experience of men to accept payment in idle words this time; I knew that, while one great revolution may be able to found a nation's liberty, several revolutions on top of each other make the enjoyment of an orderly liberty impossible there for a long time.

I still did not know what would come out of this one, but I was already certain that it would not be any result satisfactory to me; and I foresaw that, whatever might be the fate of our posterity, it was our lot to spend a wretched life between alternate swings to license and to oppression.

Mentally I reviewed the history of our last sixty years and smiled bitterly to myself as I thought of the illusions cherished at the end of each phase of this long revolution; the theories feeding these illusions; our historians' learned daydreams, and all the ingenious false systems by which men sought to explain a present still unclearly seen and to foresee the unseen future.

The Constitutional Monarchy had succeeded the Ancien Régime; the Republic followed the Monarchy; the Empire the Republic; after the Empire the Restoration; then there had come the July Monarchy. After each of these successive changes it was said that the French Revolution, having achieved what was presumptuously called its work, was finished: men had said that, and they had believed it. Under the Restoration, I, too, unfortunately hoped for that, and I continued to hope after the Restoration government had fallen; and here was the French Revolution starting again, for it was always the same one. As we go on, its end seems ever farther off and hazier. Shall we reach, as other prophets as vain perhaps as their predecessors assure us, a more complete and profound social transformation than our fathers ever foresaw or desired, and which we ourselves cannot yet conceive; or may we not simply end up in that intermittent anarchy which is well known to be the chronic incurable disease of old peoples? I cannot tell, and do not know when this long voyage will end; I am tired of mistaking deceptive mists for the bank. And I often wonder whether that solid land we have sought for so long actually exists, and whether it is not our fate to rove the seas forever!

I passed the rest of that day with Ampère[5], my colleague at the Institute and one of my best friends. He came to find out what had become of me in

---

5   Jean-Jacques Ampère, son a famous physicist, and professor of the history of French literature.

the scuffle and to ask me to dinner. At first I wanted to console myself by getting him to share my grief. But almost at once I found that his impressions were not the same as mine, that he looked with other eyes on the revolution that was taking place. Ampère was an intelligent man, and what counts for more, a warmhearted man, gentle and reliable in behavior. He was loved for his good nature. and his versatile, intelligent, amusing, satirical conversation was a pleasure; he would throw out a whole lot of remarks none of which, it is true, rose very high, but which passed the time very agreeably. Unluckily, he was too much inclined to carry the spirit of a salon over into literature, and that of literature into politics. What I call the literary spirit in politics consists in looking for what is ingenious and new rather than for what is true, being fonder of what makes an interesting picture than what serves a purpose, being very appreciative of good acting and fine speaking without reference to the play's results, and, finally, judging by impressions rather than reasons. I need not say that this peculiarity is not confined to Academicians. To tell the truth, the whole nation shares it a little, and the French public as a whole often takes a literary man's view of politics. Ampère, who was kindness itself and had not adopted the life of the coterie to which he belonged except to become too indulgent to his friends, absolutely despised the government that had fallen, and its last acts on behalf of the Swiss ultramontanes[6] had irritated him very much. His hatred for the latter, and especially their French friends, was his only feeling of that sort of which I am aware. He was mortally frightened of bores, but the only people he detested from the depths of his soul were the devout. The latter had, it is true, wounded him very cruelly and clumsily, for he was not naturally their adversary, and nothing is better proof of their blind intolerance than that they should have roused such flaming hatred in so Christian a man as Ampère. I am not saying that he was a Christian by belief, but through goodwill, taste and, if I dare to put it so, temperament. Thus Ampère needed little consolation for the fall of a government that had served them so well. Moreover he had just witnessed instances of unselfishness, even generosity and courage among the insurgents; and he was carried away by the general emotion.

I saw that he not only failed to share my feelings but was inclined to take the opposite view. Such an attitude made all the indignation, grief and anger that had been piling up in my heart since the morning suddenly erupt against Ampère; and I addressed him with a violence of language that makes me a little ashamed whenever I think of it, and which only such a true friend as he would have excused. Among other things, I remember saying:

6   By entrusting its educational system to the Jesuits in 1847, the Swiss canton of Lucerne provoked an armed conflict over papal influence.

"You don't understand anything of what is happening; you judge it like some Parisian idler, or a poet. You call this the triumph of freedom when it is its final defeat. I tell you that this people whom you so naïvely admire has just proved that it is incapable and unworthy of living in freedom. Show me what has it learned from experience? What new virtues has it discovered, and what old vices has it discarded? No, I tell you, it is always the same; just as impatient, careless and contemptuous of the law as ever; just as easily led and as rash in the face of danger as its fathers before it. Time has wrought no change in it, but has left it as frivolous in serious matters as it used to be in trifles."

After a lot of shouting, we both agreed to leave the verdict to the future, that enlightened and just judge who, unfortunately, always arrives too late.

9b8   Section 8, "The Eve of the June Days"

Personally I had no doubt that we were on the eve of a terrible struggle; nevertheless I did not fully understand all the dangers of that time until a conversation I had with the famous Madame Sand.[7] I met her at the house of an English friend of mine, Milnes,[8] a Member of Parliament, who was then in Paris. Milnes was a man of parts who did and, what is rarer, said many foolish things. I have seen a great many men in my time with two contradictory profiles: man of sense on one side, fool on the other. Never have I seen Milnes not infatuated about somebody or something. This time he was dazzled by Madame Sand and, despite the seriousness of the situation, wanted to give a literary luncheon for her. I was there, and crowded memories of the June days that followed almost at once, far from obliterating that day from my recollection, have reminded me of it.

The company was anything but homogeneous. Besides Madame Sand, there was a young English lady whose name I have forgotten, but whose agreeable and modest appearance struck me and who must have found the company she was in rather odd; then there were some fairly obscure writers and Mérimée.[9] Some of the guests did not know each other, and others knew one another too well. That was the case, if I am not mistaken, between Madame Sand and Mérimée. A short time before there had been a very tender but very ephemeral relationship between them. One was even told

---

7   A great French novelist, also known for her romance with poet Alfred de Musset and composer Frédéric Chopin. She was working among the 1848 revolutionaries.
8   Richard Monckton Milnes, politician and man of letters.
9   Prosper Mérimée, French novelist.

that they had followed Aristotle's rules in the conduct of their romance, with the whole action obedient to the unities of time and place. Our host from across the channel did not know that story and had very clumsily brought them together without warning. So they met unexpectedly for the first time after their adventure, and as Madame Sand was very offended with Mérimée for having triumphed so fast and made so little use of his success, there was great embarrassment on both sides; but they soon pulled themselves together, and for the rest of the day there was nothing to notice.

Milnes put me beside Madame Sand; I had never spoken to her, and I don't think I had even seen her before (for I have not lived much in the world of literary adventurers which she inhabited). When one of my friends asked her what she thought of my book about America, she replied: "Sir, I make it a habit only to read the books that are presented to me by the authors." I had a strong prejudice against Madame Sand, for I detest women who write, especially those who systematically disguise the weaknesses of their sex, instead of interesting us by displaying them in their true colors. In spite of that, she charmed me. I found her features rather massive, but her expression wonderful; all her intelligence seemed to have retreated into her eyes, abandoning the rest of her face to raw matter. I was struck at finding her with something of that naturalness of manner characteristic of great spirits. She really did have a genuine simplicity of manner and language, which was perhaps mingled with a certain affectation of simplicity in her clothes. I confess that with more adornment she would have struck me as still more simple. We spoke for a whole hour about public affairs, for at that time one could not talk about anything else. Besides, Madame Sand was then in a way a politician; I was much struck by what she told me on that subject; it was the first time that I had found myself in direct and familiar conversation with somebody able and willing to tell me part of what was taking place in our adversaries' camp. Political parties never know each other; they come close, jostle and grip one another, but they never see. Madame Sand gave me a detailed and very vivacious picture of the state of the Parisian workers: their organization, numbers, arms, preparations, thoughts, passions and terrible resolves. I thought the picture overloaded, but it was not so, as subsequent events clearly proved. She seemed to be herself greatly frightened by the popular triumph, and there was a touch of solemnity in her pity for our anticipated fate.

"Try to persuade your friends, sir," she said to me, "not to drive the people into the streets by rousing or offending them, just as on my side I want to instill patience into our people; for if it comes to a fight, believe me, you will all perish."

With those consoling words we parted, and I have not seen her since.

9b9   Section 9, "The June Days"

Now at last I have come to that insurrection in June which was the greatest and the strangest that had ever taken place in our history, or perhaps in that of any other nation: the greatest because for four days more than a hundred thousand men took part in it, and there were five generals killed; the strangest, because the insurgents were fighting without a battle cry, leaders, or flag, and yet they showed wonderful powers of coordination and a military expertise that astonished the most experienced officers.

Another point that distinguished it from all other events of the same type during the last sixty years was that its object was not to change the form of the government, but to alter the organization of society. In truth it was not a political struggle (in the sense in which we have used the word "political" up to now), but a class struggle, a sort of "Servile War." It stood in the same relation to the facts of the February Revolution as the theory of socialism stood to its ideas; or rather it sprang naturally from those ideas, as a son from his mother; and one should not see it only as a brutal and blind, but as a powerful effort of the workers to escape from the necessities of their condition, which had been depicted to them as an illegitimate depression, and by the sword to open up a road towards that imaginary well-being that had been shown to them in the distance as a right. It was this mixture of greedy desires and false theories that engendered the insurrection and made it so formidable. These poor people had been assured that the goods of the wealthy were in some way the result of a theft committed against themselves. They had been assured that inequalities of fortune were as much opposed to morality and the interests of society as to nature. This obscure and mistaken conception of right, combined with brute force, imparted to it an energy, tenacity and strength it would never have had on its own.

One should note, too, that this terrible insurrection was not the work of a certain number of conspirators, but was the revolt of one whole section of the population against another. The women took as much part in it as the men. While the men fought, the women got the ammunition ready and brought it up. And when in the end they had to surrender, the women were the last to yield.

9b10   Section 10, "The End of the June Days"

At that time the house in which we lived in the rue de la Madeleine had a doorkeeper with a thoroughly bad reputation in the district; he was a slightly daft, drunken, good-for-nothing old soldier who spent the time he could spare from beating his wife, at the public house. One might say that this man was a socialist by birth, or rather by temperament.

The first successes of the revolution had gone to his head, and on the morning of the day in question he had been round the local pubs announcing, among other mischievous proposals, that he would kill me that evening when I came home, if I ever did come home; he even brandished a long knife intended for the purpose. A poor woman who had heard him hurried in great distress to inform Madame de Tocqueville; the latter, before leaving Paris, sent me a note recounting the rumor and asking me not to go home that evening but to spend the night at my father's house, which was nearby, he being out of Paris. I fully intended to do so, but when I left the Assembly toward midnight, I had not the strength of mind to follow the plan. I was exhausted, and did not know whether I would find a bed ready anywhere except at home. Besides I thought it improbable that a murder announced in advance would be committed, and I was suffering from the listlessness that prolonged emotion induces. So I went and knocked at my door, having taken no further precaution than to load the pistols that in those unhappy days it was quite normal to carry. It was that man who opened the door and, as he was meticulously shutting the bolts after me, I asked him if all the other tenants were in. He laconically informed me that they had all left Paris that morning and that we two were alone in the house; I should have preferred somebody else for a tête-à-tête, but it was too late to draw back; so I looked him in the whites of the eyes and ordered him to go in front of me, lighting the way. He stopped at a door leading into the courtyard and told me he could hear a peculiar noise coming from one of the coach houses, asking me to go and investigate it with him; as he said this, he turned towards the coach house. All this struck me as very suspicious, but I thought, having gone so far, it was safer to go on. So I followed him, but I kept an eye on all his movements and had made up my mind to kill him like a dog at the first sign of any evil plan. We did hear the very peculiar noise of which he had spoken. It sounded like water flowing underground or the distant rumble of a carriage, although it clearly came from quite close by; I never did discover what it was, but then I did not spend long looking. I soon went back into the house, making my companion lead the way to my landing, watching him the whole time. I told him to open the door and, when he had done so, took the torch from him and went in. It wasn't until he saw me turning away that he made up his mind to take off his hat and bow. Did that man intend to kill me and give up the plan only when, seeing me on my guard with both hands in my pockets, he guessed that I might be better armed than he? At the time I thought he never seriously contemplated the crime, and I think so still. In times of revolution people boast almost as much about the crimes they intend to commit as they do in normal times about their good intentions. I have always thought that this poor wretch would have become dangerous only if the fight seemed to be going against us, whereas in fact, although still doubtful, the balance inclined our way, and that was enough to make me safe.

At daybreak I heard someone coming into my room and awoke with a start. It was my man servant who had let himself in with his key to my apartment. That fine fellow had left the bivouac (I had given him the National Guard uniform for which he had asked and a good musket) and looked in to see if I was back and if I needed his services. He assuredly was no socialist, either in theory or by temperament. He was not even touched by that most usual sickness of our time, a restless mind, and even at another period it would have been hard to find a man more satisfied with his station and contented with his lot. Always very pleased with himself and tolerably pleased with others, he generally desired nothing beyond his reach, and he usually did reach, or think he had reached, what he wanted. So he unconsciously followed the precepts inculcated by philosophers, but seldom observed by them, and enjoyed as a gift of nature that happy balance between powers and wants, that alone brings the happiness promised by the philosopher.

"Well, Eugène," I asked him when he came in that morning, "how are things going?"

"Very well, sir. Perfectly well."

"How do you mean 'very well,' when I can still hear gunfire?"

"Yes, they are still fighting," he answered, "but everyone is saying that it will end very well."

Having said that, he took off his uniform, cleaned my boots and brushed my clothes, and then, putting on his uniform again, said:

"If you do not need anything else, sir, with your permission, I will go back to the battle."

For four days and four nights he pursued this double calling as simply as I write it down. In those troubled days of savagery and hatred, it gave me a sense of repose to see that young man's peaceful, satisfied face.

9c To Madame de Tocqueville, his Love for her, and Some Post-February 1848 Politics

Saint-Lô, Thursday evening, March 30, 1848

I have just found, my beloved friend, your letter of last night.

Before I get started, I must say once more that I love you from the bottom of my heart. I feel my soul so full of love that I need above all to tell you about it. If one of my letters has ever caused you the least sorrow, I ask your forgiveness. To sadden you has never been my intent. If I were ever responsible for your distress, I would never forgive myself. For you are my consolation, my support, my only friend on this earth. When I say my "only" friend, I am not saying enough. I would like to find a word expressing the gentleness, devotion, and sensitivity that exists only in a woman friend; and that courage, firm reason, and good counsel that only a male friend, it is claimed, can give. I love you therefore like you deserve to be loved. I have often had an idiosyncratic and very odd way of loving. But be sure that my affection for you has a quality often not found in seemingly more tender and pleasant relationships: it is both passionate and devoted. These two words should make you forgive many sins. You are always in my thoughts as the person I love, but today I feel unusual pleasure in saying so. My heart is turned unusually strongly towards tender feelings. Why today? I don't know. Man is such an odd animal. Perhaps it is because I feel in good health or because the weather is divine, who knows?

It is important to set aside as much money as possible right now to make it through these difficult times. We cannot hope to have much income, and we'll have to use a large part of it for taxes. The tenants are going to find it very difficult to pay. We must therefore, quietly, keep as much money as possible at home, and preferably in coin. For I suspect paper money will soon lose much of its value. In circumstances such as these, our intimate love is an invaluable asset! I cannot say enough how grateful I feel when I think of our good fortune in meeting one another.

What made me want to return to Paris was that I was worrying about you. Things cannot go on like this much longer. Something serious is bound to happen in Paris between now and election day. I feel terribly awkward when I think you are alone in the city. I know all you can tell me to reassure me, but I love you too dearly to be reassured even by the best of reasons.

As for me, I am somber and even sad about my own future, but calm. I am in the state of mind I imagine an officer to be before going on campaign. I never thought I would be placed on such a stage but be assured that I will hold my place with honor. If I am greatly agitated, it is only because of the gravity of the circumstances. I can assure you that all the antics of February 24 in the Chamber of Deputies did not excite me nearly as much as when I am waiting for my turn to speak. Everything considered, of all the tensions I have felt in my life, I recall those caused by public speaking as being by far the strongest.

Adieu. I love you from the bottom of my heart.

9d   Notes for a Speech on Socialism, 1848

Some [systems] destroy property, others transform it, others limit it, and others administer it.

Almost all indirectly weaken the family.

They have in common a profound mistrust of reason and man's individual freedom.

All limit, compress, regulate, restrain, and reshape the individual.

All limit his intelligence, his rights, his future. Socialism is a new form of slavery.

I could easily show how impractical, imperfect, contrary to nature these systems are, and how little new they bring.

I will not do so.

I want only to show that these systems are totally foreign to the heritage of the French Revolution. They want to do something not only entirely different from but directly opposed to the Revolution.

If we were to find an analogy for these systems, it would be with a few of our own ancestors who, I must admit, came somewhat close to social-ist doctrines by pushing the principle of administrative centralization too far.

As for me, I am deeply a democrat; this is why I am in no way a socialist.

Democracy and socialism cannot go together. You can't have it both ways.

9e   Definition of Democracy, 1848

What is democracy? It is giving the greatest possible share of freedom, knowledge, and power to all.

What is a democratic government? It is a government which, instead of limiting human freedom, comes to its aid in a thousand different ways; a government which, instead of setting limits to freedom, opens up all sorts of vistas; instead of setting up new obstacles, finishes destroying those blocking the way; a government which does not steer freedom but instead provides the knowledge and resources that allow it to . . .

It is a government which makes it possible for every citizen, even the humblest, to act with as much independence as the highest citizen, and put his independence to equally good use . . .

A government which does not compel everybody to be equally poor, but which makes it possible for everybody to get rich with honesty, work, and merit . . .

I am appalled to see how much we have degenerated from our ancestors, how our spirit is inferior to theirs.

9f   To Gustave de Beaumont,[10] on Revolutionary Conflict in Germany: The Princes will be Victorious

Frankfurt, May 18, 1849

The newspapers must have informed you that Germany has been in a state of crisis. Nothing could be more true. The moderate party, which wanted unity without the destruction of the old order of things, having failed in its attempt to find a point of leverage on the princes and particularly on the king of Prussia, lost its balance and has fallen into the arms of the purely revolutionary party, to which it delivered itself, but with hesitations and anxieties that are paralyzing its strength. The revolutionary party has thus acquired the majority in the Diet and has put legality on its side; thus it cries "Long live the Constitution!" as "Long live the Charter!" on July 27 and "Long live reform!" on February 24 were cried. Almost all the small governments of Germany, which happen to be in the most revolutionary part of the country, are being more or less dragged along after this party. On their side, the great states, at the head of which is Prussia, are finally being cast down the road of resistance, and lean resolutely on their armies. There are therefore two laws, two governments, two German forces facing each other, between which all dealings have become impossible. You must perceive that from afar as well as I, but of what you can have no idea, is the inexpressible confusion that exists at this moment in this country, the universal agitation, the revolutionary centers that are swarming from all sides in the midst of this excessive decentralization and, most of all, the profound ignorance which everyone confesses to having about the nearest future. Moreover, yesterday in Frankfurt, the fight began officially between the Assembly and the vicar of the Empire, and at any time it may descend into the street; so, I have my bag packed and am ready at any instant to reach the railroad train and the Rhine.

What will be the result of this immense conflict? No one can say. However, I believe the princes will be victorious. They possess the only organized force that exists in Germany, the army. When I say *they*, I mean to say only the king of Prussia, because Austria is too occupied at home to busy itself with Germany, and the secondary states are not sure of their soldiers. But everything indicates that the Prussian army remains sound. The army in

10   Tocqueville's most loyal friend and travel companion.

Prussia is the homeland, and an *esprit de corps* reigns there which will apparently hold it together for some time yet. There were symptoms and even acts of rebellion in the Landwehr, but these events do not appear to be spreading. The army of Baden, however, just gave a very dangerous example to all the German armies. It expelled or killed its officers and put noncommissioned officers or soldiers in their place. Be that as it may, what I have heard gives me reason to believe that the Prussian army will remain loyal, and, if so, I believe the princes will be victorious. As an additional reason, they are up against the revolutionary party, which seems to me to be similar in every respect to our own, that is to say violent, thoughtless, and always obedient to its passions and not to its reason. But the victory of the Prussians will end nothing, I believe. This country appears to me deeply agitated and discouraged by the spirit of revolution, by disgust at existing institutions, by the vague passion for change. Moreover, because there is nowhere either a head or a center to be found, if it is difficult to make the revolution triumph with a single blow, it is impossible too to suppress it with just one. Moreover, it must be assumed that, even in the middle of this formidable crisis, Prussia is not abandoning the tradition of ambitious politics that has been its distinctive characteristic for a century. I believe that the king of Prussia has refused the supremacy the Assembly offered him in the name of the revolution only with the intention of obtaining it by repressing this revolution, and that all his acts are going to bear the imprints of an *interested* passion, which will very much increase the perils, already so great, of the position this king has taken. He plays a part in which his throne and his life are at stake, and it is very foolish of him to dream of increasing his power when he will already have so much trouble saving his old power.

The entire part of Germany that is adjacent to us is going to become an immense, very active, revolutionary center. I believe that, faced with this state of affairs, we would do well to reinforce our garrison in the east. But above all not the army for reconnaissance that has been announced. Its presence alone behind the Rhine would turn against us the revolutionary passions of Germany and would serve the restoration of the old order of things more than anything else. Speak of this and repeat it, I beg you, to those who are conducting affairs.

Although my wife's and my health have caused me many annoyances since my departure, nonetheless, the spectacle that I have before me excites my interest to the highest degree and every day presents me with a thousand new ideas, even on things I thought I knew. Frankfurt was marvelously chosen for the purpose of obtaining an idea of the revolutionary party of which it is the head. But the trip would be very incomplete if I could not go spend a week in Berlin, where the head and the center of the resistance is.

9g   To Francisque de Corcelle,[11] on Roman Affairs

Paris, June 15, 1849

I cannot tell you how impatiently I await your news. The Roman issue[12] remains, by far, our great issue. The continuation of the siege promotes agitation and unhappiness in public opinion, and the majority itself is not really sure of our right. Even though we have defeated those who wanted to create a revolution out of the Roman affair, the whole business is not disapproved of any less, and the evil which it produces, above all in certain *départements*, continues to increase in formidable proportions.

I told you, I think, in my last letter, that the Austrian envoy in Paris had assured me that his government accepted the necessity of making large reforms in the Roman states. The Spanish ambassador came yesterday to read me a dispatch his government had transmitted (the third of June, I think) to Mr. Martinez de la Rosa[13] to express the same feeling. The Neapolitan minister gives me the same assurance. But all these good wishes wind up thus: [you can have] everything you want, except the "statute." But, outside the statute or something which in a word resembles a representative element, pretty strongly constituted, it seems to me more and more that there is nothing serious to propose to France. This is the difficult part of your mission. For, independently of the fact that it is not appropriate for us to threaten the Holy Father, what good can threats do on the mind of a saint with limited intelligence? It is clearly only by conviction, and in reaching the conscience of Pius IX, that we can hope to bend his will. I have seen in our ambassadors' correspondence that the Pope seems imbued with the idea that the vote of the budget should be left to those who pay the taxes. One could perhaps take this idea which, at bottom, contains the whole of the representative system, as a point of departure from which to convince him of the idea of deliberative assemblies. If we have to take great precautions against the bad composition of these assemblies through the electoral law and by all other means, the importance of obtaining them would still be very great.

As for the other concessions about which the Catholic powers already seem to be of the same opinion as we, the most important of all, because in

11   Francisque de Corcelle, who had reviewed *Democracy in America* in 1835, served as ambassador to the Vatican when Tocqueville was minister of foreign affairs in 1849.
12   Tocqueville is referring throughout this letter to the French military expedition to restore the Pope's rule over Rome and central Italy.
13   The Spanish ambassador to the Pope.

sum it includes all the others, is a real secularization of the government. I am assured that the pope is very disposed to return to laymen the direction of all temporal affairs. What presents a difficulty to his mind and disturbs him are the mixed matters, those which simultaneously have a spiritual and temporal character, such as the ministry of foreign affairs, the nunciatures, the ministry of public education. Therefore all your efforts must tend to finding a means of clearly dividing temporal from spiritual matters, and to see if by means of this separation we could not succeed in obtaining, even by multiplying officials, that all the temporal affairs be given to laymen.

It is said that the Pope is very struck by the inappropriate use of convents and very inclined to close many of them. Nothing would be better suited to restoring his popularity than considerable and spontaneous actions in this sense. This could even make public opinion more supple about the rest.

Keep up your spirits. Good health. I embrace you from the bottom of my heart.

PS Try to get to know the Pope's confessor.

Tocqueville Retires from Political Life and Returns to Writing

10a To Louis de Kergorlay,[1] on the Project of Writing *The Old Regime*

Sorrento, December 15, 1850

I do not know, my dear friend, if you heard from my parents and our friends the news of our journey. In that case, you should know that we suffered great fatigue and still more vexation. Marie was so tired by the sea that, on arrival in Naples, she felt an extreme repugnance to re-embarking to go to Sicily. I believed it necessary to give up that part of the journey, but not the way of life I was counting on adopting in Sicily. In this respect we have not changed our plans at all. We are doing, near Naples, in a charming place called Sorrento, what we wanted to do in Palermo; that is to say, we have leased a furnished apartment, in which we have settled with our servants and in which we are living a very retiring life. The place, as I told you, is charming; the home in which we live is very well situated, very well furnished, and, in short, infinitely agreeable; the country that surrounds us is admirable, the walks are without number, and, up to now, the climate has been delightful. Among all these fine things, however, it would not be long before I grew bored if I could not create a vigorous occupation for my mind. I brought some books here. I intend to continue what I had already begun at Tocqueville this summer, with great spirit and pleasure, which was an account of what I had seen in the Revolution of 1848 and since, things and men.[2] I have

---

1 A distant cousin, best friend since childhood.
2 See selections 9a–b.

not yet been able to get back into the current of ideas and recollections which can give me the taste for this work; and, while waiting for the inspiration to come back, I have contented myself with musing about what could be the subject of a new book for me; because I need not tell you that the recollections of 1848 cannot appear before the public. The free judgments that I hold on it, both on my contemporaries and on myself, would make this publication impractical, even if it would be to my taste to produce myself on some literary theater or other, which assuredly it is not. For a long time, I have already been occupied, I could say troubled, by the idea of attempting a great work once again. It seems to me that my true worth is above all in works of the mind; that I am worth more in thought than in action; and that, if there remains anything of me in this world, it will be much more the trace of what I have written than the recollection of what I will have done. The last ten years, which have been rather sterile for me in many respects, have nonetheless given me the truest insights into human affairs and a more practical sense of the details, without making me lose the habit that my intelligence had taken of regarding the affairs of men by wholes. Thus, I believe myself in better condition than I was when I wrote *Democracy* to deal well with a great subject of political literature. But what subject am I to take up? The possibility for success lies mostly in the subject, not only because it is necessary to find a subject that interests the public, but especially because it is necessary to discover one that animates me and draws out of me all that I can give. I am the man least fit in the world for going up with any advantage against the current of my mind and my taste, and I fall well below the mediocre when I do not take an impassioned pleasure in what I am doing. I have therefore often sought for several years (every time, at least, that a little tranquillity permitted me to look around and see something else and farther than the little tangle in which I was involved), I sought, I say, some subject that I could take up; and I have never seen anything that pleased me completely or rather that seized me. However, now that we see that youth is gone by, and time marches or, to say it better, runs down the slope of mature years, the limits of life are discovered more clearly and more closely, the field of action shrinks. All these reflections, I could say all these mental agitations, have naturally brought me, in the solitude in which I live, to search more seriously and more deeply for the mother-idea of a book, and I have felt the inclination to communicate with you what has struck my imagination and to ask your advice. I can consider only a contemporary subject. Basically, only affairs of our time interest the public and interest me. The greatness and singularity of the spectacle that the world of our time presents absorbs too much attention for anyone to be able to attach much value to those historical curiosities that suffice idle and erudite societies. But which contemporary subject to choose?

One that would have the most originality and that would best suit the nature and habits of my intelligence would be an ensemble of reflections and insights on the current time, a free judgment on our modern societies and a forecast of their probable future. But when I try to find the crux of such a subject, the point where all the ideas that it generates meet and tie themselves together, I do not find it. I see parts of such a work, I do not perceive the whole; I have the threads well in hand, but lack the woof to make the cloth. I must find somewhere, for my ideas, the solid and continuous basis of facts. I can encounter that only while writing history, while applying myself to a period whose account serves me as an occasion to paint the men and the affairs of our century and permits me to make one picture out of all these detached paintings. Only the long drama of the French Revolution can furnish this period. For a long time I have had the thought, which I have expressed to you, I believe, of choosing in this great expanse of time that goes from 1789 to our day, and which I continue to call the French Revolution, the ten years of the Empire, the birth, the development, the decline and the fall of that prodigious enterprise. The more I reflect on it, the more I believe that the period would be well chosen for painting. In itself, it is not only grand, but peculiar, even unique; and nonetheless, up to the present, at least in my opinion, it has been reproduced in false or vulgar colors. It throws, moreover, a vivid light on the period that preceded it and on that which follows it. It is certainly one of the acts of the French Revolution that enables one to judge the whole play best, and permits one to say the most on the ensemble, all that one can have to say on it. My doubt bears much less on the choice of subject than on the way of dealing with it. My first thought had been to redo M. Thiers's book in my own manner: to write the plot of the Empire, avoiding only expatiating on the military part, which M. Thiers has reproduced with so much self-satisfaction and a very ridiculous pretension that he understood the profession of warfare well.[3] But, in reflecting on it, I developed great hesitation about dealing with the subject in this manner. Thus envisioned, the work would be a very long and exacting enterprise. Moreover, the principal merit of the historian is to know how to handle the fabric of the facts, and I do not know if this art is within my reach. What I have best succeeded in up to now is in judging facts rather than recounting them, and, in a history properly so called, that faculty which I know all about would be exercised only every now and then and in a secondary manner, unless I left the genre and burdened the narrative. Finally, there is a certain affectation in taking up again the road that M. Thiers has just followed. The public is rarely grateful

---

3 *Histoire de la révolution française*, 10 vols. (1823–1827). *Histoire du consulat et de l'empire*, 20 vols. (1845–1862).

to you for these attempts, and when two writers take the same subject, it is naturally inclined to believe that the second has nothing more to teach it. There you have my doubts; I disclose them to you in order to obtain your opinion.

To this first manner of envisioning the subject another has succeeded in my mind which goes as follows: it would no longer be a matter of a lengthy work, but of a rather short book, one volume perhaps. I would no longer do, to speak properly, the history of the Empire, but an ensemble of reflections and judgments on that history. I would point out the facts, no doubt, and I would follow the thread, but my principal concern would not be to recount them. Above all, in order to clarify the principal facts, I would need to illuminate the diverse causes which emerge from them: how the Empire came about; how it was able to establish itself in the midst of the society created by the Revolution; what were the means used; what was the true nature of the man who founded it; what caused his success, what caused his reverses; the passing influence and the durable influence which he exercised on the destinies of the world and in particular on those of France. It seems to me there is in that the material for a very great book. But the difficulties are immense. The one that most troubles my mind comes from the mixture of history properly so called with historical philosophy. I still do not see how to mix these two things (and yet, they must be mixed, for one could say that the first is the canvas and the second the color, and that it is necessary to have both at the same time in order to do the picture). I fear that the one is harmful to the other, and that I lack the infinite art that would be necessary in order to choose properly the facts that must, so to speak, support the ideas; to recount them enough for the reader to be led naturally from one reflection to another by interest in the narrative, and not to tell too much of them, so that the character of the work remains visible. The inimitable model of this genre is in Montesquieu's book on the grandeur and the decline of the Romans.[4] One passes there, so to speak, across Roman history without pausing, and nonetheless one perceives enough of that history to desire the author's explanations and to understand them. But independently of the fact that such great models are always much superior to every copy, Montesquieu found in his book opportunities he would not have in the one of which I am speaking. Occupying himself with a very vast and very remote epoch, he could choose only every now and then the greatest facts, and, with respect to those facts, say only very general things. If he had had to restrict himself to a space of ten years and seek his road across a multitude of detailed and precise facts, the difficulty of the work would assuredly have been much greater.

4   *Considérations sur les causes de la grandeur des Romains et de leur décadence* (1734).

I have tried in all the above to enable you to grasp my state of mind completely. All the ideas I have just expressed to you have put my mind very much to work; but it still bustles about in the darkness, or at least it perceives only half-lights which only permit it to perceive the grandeur of the subject, without putting it in a position to recognize what is to be found in that vast space. I very much wish that you could help me to see it more clearly. I am proud enough to believe that I am better suited than anyone else to bring to such a subject great freedom of mind, and to speak without passion and without reticence concerning men and things. For, as regards to men, although they have lived in our time, I am sure I do not hold toward them either love or hate; and as regards to the forms of what are called constitutions, laws, dynasties, classes, they have, so to speak, I will not say no value, but no existence in my eyes, independently of the effects they produce. I have no traditions, I have no party, I have no cause, if it is not that of liberty and human dignity; of that, I am sure; and for a work of this sort, a disposition and a nature of this kind are as useful as they are often harmful when it is no longer a matter of speaking about human affairs, but of being entangled in them.

Farewell; I am looking for a long letter from you soon. Write me in the following manner: put the scaled letter that bears my name in an envelope and on this envelope write: to *M. Desage, foreign affairs agent in Marseilles.* Prepay it to there.

I am ashamed to say that I received, a very long time ago, a very friendly letter from Mathilde. I wanted to attach a letter to her to this one, but I am so tired from talking to you of history and philosophy that I would be a very boring correspondent today. My wife intends to write yours one of these days and I will add my letter to hers. In the meantime, give our warm regards to your wife. We embrace you.

10b   To Francisque de Corcelle,[5] against Louis-Napoleon and Loss of Freedom

February 21, 1851

I received, dear friend, your long and interesting letter of the 6th and I thank you for it. You know now that I received the one you were worried about, and which I asked Beaumont to tell you had reached me. I reproach myself

---

5   Francisque de Corcelle, who had reviewed *Democracy in America* in 1835, served as ambassador to the Vatican when Tocqueville was minister of foreign affairs in 1849.

for not having written more to my friends since arriving here. What has slowed my correspondence is the impossibility of saying anything useful or interesting. There is nothing but our unfortunate French affairs which interest you, that is easy to understand, and how can I talk about them to you when there is a month between the event and the letter in which I speak of it? To reason vaguely about things that have happened but that one doesn't know about is unbearable. This is why even though I am constantly with you in spirit, I hardly write you. You understand my reason, I hope, and will excuse me.

That the state of our affairs worries me deeply and afflicts me, I don't need to tell you. You know also that I have been convinced for a long time already that we are facing a great national movement which is leading us not only out of the republic, but momentarily at least, out of freedom. Chances are certainly in favor of the President, and the probable future of the Chamber is to decline more and more in public opinion, until it is finally drowned by the universal vote. I do not believe, however, that all is lost for the Chamber. If the President, in his impatience, wants to get rid of it by force, he would have great chances of failing; if he throws himself into the arms of Lamartine and company, he will be lost. For the nation has adopted him less for himself than for the idea of authority which he represents, and at the same time out of hatred against the Revolution. I would have acted exactly as you have done throughout this most recent period; for there is no longer any means for the Chamber to retreat without falling in shame and ruin. But how I regret that things have been brought to this extreme! I was always very opposed to the idea of naming Louis-Napoleon President, because I wanted to try the republic, and I judged like you and my other friends that a *Prince*–President made the attempt impossible. But once Louis-Napoleon was elected, I immediately thought that the best thing was to try to get along with him, not in order to overthrow the republic in alliance with him, but in order to change the republic so as to create a great place for him. The leaders did not understand things this way. They only thought about their parties and themselves. They have made it very clear to the new President, he has told me so himself several times, that they despised him and at the same time that they wanted to dominate him. They have thus ended up pushing him down the slope where his tendencies and his ideas already leaned too much. So it is not they whom I lament in this moment, or who inspire the least sympathy in me. My consolation, on the contrary, is to think that these great geniuses will be ridiculed by posterity as they deserve. In fact, in all history I do not know of adventures more ridiculous than those of ambitious men finding their master in a man whom they chose to put at the head of France solely because they judged him an imbecile, which he was not, and because they thought they could get rid of him when it was time and at their good pleasure, which could not be. I therefore do not share in the least, I confess, their passions and resentments. I go further and confess to you that all in all, if in fact the nation no longer wants the republic, I would be just as happy to slide into a constitutional monarchy with Louis Napoleon, who is there, rather than with great effort to go looking for a ruler whom we don't have at hand and who would leave us as divided as we are, if I thought that Louis-Napoleon could be limited within a constitutional monarchy or wanted to limit himself to one. My resistance comes from the conviction that on the one hand the nation, once seemingly defeated, will for a while let its new leader do anything he wants, and on the other hand that Louis-Napoleon as I know him with his mixture of good and bad qualities, true and false ideas as I have seen them, will never reduce himself to submitting to even the indirect influence of a parliament. He would rather remain the temporary President of a republic than become a constitutional ruler subject to the control of an assembly. This is my reason for deciding and it is certainly sufficient. I entered public life along with liberal and constitutional institutions, I am completely determined not to stay in public life without them. I thus follow from afar the various incidents of the unequal struggle with an anxiety which you can understand. I hope that it will not speed up and that in the spring I will be able to return to share with my friends the responsibility that such a critical situation imposes on each of us. I take care of my health as best I can. Basically it is excellent now. My throat is still susceptible, but I am not sick and winter is ending now. I try to divert my mind from politics by occupying it with other things, and I make book projects for the time, perhaps near, when I will have to write rather than act. After all, I do not yet despair absolutely, although the fall seems very likely, and probably very sad. But many accidents can change the odds.

10c   To his Brother Edouard de Tocqueville, Reaction to Louis-Napoleon's *Coup d'État*

December 7, 1851

My dear friend, I have just received your letter to which I hasten to respond: there was no need to tell me not to plot against the new government. I am no child, and I know my way around. I know the coup is over, the crime committed, and that the only thing to do for the moment is submit.

It was also unnecessary to tell me that the people are quite amenable to the new regime and have already relieved it of its obligation to insure freedom and the rule of law. I knew that too, for I know this tired, nervous, half-rotten France, which asks only to obey whoever will insure its material well-being. Everything you tell me on this point, I can assure you, does not exceed my expectations.

But do not try to make me tolerate what is going on, what I am seeing, what I am hearing. This is an awful spectacle. It irritates everything that is sensitive, proud and noble in me. To be honest with you, watching these wretched people run the country is not what is most intolerable to me. They are what they are supposed to be. They do their job. What makes me regret not being in jail any longer, what would make me hide in the countryside tomorrow if only I could find a place with no Frenchmen or their business in sight, is contact with the so-called "honest" and "distinguished" classes. They accept the government of these wretches not only with resignation, as you say, but with pleasure. I see it in the eyes of those who talk to me. Yes, our souls are so base that it is not only peasants, bourgeois, or shopkeepers who readily trade freedom, dignity, and the country's honor for their peace and quiet, and the assurance they can continue sell their products or their merchandise. Every day I observe such vulgar feelings and depraved hearts among the men who call themselves the nation's elite. No need to go to Compiègne[6]; the salons of Paris are full of them. They are full of so-called aristocrats and little cowardly women who were so scared of 1852, who trembled so much for their income, that they now rejoice at the recent and unfolding events, and the ignominy of the new regime.

This is why I am finding life almost unbearable. I feel like a foreigner in my own country, surrounded by people who do not share the ideas which, to my mind, are indispensable to human dignity; people who are cold to the feelings that constitute in my eyes my moral stature, and without which I would not want to exist.

I hasten to send you these few words so that you understand my real state of mind. However painful all this may be, I will not do anything that might compromise my health, for I am more convinced than you are that there is nothing to do.

With love, from the bottom of my heart.

6   The site of Napoleon III's court.

10d   To the Comte de Chambord,[7]: Plea for a Constitutional Monarchy

January 14, 1852

I do not think that there is a reason, at present, for the Count of Chambord to explain himself in detail about political laws, or even about the exact extent of public freedom which he might have in view. The time has not come, and one cannot ask him to say what he cannot know; what he can and should make known at present is his firm and definitive intention to re-establish in France only a constitutional and representative monarchy with its chief characteristics, namely: 1) The guarantee of individual freedom; 2) A sincere national representation; 3) Freedom and complete publicity of parliamentary discussions; 4) Real freedom of the press.

I am trying, as can be seen, to take what seems to me most substantial in the regime of constitutional royalty. I think that without these four conditions just listed, this regime would not really exist, and would be only a fake; such a concession would be a lie, it would create a situation without dignity for the ruler, without guarantees for the people and without duration.

These four freedoms are necessary, but I freely admit that one can give them more or less practical application. For myself I am led to believe that after the anarchy which followed 1848, and in leaving behind the despotism which we are subject to at this moment, it will be necessary to use great prudence in re-establishing constitutional monarchy; it will be necessary first of all to give the royal power all the rights compatible with freedom, and at the beginning only give freedom those indispensable rights without which it cannot exist.

Thus, to explain my thought by two examples: a parliament where one discusses freely and whose discussions are public seems to me a condition *sine qua non* of constitutional monarchy, but this does not necessarily mean that the parliament may not at first be very limited in its functions and the period of its work very limited.

Freedom of the press again seems to me one of the necessary conditions of parliamentary monarchy, but this does not mean that, outside of pre-publication censorship, one cannot or should not take all kinds of guarantees against the abuse of this dangerous freedom.

One does not ask, I repeat, from the Count of Chambord the commitment to re-establish the freedoms of which I have spoken in the state the July

7   Grandson of Charles X and last of the Bourbons.

Monarchy left them; what is asked of him is to guarantee that these freedoms will be re-established to the extent that is indispensable for the constitutional system to be a reality and not an appearance.

10e To Francisque de Corcelle,[8] The New Aristocracy is the Army

Paris, May 13, 1852

I have received your good letter of yesterday, my dear friend. I hasten to answer as Madame Roederer[9] is leaving this evening and is giving me an opportunity which I do not want to miss. I have, however, no secret to reveal. I have had no news since your departure. Only you were keeping me abreast of what people were doing, or rather what they wished they were doing. Your departure has thrown me into complete isolation from which I have not tried to emerge. For there is only one happy event, in my opinion, worth hearing about.[10] But, as I concluded some time ago, it is not going to happen any time soon. This government must first reach maturity before one can even think about ways of taking it down. All we say or do prior to that is useless, just sterile agitation lacking in dignity. Except, of course, what preoccupied you so much recently, which was important because of its immediate influence on the attitude of the parties.

Madame Roederer will report on the review.[11] From what I have heard, the people watched it like a Franconi show.[12] They applauded the president only when he performed some equestrian prowess. The army which would have shouted its appreciation as much as desired, and as often as asked, remained quiet most of the time because there was evidently no general order given. However, the army must be, and as a whole is, very satisfied with the new regime. Although the army is subjected to arbitrary authority – its rules for promotion being constantly broken, just like all other laws – it has gained so much that the military must view themselves as the principal heirs of the republic. Day by day, the last revolution's natural and logical consequences are appearing more clearly and highlight its almost exclusively military

---

8 Francisque de Corcelle, who had reviewed *Democracy in America* in 1835, served as ambassador to the Vatican when Tocqueville was minister of foreign affairs in 1849.
9 Francisque de Corcelle's sister.
10 The improbable fall of Louis-Napoleon.
11 Military review on the Champ-de-Mars on May 10, 1852.
12 Victor Franconi was the trainer of the imperial stable.

character. The true aristocracy of the country is now the army. The army is the abusing and ruling class. It has the profits, the honor, and the power. The army is, under this regime, what the old nobility was under the Restoration, the bourgeoisie under Louis-Philippe, and the workers under the provisional government. The military spirit of the army has to be satisfied because it dominates the nation alone in the absence of all political debates. All this will unavoidably push the new government into war, unless the army is overtaken by the general enervation of morals, the enfeebling of ideas and desires, and prefers to live a quiet life in France, dominating everything, with good salaries and the prospect of good pensions, rather than risking broken bones and rheumatism in order to satisfy some higher and more violent passions. This at least is how the Chinese army thinks and reasons.

. . .

I am anxious to leave Paris, as you can imagine, and yet I don't know whether solitude will help me. I am not sure I will find the intellectual energy for big projects and big literary enterprises. I have always needed a certain respect for humanity, a certain trust in people in order to get passionately involved in ideas about the happiness and greatness of human societies. For the first time, I completely lack this respect and trust, at least towards our fellow citizens and contemporaries. At no other time in my life have I been more personally convinced of the need and superiority of free institutions. I have never seen more clearly that a people does not have real moral greatness without them. But I have also never been more certain that our defects in education or nature, our mishaps and our flaws make us incapable and unworthy of benefiting from them. I don't know anything more distressing in this regard than the current spectacle at the very top of society, among the Legitimists and the clergy. How many among the former are rallying, not *despite* the fact that it is a despotism but because it is a despotism; not because they agree to submit temporarily to a necessary yoke but because they hope to reopen for good an antechamber for their services? How many, who have shouted "Hooray for freedom" for eighteen years, have been loyal only to their old hatreds, and are eager, like their fathers, to spit in the Duke of Orleans's face when he would actually take the necessary steps to make peace with them. As for the clergy, how many priests, after having determined in 1848 that the Republic's motto derived from the Scriptures, are now treating the Republic and freedom like mortal sins. After having asked for an independent school system for twenty years, they now find it great to enslave the teachers. They are always ready to approve public tyranny so long as they are permitted to exercise a small part of it! You'll tell me that not all Legitimists or priests are like that. I know it. But those who harbor these feelings, and about whom I complain, are vocal and active. Those who do not are reduced to inaction and silence. The Bishop of Orleans is forced to retreat into a mute and powerless opposition, while a Cardinal Donnet or an abbé Sibour publicly blend in the incense they offer to God a drug uniquely of their own mixing, with which they fumigate the image of the President of the Republic. Is there a more demoralizing spectacle? For delicate minds and higher souls, I am telling you, this spectacle is more dangerous to religion than Voltaire's wisecracks, Rousseau's tirades, and the entire effort of the century's spirit of skepticism . . .

See you soon. With affectionate regards from our household to yours.

It is true that *my* Benvenuto,[13] as you call him, is a great liar and even a great prankster; but he shows the vices of his times as faithfully as his own. In so doing, he teaches much more, in my view, about the Italy of his period and his contemporaries than the most truthful of historians who, while painstakingly retelling the facts, would depict neither the spirit nor the mores of their authors.

10f   To Arthur de Gobineau,[14] denouncing the Latter's *Essay on the Inequality of the Human Races*

Saint-Cyr, near Tours, November 17, 1853

I have all kinds of apologies to make to you, my dear friend, first for not having written about your work,[15] and next for having left your last letter without a response for ten or twelve days, very much in spite of myself. As for the first misdeed, it was induced by a sort of perplexity that reading your work caused in my mind and by the confusion I was in amidst the criticism and the praises I had to address to you. As for my silence, for two weeks, it was necessitated by the obligation of rapidly reading books that were borrowed from libraries in Paris and that were being reclaimed. Now, let us come to the matter at hand: I will behave differently from most people, I will begin with the criticisms. They bear on the mother-idea itself. I will admit to you frankly that you have not convinced me. All my objections still stand. You are, however, quite right to defend yourself as not being a materialist. Your doctrine is indeed rather a kind of fatalism, or predestination if you wish; different however from that of Saint Augustine, the Jansenists, and the

---

13   Memoirs of sculptor Benvenuto Cellini, written between 1558 and 1566.

14   Author and diplomat, who served as Tocqueville's secretary in the ministry of foreign affairs; see introduction to this volume.

15   *Essai sur l'inégalité des races humaines* (1853).

Calvinists (it is these you resemble most by the absoluteness of the doctrine) in that there is with you a very tight bond between the fact of predestination and matter. Thus, you speak unceasingly of races that are regenerating or deteriorating, which take up or lay aside social capacities by an *infusion of different blood* (I believe that these are your own terms). Such a predestination seems to me, I will confess, a cousin of pure materialism and be sure that if the crowd, which always takes the great beaten tracks in matters of reasoning, were to accept your doctrine, that would lead it straight from the race to the individual and from social capacities to all kinds of capacities. Besides, whether fatality is placed directly in a certain organization of matter or in the will of God, who wished to make several human species in the human genus and to impose on certain men the obligation, by virtue of the race to which they belong, of not having certain sentiments, certain thoughts, certain behavior, certain qualities that they know about without being able to acquire them; that would be of little importance from the point of view in which I place myself, which is the practical consequences of different philosophical doctrines. The two theories result in a very great contraction, if not a complete abolition, of human liberty. Well, I confess to you that after having read you, as well as before, I remain situated at the opposite extreme of those doctrines. I believe them to be very probably wrong and very certainly pernicious.

It is to be believed that within each of the different families that compose the human race there are certain tendencies, certain characteristic aptitudes born of a thousand different causes. But whether these tendencies, whether these aptitudes are invincible, not only has that never been proven, but it is, of itself, unprovable, because it would require having at one's disposal not only the past but the future as well. I am sure that Julius Caesar, if he had had the time, would have readily done a book to prove that the savages he had encountered on the island of Great Britain were not at all of the same human race as the Romans and that, whereas the latter were destined by nature to dominate the world, the former were destined to vegetate in a corner. "*Tu regere imperio populos, Romane, memento,*"[16] says our old acquaintance Virgil. When it is only a matter of human families that, differing among themselves in a profound and permanent manner by external appearance, can make themselves known by distinctive traits in the whole course of time and be related back to a kind of different creation, the doctrine, without being in my opinion more certain, becomes less improbable and easier to establish. But when one places oneself in the interior of one of these great families, such as that of the white race for example, the thread of reasoning disappears and escapes at each step. Is there anything in the world more uncertain, no matter

16   "Be mindful you Roman that you will rule peoples with your command."

what one does, than the question of knowing by history or tradition when, how, and in what proportions men who do not preserve any visible trace of their origin are mixed? These events all took place in remote barbarous times, which have left only vague traditions or incomplete written documents. Do you believe that in taking this route to explain the destiny of different peoples you have greatly illuminated history and that the science of man has gained in certitude for having left the road traveled, since the beginning of the world, by so many great minds who sought the causes of the events of this world in the influence of certain men, of certain sentiments, of certain ideas, of certain beliefs? Again, if only your doctrine, without being better established than theirs, were more useful to humanity! But it is evidently the contrary. What interest can there be in persuading the base people who live in barbarism, in indolence, or in servitude, that since they exist in such a state by virtue of the nature of their race, there is nothing to do to ameliorate their condition, change their mores, or modify their government? Do you not see that your doctrine brings out naturally all the evils that permanent inequality creates – pride, violence, the contempt of fellow men, tyranny, and abjectness under all its forms? What are you saying to me, my dear friend, about making distinctions between *the qualities that make moral truths be practiced* and what you call *social aptitude*? Are these things different? When a person has seen for quite a while and from up quite close the manner in which public affairs are conducted, do you believe that he is not perfectly convinced that they succeed precisely on account of the very means that make one succeed in private life; that courage, energy, integrity, foresight, good sense are the true reasons for the prosperity of empires as well as for that of families and that, in a word, the destiny of man, either as an individual or as a nation, is what he wants to make of it? I stop here; allow us, please, to let the discussion rest there. We are separated by too great a space for discussion to be fruitful. There is an intellectual world between your doctrine and mine. I would much prefer to turn to what I can praise without restriction. Unfortunately, although I was not less keenly affected in this way than the other, I am obliged to be more brief, because I cannot dwell in detail on what I approved; but, on the whole, I will tell you that this book is, by far, the most remarkable of all your writings, that there is very great erudition, as far as I can judge, in the assembling of so many facts and great talent, rare perspicacity in the profit you draw from it. Those who approve your mother-idea or who desire it to be true (and in our day, after the fatigue of these sixty years of revolution, there are many people in France who aspire to just such a belief), must read you with true captivation, because your book is well constructed, proceeds very well toward the goal and leads up to it with great delight for the intelligence. I proved my sincerity to you in criticism; believe equally in my sincerity in praise. There is real and very great merit in your work and assuredly it puts you at the head and above all those who have maintained analogous doctrines. Having written all this very rapidly and with a sort of *furia francese* (I am re-entering here into your system), my hand is tired, and I ask you to let me stop here. Besides, it is not a subject that can be treated by letter. It is too complicated and too vast, but we will chat about it *abundantly*, when we see each other. Tell me only if the press is already occupying itself with you? I am receiving an English newspaper and a German newspaper (because I am applying myself bravely to learning German), but I save money on French newspapers, which, as I have told you, I believe, seem to me to have resolved a problem that was until now believed to be insoluble, which is to be more vacuous than censored newspapers. I thus know only what they contain by way of hearsay. It seems to me that the *Débats* should have readily given an account of such a considerable book.

We will be here until the month of May. I would very much like at that time to have the opportunity of finding you in Paris. You are being left buried for a very long time in your Alpine snows. I am aggrieved with it, without being able to do anything about it. I am very well. I am working a lot, and the days seem to fly. Farewell. Be assured of my very sincere friendship.

PS Do not fail, I entreat you, to remember us to Mme de Gobineau.

10g   To Francisque de Corcelle,[17] on German Philosophy and Hegel

Bonn, July 22, 1854

I had asked you, my dear friend, to send to Bonn your response to my last letter; but as you have not done so and I cannot get used to remaining so long without any communication from you, I choose to write you myself. I will do so in few enough words because I don't know anything really interesting to tell you and because, furthermore, I am overwhelmed by all kinds of tasks which I have set myself. First, our news.

So far the trip seems to be going very well. Our health is good. The road tired my wife very much. But the long rest I am giving her here has completely restored her. I think this rest will continue for some time. We are very comfortably established here. We have made many pleasant or useful

---

17   Francisque de Corcelle, who had reviewed *Democracy in America* in 1835, served as ambassador to the Vatican when Tocqueville was minister of foreign affairs in 1849.

acquaintances, and I think that I work more effectively towards the goal of knowing Germany well by first examining one part of it at leisure, rather than casting a superficial gaze here and there over a vast surface. I therefore count on staying here almost a month. After which, we will go north, to Dresden and Berlin. We are unlikely to return before the end of October. You should answer me here if you manage to jerk yourself out of your laziness.

As to my impressions of this country, they are still so incomplete and so vague that I don't know how to tell you much about them. I have hardly lived anywhere but in the Germany of a century ago; only by chance have I spoken occasionally about the Germany of today, so as not to give completely the impression of someone returned from the dead. To each time suffices its task. I am no longer a politician. I am trying to keep this firmly in mind and to replace the passions given by action with those of erudition. However, since, as you I told you, I was from time to time compelled to talk about what everyone else was talking about, I have gathered here and there some general notions which follow:

This country seems to be struck, like France, by a great political languor. This is seen by many clear signs. But the illness seems to me infinitely less deep here than among us, and is probably of shorter duration. The mind in tiring of politics has not become disinterested, as with us, in most of the studies which raise it above the material. Literary and scientific life continue to be very active, even poetry has retained its empire. A large number of books are published which find a great number of readers. Thought is constantly in action and directs itself towards points other than material well-being. Even in politics, the decline one notes comes more from the sort of confusion caused by the sight of all the stupidities that have just been committed in order to attain political freedom than from a cooling towards it. One continues to have faith in free institutions, to believe them the object most worthy of inspiring love and respect. It is the very absence of this faith which is the most frightening symptom of our illness and which I do not see among these people here. Germany is bewildered, embarrassed, ignorant of the paths it ought to follow, but it is not broken and reduced to nothing, so to speak, as we are. That, at least, is how it appears to me. As for current circumstances, everyone in this country is visibly impassioned against Russia and this passion makes them fairly favorable towards the French government, even those whose opinions ought to make them hostile to it.

I have also noted, in the political and moral order, the signs of some other facts which seem important to me. You doubtless know the role which philosophy has played in Germany for the past fifty years, and particularly Hegel's school. You doubtless are not ignorant that the Hegelian school has been the governments' protégé, because its doctrine in its political consequences established that all facts are respectable and legitimated by their existence and deserve obedience. This doctrine ended up giving birth to all the anti-christian and anti-spiritualist schools which have tried to pervert Germany for the past twenty years, above all for the past ten, and finally to the socialist schools which so much encouraged the confusion of 1848. Hegel wanted people to submit to the old and still existing fact of the established powers of his time, which he declared legitimate as a consequence of their existence. His students wanted to create for their profit other contrary facts which, by virtue of their domination, would have been equally legal and obligatory, which no longer worked in the interest of Hegel's official protectors. So from this Pandora's box has come all kinds of moral infirmities from which this people still suffers. But what is noteworthy is this: a general reaction against this materialist and socialist philosophy is beginning, it seems to me, to be seen on all sides. Not only are these doctrines no longer preached in the universities, but a large number of accredited voices have been raised against them.

Everyone tells me that, in parallel with this philosophical revolution, we are seeing a revival of religious feeling in all the different faiths which divide Germany. These are good symptoms. I particularly know some Catholic professors here (the University of Bonn is half Catholic and half Protestant). They affirm that Catholicism has regained more life than it has had for a century; which they attribute to the real freedom it enjoys, despite several fusses over details, and above all to its separation from the State, a separation still more complete because the sovereign is Protestant.

My hand is tired of writing as your mind is doubtless tired of my running on. I cannot send you anything better however, and I finish by embracing you with all my heart!

10h   To Madame Swetchine,[18] on his Literary Career

Tocqueville, January 7, 1856

It has been some time, Madame, since I have availed myself of your permission to write you. I had intended to return to Paris much earlier and see you in person, which would have been much better than writing. But a series of business matters has kept me here and will probably go on for another three weeks. I did not want to wait until then to thank you for your last letter,

18   Anne-Sophie Soymonov Swetchine, a Russian mystic who joined the Catholic church and moved to Paris where she established a famous salon.

which interested and moved me. This letter is typical of you, of your mind and your heart. I would like to deserve your goodwill because the friendship of somebody like you carries with it obligations. It forces one to be not only grateful but to do something to justify it. Thus I would have liked to shake off for good my tendency to discouragement, against which you fight in your letter. I have had this ailment, however, for most of my life, and it is not easy to do without. I have worked hard to get rid of it for some years, and I have certainly decreased its intensity. I am grateful for your letter which has helped me stay the course and made me feel better. Do not believe, Madame that the particular episode which we have discussed resulted only from this sickly sadness of mine, which has tormented me from time to time throughout my life. It derived from thinking about facts which are all too real. The more I pursue the work in which you have kindly expressed an interest, the more I see that I am led into a stream of feelings and ideas which runs in the opposite direction from those of my contemporaries, almost without exception. I continue to love passionately things for which they do not care any longer. As always, I consider freedom to be the greatest of goods. I still see freedom as one of the most fertile sources of manly virtues and great actions. For me, no comfort or material well-being can separate me from freedom. But I see the men of my own times, the most honest of them, for I do not care about the others, who think only of adjusting as best as possible under a master. Moreover, as if to confuse me even more and even scare me, they seem to be turning their new taste for serfdom into an ingredient of virtue. Even if I wanted to think and feel as they do, I could not. It is a question of my nature still more than my will. An untamable instinct forces me to remain as firm on this point as I have always been. You cannot imagine, Madame, how painful and often cruel it is for me to live in this kind of moral isolation, to feel excluded from the intellectual community of my times and my country. To be alone in the desert often strikes me as being less painful than being alone among men. For I confess my weakness to you, I have always been afraid of isolation. More than is wise, I have always needed to feel supported, to count on the sympathy of a certain number of my fellow men, in order to be happy and even calm. This profound verse was written for me: it is not good that man should be alone.[19] This state of mind, Madame, which I am confiding in you, will help you understand the profound discouragement which often overtakes me when I write. For it is above all in working for the public that it is sad to realize how different it is from oneself. I would like to be indifferent to success, but I do not have this virtue. Long practice has taught

---

19   Genesis, 2, 18.

me that the success of a book is much more due to the ideas the reader already has in mind than to what the author writes.

Do not imagine, Madame, that my book is even remotely connected to current events or personalities. But you know as well as I do that even the book most foreign to the particular circumstances of a period reveals in all its parts a frame of mind either favorable or unfavorable to one's contemporaries. Whatever the book, that is its soul, and the reason for attracting or repelling the reader.

I have been speaking much about me, Madame. My only excuse for being so weak is your kind, I daresay, friendly responses encouraging me to go on. I assure you that I don't do this often and only with a very small number of people.

I would much rather talk about you Madame, but it has been some time that I have not had any specific news of you, even though I have asked several times. Circourt,[20] who often keeps me informed, seems to be hiding in the countryside. I have written him recently but have not yet received his answer. I hope you will be good enough not to leave me without news. News not of you, but directly from you, will be much more appreciated.

Adieu, Madame, continue for many years to be loved by those who know you and respected by all the others.

10i   To Prosper Duvergier de Hauranne,[21] on Intellectual Autonomy

September 1, 1856

When I have any kind of subject to discuss, it is almost impossible for me to read any of the books which have been written about the same issue; contact with other people's ideas agitates me and disturbs me to the point of making reading these works painful. I therefore abstain as much as I can from knowing how their authors later interpreted the facts which I am considering, the judgements they have made about them, the various ideas these facts suggested to them (which, by way of parenthesis, sometimes exposes me to unknowingly repeating what has already been said). On the contrary, I take incredible pains to find the facts myself in the documents of the time; often I thus obtain, with immense labor, what I could have found easily by following another

---

20   Adolphe de Circourt, a writer, government official, and French ambassador.
21   One of the Doctrinaires and one of the organizers of the banquet campaign in 1848. See introduction to this volume.

route. This harvest thus laboriously made, I shut myself up, as in a tight space, and examine with extreme care, in a general review, all these notions that I have acquired by myself. I compare them, I link them, and I then make it my rule to develop the ideas which have spontaneously come to me in the course of this long labor, without any consideration whatsoever for the consequences that some persons might draw from them. It is not that I am not extremely sensitive to the opinion of different readers; but experience has taught me that as soon as I wanted to write from a preconceived perspective, to support a thesis, I lost absolutely all real talent, and I could do nothing worthwhile if I did not limit myself to trying to clearly render what was most personal and most real in my impressions and opinions.

Part IV

The Return to *The Old Regime and the Revolution*

Preliminary Note

Excerpting a few chapters from *The Old Regime and the Revolution* is a particularly difficult task. Much shorter and denser in its argumentation than *Democracy in America*, every chapter in *The Old Regime* plays a role in the development of the whole. Even more than usual, the reader is encouraged to read the complete texts of the work excerpted here. Nevertheless, the chapters appearing below were selected to give an idea of what Tocqueville saw as the origins and causes of the French Revolution and its significance for modern history and the contemporary world. The chapters selected emphasize the key Tocquevillean themes of equality and freedom. The excerpts from the never-finished second volume of *The Old Regime* show Tocqueville grappling with the importance of the events of 1787–89 and describing how France was ready for Napoleon's take-over in 1799. Here the master narrator of the *Recollections* once more puts in an appearance, complementing rather than replacing Tocqueville the analyst and theorist. The letters from Tocqueville's last years (13a–d) present Tocqueville's deepest and most enduring religious and political convictions, as well as revealing his final pessimism about French politics.

11

The Old Regime and the Revolution Volume One, 1856

11a Preface

This book is not a history of the French Revolution, whose story has been too brilliantly told for me to imagine retelling it. It is a study of that Revolution.

In 1789 the French made the greatest effort ever undertaken by any people to disassociate themselves from their past, and to put an abyss between what they had been and what they wished to become. In pursuit of this aim they took all kinds of precautions to bring nothing old into the new order – they put themselves under strict constraint to make themselves different from their ancestors. They overlooked nothing in their effort to disguise themselves.

I have always believed that they were less successful in their unique enterprise than observers have thought, or than they themselves thought at first. I am convinced that, despite themselves, they retained from the old regime most of the feelings, habits, and even ideas which helped them make the Revolution that destroyed it. Unintentionally, they used the debris of the old regime to construct the framework of their new society. Thus, in order to properly understand the Revolution and its work, one must forget for a moment the France of today and ask questions of a France that no longer exists. That is what I have attempted to do in this book; but it has been a more difficult task than I expected.

The first centuries of the monarchy, the Middle Ages, the Renaissance, have all given rise to great works and been the object of very extensive research, which has taught us not merely the facts about what happened, but about the laws, the customs, the spirit of the government and the nation during those different periods. But up to now no one has done the same for the eighteenth century. We think we know eighteenth-century France very well because we see its glittering surface so clearly, because we know all the details about its celebrities, because clever or eloquent critics have made us familiar with the works of its great writers. But we have only confused and often mistaken notions about the manner in which business was conducted, the real practices of institutions, the exact relations between classes, the condition and feelings of those who could not make themselves seen or heard, about the real basis of ideas and mores. I have tried to see into the heart of the old regime, so close to us in years, but hidden from us by the Revolution.

In order to get there, I have not just reread the famous books produced by the eighteenth century; I wanted to study many works deservedly less well-known, which, however poorly written, reveal still better perhaps the true instincts of the times. I have worked to understand all the public records where the French were able to display their opinions and desires on the eve of the Revolution. The transcripts of the proceedings of the provincial Estates, and later of the provincial assemblies, have furnished me with much information on the state of affairs. Above all, I have made great use of the *cahiers* written by the three orders in 1789. These *cahiers*, whose originals fill many manuscript volumes, shall remain the testament of the former French society, the supreme expression of its desires, the authentic manifestation of its last wishes. They are a unique historical document. But even they have not sufficed.

In countries where the government is powerful, there are few ideas, needs, sufferings, interests, and passions that do not sooner or later come before the authorities in their true colors. In visiting the archives of such a country one acquires not merely a good idea of its procedures, one sees the entire country revealed. If today one gave a foreigner all the secret correspondence which fills the files of the Interior Ministry and the prefectures, he would soon know more about us than we know ourselves. In the eighteenth century the government was already, as one can see in reading this book, very centralized, very powerful, and extremely active. It was constantly helping, hindering, permitting. It could promise much and give much. Already it influenced things in a thousand ways, not only public affairs, but the fate of families and the private lives of every individual. Furthermore, there was no publicity, so that no one was afraid of telling the government their secret problems. I have spent a long time studying its surviving records, in Paris and in the provinces.

There, as I expected, I found the old regime in full bloom, its ideas, its passions, its prejudices, its practices. In those records everyone spoke his own words freely, and exposed his inmost thoughts. I thus ended up learning many things about the old society of which its contemporaries were unaware, because I had before me documents which they never saw.

As I progressed in this research, I often encountered to my surprise many traits of modern France in the France of the old regime. I rediscovered there a mass of feelings that I thought had been born of the Revolution, a crowd of ideas that up to then I had thought derived from it, a thousand habits that pass for having been created by the Revolution alone. Everywhere I found the roots of present society deeply implanted in the past. The closer I got to 1789, the more I saw the spirit which made the Revolution sprout and grow. Little by little I saw the whole shape of the Revolution unveiled before my eyes. Already it displayed its temperament, its spirit, its very self. In the old regime I found not only the source of what the Revolution would do at the start, but still more what it would do in the end; for the Revolution had two very distinct stages. In the first the French seemed to want to abolish their entire past, in the second they seemed to take up again a part of what they had left behind. Many laws and political practices of the old regime disappeared in 1789 only to return a few years later, like some rivers that go underground only to reappear a few miles further on, the same stream between different banks.

The object of this book is to understand why this great revolution, which was simultaneously taking shape all over Europe, broke out in France rather than elsewhere, why it was so natural a product of the society it was going to destroy, and how, finally, the old monarchy could fall so suddenly and so completely. In my mind, this is not the end of the work. My intention is, if I have the time and energy, to follow the Frenchmen of the old regime with whom I have lived so intimately through the upheavals of the Revolution; to see how they were changed and transformed in the course of events, yet never changed their nature, always reappearing with slightly different faces, but always recognizable.

I will begin by examining them during the first stage of '89, when equality and liberty shared their devotion; when they wanted to create not only democratic institutions but free ones; when they sought not only to destroy privileges but to honor and recognize rights. It was a time of youth, enthusiasm, pride, a time of generous and sincere emotions, whose memory, despite its mistakes, will always be preserved by humanity, and which, for a long time to come, will trouble the sleep of all those who wish to corrupt or enslave France.

While rapidly following the course of that revolution, I will try to show what events, what errors and miscalculations, made those same French abandon their original course and, forgetting liberty, desire nothing more than to become the equal servants of the master of the world. I will show how a stronger government, much more absolute than that which the Revolution had overthrown, arose and concentrated all power in itself, suppressed all the freedoms so dearly bought, and put vain idols in their place. I will show how this government called the votes of electors who could neither inform themselves, nor organize, nor choose, "the sovereignty of the people"; how it called the assent of silent and servile assemblies "free taxation." I will show how while taking away the nation's ability to govern itself, destroying the chief guarantees of law, the freedom to think, speak, and write, that is, the most precious and noble of the conquests of '89 the government continued to adorn itself with the halo of the Revolution.

I will stop at the point where the Revolution seems to me to have just about finished its work and given birth to modern society. I will then consider the new society itself; I will try to figure out in what respects it resembles that which preceded it, and in what it differs, what we have lost in this immense transformation of everything, and what we have gained. I will finish by trying to see into our future.

Part of this second work is sketched out, but it is still not ready for publication. Will I be able to finish it? Who can say? The fate of individuals is still more hidden than that of nations.

I hope I have written the present work without prejudice, but I do not pretend to have written it without passion. It would hardly be possible for a Frenchman to feel nothing when he speaks of his country and ponders his times. I admit that in studying our old society in all its aspects, I have never entirely lost sight of our modern society. I wanted to discover not only what illness killed the patient, but how the patient could have been cured. I have acted like a doctor, dissecting every organ in order to discover the laws which govern the whole of life. My purpose has been to paint a picture both accurate and instructive. Whenever I encountered in our forefathers any of those manly virtues which are most necessary in our times and which have almost disappeared, I have highlighted them: true independence of mind, high ambition, faith in ourselves and in a cause. I have also taken care to cast light on the vices which, having devoured the old society, continue to gnaw at our own, so that in seeing the evil they have done, we can better understand the evil they can still do. To attain this goal, I have not refrained from offending anyone; whether individuals, classes, opinions, or memories, however respectable they may be. I have often done it with regret, but always without remorse. May those whom I have thus displeased pardon me in consideration of my sincere and disinterested purpose.

Some may accuse me of displaying too strong a taste for freedom, which, I am assured, is hardly of concern to anyone in France today. I ask those who reproach me thus to take into account that in my case this habit is very old. It was almost twenty years ago that, speaking of another society, I wrote almost exactly what I am now about to say.

In the midst of the shadows of the future we can already perceive three clear truths. The first is that today humanity is driven by an unknown force which we can hope to moderate, but not to defeat, which sometimes gently urges and sometimes shoves us towards the destruction of the aristocracy. Second, of all forms of society, the one where aristocracy does not and cannot exist is just the one which will have the most difficulty escaping absolute government for long. The third truth, finally, is that nowhere does despotism produce such pernicious effects as in just this kind of society; for, more than any other kind of government, despotism favors the development of all the vices to which such societies are especially prone, and thus pushes them in the direction in which they are already inclined to go.

People today, no longer attached to one another by any ties of caste, class, guild, or family, are all too inclined to be preoccupied with their own private interests, too given to looking out for themselves alone and withdrawing into a narrow individualism where all public virtues are smothered. Despotism, rather than struggling against this tendency, makes it irresistible, because it takes away from citizens all common feeling, all common needs, all need for communication, all occasion for common action. It walls them up inside their private lives. They already tend to keep themselves apart from one another: despotism isolates them; it chills their relations; it freezes them.

In these kinds of societies, where nothing is fixed, everyone is constantly tormented by the fear of falling and by the ambition to rise. Money has acquired an astonishing mobility, ceaselessly changing hands, transforming the status of individuals, raising or lowering families, and at the same time becoming the chief means by which to distinguish between people. Thus, there is virtually no one who is not constantly compelled to make desperate efforts to keep it or to make it. The desire to enrich oneself at any price, the preference for business, the love of profit, the search for material pleasure and comfort are therefore the most widespread desires. These desires spread easily among all classes, even among those previously most distant from them, and if nothing stops them they soon succeed in demoralizing and degrading the entire nation. But it is the very essence of despotism to favor and extend them. These debilitating passions help despotism, they occupy men's minds and turn them away from public affairs, while making them tremble at the very idea of a revolution. Despotism alone can furnish these passions with the secrecy and shadow which make greed feel at home, and let it reap its dishonest profits despite dishonor. Without despotism these passions would have been strong, with it they are all powerful.

Liberty alone can effectively combat the natural vices of these kinds of societies and prevent them from sliding down the slippery slope where they find themselves. Only freedom can bring citizens out of the isolation in which the very independence of their circumstances has led them to live, can daily force them to mingle, to join together through the need to communicate with one another, persuade each other, and satisfy each other in the conduct of their common affairs. Only freedom can tear people from the worship of Mammon and the petty daily concerns of their personal affairs and teach them to always see and feel the nation above and beside them; only freedom can substitute higher and stronger passions for the love of material well-being, give rise to greater ambitions than the acquisition of a fortune, and create the atmosphere which allows one to see and judge human vices and virtues.

Democratic societies that are not free can be wealthy, refined, even splendid, powerful because of the weight of their homogeneous mass; one can find there private virtues, good family men, honest merchants, and very worthy squires; one will even see some good Christians, for their country is not of this earth and the glory of their religion is to bring them forth amidst the greatest corruption of mores and under the worst governments: the Roman Empire in its greatest decadence was full of good Christians. But what will never exist in such societies are great citizens, and above all a great people, and I am willing to state that the average level of hearts and minds will never cease to decline as long as equality and despotism are combined.

This is what I said and thought twenty years ago. Since then nothing has happened to make me change my mind. I proclaimed my high opinion of liberty when it was in fashion, and one can hardly think badly of me for maintaining it when it is no longer in style. Indeed, in my love of freedom perhaps I differ less from my opponents than they imagine. What person could be naturally base enough to prefer dependence on the caprice of one man, rather than follow laws which he himself has helped to make, if he thought his country had the virtues necessary to make good use of freedom? I don't think such a person exists. Despots themselves don't deny that freedom is a wonderful thing, they only want to limit it to themselves; they argue that everyone else is unworthy of it. We do not differ over whether freedom is worthwhile, but over the higher or lower opinion we have of people. Thus one can state that the preference that one shows for absolute government is in direct proportion to the contempt that one has for one's country. I hope I may wait a while longer before converting to that opinion of France.

Without praising myself, I think I can say that this book is the product of considerable labor. There is one short chapter which alone has cost me more than a year of research. My pages could have overflowed with notes; I have chosen to insert only a few of them at the end of the book with references to the relevant pages in the text. There one will find examples and proofs. I could provide much more upon request if anyone thinks it worthwhile to ask.

I I b   Book One

I I b I   Chapter I: *"Contradictory Opinions about the Revolution at Its Birth"*

There is nothing more suited to instilling modesty in philosophers and statesmen than the history of our Revolution. Never was such a great event, with such ancient causes, so well prepared and so little foreseen.

Frederick the Great himself, despite his genius, did not predict the Revolution. He sensed it without seeing it. Furthermore, he acted in accordance with its spirit before it happened; he was its precursor and even its agent; but he did not recognize its approach. When the Revolution finally appeared, the new and extraordinary features which distinguished it from the innumerable crowd of revolutions remained hidden at first.

From abroad, the Revolution was the object of universal curiosity; throughout the world it gave rise to a sort of hazy notion that a new era was beginning, to vague hopes of change and reform; but no one yet suspected what the French Revolution would be. The kings and their ministers lacked even the confused feeling which moved the masses. At first they considered it one of those occasional fevers to which all peoples are subject, whose only effect is to create new opportunities for their neighbors. If by chance they spoke the truth about the Revolution, it was despite themselves. True, the chief rulers of Germany, meeting at Pilnitz in 1791, proclaimed that the danger which threatened royalty in France was common to all the old powers of Europe, that they were all menaced; but at bottom they did not believe it at all. Their secret records reveal that these were only the pretexts behind which they hid their plans or dressed them up for the eyes of the crowd.

As for themselves, they thought that the French Revolution was a mere fleeting local accident to be taken advantage of. In this light they conceived their plans, made their preparations, and formed their secret alliances; they already fought among themselves over the prospective booty, made agreements, broke them. They were prepared for everything except what actually happened.

The English, who were endowed with more experience and better understanding by the memory of their own history and their long experience of political liberty, discerned the approach of a great Revolution as if through a thick veil; but they could not make out its shape. The influence it would soon have on their own destiny and on the world's remained hidden. Arthur Young, who foresaw an imminent revolution, and who traveled through France just before it broke out, was so ignorant of its meaning that he wondered whether the result would not be an increase of privileges: "As for the nobility," he said "if the revolution gives them still more weight, I think it will have done more evil than good."

Burke, whose mind was stimulated by his hatred for the Revolution from its birth, even Burke was briefly unsure about it. At first he thought it meant that France would be weakened and virtually destroyed. "One must believe," he said, "that the military power of France has been destroyed for a long time to come; it is possible that it is permanently eliminated, and that the generation to come may say as Caesar did: *Gallos quoque in bellis floruisse audivimus* – we have heard that the Gauls too were once famous warriors."

The event was no better judged at home than abroad. In France, on the eve of the Revolution, people still had no clear idea of what it would do. Among the mass of *cahiers*, I could find only two which showed any fear of the populace. People were anxious about the power retained by the monarchy, by the Court, as it was still called. The weakness and the short duration of the Estates-Generals worried them. There was fear that the Estates-General would be intimidated. This particularly worried the nobility. "The Swiss," said many *cahiers*, "must take an oath never to bear arms against the citizenry even in case of riot or revolt." Give the Estates-General their freedom and all abuses would easily be eliminated; the reform to be accomplished was immense, but it was simple.

However, the Revolution followed its course. As the monster raised its head, it showed its unique and terrible face. After destroying the political institutions of France, it abolished the civil institutions; after changing the laws, it altered the mores, customs, and even the language. After it had destroyed the fabric of government, it uprooted the foundations of society, and finally seemed to want to challenge God himself. Soon the Revolution overflowed the boundaries of France by previously unheard-of-means: a new tactic, murderous maxims (armed opinions, as Pitt called them), an enormous power which breached frontiers, toppled thrones, crushed nations, and, oddly enough, at the same time won them to its cause. As these things happened, viewpoints changed. That which at first had appeared to rulers and statesmen like an ordinary event in the life of Europe, now seemed a fact so new, so contrary to the whole previous course of history, and yet so universal, so monstrous, so incomprehensible, that in regarding it the mind lost its bearings. Some thought that this unknown power, which nothing seemed to help or hinder, which could not be halted and could not stop itself, was going to force human society to its complete and final dissolution. Many considered it the visible work of the devil: "The French Revolution has a satanic character," said de Maistre, in 1797. Others, on the contrary, found in it the benevolent hand of God, who wished to renew not merely France but the whole world, and who was creating a new human race. Many writers of the time betray something of that pious terror that Salvian experienced at the sight of the barbarians. Burke, thinking along the same lines, wrote: "Without its former government, or rather without any government at all, it seemed that France was a fit subject for insults and pity, rather than the scourge and terror of the human race it became. From the tomb of the murdered monarchy came forth a huge, inchoate being, more horrible than any that had ever afflicted the human imagination. This strange and hideous beast headed straight for its goal, without being frightened by dangers or hindered by remorse; contemptuous of common sense and ordinary methods, it brought low those who could not even understand how it came to exist."

Was the event really as extraordinary as it appeared to contemporaries? As tremendous, as earthshattering, and as rejuvenating as they supposed? What was its real meaning, what was its real character, what were the permanent effects of this strange and terrible revolution? What exactly did it destroy? What has it created?

It seems that the time has come to answer these questions, and that today we are situated at just the right place to best see and judge this great thing. We are far enough from the Revolution to feel only faintly the passions of those who made it, but we are close enough to understand and empathize with the spirit that led them to it. Soon this will be impossible, for great revolutions which succeed make the causes which produced them disappear, and thus become incomprehensible because of their own success.

11b2 Chapter 2: "That the Fundamental and Final Objective of the Revolution Was Not, as Has Been Thought, to Destroy Religion and Weaken the State"

One of the first acts of the French Revolution was to attack the Church, and among the passions born of the Revolution the first lit and the last extinguished was this passion against religion. Even when enthusiasm for liberty had evaporated, even after people were reduced to buying peace at the price of servitude, they continued to revolt against religious authority. Napoleon, who was able to defeat the liberal spirit of the Revolution, made fruitless efforts to quench its anti-Christianity. Today, too, we have men who think they can make up for their servility towards the pettiest government officials by their insolence towards God, men who while abandoning all that was most free, most noble, and proudest in the doctrines of the Revolution, pride themselves on remaining true to its spirit because they are still unbelievers. Yet today it is easy to convince oneself that the war against religion was only an incident in the Revolution, one of its striking but fleeting aspects, a transitory product of the ideas, passions, and particular circumstances which preceded and prepared the Revolution, and not part of the Revolution's own spirit.

The philosophy of the eighteenth century is rightly considered one of the principal causes of the Revolution, and it is certainly true that that philosophy was deeply irreligious. But one must carefully distinguish between two very different aspects of that philosophy. In one part we find all the new or reinvigorated ideas about society and the principles of civil and political law, such as the natural equality of men, the abolition of caste, class, and professional privileges, and in consequence of this the sovereignty of the people, the omnipotence of the social power, and uniformity of rules. All these doctrines are not only causes of the French Revolution, they are its substance; they are the most fundamental of its works, the most lasting, and in the long run the most valid.

In the other part of their doctrines the philosophes of the eighteenth century were filled with a kind of rage against the Church. They attacked its clergy, its hierarchy, its institutions, its dogmas. They wanted to tear Christianity up by the roots. But this part of eighteenth-century philosophy, derived from the situation which the Revolution destroyed, ought to gradually disappear, buried by the Revolution's triumph. I will add only a few words here to make myself understood, because later on I want to take up this important subject again: it was much less as a religious doctrine than as a political institution that Christianity aroused these furious hatreds. The priests were not hated because they claimed to regulate the affairs of the other world, but because they were landowners, lords, tithe collectors, and administrators in this one; not because the Church could not take its place in the new society that was being created, but because it occupied the strongest and most privileged place in the old society, which was being ground into dust.

Consider how the course of time has brought this truth to light and demonstrates it daily: to the extent that the Revolution's political work has been consolidated, its anti-religious work has been destroyed. Thus to the extent that all the old political institutions that the Revolution attacked have disappeared, to the extent that the powers, influences, and classes which were particularly odious to it have been irreversibly defeated, and that as the final sign of their defeat the very hatreds that they once inspired have dissipated, to the extent, finally, that the clergy has separated itself from all that fell with the old regime, we have gradually seen the power of the Church rise and strengthen itself in people's minds. And do not think that this is restricted to France: there is hardly a Christian church in Europe which has not revived since the French Revolution.

To believe that democratic societies are naturally hostile to religion is to commit a great mistake: nothing in Christianity, nothing even in Catholicism, is absolutely contrary to the spirit of democratic societies, and many things are very favorable. History shows that the most vital root of religious instinct has always been planted in the heart of the masses. All the religions that have died found their last refuge there, and it would be very odd if those institutions which tend to make the ideas and passions of the masses dominant had the necessary and lasting effect of leading the human mind to impiety.

What I have just said about religion, I will repeat with still stronger reason about society. When one saw the Revolution simultaneously overthrow all the institutions and practices which had previously maintained a hierarchy in society, and kept people in order, one might assume that its result would be not only to destroy a particular social order, but all order, not a particular government, but government itself: one would have had to conclude that the Revolution's nature was essentially anarchic. And yet, this was true only in appearance.

Less than a year after the Revolution began, Mirabeau wrote secretly to the king: "Compare the new order of things with the old regime; from this comparison is born consolation and hope. Most of the acts of the National Assembly are clearly favorable to the monarchy. Is it nothing to be without parlements,[1] without *pays d'états*,[2] without the assembly of the clergy, without privileges or nobility? The idea of having only one class of citizens would have pleased Richelieu; equality facilitates the exercise of power. Several reigns of absolute government would not have done as much for royal authority as this single year of revolution has done." That was how a man capable of leading the Revolution understood it.

Since the goal of the French Revolution was not only to change the old government but to abolish the old kind of society, it had to simultaneously attack all the established powers, eliminate old influences, wipe out traditions, transform mores and practices, and in a way to empty the human mind of all the ideas on which obedience and respect had previously been based. From this came its singularly anarchic character. But now clear away all the debris: you will see an immense central power, which has devoured all the bits of authority and obedience which were formerly divided among a crowd of secondary powers, orders, classes, professions, families, and individuals, scattered throughout society. The world had not seen a similar concentration of power since the fall of the Roman Empire. The Revolution created this new power, or rather this power seemingly came forth naturally from the wreckage

---

1   The chief court of each region.
2   Provinces of France which still possessed traditional provincial assemblies.

made by the Revolution. The governments which were founded by the Revolution are more fragile, it is true, but they are a hundred times more powerful than any that it overthrew; more fragile and more powerful for the same reasons, as will be discussed below.

Through the wreckage of the half-demolished old regime Mirabeau already perceived this new concentration of power. Despite its size, it was still invisible to the eyes of the crowd, but time has gradually made it plain to all. Today, monarchs are especially fascinated by it. Not only those rulers whom the Revolution created, but even those most opposed to it, regard it with envy and admiration; they all attempt to destroy the privileges and immunities within their realms. They mix ranks, equalize status, substitute government officials for aristocrats, uniform rules for local liberties, and centralized government for a diversity of powers. They work long and hard at this revolutionary task. And if they encounter any obstacle, they sometimes borrow the Revolution's methods and justifications to remove it. Thus one can see them when necessary inciting the poor against the rich, the bourgeois against the noble, the peasant against his landlord. The French Revolution has been at once the scourge and the teacher of princes.

IIb3   Chapter 3: "How the French Revolution Was a Political Revolution Which Acted Like a Religious Revolution, and Why"

Every political and civil revolution has taken place within the borders of a single country. The French Revolution did not have a territory of its own; further, to some extent its effect has been to erase all the old frontiers from the map. It has united or divided people despite their laws, traditions, characters, and languages, turning compatriots into enemies, and strangers into brothers; or rather it established, above all particular nationalities, a common intellectual homeland where men of all nations could become citizens.

In all history you will not find a single political revolution which has had this character. You will find it only in certain religious revolutions. The French Revolution must be compared to a religious revolution, if you want to find an analogy to help in understanding it.

Schiller justly remarks, in his history of the Thirty Years War that the great Reformation of the sixteenth century brought together nations which hardly knew each other, and united them through their new feelings. Indeed Frenchmen fought Frenchmen while Englishmen came to their aid, and men born at the furthest extreme of the Baltic penetrated the heart of Germany in order to protect Germans whom they had never heard of before. All foreign wars took on something of the character of civil wars; in all civil wars foreigners appeared. Every country's old interests were forgotten for new interests; questions of territory gave way to questions of principle. All the rules of diplomacy were mixed up and confused, to the great astonishment and dismay of the statesmen of the time. This is precisely what happened to Europe after 1789.

The French Revolution is therefore a political revolution which acted like and began to look like a religious revolution. Observe the characteristic traits which make it resemble one: not only is it widespread, but, like a religious revolution, it is spread by preaching and propaganda. It is a political revolution which inspires missionaries, and which is preached as ardently to foreigners as it is passionately enacted at home: think what a new sight this is! Among all the unheard-of things that the French Revolution presented to the world, this was certainly the newest. But let us not stop here; let us try to proceed a little further and see if this resemblance of effects does not derive from some hidden resemblance in their causes.

Religions usually consider man in himself, without regard for what the laws, customs, and traditions of a country have added to the common base. Their principal purpose is to regulate the relationship between man and God, and the general rights and duties of men toward each other, independently of the form of society. The rules of conduct which religions prescribe relate less to the man of a particular country or time, than to the son, the father, the servant, the master, the neighbor. These rules are based on human nature itself; they can be equally accepted by all men and they are equally applicable everywhere. Thus it can be seen that religious revolutions have often had vast scope and are rarely limited, like political revolutions, to the territory of a single people, or even to a single race. And if one examines the subject still more closely, one finds that the more a religion has the abstract and general character which I have just described, the more it spreads, despite differences of laws, climate, and men.

The pagan religions of antiquity, which were all more or less linked to the political constitution or the social state of each people, and which preserved even in their dogmas a certain national and often municipal appearance, were ordinarily confined to the limits of a territory, which they rarely left. They sometimes gave birth to intolerance and persecution; but conversion was almost entirely unknown to them. Thus there were no great religious revolutions in the West until the arrival of Christianity. Christianity conquered in a short time a great part of the human race, easily crossing the barriers that had halted the pagan religions. I do not think it is lacking in respect for that holy religion to say that it owed its triumph in part to the fact that it, more than any other, was separate from all that might be particular to one people, to one form of government, to one social state, to one time or one race.

The French Revolution operated, with respect to this world, in precisely the same manner that religious revolutions have acted with respect to the other world. It considered the citizen in an abstract manner, outside of any particular society, the same way that religion considers man in general, independently of time and place. The Revolution did not only ask what the particular rights of French citizens were, but what were the general political rights and duties of men. Because it always went back to that which was least particular, in other words to that which was most natural with respect to social state and government, the French Revolution was able to make itself accessible to everyone and was imitable in a hundred different places simultaneously.

Because the Revolution seemed to be striving for the regeneration of the human race even more than for the reform of France, it lit a passion which the most violent political revolutions had never before been able to produce. It inspired missionaries and generated propaganda. Thus, in the end, it took on that appearance of a religious revolution which so astonished its contemporaries. Or rather, it itself became a new kind of religion, an incomplete religion, it is true, without God, without ritual, and without a life after death, but one which nevertheless, like Islam, flooded the earth with its soldiers, apostles, and martyrs.

Furthermore, one must not think that the procedures which the Revolution employed were absolutely unprecedented, and that all the ideas which it brought to light were entirely new. In all eras, even in the High Middle Ages, there have been agitators who, in order to change particular customs, have invoked the general laws of human society, who attempted to oppose the natural rights of man to the constitution of their country. But all these efforts failed. The same spark which set Europe afire in the eighteenth century was easily put out in the fifteenth. Indeed, in order for this kind of argument to produce a revolution it is necessary for certain changes to have already taken place in conditions, customs, and mores, which prepare the human mind to accept it.

There are times when men are so different from one another that the idea of one law applicable to all seems incomprehensible. There are others when it is enough to show them, as in a glass darkly, the image of such a law, for them to immediately recognize it and run towards it. The most extraordinary thing was not that the French Revolution did what it did, or that it came up with the ideas that it produced: the great novelty was that so many nations had reached a point where such practices were so effectively employed, and such principles so readily accepted.

IIb5   Chapter 5: "What Did the French Revolution Really Accomplish?"

The only purpose of the preceding chapters has been to throw light on this subject and facilitate the solution of the question that I posed at the beginning: What was the real purpose of the Revolution? What, in the end, was its true character? Exactly why was it made? What did it do?

The Revolution was certainly not made, as some believe, to destroy religion. Despite appearances, it was essentially a social and political revolution, and in comparison with others of its kind it did not at all tend to perpetuate disorder, to make it somehow permanent, to make anarchy into a method, as one of its principal adversaries said, but rather to increase the rights and power of political authority. It did not have to change the character of our civilization, as others have thought, halting its progress, nor even to fundamentally change any of the basic laws on which human society in our West has rested. When we detach the Revolution from all the accidents which briefly altered its appearance at different times and in different countries, in order to consider it in its own right, we clearly see that the Revolution's only effect was to abolish the political institutions which for several centuries had reigned unopposed among the majority of European peoples, and which we usually call feudal institutions. It did so in order to replace them with a more uniform and simple social and political order, one based on social equality.

This was enough to make an immense revolution, for independently of the fact that the old institutions were still interwoven with almost all the religious and political laws of Europe, they had inspired a mass of ideas, feelings, habits, and mores which were strongly connected to them. It required a frightful convulsion to destroy and suddenly to extract from the social body a part which was connected to all its organs. This made the Revolution appear even bigger than it actually was. It seemed to destroy everything, because what it did destroy was related to everything and in some sense was embedded in everything.

However radical the Revolution was, it innovated much less than is generally supposed, as I will show later on. What one can say is that it entirely destroyed, or is in the process of destroying (because it is still in progress), everything that derived from aristocratic and feudal institutions in the old society, everything that was in some way connected to them, everything that bore, in the least degree, their smallest imprint. It preserved from the old world only those things which had always been foreign to the old institutions, or which could exist without them. The Revolution was least of all an accident. True, it took the world by surprise, and yet it was the result of a very long process, the sudden and violent climax of a task to which ten generations had contributed. If it had not taken place, the old social structure would nevertheless have collapsed everywhere, here sooner, there later, with the only difference that it would have continued to fall apart piece by piece instead of collapsing all at once. The Revolution finished off quickly, by a feverish and convulsive effort, without transition, without precautions, without regard for anything, what would have been done anyway, little by little, in the long run. This was its effect.

It is surprising that what seems so easy to see today was at that time so muddled and so hidden from the eyes of the most farseeing. "You want to correct the abuses of your government," says Burke to the French; "but why create something new? Why not return to your old traditions? What keeps you from recovering your ancient liberties? Or, if it is impossible for you to rediscover the long-lost shape of your ancestors' constitution, why not look to us? Here you would have found the old common law of all Europe." Burke does not realize that what stands before his eyes is the revolution which will abolish the old common law of Europe; he does not understand that this is its sole purpose.

But why did this revolution, ripening everywhere, threatening everywhere, break out in France rather than somewhere else? Why did it have certain characteristics among us which did not appear anywhere else, or did so only partially? This second question surely deserves to be asked; its examination will be the subject of the following books.

I Ic   Book Two

I Ic2   Chapter 2: "How Administrative Centralization Is an Institution of the Old Regime, and Not the Work of Either the Revolution or the Empire, as Is Said"

I once heard a speaker, back when we had political assemblies in France, who said of administrative centralization: "That great conquest of the Revolution, which Europe envies us." I concede that centralization was a great conquest, I admit that Europe envies us for it, but I maintain that it was certainly not a conquest of the Revolution. On the contrary it was a product of the old regime and, I will add, the only part of the old regime's political constitution which survived the Revolution, because it was the only one which could adapt to the new social state which the Revolution created. The reader who has the patience to read this chapter carefully may find that I have proved my point overabundantly.

Let us leave aside what are called the *pays d'états*, that is, those provinces which governed themselves, or rather still had the appearance of partly governing themselves. The *pays d'états*, situated at the extreme boundaries of the kingdom, contained barely a quarter of the total population of France, and among them there were only two where provincial freedom really existed. I will return to the *pays d'états* later on and show to what extent the central power had subjected even them to the common rules. I want to concern myself principally with what in the official language of the time were called the *pays d'élection*,[3] although there were fewer elections there than anywhere else. These provinces completely surrounded Paris; they were geographically compact and formed the heart and most of the body of France.

When we first look at the former administration of the kingdom, there seems everywhere to be a variety of rules and authorities, a confusion of powers. France was covered with administrative bodies or isolated officials who were independent of one another, and who participated in government by virtue of an irrevocable right that they had purchased and that could not be taken away from them. Often their functions were so intermixed and so similar that they interfered with each other's work while doing their own.

The courts took part indirectly in the legislative process; they had the right to make official rules which had force within the limits of their jurisdictions. Sometimes they collided with the administration proper, harshly censuring its measures and issuing writs against its agents. Local judges made police regulations in the towns and villages where they presided.

The towns had extremely varied constitutions. Their magistrates bore different names, or took their powers from different sources: here a mayor, there consuls, elsewhere syndics. Some were chosen by the king, some by the old lord or by a prince of the royal house; there were some who were elected for a year by their fellow citizens, and others who had bought the right to govern them in perpetuity.

These were the remnants of the old powers; but gradually there was established among them something that was comparatively recent or transformed, which has yet to be described. A uniquely powerful administrative body had developed at the center of the kingdom, near the throne, which united all powers in a new way: the *conseil du roi* or Royal Council.

It was old in origin, but most of its functions were of recent date. It was everything at once. It was a supreme court, since it had the right to overrule the decisions of all ordinary courts; it was a superior administrative tribunal – all special jurisdictions were ultimately subordinate to it. As government

---

3   Those provinces of France, the majority, where provincial assemblies of Estates no longer existed.

council, it also possessed, at the king's pleasure, legislative power. It debated and proposed laws, fixed and distributed taxes. As chief administrative council, it was up to it to establish general rules to guide government agents. It decided all important matters and supervised lesser authorities. All roads led to the Royal Council, and from it came the impulses that guided everything. In itself it did not have any authority, however. It was the king alone who decided, even when the Council appeared to decree. Even when it seemed to dispense justice, it was composed only of *advisers*, as the *parlement* said in one of its remonstrances.

This Council was not composed of great lords but of people of low or mediocre birth, former intendants and other people with experience in practical affairs, all serving at the king's discretion. The Council usually acted quietly and secretly, always with less pretension than power. Also, it had no fame in itself; or rather it was lost amidst the splendor of the nearby throne. It was so powerful that it affected everything, and at the same time so obscure that history has barely noticed it.

At the same time as the entire country's government was directed by a single body, almost all control of internal affairs was given to a single agent, the controller-general. If you open an almanac of the old regime, you will find that each province had its own special minister; but when we study the government and its files, we soon see that the minister of the province acted merely on a few unimportant matters. The ordinary course of affairs was directed by the controller-general; gradually he had gained control of everything which had to do with money, i.e., almost all public administration. We see him act successively as minister of finance, interior minister, minister of public works, and minister of commerce.

At the same time as the central government had, in reality, only one agent at Paris, it had but a single agent in each province. In the eighteenth century we still find great lords who bear the title of Governor of the Province. Often hereditary offices, these were the old representatives of the feudal monarchy. They were still given respect, but they no longer had any power. In reality the intendant controlled the government.

The intendant was a man of common birth, always a stranger to the province, young, a man with his career still to make. He did not exercise his powers by virtue of election, birth, or purchase. He was chosen by the government from the junior members of the Council and was always subject to dismissal. When away from the Council, he represented it, and that is why in the official language of the time he was called a *commissionnaire départi*; a "detached" commissioner. Almost all the powers possessed by the Royal Council itself were combined in his hands; he exercised them in the first instance. Like the Council, he was both administrator and judge. The intendant was in contact with all the ministries; he was the sole agent of the government's will in his province.

Beneath him, and appointed by him, an official removable at his discretion was placed in each canton: the subdelegate. The intendant was usually a recently ennobled man; the subdelegate was always a commoner. Nevertheless, he represented the entire government in the little area to which he was assigned, as the intendant did in the larger region. He was under the intendant as the intendant was under the ministry.

The Marquis d'Argenson tells us, in his memoirs, that one day Mr. Law said to him: "I would never have believed what I saw when I was controller of finance. Know that the kingdom of France is ruled by thirty intendants. You have neither a parlement, nor estates, nor governors; it is thirty subordinate officials, detached for duty in the provinces, on whom the happiness or misfortune of those provinces, their prosperity or their poverty, depend."

These all-powerful officials were, however, eclipsed by the remnants of the old feudal aristocracy and virtually lost in the radiance the aristocracy still projected. That is why, even in their own time, they were hardly noticed, although their fingers were already everywhere. In society the nobles had the advantage of rank, of wealth, and of the respect which was always given to old things. In government, the nobility surrounded the king and made up his court; they commanded the fleets, directed the armies; they were, in short, that which most struck contemporaries' eyes and too often monopolizes posterity's attention. One would have insulted a great lord by suggesting he be named an intendant; the poorest gentleman of rank would have generally refused to accept the position. The intendants were in their eyes the representatives of an interloping power, new men, appointed to govern the bourgeois and peasants, and, furthermore, not the kind of person one would wish to associate with. Nevertheless these men ruled France, as Law said and as we will see.

Let us start with the right of taxation, which to some extent contains all other rights. We know that part of the taxes were farmed out. For those, it was the Royal Council which negotiated with the financial companies, set the terms of their contracts, and fixed the mode of payment. All other taxes, like the *taille*,[4] the *capitation*[5] or the *vingtièmes*,[6] were established and levied

---

4   The fundamental personal tax of eighteenth-century France, based on a total amount to be raised for the whole kingdom.

5   A personal tax designed in theory to strike everyone except the clergy, whether they paid the *taille* or not.

6   A five percent income tax imposed on both nobles and commoners.

directly by the agents of the central government or under their all-powerful supervision.

By a secret decision every year, the Council fixed the total amount of the *taille* and its numerous parts, and also divided it among the provinces. The *taille* thus increased from year to year without anyone being warned of it in advance by any publicity. Since the *taille* was an old tax, its basis and raising had formerly been assigned to local agents, who were all more or less independent of the government, since they exercised their powers by right of birth or election, or by virtue of a purchased office. It was the lord, the parish collector, the "Treasurers of France," the "*élus*" who had previously administered the *taille*. These authorities still existed in the eighteenth century, but some no longer had anything to do with the *taille*, and others dealt with it only in a very secondary and completely subordinate way. Even then, all power was in the hands of the intendant and his agents; he alone, in reality, apportioned the *taille* among the parishes, guided and supervised the collectors, and granted delays or rebates.

With other taxes of recent date, like the *capitation*, the government was no longer bothered with the leftovers of the old powers; it acted alone, without any interference from the governed. The controller-general, the intendant and the Council fixed the amount of everything.

Let us move from money to men. We are sometimes astonished that the French bore the burden of military conscription so patiently during the Revolution and thereafter; but it must be remembered that they had been used to it for a long time. Conscription was preceded by the militia, a heavier burden, although the number of men demanded was smaller. Periodically the youths of the countryside were required to draw lots, and a certain number of soldiers were selected, from whom were formed militia regiments where one did six years' service.

Since the militia was a comparatively modern institution, none of the old feudal authorities were involved in it; the whole operation was run solely by agents of the central government. The Council fixed the number of militia for the kingdom and divided it among the provinces. The intendant determined the number of men to be levied in each parish; his subdelegate presided over the lottery, judged the pleas for exemption, chose which militia men could live at home and which had to leave, and delivered the latter to the military authorities. There was no appeal except to the intendant and the Royal Council.

Similarly, it could be said that outside the *pays d'états* all public works, even those of the most local interest, were decided upon and conducted solely by agents of the central power. There still existed many other independent local authorities which, like the lord, the finance office, the grand overseers, could participate in this aspect of public administration. But almost everywhere these old authorities acted little or not at all: the most cursory examination of contemporary government files demonstrates this. All the highways, and even the roads which went from town to town, were constructed and maintained from the national tax receipts. It was the Council which decided on the plans and handled the bidding. The intendant directed the work of the engineers, the subdelegate gathered the *corvée* which was to execute them. Only the smallest roads were left to the care of the old local authorities, and they remained impassable.

The central government's chief agent with regard to public works was, then as now, the Roads and Bridges Corps. Here everything was like it is today to an astonishing degree, despite the different times. The administration of roads and bridges had a council and a school, inspectors who annually traveled through France, and engineers who lived onsite and under the intendant's orders and were in charge of directing the work. The institutions of the old regime, which, in far greater number than is usually realized, have continued to exist in the new society, have usually lost their names in transition while retaining their form, but this one has kept both − a rare occurrence.

The central government, with the aid of its agents, took upon itself alone the maintenance of public order in the provinces. The mounted police were spread out over the kingdom in small units, and everywhere they were placed under the intendant's authority. It was with the aid of these troops, and if necessary of the army, that the intendant dealt with all unforeseen dangers, arrested vagrants, repressed begging, and put down the endless disturbances caused by the price of bread. It never happened, as previously, that the governed were called upon to help the government in this part of its task, except in the towns, where there usually existed a city guard whose officers and soldiers were chosen by the intendant.

The judiciary had retained the right to make police regulations, and often used it; but these regulations were only applicable over part of the nation, and generally in just a single place. The Council could always overturn these regulations, and very frequently did so when it was a question of lower jurisdictions. It itself made general regulations every day, equally applicable over the entire kingdom, either in regard to matters other than those dealt with by the courts, or even on the same questions previously dealt with by the judiciary. The number of these regulations, or, as they said then, these "decrees of the Council," was immense, and grew immeasurably with the approach of the Revolution. There was almost no part of the social economy or political organization which had not been modified by these decrees during the forty years before the Revolution.

In the old feudal society, if the lord had great rights, he also bore great burdens. It was up to him to help the poor within the bounds of his domain. We find a last trace of this old law of Europe in the Prussian Code of 1795, which says: "The lord must see that poor peasants receive an education. He must, insofar as possible, feed those of his vassals who do not possess any land. If some of them fall into want, he is required to come to their aid."

In France, no such law had existed for a long time. As his old powers were taken from the lord, his old obligations were withdrawn. No local authority, no council, no provincial or parish association took his place. No one was legally obligated to take care of the rural poor any more; the central government had boldly taken it upon itself alone to provide for their needs.

Every year the Royal Council assigned to each province, from the general tax receipts, certain funds which the intendants distributed to help the parish poor. It was to the intendant that the poor peasant turned. In times of food shortage, it was the intendant who had rice or wheat distributed to the people. The council made annual decrees which established, in particular places which they carefully chose themselves, charity workshops where the poorest peasants could find work in return for a small wage. We can only presume that charity given from so far away was often blind or capricious, and always very inadequate.

The central government did not limit itself to coming to the aid of the peasantry in its distress. It also claimed to teach them how to get rich, to help them and if necessary to force them to learn how. For this purpose the government occasionally had its intendants and subdelegates distribute little pamphlets about agriculture, and it founded agricultural societies, promised bounties, and at great expense set up nurseries and distributed their products. It seems that it would have been more effective to reduce the weight and diminish the inequality of the burdens which then oppressed agriculture; but this is not something that was ever considered wise.

Sometimes the Council wanted to make people better off whether they liked it or not. There were innumerable decrees which forced artisans to use certain methods and make certain products; and since the intendants were inadequate to supervise the application of all these rules, there existed inspectors–general of industry who traveled through the provinces to keep them in hand.

There were decrees of the Council prohibiting certain crops from being sown on land which the council did not think appropriate. One finds decrees where it ordered vineyards torn up that in its opinion had been planted in poor soil. To this extent had the government already exchanged the role of sovereign for that of guardian.

11c10   Chapter 10: "How the Destruction of Political Liberty and the Division of Classes Caused Almost All the Ills of Which the Old Regime Perished"

I have just described the most deadly of all the maladies that attacked the constitution of the old regime and condemned it to death. I want to go back again to the origin of this strange and dangerous sickness, and show how many other ills had followed in its wake.

If, after the Middle Ages, the English, like us, had entirely lost their political liberty and all the local freedoms which cannot long exist without it, it is very probable that the different classes which composed their aristocracy would have separated from each other, as happened in France and more or less on the rest of the continent, and that all of them together would have been separated from the people. But freedom always forced them all to stay in touch with one another, in order to be able to reach an understanding when necessary.

It is interesting to see how the English nobility, pushed by its own ambition, has known how to mingle on familiar terms with its inferiors when necessary, and pretend to consider them its equals. Arthur Young, whom I have already cited, and whose book is one of the most instructive works which exist on the old France, tells us that, finding himself one day in the country with the duc de Liancourt, he expressed the desire to speak with some of the ablest and richest local farmers. The duke instructed his intendant to bring them to him. About which the Englishman made the following remark: "With an English lord, we would have had three or four farmers come, who would have dined with the family, and among ladies of the highest rank. I have seen that at least a hundred times in our isles. This is something for which one would search France in vain from Calais to Bayonne."

Certainly, the English aristocracy was more haughty than the French aristocracy, and less inclined to be familiar with those who lived beneath it; but the necessities of its situation required it to do so. It was ready to do anything in order to lead. For centuries no inequalities of taxation had been seen among the English, except those which were successively introduced in favor of the poor. Consider, please, where these different political principles can lead neighboring peoples! In eighteenth-century England, it was the poor man who enjoyed tax privileges; in France, it was the rich. There, the aristocracy had taken upon itself the heaviest public burdens, so that it would be allowed to govern; here, the aristocracy kept its immunity from taxation until the end, in order to console itself for having lost the government.

In the fourteenth century, the maxim "Do not tax those who do not consent" seemed as solidly established in France as in England itself. It was often cited: to break it still seemed an act of tyranny; to obey it, to return to legality. At that period one finds, as I have already said, a mass of analogies between our political institutions and those of the English; but since then the destinies of the two peoples have parted, and are becoming increasingly more different with time. They resemble two lines which, starting from neighboring points, but following slightly different directions, diverge from one another more and more the longer they extend.

I would dare to argue that from the day when the nation, tired of the long disorders that had accompanied the captivity of King John[7] and the insanity of King Charles VI,[8] permitted the kings to establish a general tax without its consent, and when the nobility had the cowardice to allow the Third Estate to be taxed provided that the nobility itself was exempted; on that day was planted the seed for almost all the vices and abuses which affected the old regime for the rest of its life, and finally caused its violent death. I admire the unique wisdom of Commynes[9] when he said: "Charles VII, who won the argument over imposing the *taille* at his will, without the consent of the estates, heavily burdened his soul and those of his successors, and made a wound in his realm that will bleed for a long time." Consider how the wound was actually enlarged over the course of time; follow its consequences step by step.

Forbonnais rightly says, in his erudite *Researches on the Finances of France*, that during the Middle Ages the kings generally lived on the revenues of their domains: "and since extraordinary needs," he adds, "were provided for by extraordinary contributions, they were borne equally by the clergy, the nobility, and the people." The majority of the general taxes voted by the three orders during the fourteenth century were indeed of this character. Almost all the taxes established at that period were *indirect*, that is to say they were paid by all consumers without distinction. Sometimes the tax was direct: it bore then, not on property, but on income. The nobles, the clergy, and the bourgeoisie were required to give to the king, for example, a tenth of their annual income. What I have said about taxes voted by the Estates-General ought to be extended equally to those which were established at that period by the various provincial estates on their territories.

---

7   John II, king of France from 1350 to 1364. He was captured by the English at the battle of Poitiers in 1356 and ransomed at great price.
8   Charles VI, king of France from 1380 to 1422. He suffered frequent bouts of insanity.
9   Philippe de Commynes (*c.* 1447–1511), author of celebrated memoirs, and adviser of Duke Charles the Bold of Burgundy and King Louis XI.

It is true that, from this time on, the direct tax known under the name of *taille* was never levied on the nobles. The obligation of unpaid military service dispensed them from it; but the *taille*, as a general tax, was then of limited use, more applicable to the manor than to the kingdom. When the king later attempted for the first time to raise taxes on his own authority, he understood that it was necessary to choose one which would not seem to strike directly at the nobility; for the nobility, who then formed a rival and dangerous class for the king, would never have accepted an innovation which would have been so harmful to them; he therefore chose a tax from which they were exempt; he chose the *taille*.

To all the particular inequalities which already existed there was now joined a more general one, which preserved and aggravated all the others. From then on, as the needs of the public treasury grew with the increase in central power, the *taille* was extended and broadened; soon it was multiplied tenfold, and all new taxes became *tailles*. Every year, therefore, the inequality of taxation separated classes and isolated individuals more deeply than ever before. From the moment when taxation had as its purpose, not to strike those most capable of paying, but those least capable of defending themselves against it, the monstrous consequence of sparing the rich and burdening the poor was inevitable. We are assured that Mazarin,[10] needing money, thought of establishing a tax on the principal houses of Paris, but that having encountered some opposition from those interested, he limited himself to adding the five millions he needed to the general bill of the *taille*. He wanted to tax the most opulent citizens; he ended up taxing the poorest. But the treasury lost nothing.

The income from taxes so badly distributed had limits, and the needs of rulers no longer had any. However, they did not wish to convoke the Estates-General to obtain grants from them, nor to provoke the nobility to demand the convocation of those assemblies by taxing them. From this came that huge and monstrous fertility of the financial mind, which so strikingly characterized the administration of public finance during the last three centuries of the monarchy.

One must study the administrative and financial history of the old regime in detail, in order to understand to what violent and dishonest practices the need for money can reduce a government that is well-intentioned but acts in secret, without check, once time has consecrated its power and delivered it from the fear of revolution, that last safeguard of peoples.

. . .

---

10   Cardinal Mazarin, minister of Louis XIII and, then, Queen-regent Anne of Austria.

Letrone[11] rightly said in 1775: "The state has only established the trade guilds in order to find resources there, sometimes through the licenses that it sells, sometimes through the new offices that it creates and which the guilds are forced to redeem. The edict of 1673 extended to their logical consequence the principles of Henry III, by requiring all the guilds to acquire letters of confirmation for a sum, and all artisans who were not yet part of a guild to join one. This miserable business produced 300,000 livres."

We have seen how towns' entire constitutions were overturned, not for political reasons, but with the intention of acquiring some money for the treasury. It was to this same need for money, joined with the wish to request nothing from the Estates, that the venality of offices owed its birth, and little by little it became something so strange that nothing like it has ever been seen. Thanks to this institution, created by the financial mind, the vanity of the Third Estate was kept in good shape for three centuries and directed uniquely towards the acquisition of public offices; this universal passion for government jobs was encouraged to penetrate into the bowels of the nation, a passion which became the common source of revolution and servitude.

As financial embarrassments increased, new jobs were created, all paid for by tax exemptions or privileges; and as it was the needs of the treasury, not of government, which determined them, in this way an almost incredible number of absolutely useless or harmful posts were created. As early as 1664, at the time of the inquiry made by Colbert,[12] he found that the capital sunk in this miserable kind of property amounted to nearly five hundred million livres. Richelieu[13] destroyed, it is said, 100,000 offices. They were immediately reborn under other names. For a little cash one thus deprived oneself of the right to direct, to control, and to constrain one's own officials. In this way there was gradually built a bureaucratic machine so vast, so complicated, so hobbled, and so unproductive, that it was necessary to let it spin its wheels, and to construct an instrument of government alongside it which was simpler and more manageable, by means of which one could really do what all those other officials were supposed to do.

We may be sure that none of these detestable institutions could have lasted twenty years, if it had been permitted to discuss them. None of them would have been established or allowed to grow worse if the Estates had been consulted, or if their grievances had been listened to, when by chance they still met. The rare Estates-General of recent centuries did not cease to protest against them. On several occasions one sees these assemblies point out as the

11   Guillaume-François Letrone (1718–1780), physiocratic publicist.
12   Jean-Baptiste Colbert, chief minister of Louis XIV.
13   Cardinal, Duke of Richelieu, chief minister of Louis XIII.

origin of these abuses the power which the king had arrogated to raise taxes arbitrarily; or, to reproduce the very expressions which the energetic language of the fifteenth century used, "the right of enriching himself from the people's substance without the consent and deliberation of the three Estates." They did not concern themselves only with their own rights; they forcefully demanded, and often obtained, respect for the rights of the towns and provinces. At each new session, voices were raised within the Estates against the inequality of taxation. The Estates asked several times for the abandonment of the guild-mastership system; from century to century they attacked the venality of offices with increasing vigor. "He who sells an office sells justice, which is an infamous thing," they said. When the venality of offices was established, they continued to complain about the abuses that were made of them. They rose up against so many useless jobs and dangerous privileges, but always in vain. These institutions were established precisely against the Estates; they were born of the desire not to convene them, and of the need to disguise from the eyes of the French the taxes which no one dared reveal in their true light.

And note that the best kings had recourse to these practices as much as the worst. It was Louis XII who finally established the venality of offices; it was Henry IV who sold them as hereditary: by so much were the vices of the system stronger than the virtues of the men who practiced it!

This same desire to escape from the tutelage of the Estates made the kings confide most of the Estates' political functions to the parlements. This confused the judiciary power with the executive in a manner very harmful to the proper conduct of affairs. The kings had to appear to furnish some new guarantees to replace those that had been eliminated; for the French, who accept absolute power patiently, as long as it is not oppressive, have never liked its sight, and it has always been wise to put up screens in front of power which, without being able to stop it, at least hide it a little.

Finally, it was the desire to prevent the nation, from which money was asked, from demanding its freedom back, that made the government constantly alert to ensure that the classes remained apart from each other, so that they could neither come together again nor join in a common resistance; thus the government would never have to deal with more than a very small number of men at one time, separated from all the others. During the whole course of the long history of the French monarchy, where so many remarkable rulers appear, some notable for their intelligence, others for their character, almost all for their courage, there is not a single one who makes an effort to bring the classes together and unite them in any way but in submission to an equal dependence. I am mistaken: one alone wanted to, and even wholeheartedly attempted to; and that one – who can fathom the judgments of God! – was Louis XVI.

The division of classes was the crime of the old monarchy, and later became its excuse; for once all those who made up the wealthy and enlightened portion of the nation could no longer agree with one another, and help one another govern, it was virtually impossible for the country to govern itself, and it was necessary for a master to intervene. "The nation," said Turgot[14] sadly in a secret report to the king, "is a society made up of different orders badly united, and of a people whose members have very few ties, where, by consequence, no one cares about anything but his own personal interests. Nowhere is any common interest visible. The villages, the towns have no more contact than do the regions of which they are part. They cannot even agree among themselves to undertake necessary public works. In this perpetual war of claims and counterclaims, His Majesty is obliged to decide everything by himself or through his delegates. They wait for your special orders in order to contribute to the public good, in order to respect someone else's rights, sometimes even to exercise their own."

It was no small thing to bring together again fellow citizens who had lived like this for centuries, as strangers or enemies, and to teach them how to conduct their affairs in common. It was much easier to divide them than it was to reunite them later on. We furnished a memorable example of this to the world. When, sixty years ago, the different classes which made up the society of old France re-entered into contact with one another, after having been isolated for so long by so many barriers, they at first only rubbed each other's raw spots, and made contact only in order to tear each other apart. Even today their jealousies and their hatreds survive them.

I I d   Book Three

I I d I   Chapter I: "How Around the Middle of the Eighteenth Century Intellectuals Became the Country's Leading Politicians, and the Effects Which Resulted from This"

I will now leave the long-term and general facts which prepared the great Revolution which I want to paint, to come to the particular and more recent facts which finally determined its place, its birth, and its character.

France had long been the most literary of all the nations of Europe; nevertheless its men of letters had never shown the spirit that they displayed in the middle of the eighteenth century, nor occupied the place that they then took. This had never before been seen among us, nor, I think, anywhere else.

14   Louis XVI's comptroller-general of finance.

Men of letters were not daily involved in public affairs as in England; on the contrary, they had never been further removed from them. They were never given any authority whatsoever, and never occupied any public office in a society already full of government officials. However, they did not remain, like most of their German counterparts, entirely strangers to politics, confined to the domain of pure philosophy and belles-lettres. They constantly concerned themselves with topics relating to government; in fact, that was their real occupation. Every day they were heard discussing the origin of societies and their original forms, the primordial rights of citizens and those of authority, the natural and artificial relations among men, the error or legitimacy of custom, the very principles of the laws. Thus penetrating every day to the roots of their era's constitution, they curiously examined its structure and criticized its general plan. Not all of them, it is true, made these great problems the object of special and thorough study; the majority treated them only in passing, and playfully; but they all dealt with them. This kind of abstract and literary politics was spread in varying degree throughout the works of the time. There were none, from the thick treatise to the popular song, which did not contain a little politics.

. . .

Above the real society, whose constitution was still traditional, confused, and irregular, where laws remained varied and contradictory, ranks were separated, status was fixed, and burdens were unequal, there was slowly built an imaginary society in which everything seemed simple and coordinated, uniform, equitable, and in accord with reason. Gradually the imagination of the crowd deserted the former to concentrate on the latter. One lost interest in what was, in order to think about what could be, and finally one lived mentally in that ideal city the writers had built.

Our revolution has often been attributed to that of America: in fact the American Revolution had a lot of influence on the French Revolution, but less because of what was then done in the United States than because of what was being thought at the same time in France. While in the rest of Europe the American Revolution was still nothing but a new and unusual fact, among us it only made more evident and more striking what we thought we already knew. It astonished Europe; here it completed our conversion. The Americans seemed merely to apply what our writers had thought of: they gave substantial reality to what we were dreaming about. It was as if Fénelon had suddenly found himself transported to Salentum.[15]

This situation, so new to history, in which the entire political education of

---

15   Abbé Fénelon, a member of Louis XIV's court, author of the *Adventures of Telemachus*, in which Salentum figured as a Utopia.

a great nation was completely shaped by men of letters, was perhaps what contributed most to giving the French Revolution its particular spirit, and made it lead to what we see today.

The writers not only furnished their ideas to the people who made the Revolution; they also gave them their own temperament and disposition. Under this long training, in the absence of any other directors, in the midst of the profound practical ignorance in which they lived, the whole nation ended up adopting the instincts, the attitudes, the tastes, and even the eccentricities of those who write; with the result that when the nation finally had to act, it brought all the habits of literature into politics.

When we study the history of our Revolution, we see that it was carried out in precisely the same spirit in which so many abstract books on government are written. The same attraction for general theories, for complete systems of legislation and exact symmetry in laws; the same contempt for existing facts; the same confidence in theory; the same taste for the original, the ingenious, and the new in institutions; the same desire to remake the whole constitution all at once, following the rules of logic and according to a single plan, rather than trying to fix its various parts. A frightening sight! For what is merit in a writer is sometimes vice in a statesman, and the same things which have often made lovely books can lead to great revolutions.

The language of politics itself then took on the quality of that spoken by authors; it was full of general expressions, abstract terms, ambitious words, and literary turns of phrase. With the help of the political passions which used it, this style spread to all classes and descended with unusual ease even into the lowest. Well before the Revolution, the edicts of King Louis XVI often spoke of natural law and the rights of men. I find peasants who, in their requests, called their neighbors their fellow citizens; the intendant, a respectable magistrate; the parish priest, the minister of the altars; God, the Supreme Being. To become mediocre men of letters, all they had to do was learn how to spell.

These new qualities were so well incorporated into the old foundation of French character that we have often attributed to our nature what derived purely from this unique education. I have heard it argued that the taste, or rather the passion, that we have shown during the past sixty years for general ideas, systems, and big words in political matters, came from I don't know what special attribute of our race, from what is called a bit pompously *the French mind*: as if this supposed attribute could have appeared all at once at the end of the last century, after having been hidden during all the rest of our history.

What is unique is that we have kept the habits we took from literature, while losing almost completely our old love of letters. I have often been astonished, in the course of my public life, to see people who never read the books of the eighteenth century nor those of any other, and who strongly despise writers, preserve so faithfully some of the chief faults which the literary mind produced before they were born.

I Id3   Chapter 3: "How the French Wanted Reforms before They Wanted Freedoms"

One thing worth remarking is that, among all the ideas and all the feelings which prepared the Revolution, the idea and the desire for political freedom proper presented themselves last, as they were the first to disappear.

We had long since begun to shake the old edifice of government; it already reeled, and it was still not a question of freedom. Voltaire was hardly interested in it: three years' residence in England had shown him freedom without making him like it. The skeptical philosophy which was freely preached among the English enchanted him; their political system affected him little: he noticed its vices more than its virtues. In his *Letters on England*, which is one of his masterpieces, Parliament is what he talks about least; in reality, he envied the English above all for their literary freedom, but hardly concerned himself for their political freedom, as if the first could ever exist for long without the second.

Around the middle of the century, a certain number of writers appeared who specialized in treating questions of public administration, and to whom several similar principles have given the common name of *economists* or *physiocrats*.[16] The physiocrats have had less renown in history than the philosophes; perhaps they contributed less to the coming of the Revolution. I believe, however, that it is in their writings above all that we can best study the Revolution's true nature. The philosophes hardly went beyond very general and very abstract ideas in questions of government; the physiocrats, however, without separating themselves from theory, came closer to the facts. One told us what we could imagine, the other sometimes showed us what was to be done. All the institutions that the Revolution was going to permanently abolish had been the particular objects of the physiocrats' attacks; none had found grace in their eyes. On the contrary, all those which may pass for the Revolution's own work had been announced in advance and ardently recommended by them; one could hardly cite a single one whose seed had

---

16   Economists and social reformers united by the belief that land was the only true form of wealth. Leading members included Letrone, Mercier de la Rivière, Quesnay, and Turgot.

not been sown in some of their writings; we find in the physiocrats all that is most substantial in the Revolution.

. . .

Of all the men of their time, it is the physiocrats who would seem the least displaced in our own; their passion for equality was so firm and their taste for freedom so vague that they have a false air of being our contemporaries. When I read the speeches and writings of the men who made the Revolution, I feel myself suddenly transported to a place and in the midst of a society which I do not know; but when I examine the physiocrats' books, it seems to me that I have lived with these people, and that I have just talked with them.

Around 1750 the nation as a whole did not show itself more demanding in the matter of political freedom than the physiocrats themselves; it had lost the desire for freedom and, in losing its use, the very idea of it. The nation wanted reforms more than rights, and, if there had then been found on the throne a ruler of the stature and disposition of Frederick the Great, I do not at all doubt that he would have accomplished in society and government several of the great changes that the Revolution made, not only without losing his crown, but greatly increasing his power. We are assured that one of Louis XV's most able ministers, M. de Machault, glimpsed this idea, and suggested it to his master. But such enterprises are not counseled: one is not made to accomplish them except when one is capable of conceiving them.

Twenty years later, it was no longer the same: the image of political freedom had presented itself to the French mind, and became more and more attractive to it every day. This was made clear by many signs. The provinces again began to conceive the desire to govern themselves. The idea spread that the whole people had the right to take part in its government, and swept up public opinion. The memory of the old Estates-General revived. The nation, which detested its own history, remembered only this part of it with pleasure. The new current carried the physiocrats themselves along, and forced them to encumber their unitary system with some free institutions.

When in 1771 the *parlements* were destroyed, the same public which had so often suffered from their prejudices was profoundly moved at the sight of their fall. It seemed that with them fell the last barrier which could still contain royal absolutism. This opposition astonished Voltaire and made him indignant. "Almost the whole kingdom is in excitement and consternation," he wrote to one of his friends; "the fermentation is as strong in the provinces as in Paris itself. The edict seems to me, however, full of useful reforms. To destroy the venality of offices, to make justice free, to forbid litigants to come to Paris from the ends of the kingdom to bankrupt themselves, to charge the king with paying the expenses of manorial justice, are these not great services rendered to the nation? These *parlements*, further, have they not often been barbarous and persecutors? In truth, I admire the 'radicals' for taking the part of these insolent and insubordinate bourgeois. For myself, I think that the king is right, and, since one must serve, I think that it is better to do it under a well-bred lion, who is born much stronger than I, than under two hundred rats of my own species." And he adds as a kind of excuse: "Imagine how I must infinitely appreciate the favor that the king does all feudal lords, in paying the expenses of their courts."

Voltaire, long absent from Paris, thought that public opinion had remained at the point where he had left it. It had done nothing of the sort. The French no longer limited themselves to wanting their affairs better run; they had begun to want to manage their business themselves, and it was clear that the great Revolution that everything was preparing was going to occur, not only with the people's consent, but by their hands.

I think that from this time on, this radical revolution – which was going to join all that was best and worst in the old regime in the same destruction – was inevitable. A people so badly prepared to act on its own could not attempt to reform everything at once without destroying everything. An absolute ruler would have been a less dangerous innovator. For me, when I consider that that same revolution, which destroyed so many institutions, ideas, and habits opposed to freedom, also, on the other hand, abolished so many others which freedom can hardly do without, I am inclined to believe that perhaps if the revolution had been accomplished by a despot, it would have left us less unfit to become a free nation, some day, than the revolution made in the name of the sovereignty of the people, and by them.

One must never lose sight of this, if one wants to understand the history of our revolution. When the love of the French for political freedom awoke, they had already conceived a certain number of ideas in regard to government which not only did not easily accord with the existence of free institutions but were almost opposed to them. They had accepted as the ideal society a people without any aristocracy other than government officials, a single and all-powerful administration, director of the state, guardian of individuals. In wishing to be free, they did not intend to depart in the slightest from this basic idea; they only tried to reconcile it with the idea of freedom.

They therefore endeavored to mix together unlimited government central-ization and a dominant legislative body: administration by officials and government by the voters. The nation as a body had all the rights of sovereignty, each particular citizen was confined to the strictest subjection: from the one, they demanded the experience and virtues of a free people; from the other, the qualities of a good servant.

It is this desire to introduce political liberty among ideas and institutions which are foreign or opposed to it, but for which we had already acquired the habit or conceived the taste, that for sixty years has produced so many vain attempts at free government, followed by such disastrous revolutions. Finally, fatigued by so many efforts, put off by a task so laborious and so sterile, the French abandoned their secondary objective to return to their primary one. Many of them were reduced to thinking that to live as equals under a master still had, after all, a certain attraction. Thus today we find ourselves infinitely more like the physiocrats of 1750 than our fathers of 1789.

I have often wondered where the source of this passion for political freedom is, which, in all times, has made men do the greatest things that humanity has accomplished, in what feelings it is rooted and nourishes itself. I see clearly that, when nations are badly led, they readily conceive the desire to govern themselves; but this kind of love of independence, which takes rise only from some particular and fleeting problems brought on by despotism, is never durable: it passes with the accident that gave it birth; they seem to love freedom, but one finds that they only hated the master. What peoples who are made for freedom hate, is the evil of subjection itself.

I also do not think that true love of liberty was ever born just from the sight of the material goods that freedom produces; for this often succeeds in hiding it. It is certainly true that in the long run, freedom always brings, to those who know how to keep it, ease, well-being, and often riches; but there are times when it briefly hinders the enjoyment of such goods; there are others when only despotism can temporarily afford their enjoyment. Men who prize freedom for only these kinds of goods have never kept their freedom for long.

That which, in all times, has so strongly attached certain men's hearts to freedom, are its own attractions, its own peculiar charm, independent of its benefits; it is the pleasure of being able to speak, act, and breathe without constraint, under the government of God and the laws alone. Whoever seeks for anything from freedom but itself is made for slavery.

Certain nations pursue freedom obstinately through all kinds of perils and miseries. Then it is not the material goods which it gives them which those peoples love in freedom; they consider freedom itself a good so precious, and so necessary, that no other could console them for its loss, and they console themselves for everything in tasting it. Others tire of liberty in the midst of their prosperity; they let it be taken from their hands without resistance, for fear of compromising by any effort the very well-being that they owe to it. What do they lack to make them free? What? The very desire to be so. Do not ask me to analyze this sublime desire, it must be felt. It enters of itself into the great hearts that God has prepared to receive it; it fills them, it fires them. One must give up on making this comprehensible to the mediocre souls who have never felt it.

IId8   Chapter 8: "How the Revolution Came Naturally from What Preceded It"

In closing, I want to bring together some of the traits that I have already described separately, and to envision the Revolution emerging naturally, as it were, from the old regime whose portrait I have painted.

If we consider that it was among us that the feudal system had most lost all that could protect it or serve it, without changing what could harm or irritate, we will be less surprised that the revolution which was going to violently abolish the old constitution of Europe broke out in France rather than elsewhere.

If we note that the nobility, after having lost its old political rights and ceased, more than anywhere else in feudal Europe, to govern and lead the population, had nevertheless not only retained but much increased its financial immunities and the advantages which its members individually enjoyed; that in becoming a subordinate class the nobility had remained a privileged and closed class, less and less an aristocracy, as I said earlier, and more and more a caste, we will no longer be surprised that its privileges appeared so inexplicable and so detestable to the French, and that at the sight of these privileges democratic envy was inflamed to such a pitch in their hearts that it still burns.

If we think, finally, that this nobility, separated from the middle classes which it had repulsed from its midst, and from the people whose loyalty it had allowed to escape, was completely isolated within the nation, in appearance the head of an army, in reality an officer corps without soldiers, we will understand how, after having been in existence for a thousand years, it could be overthrown in the course of an evening.

I have shown in what way the royal government, having abolished provincial freedoms, and substituted itself in three-quarters of France for all the local authorities, had attracted all affairs to itself, the smallest and the greatest alike; I have, furthermore, shown how by a necessary consequence Paris had become the master of the nation, when up to then it had merely been its capital, or rather had become the entire country itself. These two facts, which were unique to France, would alone be enough, if necessary, to explain how a riot could destroy from top to bottom a monarchy which during so many centuries had borne such violent shocks, and which on the eve of its fall still seemed unshakable even to those who were going to overthrow it.

France being the European country where political life had been longest and most completely extinct, where individuals had most completely lost the practical skills, the ability to read facts, the experience of popular movements, and almost the very idea of the people, it is easy to imagine how all the French at once could fall into a terrible revolution without perceiving it, those most threatened by it marching in front and breaking the trail that led to it.

Since there no longer existed free institutions, and in consequence no political classes, no living political bodies, no organized political parties with leaders, and since in the absence of all these organized forces the direction of public opinion, when public opinion was reborn, devolved uniquely on the philosophes, it was to be expected that the Revolution be directed less by certain particular facts than by abstract principles and very general theories; it could be foreseen that rather than separate attacks on bad laws there would be an attack on all the laws at once, and that there would be the desire to substitute a completely new system of government, conceived by the intellectuals, for the old constitution of France.

The Church naturally finding itself entangled with all the old institutions whose destruction was in question, it could not be doubted that this revolution would have to shake religion at the same time as it overturned the civil power; from then on, it was impossible to say what unheard of audacities the minds of the innovators would be led to, liberated at one stroke from all the limits that religion, custom, and law impose on the human imagination. And he who had carefully studied the country's situation could easily have foreseen that there was no recklessness so unheard of that it could not be tried, nor violence that could not be allowed.

"How is it," cried Burke in one of his eloquent pamphlets, "we do not find a single man who can speak for the smallest district; still more, we do not find one who can respond to another. Everyone is arrested in his home without resistance, whether it be for royalism, moderation, or anything else." Burke did not understand very well the condition in which the monarchy he regretted had left us to our new masters. The government of the old regime had already taken away from the French any possibility, or desire, of helping one another. When the Revolution happened, one would have searched most of France in vain for ten men who had the habit of acting in common in an orderly way, and taking care of their own defense themselves; only the central power was supposed to take care of it, so that the central power, fallen from the hands of the royal government into the hands of a sovereign and irresponsible assembly, and changed from good-natured to terrible, found nothing which could stop it, or even briefly slow it down. The same cause which made the monarchy fall so easily, made everything possible after its fall.

Never had religious tolerance, benevolent rule, humanity, and even good-will, been more preached and seemingly more admired than in the eighteenth century; the laws of warfare, which is the last refuge of violence, were themselves limited and made gentler. From the midst of such mild mores, however, the most inhuman revolution was going to come! And yet, all that civilizing of mores was not a false appearance; for, as soon as the fury of the Revolution was spent, one sees the same mildness immediately spread throughout the law and penetrate all political habits.

The contrast between benign theories and violent acts which is one of the French Revolution's strangest characteristics, will not surprise anyone who notes that that revolution had been prepared by the most civilized classes of the nation, and was carried out by the most coarse and ignorant. The men of the former sort not having any pre-existing link among themselves, no practice at coming to an agreement, no hold on the people, the people themselves became almost immediately the directing power, as soon as the old powers were destroyed. Where they did not rule themselves, they gave at least their spirit to the government; and if one thinks of the way in which the masses had lived under the old regime, it will not be difficult to imagine what things were going to be like.

The very peculiarities of their situation had given the common people several rare virtues. Long since freed, and long since become owners of a piece of land, isolated rather than dependent, the people showed themselves proud and sober; they were difficult to tire, indifferent to the delicacies of life, resigned to the greatest evils, firm in the face of danger; a simple and virile race which was going to fill the powerful armies under whose strength Europe would bend. But the same reasons made them a dangerous master. Since the people had for centuries borne all the real abuses, since they had lived apart, nourishing themselves in silence on their prejudices, their jealousies, and their hatred, they had been hardened by the rigors of their fate, and they had become capable of both enduring everything and inflicting everything.

It was in this state that, putting their hands on government, the people themselves attempted to finish the Revolution's work. Books had furnished the theory, the people charged themselves with the practice, and they adjusted the writers' ideas to their own fury.

Those who, in reading this book, have carefully studied eighteenth-century France have been able to see two chief passions born and developed in the nation's breast, which were not at all contemporary with one another and have not always tended towards the same goal. One, deeper and coming from further back, is the violent and inextinguishable hatred of inequality. This was born and nourished from the sight of that very inequality, and had long pushed the French, with constant and irresistible strength, to want to destroy to their very foundations all that remained of medieval institutions and, once the space was cleared, to build a society where men were as alike, and conditions as equal, as humanity could admit.

The other passion, more recent and less well-rooted, brought them to want to live not only equal, but free.

Towards the end of the old regime these two passions are equally sincere and seem equally lively. At the start of the Revolution they meet; they mix and join for a moment and then, heating each other by contact, finally inflame the whole heart of France at once. This is '89, a time of inexperience doubtless, but of generosity, of enthusiasm, of virility, and of greatness, a time of immortal memory, to which the eyes of men will turn with admiration and respect when those who saw it, and we ourselves, will long since have disappeared. Then the French were proud enough of their cause and of themselves to believe that they could be equal in freedom. In the midst of democratic institutions they therefore put free institutions everywhere. Not only did they reduce to dust the outdated legislation which divided men into castes, corporations, and classes, and made their rights still more unequal than their situations, but they broke with a single blow all those other laws, the more recent works of royal power, which had taken from the nation its free enjoyment of itself, and had put the government alongside each Frenchman, to be his tutor, his guardian, and if need be his oppressor. Centralization fell with absolute government.

But when this vigorous generation which had begun the Revolution had been destroyed or worn out, there happened what usually happens to all generations that begin such enterprises; when, following the natural course of this kind of event, the love of liberty was discouraged and weakened in the midst of anarchy and popular dictatorship, and when the lost nation began to search gropingly for its master, absolute government found immense facilities for its rebirth and foundation. These were easily discovered by the genius of he who was going to be simultaneously the continuator and destroyer of the Revolution. The old regime contained, in fact, a whole ensemble of institutions of modern date, which, not being at all hostile to equality, could easily take their place in the new society, and which, moreover, offered unique facilities to despotism. We sought for them again amidst the debris of all other institutions, and found them. These institutions had previously created habits, passions, and ideas which tended to keep men divided and obedient; we revived this and encouraged it. We returned to centralization in its ruins and restored it; and since, at the same time that it was revived, all that had formerly been able to limit it remained destroyed, from the very bowels of a nation that had just overthrown the monarchy suddenly surged forth a power more extensive, more detailed, more absolute than that which any of our kings had exercised. The enterprise seemed one of extraordinary boldness and its success unheard-of, because no one thought of anything beyond what they saw, and they forgot what had been seen before. The master fell, but what was most substantial in his work remained; his government dead, his bureaucracy still lived, and every time that we have since tried to bring down absolute power, we have limited ourselves to placing liberty's head on a servile body.

At several repetitions, from when the Revolution began down to our own days, we have seen the passion for freedom extinguished, then reborn, then again extinguished and again reborn; thus this passion will long continue, always inexperienced and badly regulated, easy to discourage, frighten, and defeat, superficial and temporary. During this same period the passion for equality has still retained possession of the depths of the hearts that it first conquered; there it clings to the feelings which are dearest to us; while the passion for freedom constantly changes its appearance, shrinks, grows, strengthens, and weakens according to events, the passion for equality is always the same, always attached to the same purpose with the same obstinate and often blind ardor, ready to sacrifice everything to those who permit it to satisfy itself, and to furnish to the government willing to favor and flatter it the habits, ideas, and laws that despotism needs in order to rule.

The French Revolution will be but a shadow for those who want to look at it in isolation; it is in the time which precedes it that we must look for the only light which can illuminate it. Without a precise understanding of the old society, of its laws, its vices, its prejudices, its miseries, its greatness, we will never understand what the French have done for the sixty years that have followed its fall; but this understanding will still not be enough if one does not penetrate into the very spirit of our nation.

When I consider this nation in itself, I find it more extraordinary than any of the events in its history. Has there ever been any nation on earth which was so full of contrasts, and so extreme in all of its acts, more dominated by emotions, and less by principles; always doing better or worse than we expect, sometimes below the common level of humanity, sometimes much above it; a people so unalterable in its basic instincts that we can still recognize it in portraits drawn of it two or three thousand years ago, and at the same time so changeable in its daily thoughts and tastes that it ends up offering an unexpected spectacle to itself, and often remains as surprised as a foreigner at the sight of what it has just done; the most stay-at-home nation of all and the one most in love with routine, when left to itself; and, when torn despite itself from its hearth and its habits, ready to go to the ends of the earth and risk all; insubordinate by temperament, and always readier to accept the arbitrary and even violent empire of a prince than the free and orderly government of its leading citizens; today the declared enemy of all obedience, tomorrow attached to servitude with a kind of passion that the nations best-endowed for servitude cannot match; led on a string so long as no one resists, ungovernable as soon as the example of resistance appears somewhere; thus always tricking its masters, who fear it too much or too little; never so free that one must despair of enslaving it, or so servile that it may not once again break the yoke; capable of everything, but excelling only at war; a lover of chance, of strength, of success, of fame and reputation, more than of true glory; more capable of heroism than of virtue, of genius than of common sense, ready to conceive vast plans rather than to complete great tasks; the most brilliant and most dangerous nation of Europe, and the best suited for becoming by turns an object of admiration, of hatred, of pity, and of terror, but never of indifference?

France alone could give birth to a revolution so sudden, so radical, so impetuous in its course, and yet so full of backtracking, of contradictory facts and contrary examples. Without the reasons which I have given, the French would never have made the Revolution; but it must be recognized that all these reasons together would not succeed in explaining such a revolution anywhere else but in France.

Here I have reached the threshold of that memorable revolution; I will not cross it this time: soon, perhaps, I will be able to. I will not then consider its causes, I will examine it in itself, and I will finally dare to judge the society that has come from it.

11e   Notes and Variants

To Preface (11a)

I am nothing, and I don't want to be anything. I expect nothing from anyone and it seems to me to me that I don't fear anything from anyone anymore. I belong neither to a clique nor to a party. I am alone. This isolation in the middle of my country is often cruel. Feeling the pain, I wanted at least to taste the corresponding pleasure, which is to express my thoughts freely, without wishing to flatter, without caring to displease, concerning myself with the truth alone.

Make a strong effort to avoid as much as possible, in *all these chapters*, the *abstract* style, in order to make myself fully understood, and above all read with pleasure. Make a constant effort to contain abstract and general ideas in words which present a precise and particular picture. Example: when I say how the Revolution has substituted an immense new social power for the dispersed old powers, recall the destroyed powers by naming them by their names, and in depicting the new social power try to use words which present the picture of government and bureaucracy as we know them and as we see them function daily. This will diminish the absolute value of the sentence in itself, since I am not only talking about France, and the thought extends beyond the space in which these words enclose it. But one writes in order to please, and not to attain an ideal perfection of language.

To Book One, Chapter 2 (11b2)

It is true that the French Revolution has left in the world a spirit of uneasiness and anarchy which seems eternal. But even this is an accidental and secondary effect of the Revolution, although more lasting than most of the others. It will come to an end like them. All great revolutions, whatever their object or their character, create a similar attitude, provided that they endure and succeed. When, for whatever reason, laws become fragile and the opinions of men unstable, when men themselves briefly raise and lower themselves by sudden and passing efforts, a taste for violence is always born in certain weak or depraved souls, a taste for instability and risk which often survives the event which created it. It is the passion for gambling transported into politics. *Circled*: This love of change for itself, this contempt for justice and for acquired rights, this attraction to tyranny and this simultaneous disgust at and horror for rules and authority, even for rules one has made and authority one has established, all these things are symptoms of the same illness. This sickness is the revolutionary disease proper, a disease endemic to countries which are in revolution or have just been, and which is born in all of them everywhere, just as typhus is born in all hospitals and ends up being a separate and particular illness, although born from the contagion of a thousand different diseases. If this disease of the human mind seems more terrible this time, and seems more durable than previously thought, this comes from the fact that the French Revolution has been the most violent, the deepest, the most fertile in catastrophes and reversals, and above all the most general revolution that there has ever been. If it had been particular to France, at the end of a certain time, whatever its anarchic violence, we would have seen minds come back to themselves, habit recover its empire and law its power. But the French Revolution struck all the peoples of Europe one after another, and still works on many of them, so that for sixty years there has continued to be a great revolutionary school open in some part of the world, where all violent, insubordinate, or perverse minds go to train and instruct themselves.

In the revolutionary disease of our times, whatever may be said of it, there is certainly something which does not let it be confused with the similar ills that all revolutions create. Above all it can be more widespread, because here the accidental illness finds itself with living roots in the permanent social state, the habits, ideas, and lasting mores that the revolution has founded.

What is or at least *seems* to be particular to it is its character as a *doctrine*. The modern revolutionary disease is not only a habit, a tendency of hearts and minds; it is a theory, a philosophy . . .

To Book Three, Chapter 2

Beyond all this there is (which I don't want to say) a natural hostility between the basis of the political principles that the writers wanted to see prevail (principles that were enemies of tradition, of intellectual authority, that were favorable to independent human reason, rooting themselves in natural law, rejecting all conventional or imposed symbols; principles which have remained the same in the new political society founded by them), a natural hostility, I say, between these principles and the natural principles of the Church, a natural antagonism which perhaps can never end, but which in any case can never end until all the ties which linked the political world to the religious world have been cut, and it is recognized that the political principles of the one are different from those of the other.

12

The Old Regime and the Revolution Volume Two

12a   Book One

12a0   Chapter 0, "Plans"

Tentative Ideas (November and December 1856)

I think that in the first part of the history of the Revolution, which is the part about which the most has been written, as little time as possible should be spent on sketching the facts and details. I would lose myself in the immensity. But which general traits, which general questions to choose?

What place to assign to individuals? They certainly played a great role in this first moment.

Louis XVI; above all the Court; Mirabeau.

My mind is drowned by details and cannot draw the fundamental ideas out of them.

I will not escape from the details if I want to write the story of that first period, even philosophically, and if I attempt anything more than a few considerations. But which ones?

Why did Reform turn so quickly into Revolution?

How was real or apparent agreement replaced by the most violent division? How could the Revolution have been made by a riot? Paris. How could the lower classes have suddenly become so furious, and the leading power?

Why the powerlessness of individuals? Why was civil war impossible?

The first thing to paint is that first period which lasts from the meeting of the Estates-General up to the fall of the Bastille and the formal establishment of the Constituent Assembly. From that moment the Revolution is made.

This is the beginning and the most difficult part of the whole book. It is on this narrow space that I must concentrate all my attention at first. I will do nothing good a priori, but perhaps from looking at the details the fundamental ideas will be born.

For this first period, to choose the issues which will end up in the formal establishment of the Constituent Assembly.

Based on this to judge the work of that Assembly. Disentangle what was fundamentally right, great, lasting in its works, then show how nevertheless it failed and did everything wrong. This is a crucial part of my work.

Apparent unanimity; good intentions; common love of freedom. First picture.

When I get to the analysis and judgement of the Constituent Assembly's work, the horizon clears: show on the one hand the greatness, the honesty, the beauty of its principles; on the other hand the lack of practical wisdom which ended up disorganizing everything.

How we suddenly fell from the old regime into the Revolution.

At the beginning perhaps pose this question first: Could the old regime have fallen without the Revolution?

12a5   Chapter 5: "How the Revolution's Real Spirit Suddenly Showed Itself as Soon as Absolutism Had Been Defeated" (from September 1788 up to the elections)

For a moment, the bond of a common passion held all classes together. As soon as this bond was relaxed, they separated; then the real figure of the Revolution, which up until then had been veiled, suddenly revealed itself.

As soon as the king had been defeated, it became a question of knowing who would profit from the victory. Having obtained the Estates-General, who was going to dominate in that assembly?

The king could no longer refuse to call the Estates General, but he retained the power to choose their form, the Estates-General not having met for 160 years. Furthermore, they were no longer anything but a vague memory. No one knew exactly how many deputies there ought to be, the relationship between the orders, the form of elections, the manner of deliberating. The king alone could say. He didn't say anything.

A unique idea on this subject came to Cardinal de Brienne, the king's prime minister, and he made his master take a decision that was unparalleled in all history. The Cardinal considered it a matter for historical research whether the number of voters ought to be limited or unlimited, the assembly large or small, the orders separate or united, equal or unequal in rights, and as a result an edict of the Royal Council ordered all local authorities and official organizations to make inquiries about the holding of the old Estates-General and about all the forms which were followed there. The Cardinal added: "His Majesty invites all scholars and other educated people of his kingdom, and particularly those who are members of the Academy of Inscriptions and Literature, to address all information to the Chancellor and report on this question."

This was to treat the country's constitution as an academic exercise and make it a topic for a competitive examination.

This appeal was immediately heard. France was flooded with writings. All the local authorities deliberated about what they should respond to the king, all the individual groups made demands, all classes thought of their special interests and sought to find in the ruins of the old Estates-General the forms which seemed most likely to guarantee them. Everyone wanted to give his opinion, since France was the most literary country in Europe, and as this was the period when literature clothed the passions of the times in the heavy garments of erudition.

The class struggle, which was inevitable but which would naturally have started only in the Estates-General itself, in an orderly way, on a limited field and with reference to particular questions, thus found limitless scope and was able to nourish itself on general ideas. It soon took on a character of exceptional boldness and unheard-of violence, which the hidden state of feelings makes comprehensible, but for which nothing had prepared people.

The movement of ideas, the movement of passions

Between the time when the king abdicated his absolute power and when elections started, [*around five months*] passed. During this space of time, there were almost no changes in the facts, but the movement which led French ideas and feelings towards the total subversion of existing society accelerated, and in the end became extremely rapid.

At first people were only concerned with the constitution of the Estates-General, and thick books of raw erudition, where one tried to reconcile the Middle Ages with contemporary views, were hastily produced. Then the question of the old Estates-General faded, the jumble of old precedents was tossed aside and people looked in an abstract and general way for what the legislative power ought to be. Ideas became more comprehensive as people went on; it was no longer just the constitution of the legislature which was in question, but of all power; people attempted to shift not only the form of government, but the very basis of society. At the beginning, people spoke only of better balancing powers, better adjusting class relations; soon they walked, they ran, they threw themselves into the idea of pure democracy. At the beginning, it was Montesquieu who was cited and commented on; in the end, they only spoke of Rousseau. He became and he was to remain the sole teacher of the Revolution in its youth.

. . .

What strikes me most, is less the genius of those who served the Revolution while wanting it, than the exceptional stupidity of those who made it happen without wanting it to.

When I think about the French Revolution, I am astonished at the event's immense size, its fame which spread to the ends of the earth, its power which has moved more or less all peoples.

I then consider the Court which had such a part in the Revolution; I see there the most ordinary pictures which can be found in history: thoughtless or incompetent ministers, debauched priests, idle women, bold or greedy courtesans, a king who had only useless or dangerous virtues. I see, however, that these petty personalities facilitate, push, accelerate this immense event. More than accidents, they become almost prime causes; and I admire the power of God, for whom such short levers are enough to put in motion the entire mass of human societies.

12a7 Chapter 7: "How for a Moment, When the National Assembly Was about to Meet, Hearts Were Joined and Spirits Raised"

No one doubted that the destiny of the human race was involved in what we were preparing to do.

Today, when the hazards of revolution have humbled us to the point that we believe ourselves unworthy of the freedom which other nations enjoy, it would be difficult to imagine how far our fathers' pride extended. When we read a writer of those times, we are astonished at the immense opinion that the French of all classes had of their country and their race, of the calm and simple confidence with which they put "French" for "men." Among all those reform projects which burst forth at the time when the government seemed to put the constitution up for an academic competition, there were almost none which deigned to imitate what was going on abroad. It was not a question of taking lessons, but of furnishing new examples. The very nature of the political ideas which filled all minds, ideas which seemed applicable to all peoples, favored this view. Therefore there was no Frenchman who wasn't convinced that he was not only going to change the government of France, but to introduce new principles of government into the world, destined to change the entire face of human affairs. There was no Frenchman who did not believe he had in his hands, not the destiny of his country, but the very future of his species.

If this feeling was exaggerated it was not wrong. And indeed we were finally going to start on the task. From up close one saw its greatness, its beauty, its risks. This clear and distinct view succeeded in seizing the imagination of all the French, and delighted them. In the presence of this immense object, there was a moment when thousands of men seemingly became careless of their own particular interests in order to concern themselves only with the common task. It was only a moment; but I doubt if anything like it has ever been encountered in the life of any people.

The educated classes then had nothing of that fearful and servile nature which revolutions have since given them. They had long since ceased to fear the royal power and they had not yet learned to tremble before the lower classes. The greatness of their plan succeeded in making them bold. The desire for material well-being which was going to end up mastering all other desires was then nothing but a lesser and impotent passion. The reforms accomplished had already disturbed private life; people were resigned to it. The inevitable reforms to come could not fail to change the situation of thousands of men; people hardly thought about that. The uncertainty of the future already slowed the movement of commerce and paralyzed industry, the economic activity of the humble [*was*] suspended or disturbed. The distress and suffering did not extinguish fervor. All individual hardships dissolved and disappeared, in the eyes of the very people who endured them, in the immense greatness of the common enterprise.

People embraced each other before being reconciled

At this moment the dangers of disunity suddenly struck all minds. People made a supreme effort to agree. Instead of looking for where they differed, they tried to concentrate on what they wanted in common:

To destroy arbitrary power, to put the nation back in possession of itself, to assure the rights of every citizen, make the press free, individual liberty inviolable, soften the laws, strengthen the courts, guarantee religious toleration, destroy the hindrances to commerce and industry, this is what they all wanted. They reminded each other of it; they congratulated each other about it. People spoke of what united them, they were silent about what still divided them. Fundamentally people didn't agree at all, but they sought to persuade themselves that they were going to agree; people reconciled without explaining themselves.

– Put here all the facts which can shed light on this. –

I do not believe that at any moment in history, at any place on Earth, a similar multitude of men has ever been seen so sincerely impassioned for public affairs, so truly forgetful of their interests, so absorbed in contemplation of a great plan, so determined to risk everything that men hold most dear in their lives, in order to lift themselves above the petty passions of their hearts. This is the common basis for the passions, the courage, and the devotion from which came forth all the great actions which were going to fill the French Revolution.

This first spectacle was short, but it had incomparable beauty. It will never depart from human memory. All foreign nations saw it, applauded it, were moved by it. Don't try to find a place in Europe so out of the way that it wasn't seen and where it didn't give rise to hope and admiration. There was none. Among the immense crowd of individual memoirs which contemporaries of the Revolution have left us, I have never seen one where the sight of these first days of 1789 did not leave an indelible trace. Everywhere it communicated the clarity, the intensity, the freshness of the emotions of youth.

I dare say that there is only one people on earth which could present such a spectacle. I know my nation. I see only too well its errors, its faults, its weaknesses and its hardships. But I also know what it is capable of. There are enterprises which only the French nation is able to conceive, magnanimous resolutions which only it dare take. Only France could one day wish to embrace the common cause of humanity and *want* to fight for it. And, if it is subject to great falls, it has sublime impulses which suddenly bring it up to a level that no other people will ever attain.

12b   Book Two: Notes Excerpted from Tocqueville's Papers Concerning the History of the Revolution

Chapter 2: "From the Fourteenth of July to the End of the Constituent Assembly [General Remarks]"

The French Revolution was made by virtue of general theories closely linked with each other and forming a single body of doctrine, a sort of political gospel where each principle resembled a dogma. The goal that was proposed inspired the French not only with enthusiasm, but to proselytize and make propaganda. Its doctrines were not only believed by them, but ardently preached, an entirely new thing in history.

Democracy. Democratic institutions. Various meanings of these words.
Confusion which results from this

What confuses the mind most is the use we make of these words: *democracy,*
democratic institutions, democratic government. As long as we do not succeed in
defining them clearly and agreeing on the definition, we will live in an
inextricable confusion of ideas, to the great profit of demagogues and despots.

Some will say that a country governed by an absolute ruler is a *democracy*,
because he governs through equal laws or amidst institutions which will be
favorable to the condition of the lower classes. His government will be a
democratic government. He will create a *democratic monarchy*.

But, the words *democracy, monarchy, democratic government*, in the true sense
of those words can only mean one thing: a government where the people
play a more or less large part in the government. Their meaning is intimately
linked to the idea of political freedom. To give the name democratic
government to a government where political freedom is not found is to say a
palpable absurdity, according to the natural meaning of the words.

Powerlessness of a particular man or even of men at the beginning of the
Revolution and as long as the Revolution's own impulsion lasted. One of the
great characteristics of the Revolution. Highlight its causes well. A great and
terrible sight.

12c   Book Three: Napoleon

12c1   Part 1: "The Convention and the Directory" – Chapter 1: "How the Republic Was Ready to Accept a Master"

We were a sad sight then: everywhere France showed the traces of that kind
of moral usury which is produced in the long run by the course of revolutions.

In truth all revolutions, even the most necessary ones, have had this effect
for a while. But I believe that ours had it more than any other, and I do not
know if one could cite from history a single event of this kind which
contributed more to the well-being of the generations which followed, and
more demoralized the generation which produced it. There were many
reasons for this, and first of all the immense mass of property confiscated by
the victorious factions. The French Revolution multiplied, in a way that had
never before been seen in any people's internal quarrels, the number of
disputed properties whose ownership was guaranteed by law, but which

worried the conscience: those who sold these confiscated goods were not very sure that they had the right to sell them; those who bought them, the right to acquire them. Among both, it usually happened that laziness or ignorance kept people from having a very firm opinion on this crucial point. Furthermore self-interest always kept most people from examining it very carefully.

This put the souls of several million men in a difficult position.

During the great revolution which brought about the religious reformation of the sixteenth century, the only revolution which can be compared to the French Revolution, the goods of the Church were confiscated, but they were not put up for public auction. A small number of great lords took them. Among us, furthermore, it was not only the lands of the clergy but those of the majority of large proprietors, not the property of a corporation but the inheritance of a hundred thousand families which was divided up. Note too that one did not enrich oneself merely by the purchase, at ridiculous prices, of a multitude of confiscated lands, but also by the token repayment of an enormous mass of debts: a profit that was simultaneously very legal and very dishonest.

If I may push the comparison further, I find that the revolution of the sixteenth century shed doubt only on a certain portion of human opinions and disturbed established mores on only a few points: honesty, which among most men has its source of support much less in reason than in habit and prejudice, was only shaken. The French Revolution attacked political and religious beliefs simultaneously, the French Revolution wanted to reform the individual and the state at the same time, and it tried to change old customs, received opinions, and old habits in all ways and at once. This produced a universal earthquake in the moral world which staggered the conscience on every side.

But what demoralizes men most in long revolutions, is much less the mistakes and even the crimes they commit in the fervor of their belief or their passions, than the contempt they sometimes acquire for the same belief or the same passions which made them act in the first place. This is the time when, tired, disenchanted, disappointed, they finally turn against themselves and decide that they have been childish in their hopes, ridiculous in their enthusiasms, more ridiculous still and above all in their devotion. One cannot begin to imagine how the energy of the strongest minds is destroyed in this fall. Man is crushed by it, to the point that not only can one no longer expect great virtues of him, but one would say that he had become incapable almost of great evil.

Those who saw the French reduced to this state thought that they were from then on incapable of ever being able to make any great moral effort.

They were wrong; for if our virtues must always worry the moralist, our vices must always leave him grounds for hope. The truth is that we never go deeply enough into either virtue or vice to be unable to change.

The French, who had loved, or rather had believed they loved liberty passionately in 1789, no longer loved it in '99, without having attached their hearts to anything else. After they had attributed a thousand imaginary charms to freedom, they did not see its real qualities, they could only recognize its difficulties and dangers. In truth, for ten years they had hardly known anything but these. In a contemporary's vivid expression, the Republic had been nothing but an agitated servitude. At what other period of history had one seen the private mores of a great number of men thus violated, and tyranny penetrate more deeply into private life? What feelings, what actions had escaped constraint? What habits, what customs had been respected? The simple individual had been forced to change his days of work and rest, his calendar, his weights and measures, even his language. While he had to take part in ceremonies which seemed useless and ridiculous to him, he was forced to exercise in secret the worship he believed he owed God. He had to constantly break laws in order to follow his desires or his conscience. I do not know if anything like this could have been borne so long by the most enduring of nations, but there is no limit to our patience, nor to our rebelliousness, depending on the times.

. . .

Political institutions are like religions, where worship usually long outlives belief. At the center of this nation, which no longer cared about freedom or believed in the Republic, where all the Revolution's fervor seemed extinct, it was strange to see the government persisting in all the revolutionary routines. In the month of May, it solemnly attended the festival of the sovereignty of the people; in spring, the festival of youth; in summer, that of agriculture; in autumn, that for the aged. On the 10th of August the government assembled public officials around the altar of the fatherland to swear fidelity to the constitution and hatred for tyrants.

. . .

The revolutionary faction which held power had also retained in its official style all the Revolution's rhetoric. The last thing that a party abandons is its language, because, among political parties as elsewhere, the vulgar make the rules in matters of language, and the vulgar more readily give up the ideas they have been given than the words which they have finally learned. When one rereads the speeches of this time, it seems that nothing could be said simply any more. All the soldiers are warriors; the husbands, spouses; the wives, faithful companions; the children, pledges of love. Honesty was never spoken of, but always virtue, and one never promised anything less than to die for the country and for freedom.

What is even worse is that most of the orators who gave these speeches were themselves almost as tired, disenchanted and cold as the rest; but that is the sad situation of great passions which long after they have lost their hold on the heart leave their mark on language. He who listened only to the newspapers might have thought himself in the midst of the nation most passionate for its freedom and most interested in public affairs. Never had the newspapers' language been more inflamed, never was their clamor more lively than at the moment when they were about to be silent for fifteen years. If you want to know the real power of the press, never pay any attention to what it says, but rather to the way people listen to it. Sometimes its passion announces its weaknesses and foretells its end. Its clamor and its peril often have the same cause. It shouts so loudly only because its audience has become deaf, and it is this public deafness which, one day, finally allows it to be silenced with impunity.

Although from then on the citizens remained estranged from the nation's affairs, it must not be believed that they were insensitive to the particular dangers that politics could subject them to. Precisely the opposite happened. Never perhaps have the French more feared the personal consequences of political events than at the moment when they no longer wanted to concern themselves with politics. In politics, fear is a passion which often grows at the expense of all others. People are easily afraid of everything when they no longer desire anything very strongly. The French, furthermore, have a kind of gay despair which often fools their master. They laugh at their problems, but that doesn't keep them from feeling them. The French were devoured by political worries right in the middle of their egoistic preoccupation with their own petty personal business and the giddiness of their pleasures; an almost unbearable anguish, an inexpressible terror, took possession of all minds.

Although the dangers which one ran in 1799 were, all in all, infinitely less great than those of the Revolution's first days, nonetheless they inspired a fear infinitely stronger and more general, because the nation had less energy, less passion and more experience. In 1799 all the various ills which had crushed the nation over ten years gathered in its imagination to form the picture of the future, and after having thrown themselves fearlessly and even without caution into the most terrible catastrophes, the nation trembled at the movement of its own shadow. One can note, in the writings of the time, that the most contradictory things were successively and often simultaneously feared: these men fear the abolition of property, those other men the return of feudal dues. Often the same man, after having feared one of these dangers, almost immediately began to fear the other; in the morning a restoration, in the evening a return of the Terror. Many were afraid to show their fear, and it was only after the crisis of 18 Brumaire[1] that one could judge, by the extent of their satisfaction and the excess of their joy, what an abyss of cowardice the Revolution had dug in those weakened souls.

However used to humanity's illogical fickleness we ought to be, it seems permissible to be astonished at seeing such a great change in a people's moral disposition: so much egoism after so much devotion, so much indifference after so much passion, so much fear after so much heroism, such great contempt for what had been the object of such violent desires and for what had cost so much. One must give up the attempt to explain such a rapid and complete change by the usual laws of the moral world. The character of our nation is so particular that the general study of humanity is not enough to understand it. It constantly surprises even those who have tried to study it in particular: a nation better endowed than any other with the capacity to easily understand extraordinary things and adopt them, capable of anything which only demands one effort, however great it may be, but unable to sustain itself very high for long, because it has only feelings and no principles. The most civilized of all the civilized peoples of the earth and yet, under certain circumstances, the people closer to barbarism than any of them; for what is proper to savages is to decide by the sudden impression of the moment, without memory of the past or idea of the future.

12c2   Part II: "The Consulate and the Empire": Section Two: "Research Notes on the Empire"

When I get to the Empire, analyze this fabric well: the despotism of a single man resting on a democratic base; the most effective combination for bringing about, in accord with the times and the men, the most unlimited despotism, the despotism best supported by the appearance of legality and by an interest which is sacred, that of the greatest number, and at the same time the least responsible. This seems extraordinary in a government which takes its origin (at least supposedly) from popular election, and yet it is true. Here, comparison. Memory of the Roman Empire. Study and summarize the nature of this government, its causes, its organization; how throughout it resembled the idea conceived by the Emperor, and still further completed and realized by his nephew. Bring in here, through some examples (there must certainly have

1   18 Brumaire (9 November),1799, Napoleon leads coup and comes to power as First Consul.

been some at the beginning of the Empire), the actions of legists inventing theories and philosophy for this power created by violence and force, the Troplongs.[2]

Above all since the study of Roman law has spread, the example of all the nations of Europe has proved that there is no tyranny which lacks for lawyers any more than it lacks for executioners. These two races abound under the hand of a despot, and there is no usurper so mediocre that he does not find a jurist to prove that violence is right, tyranny order, and servitude progress.

[*General Reflections. The Heritage of the Revolution*]
[*Mores and Feelings*]

The French Revolution produced or seemed to produce a race of revolutionaries which was new in the world

It is true that we have seen a race of revolutionaries come out of the French Revolution and survive it who seem new in the world, a turbulent and destructive race, always ready to destroy and unfit to found. A race who not only practice violence, contempt for individual rights and the oppression of minorities but, what is new, profess that it must be so: who put forth as a doctrine that there are no individual rights and effectively no individuals, but a mass to which everything is always allowed in order to attain its ends.

Something analogous has been seen after all great revolutions but there are special causes this time:

1. The democratic character of our Revolution which tended towards contempt for individual rights; towards violence since the Revolution had the lower classes as its chief instrument.
2. Its philosophical character which wanted a theory even for violence.
3. A Revolution which is not limited to a short space of time, but which has gone on for sixty years, changing only its theater, so that the revolutionary race renews itself constantly and is always found somewhere, with its tradition, its school. In such a way that for sixty years there has always been a great school of revolution open very publicly someplace in the world, where all disturbed and violent minds, men lost in debts . . . go to educate and instruct themselves.

2 Raymond Théodore Troplong was a prominent jurist who became a kow-tower to Napoleon III.

This is a particular illness, a sort of horror of rules, love of risks or danger, the combined product of all kinds of passions, errors, vices, miasmas similar to that fever which is born in hospitals and which becomes a particular and characteristic illness, even though it owes it origin to a thousand different evils.

[*Political Society*]

What is the natural government, and what ought to be the final government,
of modern society as the Revolution has created it?

Perhaps at the very end when I will say that if I stop, it is not because the Revolution is over, nor that we know definitively where it leads. Preface perhaps.

Those who have seen the first Republic have told me . . . and although I have not yet reached the usual limits of human life, I have already in my day heard it said four times that modern society, as the French Revolution made it, has finally found its natural and permanent basis, and then the next event proved that people were wrong.

The Empire, we were assured in my childhood, is exactly the government which France needs. Why . . . say why. I have seen the Empire fall.

In a society like ours, despotism is nothing but an accident, anarchy naturally engenders a despot. A moderate politics, freedom is our natural state . . . The reasons. Thus spoke the publicists and statesmen that I heard in my youth. A little later I saw the government of the Restoration pass away. I heard it said by its conquerors that . . . The reasons. They were still repeating these things when the new Revolution destroyed their work. The Republic which survived them also had its philosophers to show the causes of its duration, and its end . . . Each new government gives birth to its sophists who while it is dying still diligently seek to prove that this government is immortal.

How patriotism is justified in the eyes of Reason and appears to it not
only a great virtue but the most important

When we look at patriotism from a broad and general point of view, patriotism, despite all the great actions which it has motivated, seems a false and narrow passion. It is to humanity that the great actions suggested by patriotism are due, not to that little fragment of the human race closed within their particular limits that we call a nation and a country. At first glance it seems that those moralists, above all among the Christians, who apparently forget duty to country in order to think only of humanity, who forget the fellow-citizen for the fellow-man, it seems, I say, that they are right. It is in fact by taking a detour that we discover that they are wrong. Man, as God has created him (I don't know why), becomes less devoted as the object of his affections becomes larger. His heart needs the particular, it needs to limit the object of its affections in order to grasp the object in a firm and lasting embrace. There are only a very small number of great souls who can inflame themselves with the love of the human species. The sole means which Providence has left itself (given man as he is) to make each of us work for the general good of humanity, is to divide humanity into a large number of parts and to make each one of these fragments the object of the love of those who compose it. If every man fulfilled his duty in this (and within these limits the duty is not beyond his natural strength well-directed by reason and morality), the general good of humanity would be produced, although little tends directly towards it. I am convinced that we better serve the interests of the human species in giving each man only a particular country to love, than in wanting to inspire him on behalf of the human species, which, whatever we do, he will only consider with a distant, uncertain and cold gaze.

13

The Last Days

13a   To Mme. Swetchine,[1] on his Loss of Faith

Tocqueville, February 26, 1857

I come, Madame, to respond without too much delay to the letter I received from you.

First of all, I am not happy about the news you give me of your health. I had expected better. You confirm, it is true, that you have had a respite from your old ills; but that is far from satisfying me, if the ill which goes is replaced by a new pain. What is it, please tell me? No one told me anything about it and I would like to be informed directly by you.

I must further, Madame, reproach you a little. When I said that I didn't want to talk about myself any more, you seem to have understood me to mean that I lacked confidence in you. I declare that nothing could be more unfounded than that opinion, if you really believe it. My confidence in you is almost absolute. This feeling came to me immediately upon meeting you, and although things which come quickly go quickly, this one has lasted and seems to me incapable of diminishing or ending. I told you the pure truth, in telling you that, if I did not speak about myself any more, it was because the subject was boring for you and unpleasant for me, for I have never found the slightest pleasure in examining myself closely. It is rightly said that we never know ourselves: this is true in the sense that often we do not know how to figure out the source of the impulses that direct us; but as to

---

1   Anne-Sophie Soymonov Swetchine, a Russian mystic who joined the Catholic church and moved to Paris where she established a famous salon.

the effects these hidden motors produce on our own mind and in our own heart, these we know only too well, after having observed ourselves for a while; they constantly repeat themselves in the same way, so that (in my experience at least) the monotony of the picture ends up tiring the gaze and leads it to look towards other objects. I was thus tired of always depicting for you the same agitations, the same miseries, and above all I feared to bore you with eternal repetitions, but I see that your generosity makes you interest yourself in me, more than I interest myself. You search for causes for my weaknesses which will console me for them. You want to see my mental agitation, this fund of melancholy and discontent with myself which is always found in my mind, as the effect of aspirations higher than the results obtained by the efforts they have aroused. I do not wish to practice with you the worst of all forms of vanity, false modesty. Yes, I believe that this is true in part. I believe that my feelings and my desires are higher than my powers. I believe that God gave me the natural desire for great actions and great virtues, and the despair at never being able to seize this great object which is always hovering before my eyes, the sorrow of living in a world and at a time which accord so little with this ideal creation amidst which my soul likes to live. I think that these impressions, that age has not diminished in the slightest, are one of the great causes of this internal malaise of which I have never been able to cure myself; but to how many other less beautiful causes must it not also be attributed? Your indulgence may turn your eyes away from them, but it is not permissible for me not to see them, and, seeing them, to hide them from an eye as benevolent as yours. And to begin the confession with the worst, will you believe, Madame, that a good part of this intellectual disturbance must be attributed to that passion for success, for being known, for renown which has animated me all my life; a passion which sometimes pushes one to great things, but which in itself is certainly not great? It is the little sin which is a habit of writers. I have escaped from it less than anyone. After having published my first book, I went for so long without doing anything that this sickness natural to authors was almost cured, or at least had taken on other symptoms; but my last work has revived it. It has made the old man reappear completely with his weaknesses, his impatience, his desires always greater than the success achieved, even when the success ought to satisfy a reasonable man; but I have never been a completely reasonable man in any sense. This is a really ridiculous cause of agitation; and here is another very worthy of pity! This is the constant and always vain effort of a mind which aspires to certainty and can never achieve it; which more than any other perhaps has need of certainty and less than any other can peacefully enjoy it. The problem of human existence constantly preoccupies me and constantly overwhelms me. I can neither penetrate this mystery, nor detach my eyes from it. It alternately excites me and disheartens me. In this world I find human existence inexplicable and in the other world frightening. I believe firmly in another life, since God who is supremely just has given us the idea of it; in this other life, I believe in the remuneration of good and evil, since God has allowed us to distinguish between them and given us the freedom to choose; but beyond these clear ideas, everything beyond the bounds of this world seems to me to be surrounded by shadows which terrify me. I don't know if I have ever told you about an incident in my youth which left a deep imprint on my whole life; how, shut up in a kind of solitude during the years which immediately follow childhood, subject to an insatiable curiosity which found only the books of a large library to satisfy it, I accumulated in my mind pell-mell all kinds of notions and ideas which usually belong to another age. My life up to then had flowed in an interior full of faith which had not even allowed doubt to penetrate my soul. Then doubt entered, or rather rushed in with unheard-of violence, not merely the doubt of this or that, but universal doubt. I suddenly felt the sensation those who have witnessed an earthquake speak of, when the ground moves under their feet, the walls around them, the ceilings over their head, the furniture in their hands, all nature before their eyes. I was seized with the blackest depression, taken by an extreme disgust for life without having experienced it, and I was as if overwhelmed by trouble and terror at the sight of the road which I had still to travel in the world. Violent passions took me out of that state of despair; they turned me away from the sight of those intellectual ruins to carry me towards physical objects; but from time to time, these impressions of my first youth (I was 16 years old then) possess me again; then I see the intellectual world turn again and I remain lost and bewildered in this universal movement which overturns or shakes all the truths on which I have built my beliefs and actions. Here is a sad and frightening illness, Madame, I do not know if I have ever described it to anyone with so much force and unfortunately truth as I have described it to you. Happy those who have never known it, or who no longer know it!

I do not think, Madame, that I can be in Paris before the end of March. It is not studies which keep me here, but business which has to do with the new situation in which the death of my father has put us. We have to make a permanent establishment which will allow us to recover our freedom of movement. This requires a series of measures which it would be annoying to interrupt and which cannot be continued in our absence. I also greatly need to return to Paris for business reasons and I will come back as soon as I can; but I do not think, I repeat, that I will be able to do so before the last half of the month. I will stay in Paris for all of June. I can assure you, Madame, that among the reasons which make this delay painful for me, the pain of not seeing you until a month has passed holds first place. Believe in the sincerity of this feeling as in the tender and respectful affection I hold you.

13b To Pierre Freslon,[2] on his Melancholic Outlook Towards the Revolution

September 11, 1857

In your friendship you seem to be concerned about the conclusion of the long-prolonged study of the revolution I am making. I see you fear I will end up discouraged and in despair of the future.

In fact I often have to struggle with myself to avoid falling down that slope, for I admit that my present understanding does not extend far enough to let me see how we can act, with *our past* and what it has created, to ever establish solid institutions which are capable of satisfying people like you and me. I confess that the impossibility of finding a remedy which would cure such a great evil, that this impossibility, I say, sometimes throws me into a sort of black humor, a kind of political spleen, whose products can only be sad and ineffective. But I assure you that, on the one hand, I have a very determined intention to combat with all my power this melancholy disposition, and, on the other, that I am really persuaded that beyond this horizon where our gaze stops something infinitely better than what we see is to be found.

13c To his Nephew Hubert de Tocqueville, on Conflict Between France and Germany as a Result of the Napoleonic Wars

Tocqueville, February 7, 1858

I wanted, my dear friend, to thank you for your last letter which is one of your most interesting ones. Everything you tell me about Germany resonates well with what I have thought and known. You seem to be doing a good job of observing the state of mind. I came back from Germany three and a half years ago convinced that our neighbors on the other side of the Rhine were our most irreconcilable enemies. Regardless of whether their governments

---

2 Lawyer, member of the Constituent Assembly of 1848, briefly minister of public instruction under the Second Republic.

want to ally with us, the people will lead their leaders into other alliances. For France this is one of the worst consequences of the first Empire. If you were to read all the German literature which immediately precedes the French Revolution, you would be struck by the German attraction for all things French, and by their strange repulsion for their natural homeland which led some of them to willingly adopt ours. One detects already among German writers of the time a reaction against the French mind, but it is a purely literary reaction. Hearts are still naturally turned towards France. This remains unchanged during the first wars of the Revolution. Germany is devastated by war but the French spirit frees her from the vices of the Old Regime. The Rhine provinces much preferred our domination, despite the violence of our wars and our proconsuls, to the domination of their former masters.

It is the Empire's long, exhausting and above all contemptuous oppression of Germany that united the country against us, and ignited lasting passions against us in the heart of the German peoples. These feelings have persisted and will persist long after the causes which prompted them have disappeared. Fifty years ago, the people of Germany were still very well disposed towards our policies. Today, we never find in them a true ally no matter what we do. Our alliances are limited either to England, which accepts us only if we let her expand throughout the entire inhabited world, or Russia, whose alliance will always lead us to the brink of a global war. We have turned our natural allies into our worst enemies. The Germans' animosity against us prevents them from understanding us. I have noted it many times. Their excessive vanity, which sometimes seems ridiculous to us, makes us even more aware and resentful of their hostility towards us. The English, who have just as much pride, and more justifiably, do not feel compelled to remind us that, in their opinion, we are worthless, and that they, on the other hand, are excellent. Their company does not prompt the kind of impatience I have always felt at the national conceit of the Germans.

I hope you are using the opportunity of being in Berlin for learning to speak the language, and, if you have time, for reading a lot in German. You will never regret it.

Do you understand the current situation in Denmark and could you explain it to me? I would be very interested.

I think Lady Broomfield is Lady Clarendon's sister (the wife of the British foreign minister in London). I know the entire Clarendon family well, Lord Clarendon himself and his sister Lady Thereza Lewis. If you meet Lady Bloomfield I would be very pleased if you would tell her how much I appreciated Lord Clarendon's and Lady Thereza Lewis's reception in England, and that I have spoken to you about them with respect and affection.

Every time you have the opportunity to tell me about what is going on in

Germany, about what people are saying, and what you think of it, without breaking diplomatic rules, I would be grateful. Everything in that country interests me a lot. Adieu, my dear child.

13d To Gustave de Beaumont,[3] on Liberty and Despotism

February 27, 1858

I have wanted to write you a lengthy letter for a long time, my dear friend, but was prevented first by a pretty bad case of flu. When it was over, I found myself overwhelmed by things to do which had accumulated while I was sick. When those things were done, I fell ill again with the same thing and I still have it, not enough to make me really sick, but so that all concentration is difficult. I don't have any fever. I eat and sleep the same as when I am well; but my throat is blocked and a general malaise makes me stay in my room, which seems very hard on a man like me who is used to spending five or six hours outside every day. I hope and believe that this painful state will pass when the weather changes. For a month we have had, no doubt like you, a constant glacial north wind which dries the soil and the throats of men in an extraordinary way. Never, I think, has more arid weather been seen. The farmers pray for rain; but as doubtless elsewhere people are asking for dry weather, these contradictory wishes must have little effect on Providence.

Let me tell you right away, and before passing on to other subjects, about the joy with which we received your news about Antonin. We hoped for much from him, but this goes beyond all reasonable expectations. I have no doubt now that he will pass among the first and get his choice of service in the army. I assure you that we rejoice in your satisfaction with all our hearts. Our tender affection for your family would surely be enough to make your son's success a pleasure to us. Furthermore we find in it the kind of satisfaction given by the sight of good conduct bearing its natural fruits, sacrifices having their legitimate reward: the honest leading to the useful. Why does the world present so few sights of this kind?

I do not need to tell you how much your last letter interested me and how I agree with you about most of the things you tell me and, among others, about the value of freedom. Like you, I have never been more profoundly convinced that freedom alone can give human societies in general, and the individuals who compose them in particular, all the prosperity and all the greatness of which our species is capable. Every day this belief embeds itself

---

3 Tocqueville's most loyal friend and travel companion.

deeper in me: my observations as I make them, the recollections of history, contemporary facts, foreign countries, ours, all concur in giving these opinions from our youth the character of an absolute conviction. That freedom is the necessary condition without which there has never been a nation that was really great and virile is for me absolutely obvious. I have the faith about this point which I would like to have about many others. But how difficult it is to solidly establish freedom among peoples who have lost its use and even the very notion! What is more powerless than institutions, when ideas and mores do not nourish them at all! I have always believed that the enterprise of making France a free nation (in the real meaning of the word), this enterprise to which, for our little parts, we have devoted our lives, I have always believed, I say, that this enterprise was bold and beautiful. I find it daily more bold, but at the same time more beautiful, so that if I could be reborn, I would wish even more to risk myself entirely in this hazardous adventure rather than to bow beneath the necessity of servitude. Will others be more fortunate than we have been? I do not know. But I am convinced that, in our days, we will not see a free society in France, at least not what we understand by that word. This does not mean that we won't see a revolution here. Nothing is settled, believe me. An unforeseen circumstance, a new turn in affairs, any kind of accident could bring about extraordinary events which would force everyone to come out of their holes. This is what I was referring to in my last letter, not the establishment of an ordered freedom. For a long time nothing will be able to make us free, and for the best of reasons, which is that we do not seriously want to be free. This is, after all, the root of the problem. It is not that I am among those who say we are a corrupt and decrepit nation, destined forever to servitude. Those who fear that this is the case and those who hope it is, those who, from this perspective, display the vices of the Roman Empire, and those who take pleasure in the idea that we are going to reproduce its image in miniature, all those people, in my opinion, live in books and not in the reality of their time. We are not a decrepit nation, but a nation that is tired and frightened by anarchy. We lack the high and healthy idea of freedom, but we are worthy of more than our present fate. We are not yet ripe for the regular and definitive establishment of despotism and the government will see this, if it ever has the misfortune to establish itself solidly enough to discourage conspiracies and make the anarchist parties put down their arms and tame them to the point where they seem to disappear from the scene. The government will then be completely astonished, amidst its triumph, to find a layer of opposition under the thick layer of valets that today seems to cover the entire soil of France. I think, sometimes, that the only chance of seeing the strong desire for freedom reborn in France is the tranquil and apparently final establishment of despotism. Look at the mechanism of all our revolutions; today we can describe it very exactly: the experience of the past seventy years has proven that the lower classes *alone* cannot make a revolution; as long as this necessary element of revolutions is isolated, it is powerless. It only becomes irresistible when part of the educated classes joins it, and the educated classes only lend the lower classes moral support or their material cooperation when they are no longer afraid of them. Thus at the very moment when each of our governments for the past sixty years has seemed the strongest it has begun to be struck by the illness from which it perished. The Restoration began to die the day when no one spoke of killing it any more; the same with the government of July. It will doubtless be the same with the present government. Antonin will say one day whether I am wrong.

Pardon all this talk from a sick person who is beginning to get better, however, and who amuses himself by chattering without restraint, but also with little utility.

. . .

Adieu. I embrace you with all my heart. A thousand affectionate remembrances to Madame de Beaumont.

Suggestions for Further Reading

The list that follows is limited to English-language works in their most recent edition.

Aron, Raymond, *Main Currents in Sociological Thought*, vol. 1, *Montesquieu, Marx, Comte, Tocqueville*, New York, Basic Books, 1965.

Boesche, Roger, *The Strange Liberalism of Alexis de Tocqueville*, Ithaca, NY, Cornell University Press, 1987.

Drescher, Seymour, *Dilemmas of Democracy: Tocqueville and Modernization*, Pittsburgh, University of Pittsburgh Press, 1968.

Drescher, Seymour, *Tocqueville and England*, Cambridge, Harvard University Press, 1964.

Eisenstadt, Abraham (ed.), *Reconsidering Tocqueville's 'Democracy in America'*, New Brunswick, Rutgers University Press, 1988.

Furet, François, *Interpreting the French Revolution*, trans. Elborg Forster, Cambridge, Cambridge University Press, 1981.

Furet, François, "The Conceptual System of *Democracy in America*," in *In the Workshop of History*, trans. Jonathan Mandelbaum, Chicago, University of Chicago Press, 1984.

Goldstein, Doris S., *Trial of Faith: Religion and Politics in Tocqueville's Thought*, New York, Elsevier, 1975.

Jardin, André, *Tocqueville, A Biography*, trans. Lydia Davis with Robert Hemenway, Baltimore, Johns Hopkins University Press, 1988.

Kahan, Alan S., *Aristocratic Liberalism: The Social and Political Thought of Jacob Burckhardt, John Stuart Mill, and Alexis de Tocqueville*, New Brunswick, Transaction Publishers, 2001..

Kelly, George Armstrong, *The Humane Comedy: Constant, Tocqueville, and French Liberalism*, Cambridge, Cambridge University Press, 1992.

Lamberti, Jean-Claude, *Tocqueville and the Two Democracies*, trans. Arthur Goldhammer, Cambridge, Harvard University Press, 1989.

Lively, Jack, *The Social and Political Thought of Alexis de Tocqueville*, Oxford, Clarendon Press, 1965.

Manent, Pierre, *Tocqueville and the Nature of Democracy*, trans. John Waggoner, Lanham, MD, Rowman and Littlefield, 1996.

Masugi, Ken (ed.), *Interpreting Tocqueville's 'Democracy in America'*, Savage, MD, Rowman and Littlefield, 1991.

Mélonio, Françoise, *Tocqueville and the French*, trans. Beth G. Raps, Charlottesville, VA, University Press of Virginia, 1998.

Nolla, Eduardo (ed.), *Liberty, Equality, Democracy*, New York, New York University Press, 1992.

Mitchell, Harvey, *Individual Choice and the Structures of History: Alexis de Tocqueville as Historian Reappraised*, New York, Cambridge University Press, 1996.

Pierson, George Wilson, *Tocqueville in America*, Baltimore, Johns Hopkins University Press, 1996.

Schleifer, James T. *The Making of Tocqueville's 'Democracy in America'*, Indianapolis, Liberty Fund, 2000.

Siedentop, Larry, *Tocqueville*, Oxford, Oxford University Press, 1994.

Wolin, Sheldon, *Tocqueville Between Two Worlds: The Making of a Political and Theoretical Life*, Princeton, Princeton University Press, 2001.

Index